CW01514639

TAKING UP
THE TORCH

For Saime *with thanks*

for helping me live in the present

TAKING UP THE TORCH

ENGLISH INSTITUTIONS, GERMAN DIALECTICS
AND MULTICULTURAL COMMITMENTS

EDWARD TIMMS

sussex
ACADEMIC
PRESS
Brighton • Portland • Toronto

2 4 6 8 10 9 7 5 3 1

First published 2011 in Great Britain by
SUSSEX ACADEMIC PRESS
PO Box 139
Eastbourne BN24 9BP

and in the United States of America by
SUSSEX ACADEMIC PRESS
920 NE 58th Ave   Suite 300
Portland, Oregon 97213-3786

and in Canada by
SUSSEX ACADEMIC PRESS (CANADA)
90 Arnold Avenue, Thornhill, Ontario L4J 1B5

British Library Cataloguing in Publication Data
A CIP catalogue record for this book is available from the British Library.

Library of Congress Cataloging-in-Publication Data
Timms, Edward.
Taking up the torch : English institutions, German dialectics, and multicultural commitments / Edward Timms.
p. cm.
Includes bibliographical references and index.
ISBN 978-1-84519-385-0 (h/b : alk. paper) —
ISBN 978-1-84519-386-7 (pbk. : alk. paper)
  1. Timms, Edward. 2. Germanists—England—Biography. 3. Jews—Germany—Historiography. 4. Jewish learning and scholarship. 5. University of Sussex. Centre for German-Jewish Studies—Employees—Biography. 6. Sussex (England)—Biography. I. Title.
PT67.T56A3 2011
943'.004924007202—dc22
[B]   2010052467

Papers used by Sussex Academic Press are natural, renewable and recyclable products from well-managed forests and certified in accordance with the rules of the Forest Stewardship Council, a non-profit international organization established to promote the responsible management of the world's forests. FSC products are independently certified to assure consumers that they come from forests that are managed to meet the social, economic and ecological needs of present and future generations.

Typeset and designed by Sussex Academic Press, Brighton & Eastbourne.
Printed by TJ International, Padstow, Cornwall.
This book is printed on acid-free paper.

Contents

CONTENTS

List of Illustrations
Plates and Figures

Figures in the Text

Preface
Contexts and Questions

University teaching underpinned by research encourages self-reflection, for why should the lives of academics pass unexamined when they set so many questions for others? Hence this review of seventy-five momentous years.

How are children affected by the approach of war? Is it a blessing to have two languages laid in your cradle? If it is lawful for Christians to bear arms, shouldn't there be restrictions on aerial bombardment? How should settled citizens respond to the plight of refugees, and why are those lost at sea so easily forgotten? What role should post-imperial Britain play in Europe?

At school who decides that grammar is good for you? At college why study the literature of the enemy? Teaching in Nuremberg: Why are Germans reluctant to talk about the past? Researching in Vienna: How does satire become the scourge of the establishment? Taking up the Torch: Why choose such an ambivalent symbol for a satirical crusade, and was Karl Kraus right to foresee the Last Days of Mankind?

Sussex in the sixties: Should the new map of learning include a chapel? What exactly is the Modern European Mind, and can enduring relationships be built on shifting sand? How are we to solve Kafka's conundrum that we are forbidden to enter the door intended for us? Cambridge in transition: Could a Chinese sage succeed in putting new wine into old bottles? What is meant by the long march through the institutions? Are Marxist intellectuals responsible for student unrest? If feminists are right to define the personal as the political, does revolution begin in the nursery?

On German intellectual traditions: What did Goethe understand by 'Bildung' and why did Prussian scholars make a cult of 'Wissenschaft'? How could Heine's homeland become his distant love? Did German history really take a wrong turning, and – if so – when? Is dialectic a political theory or a 'Weltanschauung'? What is the effect of relying on dualistic categories like 'Gesellschaft' versus 'Gemeinschaft'? Why has 'Heimat' become a problematic concept? Is there an English equivalent for 'Vergangenheitsbewältigung'?

Teaching in Ankara: Why has Islam never experienced a Reformation?

Could Kemalism transform a Muslim nation? And must Hikmet's romantic communism remain a poet's dream? At conferences in Berlin and Vienna: Can imaginative writers act as the conscience of their age? And does the Austro-Hungarian Empire provide a model for multicultural creativity? By contrast in Jerusalem: How could Herzl's vision have such momentous consequences?

In divided Germany: Can the Iron Curtain be correlated with fault lines running through the German mind? Do peace activists reduce the risk of nuclear war? After the breaching of the Berlin Wall: Could this herald an era of international peace and European harmony? Or was Margaret Thatcher right to complain: 'We have beaten the Germans twice and now they're back'?

Analysts, refugees and archives: How significant is Freud's library, and what is his evidence for the claim that life is shaped by reminiscences? Why were refugee analysts so ambivalent about their European heritage? Who created the fantasy of the child–woman? And what did Derrida mean by 'archive fever'?

At Sussex in the nineties: Does postmodernism preclude a belief in progress and can transitional crises be predicted? Launching the Centre for German-Jewish Studies: What attracted Goethe to the legend of the Wandering Jew? Why did German-speaking Jews to become so attached to the nation that destroyed them? How should the Holocaust be commemorated?

After the destruction of the Twin Towers: Does Kraus's critique of militarism and the media have continuing applications? Why invade Iraq in response to an attack by Saudis trained in Afghanistan? Are we in the midst of a great war for civilization? If democracy and Islam appear incompatible, does republican Turkey offer a solution?

Facing the global financial crisis: Why should the light-touch regulation of bankers impose such heavy burdens on others? Does this signal the end of the Welfare State and equality of access to education? Can universities survive as bearers of the Promethean flame?

The issue, finally, is autobiography: Do dialectical paradigms distort the truth? And if a story has a happy ending, does this mean it has finished too soon?

Such are the questions and contexts that shape the following pages . . .

Sussex, Autumn 2010
EDWARD TIMMS

TAKING UP
THE TORCH

ENGLISH INSTITUTIONS, GERMAN DIALECTICS
AND MULTICULTURAL COMMITMENTS

CHAPTER ONE

Prelude at the Parsonage

Sitting in my office at the Arts Building were two visitors from London, Max and Hilde Kochmann. They had heard about the proposal to create a Centre for German-Jewish Studies at the University of Sussex and wanted to know more. It was the early 1990s, not long after the fall of the Berlin Wall, and there was a buzz of excitement as secret archives were revealed.

'We understand your interest in political history,' Max began, 'but why focus on German-speaking Jews?' To answer this question would require a whole book, but my reply had to be succinct.

'This is not to be a centre for Holocaust studies,' I said. 'The idea is to go back beyond Hitler to explore the creative interactions between Germans and Jews, between Lessing and Moses Mendelssohn, Goethe and Heine, Wagner and Mahler. My research has explored those tensions in the light of *Die Fackel* (The Torch), the journal published in Vienna by the satirist Karl Kraus.'

'What was so important about Vienna?' Max asked. He was proud of his links with Berlin, where he had spent his schooldays before being forced as a Jew to flee to England.

'Vienna,' I replied, 'exemplified the contribution of German-speaking Jews to modern civilization. Think of Sigmund Freud and Theodor Herzl, Arnold Schoenberg and Ludwig Wittgenstein. It was in Vienna that Hitler spent his formative years. Austria, as Kraus remarked on the eve of the First World War, became an experimental station for world destruction.'

As I outlined the case for the Centre, Hilde was watching me intently. She too had fled to England, working as a nurse in Birmingham while Max trained as an aircraft engineer. They were married in London, with flying bombs droning overhead, establishing a successful business and raising a family. With retirement approaching, they welcomed a project that focused on their cultural heritage.

There was something familiar about Hilde's smile, reminding me of the sources of my sense of mission. An image from childhood flashed through my mind, carrying me back to a half-forgotten world before Europe was engulfed by war.

That winter was so cold that we needed gloves and scarves as we set out to build a snowman in the garden of St Alban's Parsonage at Sunningdale. A snapshot from January 1939 shows its awesome bulk looming over my brother and sister, David and Helen, with a glimpse of me in the background, little more than a babe in arms (FIGURE: Sunningdale Snowman). Clasping me to her shoulder is a young German-Jewish woman also named Hilde (we called her Hilda), the refugee who shared our home. Helen and David have memories more vivid than mine, but for me the scene is full of mystery.

Do I really remember the woman – or only the photograph? Is it possible to make good the erasures of time? The quest for answers involves working through hazy memories, tattered diaries and crumpled letters. Fortunately, there is a wealth of sources to guide me back across the years,

Sunningdale snowman
(January 1939)

as I attempt to relate the formation of self to the drift of history. 'Don't be so nostalgic,' a voice whispers in my ear. 'You should live in the present!' Such precepts hardly apply to a life shaped by reminiscences and a career with its origins in the German wars.

FROM THE PLOUGH TO THE PULPIT

My parents, John Timms and Janie Axford, were country folk, and visits to the Cornish farms where they grew up were the highlight of our childhood. Rowden, situated three miles to the east of the village of Kilkhampton, was a squat building with a low-pitched roof, backing onto a sprawling shippen and a spacious dutch barn. The presiding genius was Granfer Bill Timms, a gruff hard-working character who ran the farm with the support of Grandma (his warm-hearted wife Rhoda) and their four children. She was a miller's daughter, born at Cranham Mill in Devon, while he was an orphan who had worked his way up from agricultural labourer till he owned over a hundred acres of good grazing land. The farm had had an earthy feel, and we could hardly wait to visit the animals in the byre and explore the rambling barns. Cows with bulging udders would be milked by hand, and we watched entranced as the creamy fluid spurted under Grandma's rhythmical touch.

At Rowden we could be as wild as we wished, slithering down the hayricks in glorious self-abandon. Collery, by contrast, seemed prim and proper, with a fine house facing across the valley towards Kilkhampton from the west. This was a more substantial farm, and Grandpa Thomas Axford regarded himself as a gentleman who could make a living without getting his hands dirty. As a young man he had indeed considered training for the Methodist ministry. Now he lived with Auntie, his second wife, and their formality made the household seem austere. The Axfords played a leading role in the temperance movement, and the culture of Collery was decorous and restrained. We were expected to sit in the parlour and make polite conversation, but were rewarded by freshly baked scones with lashings of cream.

Our parents first met at the village school in spring 1920. As the second child in a family of four girls and one boy, Mother was persuaded to leave school at the age of fourteen to help on the farm. After milking the cows and feeding the hens, the women would work all morning in the dairy and the kitchen, preparing hot meals to be taken out to the farm hands in the fields. To induce her to give up school, she was promised music lessons so that she could play the organ in chapel, a poor consolation for a girl with a passion for knowledge. In her final year at the village school she had been top of the class while John Timms, her future husband, came second. The Axford girls were regular prize-winners at the Wesleyan Sunday

School, whereas the only award he won at Kilkhampton was the First Prize for Ploughing. His path towards the pulpit was an uphill struggle.

It was Collery people who were visiting St Alban's Parsonage on that day in September 1936 when my story really begins. By that date my parents already had two small children, and it was tiring to cater for such a crowd. So Mother decided to rest upstairs after a busy morning. As a zealous curate, her husband was on his way to the youth club in the Church Hall when he slipped up to say goodbye – and was surprised by desire. The visitors must have been puzzled by the rumblings overhead, for the youth club had to wait as the ardour of Rowden fused with the fecundity of Collery – and the race for life began. Three months later, in church on Christmas morning, Mother felt a stirring in her womb. She was an elderly lady by the time she was ready to share the story of my conception, for she kept these things and pondered them in her heart.

If life begins by chance, identity is socially constructed, and our parents were full of stories about their formative years. Mother recalled the panic in August 1914 when war was declared and the government began to commandeer some of the horses on which farming depended. Life before the advent of tractors and motorcars was full of hazards. One of the first vehicles on the roads of Cornwall belonged to the Royal Mail, and on a dark night her father only just managed to pull his horses to the side of the road as the van approached at breakneck speed. His duties as a lay preacher on the Methodist circuit required him to drive for miles in a horse and trap, braving the storms from the Atlantic. When his carriage was swept away by floods, he survived by clinging to the branches of a tree, an episode that made headlines in the local press.

Father, as the oldest of four children at Rowden, was also obliged to leave school early. But farming proved so little to his taste that he decided to take a correspondence course, studying in the shippen by lamplight in an effort to master maths and Latin. Under such pressures it was a remarkable feat to pass University of London matriculation and qualify to study theology. Granfer provided funds to support him at college, and George – the younger son – was later to take over the farm. Those student days in the late 1920s were the highlight of Father's youth, and by the age of twenty he was the rising star of West Country Methodism. One of the books he took with him when he started his studies at Cliff College near Sheffield was *John Wesley, Christian Philosopher and Church Founder*, a splendid biography (by George Eayrs) of the eighteenth-century evangelist. This was followed by three years at Richmond College, a Wesleyan seminary affiliated to the University of London.

Father had surprisingly little to say about his theological training, which earned him the London degree of Bachelor of Divinity in summer 1930. His flair for theology, including biblical Hebrew and Greek, won him the Dr Williams Scholarship to support postgraduate studies at

Mansfield College, a non-conformist institution. During his second year at Oxford he switched to an Anglican theological college, St Stephen's House, graduating in July 1933. 'Why did you leave the Methodists,' we asked him, 'given their doctrinal disputes with the Anglicans?' He would brush such questions aside, for he was a practical man for whom pastoral activity counted for more than religious dogma. His down-to-earth attitude led him regard being a parson as a branch of the civil service, and Wesley's evangelical piety counted for less than the churchmanship of a nineteenth-century Anglican, the Reverend Sydney Smith. Asked on one occasion whether he enjoyed baptizing babies, Father disconcertingly replied: 'Does the postman enjoy delivering parcels?'

To fuse the traditions of Rowden and Collery was a formidable challenge, for temperamentally our parents were poles apart. When John and Janie announced they were getting married, one of her relatives exclaimed in alarm: 'I hope he'll treat her kindly.' She had been brought up to approach life with a proper seriousness, while he was inclined to jest. During their courting days, so Mother recalled, she had helped to organize a Sunday School outing to the seaside, loading the children on a horse-drawn wagon. But the gradients can be very steep in north Cornwall, and the toiling horse collapsed and died. When she shared this experience with her husband-to-be, counting on his sympathy, he burst out laughing. His humorous approach to life even extended to the institution of marriage, and he once observed that he was 'never really a marrying man'. This was decidedly odd, coming from the father of so many children.

It was fascinating to hear him talking of younger days, and after his death I inherited a chest full of papers, including piles of sermon notes and pocket diaries. They chronicle his clerical duties after being ordained by the Bishop of London at St Paul's Cathedral in October 1933. The first two years were spent as a curate in Finchley with a Sunday routine that included seven different services. Recognizing Father's promise, the Bishop suggested he should move to a curacy in Harrow, a busy urban parish that included the famous school. Unfortunately it proved impossible to find a house at a rent the family could afford. However, in December 1935 Father was invited to Sunningdale, a parish in the Guildford diocese which offered a spacious home at St Alban's Parsonage. To the Bishop's disgust they opted for Sunningdale.

Duties were undemanding in a parish already served by the Rector, Rev. John Archibald (Royal Navy, retired), for it was a thinly populated district, best known for its golf course. Finding that they were expected to pay formal calls, the new curate and his wife ordered visiting cards, exchanging compliments with peppery colonels and retired admirals. They lived not far from Windsor Castle, residence of the royal family, which was in one of its periodic crises. When George V died in January 1936, his eldest son Edward VIII was proclaimed king, only to be compelled to abdicate the following year as a result of his relationship with a divorced woman. He was succeeded by his younger brother, George VI, whose coronation with his consort Queen Elizabeth took place shortly before my birth on 3 June 1937. The abdication crisis coincided with Mother's pregnancy, so the choice of my name reflects sympathy for the deposed monarch.

Mother recalled that the sight of a baby at her breast provoked such unruly feelings in David, two-and-a-half years my senior, that he started rapping my head with his little fist. She decided that it would be better to breastfeed me in another room, later opting for formula milk as an alternative. The leading brand was Cow and Gate – The Food of Royal Babies, which had nourished the little princesses, Elizabeth and Margaret Rose, daughters of George VI. When Helen and David saw me being fed from those glamorous packages, they fancied it was favouritism. But neither royal food nor a regal name could transform a delicate infant into a strapping toddler, and I was slow to start speaking.

While Mother was reading us bedtime stories, Father was preparing for the pulpit. Using the backs of plain postcards that could be purchased ten-a-penny, he would compose his sermon notes in a clear hand, adding the date at the bottom of the card. The earliest to survive, dating from Finchley days, are rather conventional, as if designed to impress the Vicar rather than enthuse the congregation. Citing a biblical text, Father would elucidate the theological implications, ending with a comforting prayer. The most distinctive feature of his sermons was their affirmative view of the Old Testament. This was a period when evangelical preachers were glorifying Jesus, while theologians in Germany were constructing an 'Aryan' Christianity purged of its Judaic heritage. Much as he admired German biblical scholarship, Father took the opposite line, stressing the continuities between Old Testament and New.

THE DESTRUCTION OF JERUSALEM

During the mid-1930s Father's sermons began to address the threat of war. 'How is it possible,' he asked, 'to reconcile armed conflict with Christian conscience?' The Conservative government was making concessions to satisfy German grievances, a strategy supported by the Labour Party and the Churches. The most influential figure in the pacifist movement was Dick Sheppard, Vicar of St Martin's in the Fields, who had served as an army chaplain in the First World War. He took the lead in October 1934 by publishing a letter in the *Manchester Guardian* calling on readers to renounce war and never support another. The overwhelming response prompted him to found the Peace Pledge Union. However, Sheppard's initiative prompted Father to preach a Remembrance Day sermon in which he set out the arguments on both sides. Poets and orators may campaign for peace, he argued, but soldiers have virtues that contribute to peace in a different way. While favouring concessions to Germany, he was by no means a pacifist. His defence of the soldierly virtues echoed the stance of Winston Churchill, who delivered a speech in the House of Commons that same month warning against the weakening of Britain's defences.

Should we, Father asked, quoting Matthew 5: 39 in a sermon of August 1935, simply 'turn the other cheek'? The Quakers may follow the inner light of conscience, but the Anglican Church recognizes the compromises required by an imperfect world. Hence the principle formulated in the Thirty-nine Articles at the end of the Prayer Book: 'It is lawful for Christian men, at the commandment of the Magistrate, to wear weapons and serve in wars.' War, he concluded, is inhuman – but not unchristian. Distancing himself from Sheppard the following year, he argued that if someone threatens your family, you are entitled to fight back. The refusal to take up arms may sound impressive, but surely we must struggle if threatened by the 'gas bomb'. So seriously did he take this subject that he penned an article entitled Christianity, the Church and War, in which he chided his fellow clergy for 'flirting with militant pacifism'. For the

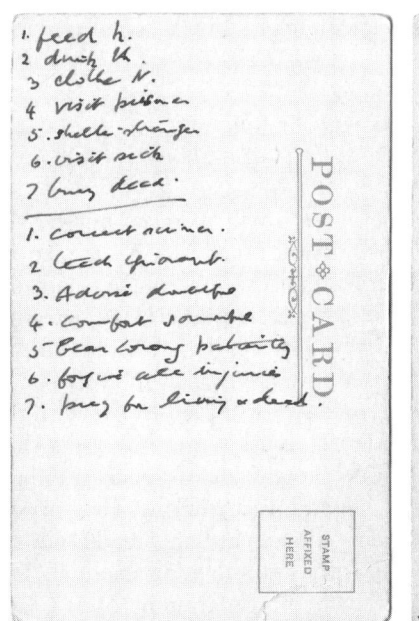
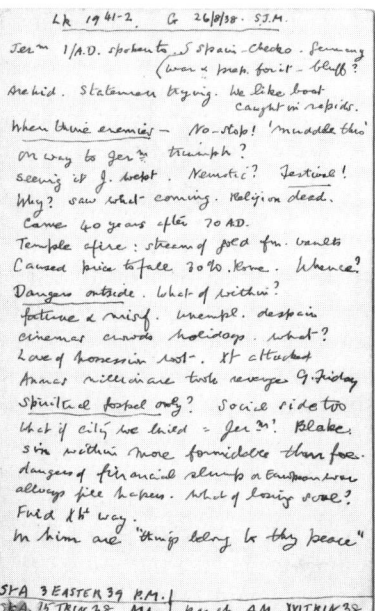

Sermon notes on postcards: Practical Christianity; and the Destruction of Jerusalem

Peace Pledge Union was carrying all before it, and in the summer of 1937 Sheppard founded the Anglican Pacifist Fellowship – with the blessing of Cosmo Lang, Archbishop of Canterbury.

Some of Father's sermons, like that on the duties of Practical Christianity, were still rather conventional. But by autumn 1938 the political crisis had become so acute that he preached on the destruction of Jerusalem, speaking from a card composed with special care.

His theme could hardly have been more topical, for the Prime Minister, Neville Chamberlain, was meeting Hitler in Munich that same week-end, hoping to secure 'peace for our time', even if it meant sacrificing Czech independence. Were German preparations for war, Father wondered, merely a bluff? The situation recalled the passage (from Luke 19: 41–42) in which Jesus, denouncing the profanation of the Temple, weeps over the forthcoming destruction of Jerusalem. What is now under threat, Father suggested, is the attempt to build Jerusalem in England's green and pleasant land, as evoked by William Blake. The threat of financial slump and European war may fill the newspapers, but for Christians there is a further peril: 'What of losing your soul?' By the time he delivered this warning to another congregation, at Easter 1939, the Germans were in Prague and appeasement was discredited.

In addition to politics, our parents had to cope with the frustrations of everyday life. The dilemma of the Anglican curate is famously defined in a *Punch* cartoon, which depicts an aspiring cleric breakfasting with his superiors:

Bishop: I'm afraid you've got a bad egg, Mr Jones.
Curate: Oh no, my Lord, I assure you! Parts of it are excellent!

Curates were expected to be grateful for small mercies, but by the spring of 1938 Father was becoming so disillusioned that he penned an article about an (unnamed) village near a famous golf course – 'a most apathetic place', consisting mainly of rich houses and their lazy servants. In a maze of winding roads with no real village centre it was difficult to find support for any communal activity until an enterprising Rector had a brainwave. He organized a weekly gym class for the choirboys with the aid of a military instructor from Sandhurst. Within a few months they reached such a high standard that their display delighted a packed Village Hall, while their singing improved beyond recognition! This article catches the panicky mood of the moment – the sense that something must be done to prevent the youth of Britain from becoming 'degenerate'. The parallel is with Nazi Germany, admired for its programme of Strength through Joy.

While Mother enjoyed parish life, Father was increasingly restless. With war on the horizon he thought of training as an army chaplain, but was discouraged by the Bishop of Guildford. A package of press cuttings reveals that in June 1938 he wrote anonymously to a Church newspaper lamenting the frustrations of curates. The sympathetic responses had no practical outcome, so the following year, on 26 May 1939, he placed a notice in *The Times*, a paper available to the clergy at half price. The laconic two-liner announced: 'BUCOLIC PRIEST (33) SEEKS LIVING: Glebe preferred; prospects solicited', followed once again by a coded address. This time he struck lucky, for after a meeting with the Bishop of Exeter he was offered a living as Rector of Combe-in-Teignhead in south Devon, a haven from the imminence of war.

HILDA'S BICYCLE

There was one response to Nazism in which anyone could join – supporting refugees. Events in Europe following the annexation of Austria, the Munich Agreement, and the pogrom of November 1938, had forced Jewish families to flee from persecution. The British government responded with a scheme that allowed approximately ten thousand German-speaking women to enter the country as domestic servants. All over Britain committees were set up to assist the refugees. The group at Sunningdale was led by Mrs William Cecil Smyly, who encouraged my parents to make room at the Parsonage for a young Jewish woman. This was the half-remembered Hilda, photographed with me in her arms beside that giant snowman. When she arrived, she was able to bring her bicycle from Germany, a sturdy machine with an elaborate skirt-guard. It was good to have help in the house during that difficult year, and Hilda accompanied the family to Devon in September 1939, the month war was declared.

Never had Britain been in greater peril than during our years at Combe. After the evacuation from Dunkirk, the country would have been demoralized but for Churchill's leadership. Panic about poison gas had prompted gas masks to be issued even to tiny children. The government was developing chemical weapons at a secret research centre (Porton Down in Wiltshire), and there was reason to believe the Germans were doing the same. Air Raid Precautions (the ARP) issued a leaflet in July 1939 entitled SOME THINGS YOU SHOULD KNOW IF WAR SHOULD COME. This contained instructions about Air Raid Warnings, Gas Masks, and the Evacuation of Children from the London area. Fear was in the air, for when we tried the gas masks on, the visors misted over and it was difficult to breathe.

Our parents anticipated the evacuation by moving us to the West Country several weeks before the Rectory became available. First Mother took us to Rowden, but the farmstead was so cramped that we moved across the village to stay with Grandpa and Auntie at Collery. Restless children got on their nerves, and as a last resort we moved to Halls, a farm belonging to another branch of the family. It was Auntie at Halls who saved the day, and the country air had unexpected benefits, for suddenly – in the arms of Uncle Jack – I began to speak. My delayed speech may have been due to Hilda, the German maid. It was one of her tasks to settle me in the collapsible cot that had served the family so well – we loved the colourful nursery-rhyme characters on its gleaming white panels. But Hilda's presence altered the bedtime ritual, for she would sing me German lullabies like Hänschen Klein, about a child leaving home, rather than Humpty Dumpty or Old King Cole. It is a mixed blessing to have two languages laid in your cradle.

Since the nation was at war, we were expected to despise the enemy, but how was this possible with a cuddly German girl in the family, helping to dress the children and wash the dishes? Hilda lived with us at the Rectory until the invasion scare that followed the fall of France. There was a sudden panic about the refugees, enemy aliens who might be spying for Germany. 'Collar the lot!' Churchill ordered, and thousands of men, mainly German-speaking Jews, were rounded up and interned. Women were treated more leniently, but they were banned from living near the coast, for fear they would assist the invaders. So Hilda was obliged to leave, obtaining a visa for Canada. I was just three years old in June 1940 when she left, but well aware of her absence, for she left her bike behind. For many years Hilda's bicycle hung on the wall in our garage – symbolizing an intangible loss with enduring consequences.

Living rent-free in the roomy Rectory made up for Father's modest stipend. Admittedly, there was no Glebe for a bucolic priest to farm, but Combe was a real village with post office, bakery and general store. The parish church, built of red sandstone, could be reached along a footpath from the Rectory. At Harvest Festival, on Sunday 1 October, Father recalled the Jewish customs described in chapter 11 of Ecclesiastes, stressing the precept: 'In the morning sow thy seed'. We can't always calculate the result of our actions, he continued, but there may be a good harvest even from corn sown on a cloudy day. In the parish magazine for December 1939, which featured his photograph, he introduced himself as a 'country lad', hoping that village people would treat him as one of themselves.

Mother, too, soon felt at home. A favourite walk took us to half a mile to Archibrook, overlooking the Teign estuary, and Father would sometimes drive us in his capacious Wolsey to the beach at Combe Sellars. But after the German occupation of the Channel Islands the fear of invasion haunted the land. Kent and Sussex were directly threatened, but there might be diversionary landings in Dorset or Devon, so the beaches were blocked with barbed wire. Fearing an invasion that would bring German landing craft up the estuary, the Home Guard began to fortify the village. Father, one of the few civilians in the group photograph, acted as chaplain, and sandbags were stacked along the hedge at the bottom of our garden.

Dad's army was hardly a fighting force, and his attitude was ambivalent. One of the first sermons he preached at Combe was entitled No Neutrality, a theme inspired by Jesus' words: 'He that is not for me is against me'. This suggests that Father shared the mood of defiance inspired by Churchill's broadcasts. 'Hitler knows that he will have to break us,' the Prime Minister declared on 18 June. 'If we can stand up to him, all Europe may be free and the life of the world may move forward into broad, sunlit uplands.' However, Father was shocked by the air attacks on German cities. On Palm Sunday, 28 April 1942, the Royal Air Force bombed the Baltic port of Lübeck. After reading reports about the destruction of military targets, he checked the plan of Lübeck in the *Encyclopedia Britannica*, discovering – as he suspected – that the ancient city centre had been flattened.

As the best-educated person in the parish, he was entrusted with sealed instructions for coordinating resistance after the invaders had landed. But talk of 'fighting on the beaches' left him cold, given the actual measures taken to resist invasion. He later told me that he was inclined to surrender the village at the earliest opportunity, believing it would be futile to resist the advancing panzers. Much as we admired his independence of mind, we'd have preferred Father to be more heroic. After all, Uncle George was in uniform, training as an officer, and we made friends with one of our neighbours, a veteran named Captain Scaife. He presented the boys with his periscope, a tubular contraption with two interacting mirrors that enabled us to keep watch for the enemy from behind the sandbags.

More alarming than the imagined invasion were the blackout curtains that covered every window to prevent us from showing lights that might invite air raids. At night the village was in total darkness, while indoors the lights were kept low, creating a spooky atmosphere for small children. The Luftwaffe concentrated its attacks on Plymouth and Exeter, but at night German planes followed the river Teign up to Newton Abbott, where they bombed the railway junction. At Combe the sky was full of mysterious sights and sounds. Rambling through the woods we discovered strips of shining foil dropped by enemy planes to confuse our radar. We couldn't resist collecting the foil, although some boys claimed they were for germ warfare. Was there a connection, I wondered, between germs and Germans?

My greatest comfort was to share Mother's bed during her afternoon rest. Attuned to the rhythm of her breathing as she slept, I once – when she stirred – murmured: 'Please don't stop'. My words woke her up, and the soporific magic ceased. Excluded from our parents' bedroom at night, I responded by fetching the elongated oil-can that Father used to lubricate his car and squirting the contents all over their bedroom wall. The children slept under the eaves of the three-storey Rectory, and it was there that my dream life began. While Helen and David shared a room, I slept on my own in a brass-knobbed bedstead known as the dreamy bed. 'Close your eyes,' Mother would say, 'and the Sandman will come'; but sometimes he brought disturbing dreams that sent me groping downstairs.

As the risk of invasion receded, it was germs that attacked us. The draughty Rectory caused ear and throat infections, for which the treatment was tonsillectomy. How proud I felt at the age of four, carrying my little suitcase as they drove me to hospital. The operation was done under anaesthetic, but the experience left an emotional scar, for relatives were not permitted to stay overnight. Worse was to follow when I was sent to recuperate with elderly neighbours who owned a quiet house with a large garden. My only companion was a tricycle, to which I would cling for comfort. How different from that cheerful bout of chicken pox shared with Helen and David! Then we had romped in the bedroom at home while Mother brought us meals on a tray. Now I pined to be back with the family, recently enlarged by the birth of my curly-headed brother Robert in July 1940.

Despite these real or imagined terrors, Combe provided a sanctuary from a war-torn world. My first taste of school was delightful, for I was allowed to join the others at Miss Hughes's kindergarten, overlooking the river at Shaldon, where we learnt raffia work and dressing-up. Miss Hughes staged the Tea Party scene from *Alice in Wonderland* with Helen as Mad Hatter and David as March Hare. Being so timid, I was cast as the Dormouse and gently dunked in the teapot. Generally we travelled to school by Balls Bus, the firm that ran a service through Combe to Shaldon, but on occasion we would be collected by Father in his car.

A person of his ability could hardly be happy in such a tiny parish, but with many priests serving with the forces his prospects improved. In autumn 1942 Father was invited to meet Robert Fleming at his home in Camberley, braving the bombing raids to reach his destination. The Fleming family were patrons of the benefice of Buckfastleigh, a mill-town midway between Exeter and Plymouth. After a searching interview followed by a meeting with the Parochial Church Council, Father was offered the living. By West Country standards the small town was industrialized, and Mother was taken aback by the narrow streets, noisy sirens and belching factory chimneys. This was very different from the farming communities in which our parents felt most at home, but with a growing family they welcomed the augmented income, so they rose to the challenge.

A Vicarage Childhood

During those early days at Buckfastleigh Vicarage we would cluster around an open fire listening to the wireless. Five o'clock was Children's Hour with its blend of songs and stories. Who needed television when *Peter Pan* could be dramatized so evocatively? We even sympathized with the villainous Captain Hook, pursued by the sound of a relentlessly ticking clock that had been swallowed by a crocodile. In the evening the BBC News brought us together. Father would sit by the shuttered window with Mother seated opposite, sewing-box at her side. Helen and David hog the couch with me squeezed between them, delighted to be staying up late with Robert already in bed. During our years at Combe the news had been a chain of disasters, but January 1943 marked a turning point. After the chimes of Big Ben we heard of victories at Stalingrad and El Alamein – outlandish names that sparked a sense of freedom.

LIBERTY HALL

The Vicarage was a Georgian building in an elevated position with views towards the surrounding hills. At first the house seemed cavernous and forbidding. The antiquated gas-lighting had to be sealed and the plumbing and wiring renewed. But Mother set to work with characteristic energy, and once a new bathroom had been installed the house began to feel like home. Five bedrooms provided scope for a child-orientated family, and soon she was pregnant again. Amid the wartime shortages we had to make do and mend, so most things were second hand. But our parents had a flair for auctions, returning with sprawling carpets and capacious chests-of-drawers.

We enjoyed frequent visits from Mother's younger sister Marion, working as a midwife in Plymouth. She was at the Vicarage in September

1943 for the birth of Christopher, assisted only by Father. Chris was the first child to be born at home and we were thrilled when she brought the newborn baby into our bedroom – but why was his penis so long? Marion laughingly explained that this was the umbilical cord. During the following years there was almost always a baby to be settled in the Humpty Dumpy cot brought from Combe: Jonathan born in April 1945, Margaret in February 1947, Simon in April 1950. There was also space for a live-in maid, a buxom country girl named Brenda who quickly gained our affection.

Father thrived on his new social and pastoral responsibilities. Holy Trinity, the parish church, stood high above the town, a formidable walk for worshippers. 'Why was it built so far out?' we asked. The medieval village must have been near the church, he explained, but later the population gravitated to the banks of the Mardle, the moorland stream that courses through the town servicing the woollen industry. The spire was visible for miles around, forming an important landmark. After the dissolution of the monasteries a fine peal of eight bells had been acquired from the Benedictine abbey at Buckfast. During the invasion scare of 1940, Churchill had imposed a ban on bell-ringing – they were only to be rung as a signal that the enemy had landed. By the spring of 1943 the threat of invasion was over and the ban on bells was lifted. It was a glorious moment when they rang out again, calling the faithful to celebrate the approach of peace.

From the churchyard with its sprawl of lichen-encrusted graves there were glorious views towards the moors. 'Why does this look more like a prison?' I asked, pointing to a penthouse near the porch. Peering through the metal railings, we could see a tomb sealed by a massive slab. The vault contained the body of Richard Cabell, a Dartmoor landowner who died in 1677. His evil reputation gave rise to the legend that black dogs breathing fire were found howling around his body. It was this folktale, Father explained, that inspired Arthur Conan Doyle to write *The Hound of the Baskervilles*, that most macabre of Sherlock Holmes mysteries. Superstitious souls insisted that the vault should never be disturbed. Two years before our arrival iron railings had been removed from the churchyard to be melted down for the war effort, but no one had touched the Baskerville tomb.

Although by no means as ancient as the church, the Vicarage had quite a history. It stood next to Glebelands, the farm formerly attached to the living, which had been sold before the war. It was exciting to cross the Big Field, which still formed part of the grounds, and play in the derelict outbuildings and abandoned horse-carts. At the entrance to the field stood a large mounting block, where earlier Vicars had saddled up to visit their flock. They had also run their own school, for next to the house stood the imposing Schoolroom with storehouses underneath. The School in its heyday had included James Anthony Froude among its pupils, a noted historian. Now the Schoolroom was used by community groups, including a brass band that would come once a week to collect their instruments.

A large cellar ran the whole length of the Vicarage, with cobbled rooms where horses had been stabled. It was now used to store apples and pears from the orchard, harvested by Father with help from the children. Among piles of discarded books stood a venerable wind-powered organ on which you could play haunting chords, enhancing the mystery of that nether world. We felt safer in the attic, reached up four flights of stairs, which had once served as sleeping quarters for children attending the School. It was here among the trunks and suitcases that we dumped our gas masks, thankfully no longer needed. Nearby was a crystal set from which we tried to transmit coded messages and a metal canister designed for making ice cream. Try as we might we never succeeded in producing the longed-for delicacy. There was no heating in the bedrooms, and on winter evenings we would dive under the bedclothes, cuddling hotwater-bottles filled by Father to take the chill out of the sheets. It was his task to prevent the house from freezing, and he kept good fires blazing downstairs.

The Vicarage with its grounds and outbuildings was a paradise for children. Halfway down the garden there was a brick tool-shed, ideal for use as a playhouse, and there was a harum-scarum temper about our lives, sliding down the banisters, chasing chickens in the fields or building dens in the bushes. Father's patience was sorely tried by the din we made. 'Don't mind me, this is Liberty Hall!' he would cry in mock despair echoing a favourite play, *She Stoops to Conquer*. 'You may do as you please here!' Like Goldsmith's peppery paterfamilias, he had to cope with high-spirited youngsters claiming the run of the house. Fortunately for us, Father was not a traditional disciplinarian. 'Tact!' he would cry in an effort to calm our squabbles, or 'Path!' if our toys threatened to cover the whole floor. Faced by the rising tide of tearaways and toddlers, he would retreat to his study or escape in his car.

Petrol rationing meant that most private cars had to be laid up for the duration including our thirsty Wolsey, parked in the coach-house underneath the Schoolroom. Hilda's bicycle was stored nearby, suspended from the wall to avoid damage. Father was able to eke out the modest petrol ration allocated for his duties of a parson by acquiring a more economical two-door Morris, so he had fuel for a limited weekly mileage. The car provided a quiet place where he could sit and think, sipping tea from a thermos, and sometimes he would take us with him as he drove off for a meeting or a pastoral visit. Did we realize how privileged we were? Motoring was an unimpeded pleasure when he drove across the moors for the monthly meeting of the Clerical Society. Even in wartime the South Devon clergy would gather for learned discussions of New Testament Greek. Mother would take us for country walks with bikes for the older ones and prams for those with shorter legs. It was only on Sundays that we became copybook Vicarage children, trooping up the hill to the parish church in our smartest clothes, or to evening services at St Luke's, a more practical but rather dingy building in the town centre.

The Vicarage was a haven for a family addicted to games. The dining room storage cupboard was converted into a home for jigsaw puzzles, which would compete with board games for space on the mahogany table. From a chaotic jumble of pieces would emerge a Beatrix Potter figure or a fire engine racing through a farmyard. We also had a kaleidoscope which produced amazingly colourful configurations when rotated. But I was a jigsaw-puzzle person, patiently fitting pieces together rather than making leaps of the imagination. With the younger children Mother would play Ludo or Happy Families, and card-games became an evening ritual as Father introduced us to Bridge and the art of finesse.

The Vicarage was a bookish place with shelves in every room: fairy-tales and adventure stories in the bedrooms, more edifying publications in the dining-room, history in the drawing-room, theology in Father's study, and lighter reading in the lavatory. There would even be books at bath-time. While we relaxed in the tub, Mother would read us the charmingly illustrated Bible Stories for Little Folks. The final line from the

The Co-operative
Wheatsheaf symbol

The Squander Bug
(from a poster of the
1940s)

parable of the Lost Sheep was so reassuring: 'Rejoice, for that which was lost has been found'. Then we might be tucked into bed with a chapter from *The Wind in the Willows* or *The Family at One End Street*. Sharing a room with Robert encouraged my own story-telling skills. Following the example of folktales like the Billy-Goats Gruff, I would divide each episode into three parts – a dialectical pattern that is with me still.

There were no books in the breakfast-room, hub of family life with a sturdy Aga stove. Mother would be up early cooking breakfast and peeling potatoes or apples for delicious pies. Junket, saffron cake and prunes were further favourites. After meals, piles of dishes had to be washed and dried, generating a cosy conversational rhythm, especially when Aunty Marion lent a hand. As a nurse she had a fund of anecdotes, amusing us with stories about people clamouring for medicines when all they really needed was a 'dose of common sense'! In the evening Father would emerge from his study to tackle the *Times* crossword with an occasion contribution from the children. Mother, too, developed a flair for crosswords, almost matching her genius for Scrabble.

The shortages taught us to share – a bar of Cadbury's chocolate had to be divided into eight pieces. With so many ration books Mother managed rather well, shopping at Heywood the Baker, Hoff the Butcher and Jeffrey the Grocer as well as the Co-operative Society, which owned the woollen mill. Almost everyone shopped at the Co-op – there were about two thousand inhabitants in the town and our family's membership number was 698. But the thrift and patience symbolized by the Co-op's Wheatsheaf emblem (FIGURE: The Co-operative Wheatsheaf) were challenged by the wicked Squander Bug (FIGURE: The Squander Bug). This cartoon character, adorned with swastikas, was designed by the National Savings campaign to convey the message that self-indulgent spending would undermine the war effort.

We learnt that nothing should be wasted – potato peelings were taken out to the field to feed the geese. They were supposed to keep the grass cropped, but would often escape through a half-open gate. 'Chase the geese back into the field!' Mother would say, a simple task for someone brought up on a farm. Armed with an iron bar I toddled down the path to fetch two geese lurking in a shed, little realizing that it was mating time. The gander swooped, I turned and fled, tripped on the cobbles and fell flat on my face. In a flash the monster was upon me, pecking the back of my neck until my screams were heard.

VALIANT SOLDIERS

Even our sheltered childhood was shadowed by war. The sky was filled with barrage balloons, and we learnt to distinguish the wail of the siren from the hooter calling workers to the mill. Soldiering was in the air, and when Uncle George visited us in uniform, he presented us with a sleek black automatic captured from the enemy. Next to the cabinet in Father's study which contained the communion plate stood a double-barrelled shotgun used for shooting pheasants and scaring rooks. Fascinated by weapons of every kind, we mimicked the jargon of combat: blitz, straf, flak, panzer and stuka crumbled under the attack of ammo, joystick, spitfire, prang and gone for a burton. The British were always victorious on our drawing-room carpet, where we constructed fortifications with the massive crimson tomes of the *Times History of the First World War*. When David was given an airgun for his birthday, we were soon hitting the target which Father had fixed to a gatepost, the lid of one of his Players Navy Cut tobacco tins.

The airgun pellets could do serious damage when pushed deep into the breech to increase velocity. David and I would pepper the geese from long range, making them squawk with surprise. Worse was to follow one evening when we were chatting with Brenda in the kitchen, with the airgun beside us. Feeling left out, I cocked the gun, failing to notice that David had already inserted a pellet. Pointing the gun at Brenda, I hoped that the loud report it made, even when unloaded, would win me her attention. She screamed as the pellet hit her breast, but fortunately she was wearing thick winter clothing, so she only suffered a bruise. A few months later this lovely young woman left us to get married – had I scared her away?

Although the cowboys were the heroes in the films we watched at the local Picture House, my sympathies lay with the long-suffering Indians. Father's archery equipment, kept in a corner of the Pantry, was almost too heavy to handle, while the fearsome arrows had sharp steel tips. Quoting his favourite tales from Homer, he would warn us that it took a man to string Ulysses' Bow. Having been given a brilliantly coloured Red Indian headdress as my birthday present, I began to pester my parents for a tent. Wartime shortages meant that there was no such thing in the shops, so they placed an advertisement in *The Times*: 'Big Chief Needs Wigwam'.

Ten days later we were erecting a brightly coloured tepee on the lawn and fetching Father's bow and arrows. We were joined by a charming squaw named Ann Williams, daughter of the local woman who came to help with the housework. Robert was to represent a rival tribe hunting buffalos on the lawn – actually they were goslings, just hatched from a clutch of eggs. That afternoon, aiming at Robert one of the steel-tipped arrows, I challenged him to dodge behind the acacia tree. I fired, he dodged, and the arrow pierced a passing gosling. We were grief-stricken about the gosling, which died the following day, but Mother wondered what would have happened if Robert hadn't dodged.

Looking back on our adventures at the Vicarage, it seems a miracle that no one was gravely hurt. From the attic there was a small window which was left unlocked, leading out onto a broad lead gutter. There was nothing to stop us from crawling out and even clambering across the roof to retrieve tennis balls, ignoring the risk of a thirty-foot drop. Games of cricket in the front yard were only slightly less hazardous, since a forceful drive was likely to shatter the windows of Father's study. So many panes were broken that our parents would block them with cardboard, for it was not worth getting them repaired until we were back at school. Mother would then call the glazier and take him around the house, pointing out the windows to be repaired. After one such tour, he inquired with a sympathetic smile: 'And how are the dear children?'

It was impossible to ignore the drone of war. Hearing enemy planes on their way to bomb the docks at Plymouth, we wondered how Aunty Marion was surviving. On my father's advice she made a will, which she posted to him for safekeeping. A few weeks later a patched-up package arrived with a note from the Royal Mail saying 'Found in the street next to a letter-box destroyed by bombing'. In autumn 1943 the troops began to arrive on our doorstep. Only Father was aware that people had been evacuated from villages near the South Devon coast to make way for the

US army, so we were surprised to see American soldiers in town. They would gather for an evening drink in one of the pubs – the Valiant Soldier, the Waterman's Arms or the Sun Inn at the bottom of Silver Street. From our bedroom window we could hear them carousing as they spilled out into the street after drinking pints of scrumpy, a potent local cider. Sometimes a soldier would be carried out and laid in the orchard to sleep off his hangover under our apple trees.

In the spring of 1944 an incessant rumbling prompted us to race down to see what was happening. We could scarcely believe our eyes: Armageddon at the bottom of our garden! We watched entranced as a stream of military vehicles poured along the road, gearing up for manoeuvres on Dartmoor. This was part of the greatest army ever assembled for a seaborne invasion – the D-Day landings. Those really were valiant soldiers for the casualties were horrendous (Uncle George was among the wounded). The invasion took place three days after my seventh birthday, so the book given me by my parents was well chosen – the Victorian children's classic *Giant-Land*. As the troops fought their way up the Normandy beaches, my imagination was pursuing monsters with Little Tim's trusty sword.

David and I devoured books about modern military conflict. From Uncle George we had inherited a taste for *Champion*, the boys weekly featuring heroes like Sergeant Bill Ross, leader of the lost commandos, and Rockfist Rogan of the Royal Air Force. And there was no end to the yarns of imperial conquest like *Keepers of the Khyber*, *The Bengal Lancers* and *Deeds that Thrill the Empire*. It felt as if our country had been at war for ever. From a battered copy of Jane's *Fighting Ships* we learnt the difference between the British dreadnoughts and German battle cruisers of the First World War, and the excitement of sailing was evoked by Arthur Ransome books like *We didn't Mean to Go to Sea*. A further favourite was *When the Vikings Came*, an account in archaic English of resistance against foreign invaders.

As the Allied armies advanced towards the Rhine, the Church of England held a National Day of Prayer. Taking the Sunday services on 3 September 1944, Father read out a prayer of thanks 'for the courage and devotion of men and women in Navy, Army and Air Force; and for the unity and constancy of our whole people'. In his sermon he stressed that deliverance depended not on a single day of prayer, but on being faithful to truth and right 'day by day and week by week'. The following spring there was nothing triumphalist in his sermon for St George's Day, at the moment of victory. After reviewing the legends about defeating dragons, he highlighted the essential message: the 'defence of the weak against the strong'. More important than the emblem of St George was the work of the Geneva-based Red Cross.

A further opportunity to discuss strategic questions arose during the final phase of the war. The housing shortage prompted my parents to share the Vicarage with a Royal Air Force family, Flight-Lieutenant Mitchell with his wife and two sons, Johnny and Neil. Since the raids on Lübeck, Father had been opposed to the destruction of German cities. Like George Bell, Bishop of Chichester, he believed that carpet bombing was both immoral and counterproductive. Such debates were above our heads as we conducted war games, but we knew that ground forces held the key to victory. Our model aircraft had undeniable glamour, but tanks and field-guns were needed for the final advance. In May 1945 Victory in Europe was celebrated with a party outside the Sun Inn, with trestle tables set up to feast several hundred children.

Homely Schooling

It was not only thousands of children that were evacuated during the war, but schools complete with their staff. Alleyn Court, a boys preparatory school from Essex, had taken over Bigadon House, formerly the residence of the Fleming family, a handsome building overlooking the town. In autumn 1943, after making various inquiries, our parents enrolled me as a dayboy at Alleyn Court together with my brother David. Given the shortage of teachers, Father was asked to take classes in maths and scripture, so the fees were waived. Every morning he would drive us up the winding road through the woods. Most days we would be accompanied by Joseph Van Biene, a distinguished-looking Dutchman who had found sanctuary in England and also helped out with teaching. Van Biene lodged near the Vicarage with a garrulous woman whose husband had recently died. 'What a terrible death!' he would mutter, as he tried to close his ears to her chatter.

Alleyn Court had a reputation for both teaching and sports, but we were made to feel inferior to the boarders, and although I enjoyed playing games in the woods, class work proved a trial. There were spelling tests that required you to recite the letters out loud, exposing you to ridicule if you got things wrong. Worse still was Mr Yelling, a martinet who lived up to his name by terrorizing his charges. As a matter of principle he would refuse the request to 'be excused' from boys who needed the toilet. Consequently, there were days when my desk would be surrounded by a pool of water. My diffidence is captured in a family photo showing me with hands in pockets (front left), looking frail with shifted shoulders and spindly legs, while David and Robert stand sturdily beside me.

Walking back from school was a further ordeal. Father would drive home mid-morning after his classes, so we were on our own. It was two miles down a country lane and back through the town, but first we had to cross a farmyard patrolled by dogs. Taking his courage in both hands,

David would make the dash for safety, leaving me to scramble after him with the hounds in hot pursuit. Sometimes the farmer's wife would call the dogs to heel, but the anxiety was hard to bear. In Buckfastleigh, too, there were dogs on the prowl, and one day local boys formed a crowd to watch a fight between a mastiff and a cocker spaniel. Against such an adversary the spaniel had no chance, and its floppy black ears were soon dripping with blood. What alarmed me most was that the boys were cheering the mastiff, while I identified with the spaniel. Fearsome beasts were soon haunting my sleep, snarling like the hound of the Baskervilles. If we heard on the wireless that a convict had escaped from Dartmoor Prison, we would lie awake at night wondering whether he would come our way. In a recurrent nightmare there were dogs lurking in the closet, but no one could hear my stifled cries for help. Such dreams would send me across the landing to snuggle next to Mother in the double bed. But Father took up so much space that I'd be shivering on the edge until I finally crept back into my room.

It was not the struggle in Europe that caused panic in a seven-year-old, but heavy-handed schooling. Having gifted siblings was an incentive, but would I ever be as cheerful as Robert, as sturdy as David or as creative as Helen? Much to my relief my parents withdrew me from Alleyn Court after discovering that another boy my age, John Moat, was finding the regime equally unbearable. John was now being tutored at home by a governess named Miss Burge, and since they lived only a couple of miles up the road towards the moors it was arranged that I would join him. Father would drop me off at their thatched house, set by a stream in a rambling garden. Here we enjoyed a homely form of schooling, and lessons ceased to be an ordeal. John had a flair for composition while my maths improved under Miss Burge's guidance. She set me homework from a well-designed primer with eye-catching illustrations, Ballard's Arithmetic. Shopping was one of the most attractive features, with each item priced in the illustrated shop-windows at so much per ounce. It was fun to work out the cost of a basket of groceries, reckoning twelve pence to the shilling and twenty shillings to the pound.

After lessons, John and I would explore the garden and paddle across the stream, a paradise for adventure learning. Miss Burge must have had mixed feelings as she watched us carving wooden boats with our pocket-knives and constructing dams out of pebbles. But she would not have been the first to see a flowing brook as the wellspring of wisdom. Those boys would surely grow up to become engineers or architects, rather than poets or scholars! This time there were no dogs to waylay me on the solitary walk back home. There were joyful encounters when Mother walked up the hill to meet me, accompanied by five-year-old Robert. This provided the bonus of a botany lesson, as we gathered flowers from the hedgerow, learning the difference between Sweet William and Bird's Foot Trefoil.

The interlude with the governess left formal education in limbo (even my fumbling efforts at the piano ended in failure). But salvation came in the form of two middle-aged spinsters, dumpy Miss Hunter and willowy Miss Boustead. They seemed an odd couple, but their combination of talents enabled them to establish Rock Preparatory School at their house on the road to the station. Turning their home into a school proved a winning formula. After opening with eight pupils in April 1946, the school went from strength to strength, providing a basic education for no less than six of the Vicarage children. In the senior class, the over-eights, there were initially just two pupils – myself and a delightful girl named Rosemary Bolton. Robert joined the junior class with five other children, including Nicholas Coulton, who was later to have a distinguished career in the Anglican Church.

Neither teacher had been formally trained, so their methods were unorthodox. When Rosemary and I arrived in the mornings, we would be given copy of *The Times*, which the ladies had been reading over breakfast. Certain words had been underlined, and we were instructed to learn them by heart, since we would be tested later. Rosemary, with her verbal skills, could cope pretty well, but I managed to get most of them wrong. It seemed unfair to ask us to memorize long words like 'nationalization', but my parents said we were lucky to have them underlined in advance. While Miss Hunter's manner was severe, we could relax with Miss Boustead, who made learning French seem fun. For the first time I actually enjoyed going to school. This was due partly to Rosemary's charms, partly to walking home with Robert. The route through the town took barely ten minutes, but sometimes we would climb the Two Hundred Steps to the Parish Church, returning home along country lanes.

One of the strongest bonds between us was the pleasure of reading. It was not only outgrown clothes that were handed on, but the books we all enjoyed. Mother would read to us from an edition of *The Water Babies* with sensuous images of scantily clad children, or from Kipling's *Jungle Book* with Mowgli pictured among the wolves and Rikki-tikki-tavi confronting the cobra. The social satire in the *Just William* stories by Richmal Crompton was also vividly illustrated, and we enjoyed the exploits of Greek heroes like Jason capturing the Golden Fleece and Odysseus outwitting the Sirens. But if educationally life was an open book, emotionally we learnt to be reserved. Difficulties were to be resolved not through open discussion, but by nightly saying our prayers. Feelings were kept at a distance, but family life was enhanced by a conversational code that blended social precepts with literary allusions. 'Tact!' Father would say to calm a children's quarrel and 'Science!' when we resorted to brute force. Or he would soothe a fretful infant by quoting from Lewis Carroll: 'Come to my arms, my beamish boy!'

'What is the good of books without pictures and conversations?' Alice

The Mad Hatter's Tea Party (by John Tenniel, 1865)

asks on the opening page of *Alice in Wonderland*, and the illustrations came to life as we gathered around a tea table that could be as whimsical as that in the story (FIGURE: The Mad Hatter's Tea Party).

We had loved the Tea Party scene since kindergarten days, when I was a dreamy dormouse. Now we responded more consciously to the melody of Carroll's wordplay and the counterpoint of Tenniel's figures. Father would recite lines from the Hunting of the Snark, as well as verses by Edward Lear about the Jumblies or the Pobbles. And there were moments when the breakfast-room was transformed into a field of nonsense littered with hatters and hares, jabberwockies and treacle wells. Our talk was enlivened by phrases like 'frabjous day', 'curiouser and curiouser' or 'it was the *best* butter'. Soon we were picking up echoes from P. G. Wodehouse stories about parsons preaching interminable sermons or effete young men pursued by formidable aunts. This unconventional literary education provided a foretaste of the verbal play of satire.

The house became full of melody when Helen practised the piano, performing the hymn tunes that Mother loved or Father's impassioned favourite, the Arrival of the Queen of Sheba. There was none of the sententiousness you might expect of a parson's family. Framed inscriptions like The Lord is my Shepherd made way for delicate watercolours by Eric Walker, an artistically gifted friend from Father's student days. Vicarage culture was surprisingly secular, for we learnt about the natural world from the *Children's Encyclopedia*. The ten blue volumes, edited by Arthur Mee, were read so often that they began to fall apart, and the brilliant colour plates caught my imagination long before I could cope with the multifarious text. In 1943 my sister Helen, who had been attending Haccombe House as a weekly boarder, won a place at Christ's Hospital school for girls. Opening the relevant volume of the *Encyclopedia*, Father proudly showed me the Christ's Hospital crest.

It was Arthur Mee who opened our eyes to the wider world. His approach to the universe of knowledge was firmly scientific, but he succeeded in conveying complex processes in visual terms: the planetary system, the emergence of the earth out of a ball of gas, the evolution of primates and the life of plants. Mee also gave ample space to religion and history, art and literature. Darwin and Jesus both received their due, in separate narratives. The Bible was presented as the 'greatest story ever told', but it was made clear that it was a story – a narrative with a history of its own. Thus the account of the earth being created in seven days was described as 'an inspired vision, placed first in their sacred book by the Hebrews, wonderful in its imagination'. Within this pluralistic framework, religious faith coexisted with scientific inquiry and technical innovation, artistic imagination with ancient legend. Among a multitude of picture stories there were also nursery rhymes, answers to questions that all children ask and guidelines about things to make and do. Prompted by pictures of the Boy Carpenter, I couldn't wait to have a tool set of my own. . .

The breakfast table was strewn with magazines and newspapers, for *The Times* and the *Western Morning News* would be delivered in the mornings, the *Church Times*, *Punch* and *Radio Times* every week, together with our favourite comics *Champion*, *Dandy* and *Beano* until they were replaced by the more educative *Eagle*, *Swift* and *Robin*. They had to compete with the *Totnes Deanery Magazine*, much of it written by Father. Parish magazines tend to be sanctimonious, but he contributed ironic reflections on current affairs, and his Vicar's Notes could be mildly subversive. 'If you should ever be expecting a baby, and ought not to be,' he wrote in December 1944, 'don't write to an agony aunt, but contact your moral welfare officer. She has heard your story many times and exists to help you.'

Father was alert to the compromises required to sustain Christian faith in an increasingly secular society. His open-minded approach also prompted him to give evening classes in Comparative Religion, elucidating the claims of other creeds. At a time of intense rivalry between Anglicanism and other churches he worked for Christian unity, welcoming the appointment of a new Roman Catholic parish priest and cooperating with the Abbot at Buckfast. Before sending his text to the printer, Father would try his ideas out on the family, revising his typewritten drafts in order to achieve a studied informality with humorous undertones. Thus in February 1949 he printed details of an artist's account for touching up the wall paintings of a church, including the following items: 'Correcting the Ten Commandments; putting a new tail on St Peter's rooster; and mending the shirt of the Prodigal Son.'

We listened to Father's sermons with increasing attention – and a growing respect for of his pragmatic Christianity. 'The children of this world are wiser in their time than the children of light', he would say, echoing St Luke's Gospel. After all, he was a farmer's son, brought up to work with his hands, and he valued practical wisdom above other-worldliness. But he combined this with theological scholarship, as reflected in his commentary on the story of the Good Samaritan. The moral message of helping those in need was only the surface meaning, for the parable encapsulated Jesus's debt to his Jewish heritage – the law and the prophets on which Christian faith was founded.

Father's knowledge of ecclesiastical history led him to highlight the links between the Church of England and the Royal Family. A sermon of January 1949 defended Charles I against the Whiggish view that he was a 'bad king' who deserved to be beheaded. Responding, around same date, to what he felt to be an over powerful Labour government, he questioned St Paul's emphasis (in Romans 13:1) on obedience to the state: 'Are we to obey when the State is wrong? German Christians said Yes'. Nationalization, he suggested, was an abuse of state power. Instead, he argued for a 'modern middle way', balancing the need for social reforms against the claims of private property. Priests are supposed to be non-political, but Father's commitment to community service won him election – as an Independent – to the County Council. Education and Health were his twin passions. Convinced that local children could better themselves through further education, he encouraged a former choirboy named Ronald Weeks to train as an architect and was delighted to see him win an international reputation.

As the family expanded it was natural that we should pair off with the brother or sister closest in age: Helen with David, Edward with Robert, Christopher with Jonathan, and Margaret with Simon. I felt lucky to be in the middle, not too young to interact with Helen and David, but not so old as to lose touch with the younger ones. As the oldest, Helen would demonstrate her power by pinning me to the ground and tickling me – a delicious torture. At the junior end Simon shared with us a passion for horse racing. Buckfastleigh had its own National Hunt races, festivals for the whole community. Unlike his more straitlaced Free Church brethren, Father enjoyed the occasional flutter, and he would smuggle us into the unsaddling enclosure. We would return home clutching a bundle of discarded betting-slips to organize imaginary races, with Simon triumphantly astride the rocking horse in the hall.

The advent of television was a significant watershed. Hearing in 1953 that the coronation of Elizabeth II was to be broadcast by the BBC, Father arranged for an aerial to be erected at the parish church so that parishioners could gather to watch the ceremony. Soon transmissions could be accessed from most houses in the town, although our parents were reluctant to install a set at the Vicarage. It was a different story in the Victorian cottages on the other side of Silver Street, where TV sets rapidly became the norm. My brother Christopher, the first enthusiast in the family, would often slip across to watch with our nearest neighbours. One afternoon he agreed to join a walk on Dartmoor strictly on condition that we were home in time for his favourite programme. It was lovely weather, ideal for relaxed conversation as we went striding across the turf, but we were less than halfway when Chris checked his watch and reminded us of our promise.

There were also significant changes in reading habits. Growing up in a country at war, the older ones were weaned on adventures set in remote corners of the Empire. Girls were expected to enjoy stories like *The Quest of Honor*, given to Helen at the age of twelve, which describes the mission to India of an intrepid young woman pilot. For the younger children, attuned to a more peaceful world, this militaristic fare was no longer appropriate. The new illustrated books featured their favourite TV characters, while the *Children's Encyclopedia* appeared out of date. The narratives of Richmal Crompton presupposed a polite upper-class ethos against which William's gang was in revolt; but as that social setting became increasingly implausible it was the stories of Enid Blyton that captured the imagination. It was now Noddy and Big Ears that appealed, rather than the Pobble or the Snark.

Father was becoming so absorbed in public affairs that there was less time to spend with the children. Ten years earlier he had found time to construct a go-cart, mend our bicycles or teach us target practice. In return we would help him with apple-picking, an autumnal pursuit that kept him in touch with his farming days. But later he became more withdrawn, beavering away at the typewriter in his study between cups of tea before dashing off in the car to the next appointment. To escape from the racket of family life he would often work at night, sleeping on in the mornings despite our efforts to rouse him to meet unexpected callers. A telling episode occurred when Margaret brought a school friend home for a visit. Just as she was about to leave, the friend asked a question that had been puzzling her for days: 'Who is that strange man who keeps coming into the kitchen to pour himself a cup of tea?'

After a decade at Buckfastleigh our parents were in their prime, photographed under the acacia trees. That spring Father published an extended essay in the Parish Magazine, reflecting on the first ten years. His motto was a phrase from the coronation service for Elizabeth II – the prayer that the Queen should be supported by 'a learned and useful clergy'. In his own case an excess of usefulness had diminished his learning, for he now scarcely found time to attend the Clerical Society. 'How does a parson use his time?' he asked. His answer was that, apart from church services, his days were filled with what people call 'consultation'. Parishioners would come to him for advice on any subject under the sun: from housing, wills and probate to pensions, tax and insurance. But often, he added, it was 'only a matter of listening for an hour to someone's troubles, and saying almost nothing in reply'. Advising young couples contemplating marriage required special sensitivity: 'My children have observed that this takes me about an hour and a half'. It sounds as if we were watching the clock. He was also skilled in relationship counselling during the breakup of marriages. 'Oh my giddy aunt,' he might exclaim after one of those sessions, 'they couldn't have made life more difficult for themselves even if they'd tried to do so!'

As Britain emerged from the strains of war, social cohesion became blended with openness to new ideas. Buckfastleigh was a good place to be during the post-war reconstruction led by Clement Atlee's Labour government. The National Health Service meant no more medical bills, Family Allowances were paid to mothers, and there was free orange juice, cod-liver oil and school milk for children. The woollen mills were thriving, and more than a hundred council houses were built at Glebelands, providing affordable modern homes in an airy hillside setting. Aunty Marion, now employed by Devon County Council as a Health Visitor, rented number 77 – just a short walk across the Big Field.

The Vicarage remained our stronghold as we reached the threshold of puberty. A snapshot taken outside the front door marks the rite of passage as our carers bid goodbye to one of their fledglings. Mother stands boldly upright, the abundant heart of the family, while Marion is about to join her, equally devoted in her practical way. In the porch Father is just visible, always ready with wise counsel. This triad gave our upbringing an enduring strength, but we were over protected – and under prepared for the outside world. What if it turned out that life was not a jigsaw puzzle with the pieces neatly boxed? What if a vital piece was missing?

CHAPTER THREE

Lessons of Boarding School

Nothing prepared us for the shock of being packed off to boarding school. Seeking more sophisticated teaching than any local school could provide, Father succeeded in sending six of us to Christ's Hospital, the bluecoat school for boys at Horsham in Sussex with a girls school at Hertford. Helen was the first to pass the competitive entrance exam, starting in autumn 1943, while David was admitted two years later. For me there was an easier path to admission made possible by charitable endowments. Benefactors who had made substantial gifts to the foundation were entitled to present a deserving child, who would take a simpler exam.

Father must have written dozens of letters before he succeeded in obtaining a presentation for me (a feat he was to repeat for my brother Christopher). Early in 1946 we travelled London for the entrance tests at the school office in Great Tower Street. English caused few problems, but long division was beyond me, leaving me feeling despondent. As a reward for my efforts I was taken to watch the celebrated magician Jasper Maskelyne, who dazzled us by beaming a glamorous young woman from a sealed box on stage into an identical box suspended from the rafters. The magic must have rubbed off on me for I was awarded a place at the Preparatory School.

RELIGIOUS FOUNDATIONS

Normally the cost of sending a child to boarding school is beyond a parson's purse, but Christ's Hospital was exceptional. As a religious foundation dating from the dissolution of the monasteries, its endowments enabled it to educate children from lower-income families for a nominal fee. Files from the year 1948 show that the annual income on which our parents were raising seven children totalled £539, plus £78 in Family

Allowances. When the school calculated our required contribution, the answer was 'nil'. This zero rating lasted for twelve years, and in the early 1950s there were four Vicarage children at the school, all boarded, fed, clothed and educated free of charge. This included the cost of the splendid Tudor-style uniform worn by the boys, with its long blue cloak, black breeches, silver buttons and yellow stockings. It was only in the 1960s, after Christopher was admitted, that a modest fee was charged.

Two of the younger children enjoyed a more gradual initiation. Before starting at St John's Leatherhead in Surrey at the age of fourteen, Jonathan attended Woolborough Hill in Newton Abbott, which provided a bridge between home and boarding school. Margaret, the seventh of the Vicarage children, also experienced a more gradual transition. For a time she travelled with her friends on the Dart Valley Railway to Totnes Grammar School, and she was almost twelve when she started as a boarder at St Brandon's School in Somerset. By contrast Simon, the youngest of the family, was sent as a boarder to a prep school in Birmingham at age of eight, before transferring to Christ's Hospital three years later.

Christ's Hospital, affectionately known as Housey, has an enviable reputation, and we owe the foundation an enormous debt. Dramatic buildings in a spacious setting endow the school with grandeur, and our lives were transformed by the spirit of endeavour and the quality of the teaching. But gratitude does not alter the fact that Housey was a hard school. The Spartan ethos was accentuated by post-war austerity, and my first year coincided with one of the coldest winters on record. Snow began to fall on 23 January 1947 and lasted the whole term. David and I had each been given a multicoloured rug to make the dormitories feel cosier, but then our parents decided that those fine fabrics were too delicate for the rough-and-tumble of boarding school, so we packed grey utility blankets instead. We grieved for those homely comforts, but sixty years later one of those glorious rugs survives as a memento.

Being away at school increased the habit of hoarding. Several letters from home survive from those early days, handwritten by Mother, typed by Father so that carbon copies could be posted to other children. He diverted us with quirky anecdotes, while she showed greater sensitivity to the pains of separation, sending us tuck parcels of home-baked delicacies. What I missed most was the company of my brother Robert, but he was to spend three more years at Rock School before joining us at Christ's Hospital. Fortunately I made friends with a boy named Malcolm Postgate, a cheerful character who became like a brother. In the dayroom we would create endless Cat's Cradles with pieces of string, while our favourite playground game was 'Will you be my Robot?' – mimicking a machine that only moved when your friend pressed the right button. Did we sense that there was something robotic about the school routine? It was a relief on Sunday afternoons when David called round from the Upper School to take me out for a country walk, producing a bar of Kit Kat from his pocket. After Robert was admitted to the Prep, it would be my turn to provide the consoling chocolates.

The teachers in the Prep School seemed larger than life. Our long-serving housemaster, M. H. Jones, was known as Jonah – a tribute to his survival skills. Like most teachers he was very patriotic. The project he set us early in 1947 focused on HMS *Vanguard*, the largest battleship ever built for the British navy, which was taking members of the royal family on a tour of South Africa. We made drawings of a magnificent flotilla, pinning them to the classroom wall. During those final years of Empire, George VI was King of South Africa as well as Emperor of India, and we nine-year-olds were being coached in patriotism. However, on Sunday evenings Jonah would relax, sitting in the centre of the dormitory to read us hilarious episodes from *Three Men in a Boat*.

Classroom learning was augmented by activities like Chess and Book Binding. I could hardly wait to join the Butterfly Club, a childhood passion ever since Father took me to see the collection of the naturalist William Keble Martin. At home the buddleia would be ablaze with Tortoiseshells, Peacocks and Jersey Tigers, while at school those fragile creatures lifted our spirits. We would pursue Painted Ladies across the fields and discover Five-Spot Burnets coupling in the long grass. Learning

LENT TERM, 1949

LIST OF FORMS.

Classical Grecians......Mr. D. S. Macnutt	Great Erasmus F...Mr. G. W. Newberry
Mathematical Grecians	Upper Fourth A.........Mr. C. O. Healey
Mr. W. Armistead	Upper Fourth B.........Mr. E. G. Malins
Science Grecians A......Dr. G. van Praagh	Upper Fourth C...The Hon. D. S. Roberts
Science Grecians B.........Mr. R. Crosland	Upper Fourth D.........Mr. J. H. Edwards
Science Grecians C...Mr. P. G. Matthews	Upper Fourth E...........Mr. J. H. Page
Modern Language Grecians	Little Erasmus A............Mrs. H. Wheeler
Mr. R. A. Dean	Little Erasmus B.........Mr. E. G. Malins
Music Grecians	Little Erasmus C...Mr. M. T. Cherniavsky
The Reverend W. C. M. Cochrane	Little Erasmus D...........Mr. J. C. Tod
History Grecians The Hon. D. S. Roberts	Little Erasmus E.........Mr. E. C. Aitken
Classical Deps...........Mr. A. H. Buck	Lower Fourth A.........Mr. E. C. Aitken
Science Deps. 1...........Mr. T. G. Jarvis	Lower Fourth B...............Mrs. R. Hurst
Science Deps. 2.........Mr. G. W. Deakin	Lower Fourth C...Mr. M. T. Cherniavsky
Science Deps. 3.........Mr. C. F. Kirby	Lower Fourth D.....Mr. G. W. Newberry
Modern Language Deps. Mr. J. E. Massen	Lower Fourth E...............Miss M. Eller
Geography Deps............Mr. J. H. Page	Third Form A...............Miss M. Eller
General Deps.................Mr. J. H. Page	Third Form B.........Mr. J. H. Edwards
Agricultural Form	Third Form C...............Mrs. R. Hurst
Mr. J. M. Wolstenholme	Prep. I.....................Mr. G. W. Pink
Great Erasmus A.........Mr. E. C. Aitken	Prep. II....................Mr. A. L. Eagle
Great Erasmus B.........Mrs. H. Wheeler	Prep. III..................Mr. D. G. Bourne
Great Erasmus C The Hon. D. S. Roberts	Prep. IV..................Mr. P. N. V. Keep
Great Erasmus D...........Mr. J. H. Page	Prep. V.........Mr. C. M. F. Rathbone
Great Erasmus E.........Mr. L. M. Carey	Prep. VI...................Mr. M. H. Jones

The Christ's Hospital hierarchy: From Classical Grecians to the Prep (1949)

to swim was equally liberating. Our swimming coach was G. W. Pink, notorious for a hands-on method of classroom teaching known as Pinker's Torture. He would stand behind a pupil struggling with a knotty question and massage his collar bone until the squirming boy came up with an answer – an idiosyncratic technique that would have been unthinkable in a more conventional school. Our singing teacher was the portly Philip Dore, who taught us a medley of songs like Drink to Me only with Thine Eyes. The drawback was that Pip Dore would separate the choristers from those he regarded as 'crows'. Housey offered a wealth of opportunity to the musically gifted, but that was not my scene.

Gymnastics were the province of a muscular ex-army man named Sergeant Usher. Lacking physical coordination, I found it impossible to launch myself over the vaulting horse, and the ensuing crash landings were humiliating. When I shared my distress with my parents, they consulted a friendly teacher, who assured them that – compared with the Upper School – the Prep was a picnic. If this was intended to console me, it had the opposite effect, making me dread the ordeals that lay ahead. For the senior staff included formidable figures like the irascible Derrick Macnutt, who taught Classical Grecians at the apex of the academic hierarchy (FIGURE: The Christ's Hospital hierarchy). The title of Grecian, originally conferred on scholars of Greek, had been extended to include proficiency in other subjects.

To do as well as David, whom I now joined in Thornton A, had always been my dream. Having an elder brother in the same boarding-house proved a comfort, given the rigidity of school routine. Every activity was timetabled: rising bell at 6.55, breakfast over by 8.15, morning chapel at 9.00, followed by 90 minutes of lessons, 30 minutes for Physical Training, then a further 90 minutes of lessons. It was not until 12.15 that the blessed moment arrived when we had time to ourselves: to relax in the dayroom or pay ball games on the asphalt behind the houses. In the afternoons we had to participate in organized sports, and there was homework in the evening. The week-ends were more relaxed, and after Sunday morning Chapel we would write a letter home.

The diaries kept throughout the following years reflect the routine of lessons and services, games and meals. There were moments of sheer misery, but that was not the whole story. My diaries devote most space to fun with friends and sporting activities, which introduced an unpredictable element into our regimented lives. Further relief was provided by the Boys Magic Service, based at Prestatyn in Wales, which supplied tricks through the post. Memories of Jasper Maskelyne inspired me, wand in hand, to make bunches of flowers disappear. Comparing notes with a fellow member, the musically gifted Francis Warner, I discovered that he too was a parson's son. This may explain why changing water into wine was our favourite trick.

St Paul Shipwrecked (detail by Frank Brangwyn, mid-1920s)

At home Christian teaching was applied with a light touch – Father rarely wore a parson's collar, and we did not say grace before meals. But at school religion was taken seriously. There were classes in Divinity twice a week, ensuring we were grounded in the gospels, and every weekday evening we had Duty – a bible reading followed by prayers conducted by one of the senior boys. There was also compulsory Chapel every day (twice on Sundays, plus optional Holy Communion). After eight hundred boys had filed into the cavernous building, the Headmaster, Oswald Flecker, would read the Lessons in a voice that lifted the rafters. Aurally we were uplifted by the sonorous Anglican liturgy, visually by Frank Brangwyn's bold cartoons depicting the Spreading of the Gospel.

My imagination was caught by ST PAUL SHIPWRECKED (FIGURE: St Paul Shipwrecked), a panel based on Acts 27. After Paul's Christian witness had provoked the Jewish community, he embarked on the hazardous voyage to Rome so that his alleged offences could be judged. When the ship ran aground in a storm, all escaped safe to land.

The figures struggling half naked from the sea, while St Paul raises his hand in benediction, provided a daily reminder of the drama of early Christianity, as well as the strenuous effort required by our studies. I also sensed St Paul's significance as the pivotal figure in the transition between Judaism and Christianity.

Our worship was enhanced by choral singing led by the Director of Music, the Reverend Cecil Cochrane. The nickname Corks suggested it was not only music that he enjoyed, and the rehearsals he conducted in Chapel were like stage performances. holding eight hundred boys under his spell. There was an inclusiveness about congregational singing, with certain lines from Stanford's setting of the Magnificat making a profound impression: 'He remembering remembering his mercies hath holpen his servant Israel: as he promised to our forefathers, Abraham and his seed forever'. Drawing our deepest breath to express 'holpen' with its archaic echoes, we became part of a community that reached beyond the school to the Judeo-Christian tradition on which it was founded.

DISCIPLINE AND DESIRE

At school we were disciplined in every sense. Boys were not permitted to return home at Half Term, though occasional visits were allowed from parents. We were invariably addressed by our surnames, avoiding any hint of intimacy. To distinguish me from my brother, I was known as Timms E (Ted to my friends). There were elaborate rules regulating everything from fastening your collar to walking on the grass. We were marched like military units from our residential houses to services in Chapel and meals in Hall, with the school band lifting our spirits at lunchtime. Grumbling about the food, we used derisive names like skiffage pie for dishes we disliked. Bowls of tea were known as kiff, butter as flab and bread as crugs, though this hardly did justice to the delicious loaves supplied by Prewetts Bakery in Horsham. Food was still rationed, but the diet was nutritious, for breakfast often included kippers, haddock or herrings, served after a bowl of porridge.

There were further ordeals in the barely heated dormitories. Twenty-five boys slept in each of the two dorms, barn-like spaces bereft of privacy, for there were no screens to separate the rock-hard beds, arranged barrack-room style in two long lines. 'Stop talking!' we juniors would be told as the Monitors switched out the lights, but we couldn't stop chattering about the events of the day: unfinished homework (and the threat of detentions); the masters (using derisive nicknames); sports (surely we would win next time); and sex (sharing smutty stories to conceal our ignorance). No one seemed interested in politics, for if we worried about the setbacks suffered during the Korean War, it was the cricket scores on the back page that excited us. Nor did we talk about money, for we had none – apart from sixpence to spend at the tuck shop.

In the cavernous dorms there were just two radiators – no wonder there were so many coughs and colds! However, the Infirmary (the Sicker) alleviated our complaints, for there were nurses with a feminine touch. To speed recovery, Matron would put us on starvation diet, asking each morning if we had opened our bowels and administering doses of the dreaded Black Draught to restore proper function. The Sicker offered respite from the rigours of school, for as we recovered, we could relax in the dayroom with copies of Wisden recording the exploits of English cricket or Sherlock Holmes stories in the original Strand magazine. The medical officer, Dr Thomas Scott, must have realized that my needs were as much emotional as physical. He would issue a Pass that made it possible to return to classes while exempted from strenuous sports.

At that time the ages in each house ranged from eleven to eighteen, divided into Seniors and Juniors. Sportsmen enjoyed the greatest esteem, and it was the height of glory to play for the school. Academically, the dream was to be 'awarded your buttons', that is to wear the distinctive Grecian's gown with floppy velvet cuffs and large silver buttons. Scholars in their final-year were known as First Parting Grecians, followed in descending order by Second Parting and Third Parting, Probationary and Deputy Grecians, and even Probationary Deputy Grecians. The gown endowed senior boys with an awesome authority.

Discipline was enforced by corporal punishment. Our Housemaster, Fred Haslehurst, rarely caned anyone himself, for the right to chastise wrongdoers was delegated to Monitors. They enjoyed unchallenged privileges, having juniors known as Swabs at their beck and call, and there was no appeal against a beating. In place of a cane they used the leather Housey girdle, plaited into a pliant truncheon. One night a Monitor was so enraged by some harmless oversight that he thrashed an unlucky junior a dozen times before he could be restrained. So strong was the taboo on sneaking that no one reported an act of savagery that took place before twenty-five witnesses. After that Monitor had left school, we heard he was driving a grocery van. How could such a nonentity have wielded such power? The answer lay with a culture of bullying that had become institutionalized, as young men boarded in the same house as delicate boys, while teachers turned a blind eye to a regime crying out for reform. Even Top Tablers, next senior after the Monitors, were entitled to inflict a 'fotch', slapping the face of a junior at considerable risk to eyes and eardrums.

A more judicious penalty was punishment drill – having to double around the asphalt in our sports clothes for ten or twenty minutes, depending on the seriousness of our offences. House drills took place under the watchful eye of a Monitor during the 12.15 break, depriving us of precious leisure time. Although resented, they contributed to our physical fitness as a form of compulsory jogging, long before that term was invented. School drills were supervised by Sergeant Usher with parade-ground panache. In those years military discipline was not merely a metaphor, for several teachers were ex-army men, and at the age of fourteen we were required to join the Cadet Force. Once a week for five years, usually on Fridays, we would parade in khaki uniform, transforming the school into a barracks. Each summer there was a Field Day, when miniature campaigns were conducted across the Sussex countryside, and at the tender age of fifteen I joined my friend Spencer White at a corps camp near Pirbright, sleeping in tents surrounded by professional soldiers. With our own hormones playing havoc, we were shocked to find the sexual hang-ups of grown men expressed with such coarseness. After this glimpse of soldiering I was ready to become a pacifist.

Although there was merit in exercises like map reading, the rituals of the parade ground filled me with dread. When promoted to company sergeant, it became my duty to marshal the troops, but so casual was my bearing that the commanding officer yelled across the parade ground: 'Pick Your Feet Up!' It may have been this episode that led me to pen a satirical poem:

> Again the day has dawned, that day of doom,
> again that dreaded Friday afternoon,
> when sane, right-minded boys are made
> to don ill-fitting khaki suits,
> to fall in smartly on parade
> and play with heavy hearts and boots
>   at soldiers.

The finally strophe blamed our misery on teachers who 'loved to throw their weight around / while giving drills and reprimands / like soldiers!'

This was unfair. Several of the staff had seen active service only a few years earlier, including the senior French teacher, Arthur Rider. On rare occasions he would describe his experiences after the Normandy landings instead of testing us on irregular verbs. The school had a shooting-range where we trained with live ammunition, for the cadet force was not a game – we were gearing up for two years of compulsory National Service. British forces had suffered grievous losses in Korea, and a recent school leaver reappeared in lieutenant's uniform with tales of guerrilla warfare in Malaya. Those who wished to remain at school after the age of eighteen had to apply to the Ministry of Labour and National Service for deferment, enclosing a certificate signed by the Headmaster.

If discipline was tough, friendships were rewarding. We loved spadging – sauntering down the Avenue after lessons arm-in-arm. My closest companion in early days was Hugh Barton Jayne, who challenged the primacy of rugby by bringing a soccer ball to school. On winter evenings we would slip out to play a solitary game, alternating in the roles of goalie and striker. This prompted impassioned debates on the merits of our favourite teams (he supported Reading while my team was Blackburn Rovers). Hardly had Jayne reached the age of fourteen, however, when the incomprehensible occurred: he was hospitalized after contracting 'water on the brain'. My letters were read to him by his devoted mother, to whom he dictated his replies (I have them still). The news of his death in March 1952 left me feeling responsible for an unlived life.

At the other end of the spectrum was Terry Moore, a gifted Londoner who excelled at every sport. When he was made captain of the school rugby team, I was left in the second fifteen. Was I never to become Big Chief? Roller-skating left me standing, amazed to see others waltzing around on wheels, but ball games were more rewarding. After an inauspicious start as a cricketer I became a demon bowler, and with my brother Robert bowling leg-spin from the other end, we made a formidable combination. In winter there were cross-country runs, more enjoyable as my stamina improved, but my sporting prowess was affected by short-sightedness. There were dire warnings that 'if you read too much, you'll ruin your eyesight' and 'if you masturbate, you'll go blind!' But how could a teenager renounce such pleasures?

Those chilly dormitories offered compensations, for bath-time encouraged intimacy. At the Vicarage, while the children splashed in the tub, Mother had warned: 'We don't play with penises!' But no one had explained the facts of life so that first ecstatic spurt astonished me. It was assumed we would discharge our energies through contact sports, but physical vitality encouraged bonding. One afternoon a harmless romp in the changing-room with a handsome boy my own age escalated into horseplay. Overwhelmed with desire we took refuge in the toilets, where he liberated me with a practised touch while I returned the compliment. This initiation proved inspiring. We would gaze at each other during homework, touching feet under the table, and at night he would slip into my bed reciting his favourite poems. When the school took the first steps towards sex education, a psychiatrist named Dr Matthews explained that homosexual love could be a normal phase. For me it was a sensuous apprenticeship, but others were less fortunate, enduring abuse that cast a long shadow.

Amid the hubbub of the dayroom we would listen to the Dick Barton radio series in the evening and play table tennis or cards at week-ends. Marathon games of Bezique or Bridge strengthened the bond between two pairs of brothers. The oldest was my friend Peter Britton, who was studying mechanical drawing with a view to becoming an engineer. His brother Michael, a regular clown, was best friends with my younger brother Robert, whose quicksilver humour enlivened our exchanges. We became so close that their mother invited us to spend a week's holiday at their home in Swanage, enabling us to explore the Dorset coast. This visit was made more poignant by the knowledge that she came from Germany while their father, a decorated British soldier, had been killed in battle.

Our housemaster, Fred Haslehurst, was both feared and revered. His saturnine features bore a scar, attributable (we assumed) to being wounded in the First World War. For his study was decorated with cartoons showing plucky Tommies crouching in their dug-outs under fire from the Huns, with captions like: If you knows of a better 'ole, go to it! or There goes our blinkin' parapet again! (FIGURE: There goes our blinkin' parapet again).

Fred (as we called him) was a disciplinarian who insisted on cold baths every morning. 'When will he come out of his shell?' he asked in my first report, appalled by my timidity, and at the end of my first term of Greek

'There goes our blinkin' parapet again'
Bruce Bairnsfather, *Bystander*, 1915

'There goes our blinkin' parapet again' (cartoon by Bruce Bairnsfather, 1915)

he wrote: 'He has a long way to go'. But there were occasions when he would relax, especially when organizing the end-of-term play assisted by his wife, a charming woman who worked as the Headmaster's secretary. Her weekly play-readings included amusing farces like Ben Travers's *A Cuckoo in the Nest*. Fred would join the group later in the evening to regale us with stories, puffing at his pipe.

In summer 1950 we were to choose subjects for advanced study. My favourites were English and History, the provinces of two exceptional teachers. English earned me high marks, for there were incentives to write well at a school that had nurtured the talents of Coleridge, Charles Lamb and Leigh Hunt. It was easy to see how the Head of English, the elegant Edward Malins, earned the nickname Ego. His self-assurance led him, on one occasion, to use the letters of his name to grade our work. 'M' meant excellent, 'A' good and 'L' satisfactory, while stragglers received an 'I', 'N' or 'S'. Despite such quirks of character he was a stimulating teacher, introducing us to Eliot's *Waste Land*, Beckett's *Waiting for Godot* and Salinger's *For Esmé with Love and Squalor*. Senior boys would be invited to his home for literary evenings, and he even organized trips to the theatre.

The Head of History, D. S. (Daddy) Roberts, encouraged an imaginative approach to the past, tinged with nostalgia for imperial grandeur. The civilizing mission of the British Empire was beyond question, but this was not a narrow-minded nationalism for we learnt that wars are won by coalitions. The message, in the classroom as on the playing fields, was that success depends on teamwork. Textbooks with evocative titles like *Beyond the Sunset* highlighted the voyages of exploration and exploits of the conquistadors. To illustrate the career of Cecil Rhodes, Roberts took us outside and marked out a grassy area half the size of a tennis court. Such was the concession in South Africa where Rhodes first struck gold, before pursuing the dream of an Empire that was to stretch from the Cape to Cairo. Only through visualization, Roberts insisted, could we grasp the dynamics of history. Being taught by such inspired eccentrics marked us for life. We learnt a great deal at Housey, but we also had a lot to unlearn.

For some reason English and History were not available as advanced options, so when Haslehurst summoned me to his study to discuss special subjects, he announced that I'd be starting German. This left me speechless. There I stood surrounded by cartoons of the dreaded Huns, trying to grasp that German would be my destiny. It might have been possible to protest, had there been an alternative, but I had no gift for Classics (the subject chosen by my brother David) and no taste for Natural Science. So I shrugged my shoulders and began to study the language that had shadowed my childhood: no longer 'Panzer' and 'Stuka', but 'Buch', 'Stuhl' and 'Bleistift'.

THE GRAMMAR OF VOCATION

Modern Languages were modelled on the study of Greek and Latin with the prestige attached to authors like Vergil transferred to the French and German classics. This programme was taken so seriously that Modern Linguists spent over half their time (18 lessons out of the weekly total of 33) on French, German and Latin. The only other subjects assigned more than two hours a week were English and Maths. As if this curriculum were not sufficiently skewed, life in contemporary Europe was largely ignored. France had hardly recovered from the trauma of defeat while Germany lay in ruins. Our introductory textbook, *Deutsches Leben* by A. S. Macpherson, focused on life before the rise of Hitler. Line-drawings by Adrian Hill evoked a country in which the only figures in uniform were the station master and the postman. There was a piece on the production of Dresden China and another on the Leipzig Fair featuring the technology of the 1920s. Growing up under the shadow of the Cold War, we were introduced to a Germany remote from the realities of military occupation.

This approach privileged linguistic accuracy rather than communicative competence, with the emphasis on textual comprehension and accurate translation. 'Grammar is good for you!' might well have been the school motto. The Headmaster was joint author of a Latin primer with the head of Classics, Derrick Macnutt, an authority on crossword puzzles. Classes with Macnutt were excruciating, for he would bellow at you in a voice that earned him the nickname Boom and give you a detention just for looking out of the window. Trouble with French irregular verbs led to group detentions described by our teacher, A. L. Johnstone, as Johnny's Tea Parties. Arthur Rider could be even fiercer, intimidating younger boys by kicking their desks when they made a mistake. The combination of tedium and terror might have put us off languages for life, but for our German teacher J. E. Massen, known as Jem. Where Macnutt raged and Rider scolded, Massen explained. He began with the principles of English grammar – cases and tenses, pronouns and prepositions. This helped us to understand why German still made sense even when the sentence ran backwards. The case inflections ensured that 'Den Mann beisst der Hund' could not possibly mean 'The man bites the dog'.

For the first two years I struggled, filling my diary with comments like 'Foul day!!!! Double German', but towards the end of 1952 there was a change of tone. 'Feeling very happy', reads an entry in December (emotional fulfilment was boosting my confidence). In French we were introduced to the poetry of Lamartine by the genial Reggie Dean. We wrote literary-critical essays in English, and it was a relief for a tongue-tied student to be studying poems and plays. The Advanced Level syllabus makes impressive reading. In addition to Prose and Unseen (translation from and into the foreign language), there was an Essay in each language, a three-hour Literature paper, a Dictation and an Oral. Our set texts in French were Corneille's *Le Cid*, Racine's *Athalie*, Moliere's *Femmes Savantes* and La Fontaine's *Fables*; in German Lessing's *Emilia Galotti*, Meyer's *Das Amulett*, Carossa's *Eine Kindheit*, and *The Evolution of Prussia* by Marriott and Robertson. For a bookish person this was rather attractive, and I began to spend my leisure in the library.

Carossa's account of his childhood provided my first taste of autobiography. The school edition of *Eine Kindheit*, edited by Jethro Bithell, was first published in 1941. This hundred-page text, densely printed in Fraktur, was framed by a further hundred pages of biographical details and explanatory notes. The introduction left us floundering: we knew about Hitler's Third Reich, but how was that to be squared with the idea of a Third Realm of the spirit, defined as the final goal of Carossa's teaching? Fortunately, Bithell's endnotes brought clarity into Carossa's poetic prose. This was the language of a rural Germany that abounded in quaint traditions, and we could identify with the experiences of an impressionable child before the First World War. *Eine Kindheit* inspired my first literary-critical essays – on Carossa's Attitude to Physical Suffering and on the Influence of Schoolfriends on a Child's Evolution.

German became more fascinating when we began reading Goethe. We learned by heart the love poem that begins 'Es schlug mein Herz' – literally 'It throbbed my heart'. There was something strange about German pronouns. What was that impersonal 'es' that introduced the thrill of feeling? It suggested a divided self, simultaneously subject and object of desire. Hence the frequency of reflexive verbs: 'I can't remember' translates as 'ich kann mich nicht erinnern' – literally 'I can't myself internalize'. The use of the first person pronoun proved equally intriguing. In English the word 'I' proudly precedes the verb, affirming the autonomy of the subject. But in German, instead of 'I realized' you would find 'Es fiel mir ein' ('It slipped into my mind'), suggesting an involuntary process. The first-person singular 'ich' might even come towards the end of the sentence, as if it were less the agent than the conduit of experience. Or it might be placed at the beginning in the dative case: 'Mir träumte' ('Me dreamed'!). This sounded like poetry, recalling the Shakespearean 'Methinks'. Modern English seemed less subtle, having even lost the intimate 'thou'.

Such thoughts encouraged self-awareness as I entered an introspective phase, but my progress was patchy. All my group were entered for Advanced Level, but in autumn 1953 my parents received a letter from the Headmaster saying that their son would leave school the following July unless his work showed so much promise that they could 'recommend his retention'. This reflected the school's draconian policy that boys should be discharged at sixteen unless likely to win an Oxbridge award. No allowance was made for late developers, and the news left me with a sense of failure. However, Father had mentioned the idea of switching to theology, knowing that boys wishing to be ordained were kept for university entrance despite an uneven academic record. There was thus a double motive behind my decision to talk to the chaplain, the Reverend Ron Pullin, about studying for the Ministry.

At his suggestion I attended a conference of the Advisory Council of Training for the Ministry at Jesus College Oxford in April 1954. The participants included a contemporary named Simon Hoare with similar interests. To their credit, the organizers did not create a climate of incense-laden piety, for the theme was The Church in the World. The lectures stressed the value of secular life, while a sermon by the Bishop of Peterborough suggested that by setting yourself a high professional standard you could serve God whatever your choice of career. During those spring days Hoare and I went boating on the river, discussing the book he was reading – the correspondence between Vincent van Gogh and his brother Theo. This showed that spirituality could also express itself in artistic forms.

The question of vocation continued to trouble me. One of the most memorable sermons preached in school chapel was by George Bell, Bishop of Chichester, on the biblical text 'You have not chosen me, but I have chosen you'. His sonorous voice had extraordinary power, but his message begged the question: How do you *know* that you have been chosen? It dawned on me that vocations are not delivered from on high in the form of 'Come hither, my child!' They constitute themselves through a commitment to the task at hand. Staking out the possibilities of theology helped to restore my confidence, but it was the desire to learn that drove me. Fortunately, my grades began to improve thanks to coaching from John Woods, a kindly older boy.

The learning process continued during the summer holidays. Traditionally, we would spend a few weeks at Collery farm, helping with the harvest. But in August 1953 I visited the family of Pastor Schönfelder at Woltersdorf, near the river Elbe. The village seemed untouched by the twentieth century while the family might have stepped out of a picture-book. The boys wore Lederhosen, making my trousers with their synthetic fibres feel effete, and there was a down-to-earth approach to sanitary arrangements. Didn't I know that WC pedestals were less healthy than squatting on your hams? The bikes on which we toured the countryside were fine for the rugged terrain, but when the horses were to be taken out to pasture, we had to ride bareback. People farmed with oxen yoked to primitive carts, the vegetables served at meals came straight from the garden, and when there were eels for breakfast we had to kill them the night before. There could hardly have been a greater contrast to impressions formed in France during an exchange with a doctor's family near Rouen. There we would buzz into town on solex motorcycles, before spending exciting days in Paris. But if France had joined the modern world, rural Germany was in a time warp. The only reminder of defeat in war was the border with the Russian zone, just across the Elbe. 'Attitude to the past,' I wrote in my diary: 'best forgotten!'

That autumn Mr Massen set his German specialists an unconventional task. We were each to deliver a short lecture in English on a subject of our choice, based on a single sheet of handwritten notes. The subject I chose was Otto von Bismarck, the statesman notorious for 'blood and iron'. For two weeks I immersed myself in the subject, covering a huge sheet of paper with notes in miniscule handwriting. When it was my turn to speak, I stood boldly before the class and delivered the first – and probably the longest – lecture of my life, speaking for seventy minutes while fellow students listened in amazement. Even Massen sat riveted to his chair, for under the agreed conditions he had no right to intervene.

The interest in theology continued for several years, but my French and German improved so dramatically that I was allowed to stay on for university entrance. The Bismarck episode may have tipped the balance, for I was encouraged to give a second lecture – shorter this time – on the Art of Albrecht Dürer. Speaking foreign languages was also becoming easier. My French was halting, for Arthur Rider's perfectionism meant that every construction had to be checked through in your mind before you opened your mouth. But when Massen asked each member of the class to read out a tricky passage of German, I did so with an ease that surprised him. Some intangible factor gave German rhythms an irresistible appeal – was it some preconscious memory of Hilda singing me nursery rhymes?

Ballads like Goethe's 'Erlkönig' and Heine's 'Lorelei' proved easy to learn by heart, captivating the imagination by leaving so much unexplained. Why is Heine's fisherman unable to resist the lure of the Rhine maiden? What leads Goethe to celebrate the forces that steal the life of a child as the father gallops through the night? French, we were repeatedly told, was the language of intellectual clarity, but German had undertones of mystery. This was intensified by melancholy stories such as *Immensee* by Theodor Storm and *Tonio Kröger* by Thomas Mann, with their images of unattainable beauty. Further excitement arose from reading the *History of the German Novelle* by E. K. Bennett, especially when we learnt that the author was coming to conduct the Oral Exam. The day before he arrived I fell into a fever, but he came to the Infirmary and conducted the exam at my bedside, generously allowing a barely coherent pupil to pass.

The tension between competing images of Germany, poetic and political, was intensified when a friend smuggled into the dormitory a book of photographs of the liberation of Belsen. Nazi concentration camp guards could be seen next to skeletal Jewish prisoners. How was this possible? The question became more poignant when my friend Peter Mckenzie brought a German exchange student named Gisela Pollich to visit the school. 'You can call me Gila,' she said as she perched on a window-sill in the dayroom, surrounded by uncouth boys. She seemed like a creature from another world – the romantic Germany of my favourite ballads and stories.

When at last we became Grecians, our duties included reading grace in Hall, a building that seated over eight hundred students and staff, decorated with monumental paintings. The text was a tongue-twister beginning 'Blessed Lord, we yield Thee hearty praise and thanksgiving for our Founders and Benefactors, by whose charitable benevolence Thou hast refreshed our bodies at this time.' When the Hall Warden, the imperturbable Noel (Sam) Sergent, banged his gavel to mark the end of the meal, there was silence as you climbed the pulpit. For me the words had a personal face, for the benefactor who had presented me, Miss Katharine Harben, would invite me to visit her at her home near Horsham.

Social life became more relaxed, for we were now allowed to stay up late, brewing coffee and baked beans on toast during winter evenings. We also developed a more mature relationship with our teachers. The Modern Language Grecians had a room of their own designed for seminar-style teaching. Academically we learnt most from mainstream teachers like Massen, Dean and Rider, but the eccentrics could be equally inspiring. The physicist Dr Gordon Van Praagh would spice his course on Science for Non-Scientists with allusions to Gilbert and Sullivan. The Art School was the empire of one of the few women teachers, the idiosyncratic Nellie Todd. She played us classical music while we painted, correlating Schubert with Caspar David Friedrich, Debussy with Renoir. Academic routine was also enlivened by the Debating Club, where I began to make cautious interventions; and the Literary Society, where my friend Robin Kinloch and I presented a paper about the dramatic traditions of seventeenth-century France and Restoration England. When I became secretary of the Franco-British Society, we screened films by Jacques Tati that attracted half the school.

Towards the end of my time a cohort of innovative younger teachers arrived. The debonair David Jesson-Dibley, affectionately known as J-D, helped us cultivate a more pithy English style by introducing us to prose rhythms (of which I'd never heard) and encouraging emphatic condensations. We learnt to replace empty phrases like 'somewhat surprised' or 'quite nice' by 'astonished' or 'splendid' – his favourite word. Another English tyro, Olive Peto, introduced us to the poetry of Gerald Manley Hopkins. My imagination was captured by certain lines from *The Wreck of the Deutschland*, dedicated to the memory of five Franciscan Nuns exiled from Germany by the Falck Laws and drowned off the Kentish coast in December 1875: 'Hope was twelve hours gone; / And frightful a nightfall folded rueful a day.'

How was it possible to grasp God amid the tumult of souls plunged into the deep? New teachers were reshaping our ideas about religion. Patrick Daunt encouraged us to write freely about Christian doctrine, balancing faith against reason. His antipode was Russell Grice, a student of analytical philosophy. Sitting at the head of the table during lunch, he would challenge any statement of religious faith. While questions of belief remained unresolved, the study of German was transformed by Patrick Cullen, a free spirit fresh from Cambridge. During conversation groups over tea in his den, it dawned on us that foreign languages were not reserved for literary declamations, but could be used to ask for the sugar. Now I ceased to picture teachers and pupils as hostile camps, and when one of the linguists fell ill towards the end of my final year, his classes were assigned to me. It was not easy to keep order among twittering twelve-year-olds, but this enabled me to reciprocate the benevolence of the school.

The mid-1950s saw the inauguration of reforms that were to transform Christ's Hospital into one of the best regulated schools in the country. The changes were led by George Seaman, affectionately known as Clarence, a soft-spoken new headmaster with admirable firmness of purpose. Recognizing the drawbacks of having boys between the ages of eleven and eighteen cooped up together, he divided the school into Senior and Junior houses (a reform introduced after my time). And to balance the influence of bachelors of the old school, he fast-tracked the appointment of younger married teachers, providing new-built homes to match. A turning-point came during my final year with the dismissal of a popular housemaster, who had compromised himself by making sexual advances to one of the boys. A more traditional head might have turned a blind eye, but Seaman acted decisively.

Where Flecker had been remote and autocratic, Seaman would invite the Grecians to discussion groups at his house, giving us a foretaste of Oxbridge tutorials. Several boys seemed destined for academic distinction, including the artistic Anthony Arblaster and the erudite Jasper Griffin. While their progress appeared effortless, mine had been a continuous struggle, but by autumn 1955 my confidence was growing. My sister Helen had just completed her studies at Girton, while David had won a scholarship at Oriel College Oxford. Now it was my turn to face the examiners, travelling to Cambridge in my velvet gown. Nervousness left me tongue-tied during the French oral, but I took the translation papers in my stride and enjoyed literature papers that included favourite themes, from the dramatic power of La Fontaine's *Fables* to an appreciation of any poem by Goethe. Having 'Erlkönig' by heart meant that my ideas came pouring out, contrasting the fevered imaginings of the child with the father's despairing reassurances. Back at school there was not long to wait. In mid-December a telegram arrived awarding me a scholarship at Caius – the Christmas present of a lifetime.

CHAPTER FOUR

Colleges, Languages and Mentors

Although life in Britain was comparatively tranquil, the international conflicts of the 1950s extended from Korea to Cuba. Western governments felt threatened by the communist advance, while colonialism was under pressure from Aden to Algeria. Young men of my generation, including those destined for university, were required to complete two years of National Service after leaving school, for eighty thousand troops were stationed at the Suez Canal, making huge demands on manpower. But those who had gained entrance scholarships were allowed to defer military service until their studies were complete. My call-up papers would have arrived in autumn 1956 had my father not persuaded me to go straight to Cambridge. College life was surely preferable to being drafted to some outpost of Empire.

Caius (pronounced 'keys') was a good choice for Modern Languages, for the Senior Tutor, Ian MacFarlane, was an expert on the French Renaissance, while Eric Blackall, a Goethe scholar, was responsible for German. Moreover, Francis Bennett, the doyen of German studies, was still active as a college supervisor. The eleven Freshmen who arrived to read Modern Languages at Caius in autumn 1956 all had rooms in college during their first year. Although we received maintenance grants, we had to live frugally if our funds were to last the year. The term Freshmen was apt, for it was an all-male college and we were decidedly immature. None of us came from the elite schools that dominated the college Boat Club, but we enjoyed an easy-going camaraderie. My closest friend was John Woods, two years my senior at Christ's Hospital, who after National Service was in the same intake at Caius. We formed a triad with John Rice from Scarborough High School, a chess-player with a passion for classical music.

GATES OF KNOWLEDGE

During the dinner to welcome new students, the Master, Sir Nevill Mott, explained the symbolism of the gates designed during the Renaissance by his predecessor, John Caius. Entering the college from Trinity Street through the Gate of Humility, we would pass through the central arch symbolizing Virtue and Knowledge, to leave the college at the end of our course through Dr Caius's masterpiece, the Gate of Honour. This account was undercut by irony, for Mott added that in the Victorian period, when the Waterhouse building overlooking Trinity Street was constructed, the original Gate of Humility was removed to the Master's garden. 'Do you think the Victorians lacked humility,' he asked, 'or were the Fellows sending a message to the Master?'

Gates featured prominently in College Regulations: 'The gates are closed at 10 p.m. No person other than a member of the College may enter after 10 p.m. except with written permission of a Tutor.' Our movements were monitored by the Porters, and written permission had to be obtained from the Dean if we planned to be away for the week-end. A further regulation decreed that 'no student may entertain women visitors in College after 11 p.m.' To evade these rules, we had to become nimble climbers, scrambling over the walls at the risk of injury from the spikes that adorned them. We were not regarded as adults until we reached the age of twenty-one, and the colleges took a paternalistic interest in their charges, swaddling them in rules about eating dinners and wearing gowns. Scholars were required to take an oath committing them to diligence and good conduct.

Mostly, we accepted the authority of our Tutor or Director of Studies – in our case Ian MacFarlane. He and his wife would invite us to sherry at their home in Huntingdon Road, but he had a sharp an eye for infringements. To compensate for these restrictions, we were treated as young gentlemen by the bedders, middle-aged women employed to clean our rooms. We would be woken by these cheery souls every morning, while another college servant cleaned our shoes. Some students found this system so irksome that they were delighted to move into lodgings in town, but my scholarship entitled me to rooms in college for all three years.

There was no escaping the fact that Cambridge was a fortress of male privilege with about nine thousand undergraduate places available for men, but less than one thousand for women, mainly at Girton and Newnham. There was still some resistance to women's emancipation, for admissions were controlled by the colleges, and the men's colleges (including Caius) had statutes that excluded women. It seemed that the only way to increase opportunities for women was to create new foundations, a prohibitively expensive project. A start had been made with New Hall, but this hardly altered the distribution of resources. The men's colleges had endowments which they used for the benefit of their own members, apart from a modest payment to central university funds.

Among Modern Linguists we might have expected a better gender balance, given that women often excel at languages. But at lectures we looked almost in vain for women who might have brightened a room filled with men in drab college gowns. Teaching staff in the German Department were exclusively male, and scarcely a single woman author was included on the reading lists. At least in French there was a chance of being taught by the glamorous Odette de Mourgues, author of romantic novels. Students with the maturity gained from two years of National Service had a better chance of acquiring girlfriends, but for young men straight from school the chances of such relationships were remote. There was little outlet for burgeoning emotions, let alone for frustrated sexuality.

Despite these difficulties, we settled into a comfortable routine, cycling across town with flowing gowns to attend lectures. There were three or four written assignments each week and a long list of prescribed authors, leaving little scope for reading outside the curriculum. After classes we would switch into sporting mode for a game of squash or tennis, while after dinner we would play darts over a glass of beer. The Freshers Fair publicized the activities of an extraordinary range of societies from the Conservative Club to the Heretics, an anti-establishment group supported by the novelist E. M. Forster. In return for a hefty subscription we had access to both social facilities at the Union Society and gladiatorial confrontations in the Debating Chamber. That women were excluded from membership was taken for granted, so strong was the patriarchal ethos – public argument was thought unseemly for the gentle sex. The debates dealt with general propositions, sometimes political, sometimes comic. 'If music be the food of love, play on' was the theme of an uproarious encounter between the bandleader Johnny Dankworth and the cartoonist Gerard Hoffnung. There was also a large audience for the motion 'This House has no confidence in Her Majesty's Government', which the conservatives won by 300 votes to 228 (I sided with the conservatives).

Cambridge with its gates and gowns could feel like a closed community, especially on a dismal Sunday afternoon. But it was then that the doors of perception opened at the Arts Cinema, home of the Film Society, which screened a marvellous range of films with programme notes by such luminaries as Leslie Halliwell and Peter Hall. The show would begin with a short like Grierson's *Night Mail* or Renoir's *Une partie de campagne*, and we were soon on intimate terms with Eisenstein, Capra, Kazan, Lubitsch, Bunuel and Visconti. It was enchanting to watch René Clair's *A nous la liberté*, and my diary described John Ford's *The Sun Shines Bright* as the most remarkable film I'd ever seen. While most impressed by films with a message, such as *All Quiet on the Western Front*, we also enjoyed the anarchic comedy of Charlie Chaplin and Buster Keaton.

Visits to the cinema inspired long conversations with friends, two of whom questioned the cosy academic ethos. George Hughes was beginning to look beyond the course towards a business career while Cyril Swindley, another shrewd northerner, had a passion for self-help manuals like Norman Peale's *Power of Positive Thinking*. Although we took a lively interest in international affairs, none of the group was politically sophisticated. Hence our confusion when our first term coincided with a double crisis: the Hungarian Uprising, crushed by Soviet tanks, and the nationalization of the Suez Canal by Nasser, followed by military intervention in the Canal zone by an Anglo-French force in collusion with Israel. Few of us were clear-sighted enough to recognize that the Suez affair was a monumental blunder. Bewilderment reigned as we tried to work out some way of justifying British military action while condemning that of the Soviets. I was moved by the tragic fate of the Hungarian leader Imre Nagy and had fantasies of going to Austria to help the refugees pouring over the border.

What distinguished us from our contemporaries was a lively curiosity about Europe. For linguists, the Channel ports formed gates to a wider world. British attitudes seemed oppressively insular, although the Empire threw a long shadow, especially for veterans boasting about their exploits in Hong Kong or Gibraltar. But foreigners were regarded as figures of fun, and the general public, led by the conservative media, showed little interest in efforts to create a European Common Market, while Charles de Gaulle as President of France created a further barrier. The Cambridge system discouraged us from spending a year abroad, but studying languages enabled us to escape the provinciality of our upbringing. We read foreign newspapers, corresponded with friends abroad, and organized trips to the continent at every opportunity.

France was the goal of the motoring tour planned for the summer of 1957 with John Rice and John Woods, together with a school friend named Andy Kerr. This was a delightfully collaborative venture. First, we stayed for three weeks with the Rice family near Scarborough, working at a hotel to replenish our finances. We also found time to attend the celebrated Theatre in the Round, seeing *The Glass Menagerie* by Tennessee Williams and *An Inspector Calls* by J. B. Priestley. Later that summer we persuaded my father to lend us his Wolsey, which had been laid up during the war. After an overnight stay with the Woods family in Dulwich, we crossed to Boulogne, to be welcomed by French friends with the finest food and drink Normandy could provide. After a week camping in the Loire valley, we drove through Alsace into Switzerland. When disaster struck on a remote country road, we were saved by the generosity of a young Swiss garage owner, who allowed us to camp in his garden for while he repaired the engine block.

Crossing into German-speaking territory brought a change of mood, for there was something archaic about the half-timbered buildings of Alsace and the gothic lettering adorning the shops in Basel. The feeling grew stronger as we arrived in Heidelberg, the university town overlooking the Neckar. Here we were taken by Andy Kerr to visit Gila, the schoolgirl who had caught my imagination when she visited Christ's Hospital, dazzling a room full of boys. Now she seemed irresistible as we sat talking about art and life and looking at pictures – including her own. She gave me a drawing in dazzling black and red expressing her idea of 'Chaos'. Thus began a relationship that was to transform my attitude to Germany.

DISTANT LOVE

During our Freshman year we had studied two languages in almost equal depth, but were only required to take one literature paper – in my case German Literature from 1815-1870. Heine had been a favourite since schooldays and one of his poems written in Paris caught my feelings about French and German culture:

O Deutschland, meine ferne Liebe,   O, Germany, my distant love,
gedenk ich Deiner, wein' ich fast.   thinking of you, I'm close to tears.
Das muntre Frankreich wird mir trübe,   The joys of France have lost their verve,
das leichte Volk wird mir zur Last.   its facile glamour disappears.

France and Germany represented competing models of identity, the one associated with clarity and charm, the other with a problematic profundity.

During our second-year we had a range of options in Literature, Thought and History. While some students found their enthusiasm waning, my interest in German was heightened both by Gila's charm and by the courtesy of my supervisor, E. K. (Francis) Bennett. Generous public funding enabled the colleges to teach groups of just two or three students, which gave us access to some of the most erudite scholars in the land. When we began weekly supervisions in autumn 1957, Francis's avuncular warmth quickly won our hearts. As an undergraduate at Caius in 1914 he had opposed the First World War, a welcome contrast to those ex-army teachers who had made my life such a trial. His rooms radiated a love of literature, art and music. What caught the eye as you entered was a majestic grand piano – 'not used since Benjamin Britten was last here,' he remarked.

For Francis, life and literature were intimately connected. Our supervisions on the Sturm und Drang focused on Goethe's novel of unrequited passion, *Die Leiden des jungen Werthers*. A love story written in letters at first seemed rather weird, but Francis helped us appreciate Werther's outpourings. A similar sense that unattainability intensifies desire began to colour my letters to Gila. However, as German became more emotionally charged, French was losing its charm. The subject had not yet made the turn towards Theory that was to transform cultural studies around the globe, and the traditional Great Authors approach downplayed the historical context. Corneille and Racine took precedence over Camus and Sartre, and there was little interest in the ruptures caused by war and revolution.

Sent for supervisions to Miss Wallas at Newnham, we plodded through *Polyeucte*, a martyr drama familiar to me from school about which there seemed to be nothing new to say. In reaction, as my diary noted on 4 November, I turned to something more topical, the *Autobiography of a German Pastor* by Hans Ehrenberg. This account of the struggle to live as a Christian under Nazism made Corneille's treatment of religious conflict appear contrived. The turning point came with René Descartes, whose cerebral *Discours de la méthode* proved even less congenial. So defying the advice of my Director of Studies, I decided to concentrate exclusively on German. Fortunately, Francis was willing to supervise me for all four German options: Essay, Eighteenth-Century and Nineteenth-Century Literature, and Weimar Classicism. He guided me, between January and May, through a plethora of texts from Goethe's *Faust* to the poetry of Stefan George.

Lectures were optional and their quality uneven. Professor Walter Bruford lectured on *Faust* with precisely the kind of pedantry that Goethe derided, while his attempts to quote from memory could be comical: 'Zwei Seelen wohnen, ach' – um? – er? – 'in meiner' – no! – 'in *dieser* Brust'. For him, the genesis of the play seemed more interesting than its content. His book on *Theatre, Audience and Society in Goethe's Germany* impressed me by its wealth of information, but it lacked the sparkle of his predecessor, Elsie Butler, whose *Tyranny of Greece over Germany* had inspired me to study Weimar Classicism. My diary entries highlight the excitement – not of the lectures – but of the supervisions with Francis:

> More Faust read before a lecture on the subject by Prof. Bruford at 11 and a supervision with Bennett at noon. The play fascinating, Bruford factual but dull, Bennett most forthcoming on Faust's view of life and his own, the advantages and disadvantages of the university education and life, and what we are to do with our life and the world. I count it a privilege to have Bennett as my supervisor. He is an excellent tutor for life if not for examinations.

Francis transformed my understanding of what Goethe understood by 'Bildung' – a process of self-cultivation that harmonizes our intellectual, aesthetic and moral powers.

Could Christian faith be combined with Faustian striving? The devotional life of the college was nurtured by the Dean, Hugh Montefiore, who created a network of acolytes known as the Church in Caius. One of its 'cells', which included Martin Conway and briefly also John Woods, used to meet in my rooms in St Michael's Court to discuss topics like the Retreat of Christianity, Holy Worldliness, and the Hydrogen Bomb. It was Conway, an erudite theology student, who encouraged me to read the apocalyptic novels of Charles Williams, including *All Hallows Eve*. But the practical Christianity of Mervyn Stockwood held a stronger appeal, for he transformed Great St Mary's into the vibrant hub of the university as a forum for challenging debates and innovative performances. It was there, in February 1957, that we witnessed a memorable production of Eliot's *Murder in the Cathedral* by the Pilgrims Way Players (FIGURE: Cambridge University Church), directed by my Christ's Hospital friend Francis Warner with another Old Blue, the saintly Roger Martin, playing Thomas Becket. For me, at this stage in my own pilgrimage, this was the 'only great play' of the early twentieth century.

Cambridge University Church: Pilgrims Way Players (theatre programme, 1957)

Cambridge was a cornucopia for the inquiring mind. Every week there were Amateur Dramatic Club productions that put student actors through their paces – for example, Derek Jacobi and Clive Swift in Ibsen's *The Pillars of the Community* in December 1957, with the aspiring author Margaret Drabble in a minor role. That same year the German Society staged Kleist's *Der zerbrochene Krug* with drunken Judge Adam played by Richard Marquand, later to become an avant-garde film director. Given these stimuli, I took the Preliminary Exams in my stride and began to plan a further European trip with my friends. Before leaving college, we called on Francis Bennett for advice about vacation reading, and he sent us on our way with a cheery wave. Back home, leafing idly through *The Times*, my eye was caught by an obituary: 'Mr E. K. Bennett, Fellow of Gonville and Caius College'. There could be no mistake: our gentle teacher was dead. He had collapsed suddenly in his rooms on the evening of 13 June, just six days after we had left him in such good spirits. Earlier that year, echoing Goethe, he had told us he was 'an ancient heathen' ('ein alter Heide') – he believed not in God but in love. The news of his death prompted me to improvise a memorial service, combining passages from the Prayer Book with lines from *Faust* about awakening from a healing sleep. His teaching would continue to inspire the students whose minds he had touched.

The vacation provided welcome distractions, including sailing trips with a neighbour named Christopher Gamble, a retired solicitor from Edinburgh who needed a crew for his yacht moored at Brixham. 'I hope he's not a pansy man,' said Mother, alarmed at the thought of her sons out at sea with a stranger. But Father, a good judge of character, was able to reassure her: Gamble's passion was for boats, not for boys. He proved such a good friend that he even loaned me one of his cars, an antiquated shooting-brake constructed on the chassis of a London taxi. The plan was to drive all the way to Turkey accompanied by my brother Robert and two college friends, John Rice and Andrew Kerr.

Although jokingly known as 'the hearse', the vehicle had proved its value in July by conveying wedding guests to Oxford for the marriage of my sister Helen to Peter Petter, one of David's college friends. Now in August it provided ample space for camping equipment and four passengers. Our guidebook opened with the words: 'The traveller to Istanbul cannot afford to tarry'. But tarry we did, first by choice, visiting Gila at a lakeside camp in Carinthia, and later by necessity. The coastal road in Croatia petered out into a dust-track and it proved almost impossible to erect our tents on the rock-hard terrain. When at last we found an idyllic spot to camp near the lakes at Plitvice, we were arrested for entering a military zone. Discouraged by our experiences in Yugoslavia, we turned back, spending ten days touring northern Italy instead. So the mysteries of Turkey remained unexplored.

PASSPORT TO THE WORLD OF LEARNING

Returning to Cambridge in October 1958, I learnt that my marks in Prelims had fallen short of First Class by only a few percentage points. The fascination of my studies had been strengthened by that meeting with Gila amid the mountains of Carinthia, but an even stronger impulse arose from mourning for Francis. Even before his death the College had appointed a successor, Dr Freddy Stopp, a scholar committed to rigorous research. The reading list for his favourite subject, the German Reformation, would have seemed formidable even for a graduate class, and he conducted supervisions in seminar style. Sitting at a table with his three students, Geoffrey Ashcroft, John Woods and myself, he would call on one of us to introduce each week's topic. There was no Francis to coax us through an embarrassed silence, but a supervisor whose searching gaze left no place to hide.

Francis had already set me on the path leading from 'Bildung' (self-cultivation) to 'Forschung' (scholarly research). If we were baffled by some arcane motif, such as the Walpurgisnacht scenes in *Faust*, he would say 'it's all in the Beit!' Did he mean the German Bight, the stormy region of the North Sea that featured in shipping forecasts? We had never heard of the Beit Library, the sanctum for advanced students, so we listened entranced as Francis took us back to the year 1913, when he had arrived at Caius. 'There was such hostility towards Germany,' he said, 'that people thought war inevitable. But Otto Beit decided to do something about it.' As a Jewish businessman from Hamburg who had become thoroughly anglicized, Beit longed for the two nations to be friends, so he endowed a German library. Hardly had the books begun to arrive when war broke out. 'Walter Bruford and I were among the first to sign on as members of the Beit,' Francis recalled. As a pacifist, he had found it hard to justify his passion for German literature to bellicose fellow students. While the majority could hardly wait to fight the Hun, he had campaigned against the super-patriots in the pages of the *Cambridge Magazine*, before joining an ambulance corps.

During the war the Beit Library had expanded under the guidance of Professor Karl Breul, another bridge-building anglophile, born in Hannover. 'My main interests originally lay with Italian,' Francis explained, 'but the holdings of the Beit helped me to become a Germanist'. During the 1920s the Library was located in the Arts School near the Cavendish Laboratory. 'We were dismayed,' he recalled, 'when the Library was moved to an attic in the Old Schools in the mid-1930s'. Protesting against the disruption, Francis and his students improvised a verse play – a parody of *Faust*, in which a group of scholars lament the loss of their books. The play also included a passage denouncing German nationalism – 'Deutschtum'. The implication was that books cherished by British academics were banned in Hitler's Germany.

Suitably inspired, we set out in search of the Beit, located close to Caius – just fifty yards down Senate House Passage and up a winding staircase. Untold riches awaited us – the broad sweep of German culture from medieval poetry to modern politics. Which options should we choose for our final year? Medieval Literature should have been a priority – the province of Dennis Green. The legends of the Nibelungen had fascinated me since schooldays, but the supervisor was as important as the subject. Dr Green's scholarship extended to Old Norse, but during my first year I'd found his teaching brusque and uninspiring. So I steered clear of medieval studies, opting for the other extreme, Literature, Thought and History since 1890. That autumn we were supervised by Ronald Gray, whose language classes had proved so stimulating during our first year. Since he had no college Fellowship, we met at his home in Abbey House, the oldest and most ramshackle domestic building in Cambridge. The habitat suited the man, for Dr Gray's approach was delightfully informal. If the topic was German Expressionism, he would embark on a discussion of Buddhism, and after an enthralling lecture on Kafka's religious aphorisms, he startled us the following week by retracting everything he had said.

The appeal of German lay in the eclectic mix of literature, thought and history with its political subtext. Students flocked to A. H. J. Knight's lectures on German History since 1871. His delivery was dramatic but he needed a run-up, since he actually started with the Congress of Vienna. By the end of the first term he had only reached Bismarck's social reforms in the aftermath of the Franco-Prussian war, and he had lost half his audience for it was the Nazi period we wanted to hear about. Paul Roubiczek's lectures on German Philosophy, delivered with a strong central European accent, enhanced the mysteries of Kant and Hegel, introducing us to categorical imperatives and historical dialectics. It was a relief to arrive at Marx, who famously turned the dialectic right side up, placing historical contradictions within the framework of class conflict.

It was only in the New Year that the rising star of the department came into view. My diary of 16 January 1959 records 'one of the best lectures I have ever heard, by Dr J. P. Stern, arrived 3 a.m. this morning from the States, on nineteenth-century German prose'. Students nurtured on Bennett's *History of the German Novelle* were astonished by Peter Stern's verbal fireworks. Where Bennett had placed his narratives in a provincial context, Stern explored texts that challenged our grasp of existence. This was exemplified by *Lenz*, the story by Georg Büchner about a man on the verge of a mental breakdown. The limitations of the short story, supposedly a minor genre compared with the social novel, proved to be a source of strength, unsettling our sense of a reality.

Peter Stern took over as our supervisor for twentieth-century poetry. On 29 January I noted: 'supervision with Dr Stern, who placed Rilke very clearly in his intellectual context in a lecture in miniature. I kept silence'. This sounds unpromising, for Stern as a supervisor could be as intimidating as he was inspirational as a lecturer. My first essay – on Rilke – was a flop. Fortunately, this was balanced by the encouragement received from Freddy Stopp, supervising me on the Reformation and for nineteenth-century texts like Goethe's *Die Wahlverwandtschaften*. Conversations with friends could be equally stimulating. My diary also records a discussion with George Hughes that went well beyond the banalities of university life. Our starting point was Gottfried Keller's novel *Der grüne Heinrich*, which explores the dilemma of a young man caught between two women, one seen as ethically responsible ('sittlich'), the other as sensuously appealing ('sinnlich'). Could this distinction be valid in real life? If inexperienced young men were struggling to make connections between imagination and experience, the situation was no easier for women, some of whom were equally unsure of themselves. In February 1959 we heard that a final-year student at Girton, Enid Harmer, had disappeared under ominous circumstances. A week later her body was found in the Cam. Her brooding presence at the back of lecture rooms

Books Read for the Modern Language Tripos (from a diary of 1959)

had suggested that she was extremely shy. Perhaps the fault had been on our side – for failing to make contact with someone so isolated.

The circumstances of Enid's death were elucidated by my friend John Rice, her supervision partner for History of the German Language. He had come to know her well, inviting her to his lodgings for tea and lending her two of his essays. Students often learn as much from their friends as from their supervisor, who in that case was an inexperienced postgraduate. However, the real problem lay elsewhere. Enid confided in John about the difficulties she was experiencing with her supervisor for Old Norse. At Oxford, J. R. R.Tolkein was inspiring a revival of interest in heroic sagas, but at Cambridge we were less fortunate. Enid found her teacher's manner so forbidding that she said it would drive her to suicide. John took this lightly, consoling her with a few kind words, until Enid's bicycle was discovered near the river.

The stresses of our final year were compounded by the need to choose a career. While others in my group were making plans, I was casting around for a way to avoid conscription into the army. The turning point came two weeks later when Freddy Stopp invited me to attend a colloquium normally reserved for dons and researchers. By this date I had produced a second more carefully argued essay for Peter Stern on the *Duino Elegies*. Clearly, Freddy wished to give me a taste of a research community, and the paper on approaches to Brecht – by John Willett – did not disappoint. Better still, Dr Stern was also there to welcome me, commending my essay as a fine piece which he 'liked very well'. This came at the right moment, prompting me to stay on for two weeks after the end of term for additional reading.

Perched in the eyrie of the Beit Library, I developed a taste for research based on the principles pioneered by German scholarship: 'Wissenschaftlichkeit' (scientific rigour) and 'Quellenstudium' (the analysis of sources). Solitary study made it possible to read well beyond the syllabus, from Theodor Fontane and Thomas Mann to more popular authors like Hans Carossa, Ernst Wiechert and Hermann Hesse. Freddy Stopp continued to act as my mentor, inviting me to tea in Regent House, the faculty club, to discuss the idea of postgraduate studies. The most promising subject was the poetry of the seventeenth century, which we discussed on 21 March. The religious epigrams of Angelus Silesius appealed to a mind immersed in devotional matters, although by this date all idea of training for the priesthood had been abandoned. The experiences of my second year had included a Retreat at Westcott House, the Anglican theological college. While others were deep in prayer, I was in the library, intrigued by the historical exegesis of the Bible. If the scholarly impulse had displaced the pastoral, mystical poetry might combine them.

It was in this frame of mind that I returned home for Easter. Aware that my mother was convalescing after an operation in London, I had become too self-absorbed to realize that all was not well at the Vicarage. My presence may have increased the tensions, for shortly after my return I experienced a night of extreme unrest. Despairing of sleep, my mind evolved an autobiography in the form of a testament left 'after committing suicide' (8 April). The following day a blazing row erupted between my parents, John and Joan, as we were now beginning to call them. The issue, according to my diary, was whether she should employ domestic help during her convalescence. My response was to bury myself in my books: Eight hours spent reading Fontane's *Der Stechlin* – a novel about a family in decline.

There was no place to hide three days later, when my father suffered an attack of vertigo in the pulpit and had to discontinue his sermon. In retrospect it seems that both parents, then in their early fifties, were passing through a mid-life crisis. His way of coping was to immerse himself in public duties, with his work as a County Councillor competing with his obligations as a pastor, while she, in addition to running the household, found time to organize meetings of the Mothers Union. There were bound to be tensions between two such contrasting personalities. Aunty Marion was there to mediate, but this triangle, a source of strength in younger days, may have exacerbated the tensions.

Growing up at the Vicarage, with long absences at school or college, we had failed to notice the danger signs. Helen was married and living near London, while David had been called up for military service. He would spend his occasional visits tinkering with his motorbike in the garage, increasingly withdrawn. Robert, during his final year at Christ's Hospital, had won a scholarship to study Maths at Cambridge. In his leisure time he was perhaps too absorbed by his favourite football team, Plymouth Argyle, to have picked up the vibrations at home. Christopher, Jonathan and Margaret were also at boarding school, and even eight-year-old Simon had started at the Bluecoat School in Birmingham. Mother had to cope with the empty nest, but it was Father who now became severely depressed.

My response took two main forms. On a practical level I escorted Simon on the train back to school, thus saving my father an arduous journey. On the academic plane my path was clear. Nothing would delight my parents more than scholarly success, so I redoubled my efforts. Back at Cambridge the demands of revision were so great that there was scarcely time to keep a diary. Anxieties about my parents were alleviated by a well-timed visit from my father on 23 May. For once he spoke freely about his health problems, explaining that he was being treated by a faith healer in Harley Street, while taking a rest cure at St Luke's Nursing Home. Mother was also enjoying a break, staying with my sister Helen, her husband Peter and their newborn son Timothy.

It was thus in a calmer frame of mind that I approached my Finals. The papers covered German literature, thought and history from 1500 to the present, so comprehensive revision was impossible. On the eve of examinations, a Sunday, I decided to concentrate on my favourite author, Adalbert Stifter, whose vision of nature mitigated his awareness of tragedy. Later, with the bells of Great St Mary's calling from outside my window, I found peace of mind at Evensong. My prayers were answered for the following morning the Essay paper included my favourite topic – Stifter's treatment of the theme of nature! The ideas simply flowed during further papers which enabled me to write extensively on other favourites like Goethe and Kafka, Grimmelshausen and Theodor Storm. Each script ended with the cryptic dedication 'IMFB' (In Memory of Francis Bennett).

For most students Cambridge in June is a paradise of punting on the river and all-night balls, but my impulse was to escape. The occasional visit to the races – Newmarket for the Guineas or Epsom for the Derby – brought some relief, but a more exciting opportunity arose when Cyril Swindley announced one evening that he'd decided to hitch-hike to visit friends in Holland – and would pay the expenses of anyone who joined him. So the two of us climbed out of college and caught the ferry to Ostend. Hitchhiking proved a testing experience. As busy Belgians buzzed by, the power of positive thinking began to fade. One night was spent sleeping rough on benches in what turned out to be the open-fronted pavilion of a village sports club. But we finally reached Rotterdam, where we enjoyed relaxing days and sumptuous meals with Cyril's friends. Although this escapade eased post-examination tensions, it caused problems back at college. Our absence was reported to the Senior Tutor, Ian MacFarlane, who might have called police if John Woods had not explained where we were. Hauled over the carpet after our return, we were relieved to be let off with a fine, though my fine was doubled for infringing my scholar's oath.

My final interview with MacFarlane left a deeper mark. 'Quite a useful three years,' he observed, implying that I had fallen short of his ideal – the good college man, so I left under a cloud to face an uncertain future. Some of my chattels were stored in college so that they could be collected by my Robert when he started his studies at Queens that autumn. Then my elder brother David, on a break from military service, collected me in the family car and drove us to London, where my father was about to be discharged from the nursing home. As Father and I travelled home, he allowed me to take the wheel – a sign that he at least had confidence in my abilities. The atmosphere was unsettled, as my parents, still not completely fit, were planning to holiday in Folkestone. Fortunately, there was another mentor to guide me through the anxious weeks before the exam results. Christopher Gamble, the friend who had lent us his car the previous summer, was planning to sail along the coast to Cornwall and invited me to join him.

The port of Brixham was bathed in sunlight when we arrived. Fishing boats crowded the quay, but there were also moorings in the harbour for pleasure craft. It was here that Gamble kept his yacht, affectionately known as *Ming*. As the two of us rowed out, he unfolded his plans for a ten-day voyage. At just over thirty feet, *Ming* had three berths, a loo and a galley, together with an engine for use in emergencies, so we would be self-sufficient. Tacking into a stiff breeze, I soon got the feel of the tiller with one eye on the swaying compass and the other on the fluttering burgee. We were heading for Falmouth on the southwestern tip of England, anchoring at night in the secluded estuaries that punctuate the coastline. What a relief to put open water between us and the cares of the mainland!

Gamble, a diverting conversationalist, shared my aversion to British insularity – that purblind attitude encapsulated in the famous newspaper heading 'Fog in the Channel: Continent cut off'. The government was edging towards a rapprochement with Europe, although few people showed any enthusiasm. But Gamble, who had travelled extensively in his youth, had cosmopolitan tastes (his reading on that voyage was Pasternak's *Doctor Zhivago*). Although a practising Anglican, it was the classical world that provided his norms. His definition of a civilized nation was to have been occupied by the Romans, cultivate olives, and produce your own wine. Our conversations, ranging from classical history to experimental sexual technique, made me aware of my cloistered upbringing.

The following morning the coast really was shrouded in fog, and we were marooned at Salcombe for two days. There was nothing to do but chat and read, before rowing ashore for supper. The copy of *The Times* purchased in the village store contained the Tripos results for Classics and Geography, but no trace of Modern Languages. At Salcombe we were joined by another of Gamble's friends, a physical chemist from Cambridge named Dennis Hayden who was a Fellow of Trinity Hall. Next day the fog lifted and we headed out to sea with a stiff breeze behind us. We had just passed the Eddystone lighthouse when the wind dropped and visibility worsened. Fortunately, we managed to start the engine and grope our way through the mist, until Gamble's navigational skills brought us round St Anthony's Head.

We awoke to find Falmouth sparkling in sunshine. Rowing across the estuary, Gamble regaled us with tales of three-masted clippers like the *Cutty Sark* which had sailed all the way to China. Falmouth was open towards the Atlantic, hinting at exotic climes. Subtropical plants were flowering on the footpaths, and the scent of foxgloves was intoxicating as we strolled into town for lunch. As my friends lingered over coffee, I set out in search of *The Times*. My exam results should have been published the previous morning, but where can you find yesterday's paper? At last I discovered a crumpled copy of the *Daily Telegraph*, and there, on an inside page, was the list for Modern Languages – with my name in the First Class. That evening *Ming* became the scene of raucous celebrations. Gamble, proud of the pass degree he had taken at Oxford in the 1920s, suggested that standards at the other place must be slipping, but my eyes were on the horizon with a passport to the world of learning in my pocket.

CHAPTER FIVE

Exploring the New Germany

We set out later that summer in a vintage Austin convertible, purchased with the help of my parents. My companion John Rice, who had enrolled for a teacher's training course in Cambridge, had few doubts about his vocation, but was I on the right track? Earlier that year, when fellow students were considering careers with banks and insurance companies, the Central Bureau for Educational Exchanges had appointed me as an Assistant in Germany. In addition to giving me a taste of teaching English, this would delay my call-up for military service by a further twelve months. The school was in Bavaria, and John had agreed to accompany me on the first stage of the journey. Heading south down the Rhine valley, we passed the Germania monument at Rudesheim, a gigantic figure with crown and sword symbolizing the triumphs of the Wilhelminian Empire.

The new Germany was represented by the delicate figure of Gila, the girl from Heidelberg. Arriving at the apartment where she lived with her parents, we spent the morning looking at books and photographs. In the afternoon she suggested an excursion to Schwetzingen, the former royal palace situated in an extensive park. Sensing my feelings, John opted to spend the afternoon in town, checking the record shops for new releases. So Gila and I were alone as we drove to Schwetzingen and strolled through the enchanted gardens. Eye contact counted for more than words as we sat among the squirrels frisking under the trees. We always spoke German, but no one had taught me the language of endearment. Did she really return my feelings? Gila was to spend two months in England as an au pair, while I started teaching in Bavaria, but as we parted she invited me to spend Christmas with her family.

UNANSWERED QUESTIONS

Leaving John to catch the train back to London, I drove on in a dream. Initially my assignment was to a school in Erlangen, a tranquil university town. However, it turned out that, due to a mix-up at the Ministry, a teacher from Scotland named Allan McLay had already been posted to that school. It took almost a month to sort out the muddle, during which I became firm friends with Allan and his wife Christine. Erlangen is at the heart of the region known as Franconian Switzerland, and I enjoyed exploring the countryside while awaiting another posting. In the third week of September I was transferred to schools in the Nuremberg area – an exciting prospect, for the city was far more typical of the modern republic rising out of the ruins of war.

My lodgings were in a quiet residential district where Frau Zahn, a recently widowed singer, made me feel at home. Although the ancient centre of Nuremberg had been bombed beyond repair, the massive ramparts were being rebuilt. Given my interest in Albrecht Dürer, I was intrigued by this attempt to restore the profile of the city as depicted in engravings of the Reformation period.

The contrast between weathered masonry and fresh pink stone reflected the city's fractured past, for Nuremberg with its picturesque houses, churches and fountains had been the scene of the great Nazi rallies. After the devastation caused by the Allied bombs, the castle and the principal churches had been restored, but it proved impossible to re-construct the tightly packed medieval houses. So the new urban centre was a conventional mix of flats, offices and stores that made the ramparts seem even more archaic.

At first, it was a disappointment to find that my teaching was divided between two schools more than five miles apart. The Martin Behaim Ober-Realschule, newly constructed in a residential suburb, was a boys school serving upwardly mobile families. Lessons often started at 7.45 a.m., which meant getting up very early, but school was over by 1.30 p.m.,

Old Nuremberg (engraving of 1579)

leaving plenty of leisure time. Students in their final year took five advanced subjects with the goal of passing the coveted Abitur, the school leaving exam that guaranteed access to higher education. My job was to provide classroom support for lessons in English, including grammar, conversation, play readings and current affairs. From Nuremberg it took twenty minutes to drive to the school in Fürth, which was my second assignment. This dour manufacturing town offered a surprisingly warm welcome. The Ober-Realschule was a cavernous building dating from the late nineteenth century, where the pace of life seemed more measured. Here I was given greater responsibility, conducting both classes for restless teenagers and seminars for trainee teachers. There was also a French Assistant, a young man from Paris named Dominique Tassel, who became my companion on tours through the countryside.

For someone brought up in rural England, it was exciting to live in a sprawling conurbation. Erlangen was a small town dominated by its university, but Nuremberg offered a broad social spectrum from working-class teenagers to bustling businessmen, although there were few female contacts (all my colleagues were male). Middle-class women were still expected to stay at home caring for the family. It was unusual, at a shop in Erlangen, to find a well-qualified young woman working as dispensing chemist. My friend Allan, who had a wicked sense of humour, prompted me to go into the shop and ask for 'zehn Stück London'. It was only as the young woman was wrapping the package that I realized it contained ten condoms, products of the London Rubber Company.

The economic miracle was well under way with motorways carving their way through the countryside. As the dashing new Opels and Audis overtook my vintage Austin, I sensed that England was falling behind. The main station at Nuremberg was the hub of an integrated transport system with tramlines radiating in all directions, and the electrification of the railways was well advanced. Politically, too, the Federal Republic struck a good balance between the powers of central government and the spheres delegated to regions, which included health and education. Parliamentary elections had produced a stable democracy led by the conservative coalition of Konrad Adenauer. One my tasks was to explain the vagaries of the British electoral system. In the election of autumn 1959 the Conservatives, led by Harold Macmillan, had been returned to power with a large majority of seats, despite receiving well under 50 percent of the national vote. It took considerable ingenuity to explain this to pupils accustomed to a finely calibrated system of proportional representation.

Teaching duties left ample time for excursions. While foreign observers were praising the country's stunning economic success, we began to explore a Germany virtually hidden from view, driving off the beaten track in my little Austin. Village inns offered instructive contrasts. While priding themselves on wholesome home cooking, they would have a jukebox in the corner playing the latest Elvis Presley. A picture emerged of a country caught between two impulses: a dynamic striving for modernity on the American model and a nostalgic attachment to traditional country ways. Coca-Cola was on sale everywhere, but in this hop-growing region each little town had its distinctive brewery. No household was complete without a refrigerator, but the restaurant around the corner was likely to have its own abattoir, proudly announcing that on Slaughter Day it would be serving blood-and-liver sausage. This was not for the fainthearted, as we discovered to our cost; but in a sense the whole country was suffering from digestive difficulties. Huge articulated trucks thundered along the motorways, but the landscape was criss-crossed by tranquil footpaths, showing that anti-industrial ideals were still alive in the minds of week-end ramblers.

To my mind, the phrase Divided Germany denoted not merely the Soviet satellite in the East, but a syndrome affecting the whole nation. Germans were finding it difficult to come to terms with their past, which was selectively cherished and denied. The traumas caused by two World Wars were the latest in a series of fissures that undermined historical continuity. What had caused the demise of those thriving free cities of the early modern period like Nuremberg and Augsburg? How could a Thirty Years War have been fought over issues of religious allegiance? Why had the courtly culture of the eighteenth century left such an authoritarian legacy? These questions were inscribed in the built environment: fortified churches, medieval monasteries and Renaissance town halls, opulent Baroque palaces and bombastic imperial monuments, the grandiose parade ground near my school where Hitler presided over the Nuremberg Rallies and the bleak building on the road to Fürth where the War Crimes Tribunal had sentenced Nazi leaders to death. How could you reconcile such contradictions?

Constructing a coherent picture of Germany was an elusive task. My social experiences were recorded in long letters home, while more personal feelings were confided to my diary. Almost obsessively, my reflections returned to two magical moments that had transformed my life. It was still hard to believe that my Cambridge degree had opened the path to research for a doctorate. My thoughts about possible topics were extremely confused, but the apprenticeship in Germany would help me to make an informed choice. Secondly, the afternoon with Gila in Schwetzingen had left me suspended between hope and apprehension. When I wrote to Gila saying that she was continuously in my mind, there was a long pause before her reply arrived, but it filled me with joy. 'She thinks of me just as often,' I noted, 'and asks how deeply I feel for her.' It was a glorious autumn, and solitary drives to favourite haunts in the countryside enabled me to absorb her latest letter undisturbed, confiding to my diary 'the key question, her name: Gila; her occupation: enchantress; her victim: me'.

There are undertones of euphoria in my letters home, describing the delights of weekend excursions with the McLays and Dominique. Visits to the picturesque towns of Bamberg and Rothenburg inspired such eloquence that Mother saved my letters. The topographical detail suggests that the Franconian countryside was being studied with the eyes of a cultural historian, noting the distinctive character of castles and churches, farmsteads and market towns. 'Everything is new and interesting,' I wrote on 30 September. 'Whether in the heart of Nuremberg or out on the atrociously surfaced country roads there is no limit to the things to wonder at: oxen pulling lengthy farm wagons, the farms themselves with rich dung-heaps and massive barns, and women, many of them widows, working all day in the fields'. Two weeks later I wrote with equal excitement about the autumn fair in Fürth and the top-hatted chimney-sweeps on the streets of Nuremberg.

A teaching break in November provided a chance to visit Berlin, travelling with Dominique and the McLays in their car. Since Alan still had to pass his driving test, I was in the driving seat, feeling very German at the wheel of a Volkswagen. But Berlin seemed a city of ghosts, with the historic core in the Soviet zone while the new centre in the West consisted of modern blocks surrounded by devastation. The political climate was tense, for this was just a few months before the building of the Wall, but we had no difficulty in driving through the Brandenburg Gate after routine questions from communist border guards. That Sunday we heard Handel's Messiah sung in St Mary's Church by an East German choir. 'Paul Gerhardt preached here,' said a mournful church-goer, reminding us of the power of religious poetry. The sermon by Otto Dibelius, Evangelical Bishop of All Berlin, alluded to the limits of temporal power. We gathered that the large congregations he attracted were causing consternation for the authorities.

Berlin left me feeling drained. Driving back along the monotonous motorway, I would have fallen asleep at the wheel had not Dominique jogged my arm. The letter from Gila waiting at my lodgings brought an even more dramatic awakening. On her return to Heidelberg, she explained, she had been reunited with an earlier boyfriend. As I read her wounding words, my world fell apart. It was small comfort that she asked me to continue writing, since she treasured my letters. The following day I sat down to compose a reply, trying to be as stoical as possible. Gila, who had just moved to Karlsruhe to study architecture, had sent me her new address. But when I came to write 'perhaps we shall never meet again' something snapped: Why not go to Karlsruhe? It seemed crazy to drive three hundred miles to see a girl, but the impulse was overwhelming.

Cutting school the following morning, I set off in the Volkswagen at such a lick that I was fined for speeding. It took several hours to track Gila down, since she had no idea I was coming. At last, as my diary records, there she was:

> It was a meeting full of shock (for her), joy (for me), and sorrow (for both of us). Tense and then emotionally unrestrained; tender and yet we could only grope towards a new relationship. As a gesture more meaningful than words she gave me a picture she'd painted and a little horse she'd made. At midnight I walked her home and we parted with an embrace in the rain.

Back I drove for several hours before stopping by the roadside and curling up in my sleeping bag. There followed a period of hibernation. With my next letter I sent Gila a delicate metal ornament in the shape of a squirrel, symbol of our enchantment. 'Do I still have hopes that she may love me one day?' I asked myself. Allan generously accepted an evasive explanation for the long trip in his car, for my diary was my only confidant. Under Gila's spell I had imagined that 'the intricate jigsaw puzzle of my life was beginning to take shape'; but now 'I fumble in the dark'.

Probing the Past

That enchanted autumn was followed by chilly days, but there was little time to brood as my teaching load increased. In my zeal to discover the real Germany I had forgotten how cold continental winters could be. The Austin, stalled by the arctic conditions, had been laid up for the winter, and classes began so early that sometimes I'd rise in pitch darkness to travel by tram across the Nuremberg–Fürth conurbation. My breakfast, as I changed trams at the teeming junction known as the Plärrer, would be frankfurters with lashings of mustard. An evening class at the Volkshochschule in Fürth, teaching elementary English to underprivileged young adults, involved a further trek across town. Coping with such a large class proved extremely testing, but the extra income enabled me to buy warmer clothes.

With the streets buried in snow German hospitality was all the more welcome. Scarcely a week passed without an invitation to join a teacher's family for supper, often accompanied by Dominique. Fluent in German and widely read, he was planning a thesis on Kleist's *Michael Kohlhaas*, which he regarded as the greatest German political novel. One week-end we were taken flying kites by the music teacher, Herr Koch, with his twelve-year-old twin daughters, followed by a simple meal served by his wife. It turned out to be St Martin's Day, and a sudden knock on the door revealed a cloaked figure carrying a book in which the deeds of children were supposedly recorded. The saint had arrived to reward them, with birch-strokes or with presents, and the twins responded with favourite songs. The hospitality offered by Helmut Offenwanger, Head of Languages at Fürth, was just as generous. In a lounge teeming with house plants we were treated to coffee and cakes, with apricot brandy as an appetiser, followed by dozens of different meats and cheeses, washed down with Franconian wine. So much good food was clearly not good for the figure, but Offenwanger was an excellent linguist, well versed in the culture of France, where he had studied, and England, where he had been a prisoner-of-war. The camp at Trumpington near Cambridge, he claimed, was so well run that those months were among the happiest of his life.

In Nuremberg I had the good fortune to be invited to rent a room by Gerhard Glockzin, a youthful teacher of English who was moving into a new terrace house with his wife Trude and their two young sons. They offered me a centrally heated room on the ground floor with its own bathroom and a door opening to the garden. The house was a mere fifteen-minute walk from the school, and the atmosphere was so relaxed that we would often share a convivial lunch or an evening bowl of punch brewed with brandy and sugar, a 'Feuerzangenbowle'. Trude had a sparkling sense of humour, while Gerhard, who had spent a year in the United States, combined a flair for languages with an interest in the wider world. One evening he took me to watch American soldiers in cabaret acts, including a hilarious bedroom scene involving cross-dressing.

The teaching routine was alleviated by frequent religious holidays both Catholic and Protestant, providing scope for further excursions. Early in December, Dominique and I spent five rewarding days in Munich exploring the thriving city with its broad boulevards, sleek blue trams and fascinating art galleries. On our return we found Nuremberg deep in snow, putting us in the mood for Christmas. The centre was transformed by the Christ Child Market with stalls selling the celebrated Lebkuchen (spicy chocolate biscuits), the ideal present for my family back home. We clubbed together to present Allan McLay with a bottle of whisky, but the best news was that his wife Christine was expecting a baby. They were in such good spirits that they agreed to join me on a trip to celebrate Christmas in Vienna. After attending a Haydn Mass at the cathedral, Allan and Christine enjoyed Humperdink's *Hansel and Gretel* while I watched an ambitious version of Schiller's *Wallenstein* trilogy, starting with a Brechtian prelude and culminating, after an early evening break, in the grandeur of Wallenstein's Death. It was not hard to identify with a hero struggling to piece the shattered world together by dint of his own power.

We could now compare the three principal German-speaking cities. Munich felt like the artistic capital, but the city (as I wrote home) seemed 'to have been bypassed by the mainstream of progress'. Berlin, by contrast, struck me as a 'hollow city, highly artificial, no longer the great capital it was when Christopher Isherwood was writing his sketches'. Its symbol was 'a postcard of a bear in a cage', purchased in the Russian zone. It was the visit to Vienna that proved most inspiring. Austria had regained its sovereignty three years earlier and the city seemed poised to recapture past glories. For an aspiring cultural historian there could hardly be a more tempting destination.

My New Year's resolution, once back in Nuremberg, was to improve my social skills by attending a Dancing School. Here we learnt modish steps like the rumba and cha-cha-cha in delightful company, as well as formation dances like the Polonaise. Further social activities were organized with the student teachers from Fürth, while giving private lessons earned me a growing circle of friends. Teaching English to the wife of a lawyer introduced me to a family of expellees from the Sudetenland, who proved to be life-long Social Democrats. Further social contacts were made when I acted as interpreter at the annual Toy Fair. However, in most conversations with older Germans something was missing. That something was Nazi Germany, the blanked-out period between the nostalgically remembered Heimat of their youth and the thriving modern Bundesrepublik. Paradoxically, the War Crimes Tribunal provided an alibi. Hadn't the guilty men been punished?

Why were my colleagues so evasive? Many of them had been in the forces, including the genial Herr Kohl, a veteran with a pronounced limp. And it was rumoured that one of the younger teachers, Herr Ritter, had served on the *Tirpitz*, the battleship sunk by the RAF in November 1944. But it was unusual for anyone to mention to the war. The tone was set by the ebullient Offenwanger, who recalled his time as a British prisoner-of-war with great affection, but had nothing to say about the Wehrmacht. However, a more enlightened teacher named Herr Hock took me to see *Der Nürnberger Prozess*, a film about the War Crimes Tribunal incorporating documentary footage of the Nazi movement and the concentration camps. 'Suddenly the dark side of the German soul is thrust upon one', I noted, 'unimaginably brutal. What is more real, that film in the darkened cinema or the sunshine outside?'

There was also one teacher in Nuremberg, Dr Beckstein, who tackled politics more directly, warning me not to refer to the German Democratic Republic as East Germany. That phrase should be reserved for the lost territories, now under Polish administration. On another occasion he mentioned the fate of the Jews, claiming that the Germans had no quarrel with their Jewish fellow citizens. It was the flood of immigrants from the East, the so-called 'Ostjuden', that had provoked hostility. The tendentiousness of these comments soon became clear. In January the post brought me books chosen as a college prize, including a recently published history of Franconia: *Franken: Land, Volk, Geschichte und Wirtschaft*, edited by Conrad Scherzer. Marginal notes show how attentively I read the colourful narrative. It was not until page 132 that there was any reference to the Jewish population, which was said to have been not very numerous. After noting that Jews had settled in Bamberg and Fürth and contributed to the brewing industry, this brief passage concluded by drawing a contrast between 'old-established liberal Jews' and 'the numerous orthodox Eastern Jewish immigrants'. Such passages showed how deviously the historical record was being distorted. The suggestion that even liberal Jews resented the influx of 'Ostjuden' provided antisemites with an alibi.

There was a conspiracy of silence about the anti-Jewish crusade launched by Julius Streicher, the self-styled Führer of Franconia, and no one at the school in Fürth breathed a word about the Jewish community that had flourished before the war. Reading Scherzer, one would never have guessed that eighteenth-century Fürth had been such a centre of Jewish learning that it was dubbed the Franconian Jerusalem. Little did I know that around 1800 its Hebrew printing press had produced handsome volumes like *Derech S'lulah* (The Straight Path), printed by Isaak

Frontispiece of *Derech S'lulah*, printed by Isaak David Zirndorfer (Fürth, 1802)

David Zirndorfer, with a frontispiece showing Moses and Aaron standing on either side of the Tables of the Law.

So strong was the taboo that no one mentioned the Jewish cemetery on the banks of the Regnitz, only a short walk from the school. Perhaps one of those friendly teachers would have responded if I had asked the right questions. Seduced by the glamour of cultural centres like Nuremberg and Vienna, Heidelberg and Munich, I had yet to learn that history reveals a different face when viewed from the margins – and that excluded figures provide the key to a more complex ensemble.

This silence formed part of a larger problem of public memory. As we toured the towns and villages of Bavaria, we looked – often in vain – for memorials to those who lost their lives in two World Wars. One of the most moving was in the hillside village of Egloffstein, a simple cross supported by two slabs bearing the names of the dead (more in the Second World War than the First). The inscription read: 'May their sacrifice not be in vain and may earth and heaven accept it'. Recalling the memorials erected in village squares throughout England, I began to reflect on the difficulty of commemorating defeat. Those killed in a war of criminal aggression could hardly be venerated as Our Glorious Dead. That rhetoric had collapsed with the defeat of Nazi Germany, although there were still occasional traces. In a church at Ansbach we were astonished to discover a stained-glass window portraying a saintly Hitler in shining armour. And why had no one removed from a small country church that framed tribute to a soldier who died for 'Volk, Führer und Vaterland'?

Such questions were intensified by a memorable trip to Prague. At Cambridge we had learnt to approach literature contextually – who could study Kafka without appreciating the fate of the German-speaking Jews? Now my car was back on the road, I arranged for my brother Robert and his friend Michael Britton to join me on a ten-day excursion through the Czech Republic. Once we had crossed the border, we became lost in a maze of minor roads from which all signposts had been removed. After numerous detours we arrived at Karlstein Castle, built by Charles IV to house the crown jewels of the Holy Roman Empire, later in Nuremberg and now in Vienna. Standing on the battlements, we relived the days when Bohemia formed a bridge between East and West.

Prague felt like a pilgrimage. The architecture hardly seemed to have changed since the Thirty Years Wars, when the Habsburgs reimposed their rule, creating a panorama of statues, churches and palaces. Guide-book in hand, we reverently crossed the Charles Bridge and gazed up at Hradschin Castle, but even the most solemn situation couldn't suppress Michael's boisterous spirits. We had just visited the chapel where Jan Hus launched the Czech religious revival when he and Robert started joshing each other around Bethlehem Square. This caught the eye of Mira Bartosova, a woman who lived nearby with her twelve-year-old daughter

Blanca. Sensing that we were too harmless to be watched by the secret police, she introduced herself, and we spent the evening discussing every conceivable subject from socialist child care to the oppressiveness of communism. 'Think of me as you cross the Charles Bridge,' Gila had written in a letter recalling her own impressions of Prague; but on the return journey it was Blanca who was on my mind, symbol of a nation longing for freedom.

The experiences in Prague overflow the pages of my diary: the Strahov monastery with its rococo library; the football stadium (a must for Robert) to see Prague draw with a Soviet team under the shadow of Stalin's gigantic statue; a night at the opera and an entrancing puppet play. Sauntering through the narrow streets we found revelations around every corner, from St Nicholas Church to the Old New Synagogue. But the most lasting impression was the visit to Lidice. In June 1942, as a reprisal for the assassination of Reinhardt Heydrich, all the male inhabitants of this mining village were taken from their beds and shot. The women and children were dispersed and the village, which had allegedly sheltered the assassins, was erased from the map. With proverbial thoroughness the Nazis made a film documenting their crimes, now shown to visitors. As we sat in the memorial garden, we struggled to understand. Was it still possible to believe in the basic goodness of man?

A CRITICAL HERITAGE

It was time to start thinking about a subject for research. My tutor Freddy Stopp had encouraged me to visit the Germanisches Nationalmuseum, but afternoons spent in the catalogue room proved frustrating. Like the rebuilt city ramparts, its holdings seemed designed to distract from the essential question: How could such a civilized nation be responsible for the atrocities of the Nazi period? This was not a question anyone would ask in conservative Bavaria, but things were beginning to move in the Social Democratic municipality of Fürth. For teachers at the local Volkshochschule they organized a full-day seminar on National Socialism, including a lecture on Hitler's foreign policy, a film about his seizure of power, and finally – after beer and sausages – a gripping account of German literature under Goebbels.

This set me thinking in new directions, concentrating on two authors who offered contrasting perspectives on Nazism: Ernst Wiechert, a conservative author imprisoned for his beliefs, recommended by Gila; and Arnolt Bronnen, a Nazi fellow traveller whose autobiography, *Arnolt Bronnen gibt zu Protokoll*, was presented to me by my friend Allan McLay. Bronnen's narrative, as noted in my diary, provided a 'new angle' on the Nazi movement. It might prove rewarding to write about a left-wing radical who became a fanatical Nazi, rubbing shoulders first with Brecht and then with Goebbels..

Fortunately, there was a group of student teachers with whom these issues could be discussed. Once a week we met for a seminar on topics of their choice, from the history of Stonehenge to Bertrand Russell's *New Hopes for a Changing World*, a challenging book that set out proposals for world government and a life without the fear of war. This seminar embodied the new Germany – young men and women committed to international reconciliation. The most approachable was Hans Keith, a burly fellow from Rothenburg identified in my diary as the best of those at Fürth. We enjoyed long conversations at his lodgings, packed with books and pictures. 'Why were there so few really critical authors in the early twentieth century?' I asked. I was casting around for German equivalents of Aldous Huxley or Grahame Greene, but he took the question differently, citing the two outspoken satirists. 'Read Kurt Tucholsky,' he urged, 'and Karl Kraus'. The names were new to me, for at Cambridge we had studied unpolitical authors like Hermann Hesse and Thomas Mann. But Tucholsky was a left-wing journalist whose articles in *Die Weltbühne* provided a running commentary on the crises of the Weimar Republic.

On 17 March a public reading from the works of Tucholsky was organized at the Technical University. 'Jew and brilliant journalist,' I noted, 'very entertaining'. The post-war moratorium on asking awkward questions was coming to an end, as Fischer Verlag launched a documentary series starting with *Die Zerstörung der deutschen Politik* (The Destruction of German Politics), edited by Harry Pross. The copious annotations in my copy show that the book made a deep impression, for it focussed not the deeds of great men, but on discourses and ideologies. Harry Pross provided an antidote to Conrad Scherzer, whose history of Franconia represented the 'völkisch' tradition. In a country noted for conformism I was discovering a critical heritage. A further provocative paperback, *Die Zerstörung der deutschen Literatur* (The Destruction of German Literature) by Walter Muschg, showed how closely the arts of the early twentieth century were linked to German politics. The concept of a unified national identity was displaced by an awareness of fractures and fissures. Creativity might emerge out of disaster, as in Wolfgang Borchert's vision of Hamburg, which left me feeling that I too might have something to say.

Hans Keith was an idiosyncratic character who lived life against the grain. The group that met at his lodgings included the alarmingly erudite Helmut Schwimmer, a teacher at the Melanchthon Gymnasium. After Helmut had tried to convince us of the merits of the latest electronic music, Hans would take us back to the Munich of the 1920s by playing recordings from the subversive cabaret act of Karl Valentin and Liesl Karlstadt. On another occasion a discussion of Dada prompted us to create a collage, pasting scraps of texts and images into an anarchistic composition. Hans combined avant-garde with antiquarian interests, decorating his room with photos of the cherubic figures from Bavarian churches. One of his missions was to persuade lovers of Gothic architecture to cultivate a taste for the Baroque.

As the days lengthened it became possible to make longer excursions, including one as far as Strasburg with Dominique. In mid-June, Hans Keith and I drove across to Lake Constance, staying overnight in rural hostelries. As we cruised along bumpy roads, the steering of my Austin developed an alarming wobble and we almost lost a wheel. Later a flash-flood made it necessary to dry out the distributor, but nothing could damp our spirits. On the island of Reichenau we discovered three churches untouched by time, serving a population of perhaps three hundred. 'A magical land!' I noted, as we headed into Swabia, exploring the landscape celebrated in Mörike's poems and meeting an innkeeper's wife who seemed to have stepped out of one of his folktales.

Hans was a mentor whose knowledge proved empowering. On his advice I purchased a selection of satires by Karl Kraus, just issued as an inexpensive hardback. The introduction by Heinrich Fischer recalled that Kraus had edited his journal *Die Fackel* (The Torch) in Vienna from 1899 until his death in 1936. Kraus, like Tucholsky, engaged with the political events of his day, but there the parallel ended. Reading a text by Tucholsky, one could immediately grasp the message, but Kraus's prose was opaque. His style was wittily adversarial, but what was the significance of his targets, those ephemeral figures that peopled his pages? While Tucholsky's writings had obvious power, Kraus's required continuous decoding. However, one thing was clear: there was scope for research on two gifted satirists.

It would have been good to return to England with a sense of achievement, but the pieces still wouldn't fit. Constructing a new Germany might have been easier with Gila's support, for I had dreamed of an intimacy that would reveal essential truths. Our correspondence continued, and on 8 March my hopes revived when she informed me that she had separated from her boyfriend; but a visit to Karlsruhe in May left a feeling of emptiness. On the return journey I paused in Schwäbisch Hall, spending half-hour in the Gothic church. The organ was playing and the staircase to the tower was unlocked, giving access to the void above the nave. There I stood, alone among the pigeons, in floods of tears. Driving home, I started to plan a fairy tale entitled In Search of the New Germania, which (according to my diary) 'could be good if it ever comes into being'. It was not only romantic love that had proved a fairy tale, but the quest an integrated identity. Early in June we met again in Heidelberg for what proved a thwarting day. When Gila declared that we were completely mismatched, there was nothing more to say. But on the return journey I stayed in Rothenburg with Hans Keith and his parents, comforted by the warmth of their welcome.

At least I was in a position to counteract the negative images of Germany that proliferated in Britain. In autumn 1959 the visit of Chancellor Adenauer to London had provoked anti-German outbursts in the press, linked with accusations that he was protecting former Nazis. 'It is hard to get to the truth in these matters, which are discussed with reticence by older Germans, who were of course mainly fellow-travellers with the Nazis in the 1930s,' I explained in a letter home. During the following months my contacts with Germans in all walks of life discredited the concept of a nation indelibly tainted by Nazism – a fixed idea with sections of the media. It was conveniently forgotten that the British bombing raids on Hamburg, Nuremberg and Dresden could also be regarded as war crimes.

Only fifteen years earlier Allied planes had been destroying German cities with a callous disregard for the lives of civilians. Now people welcomed me into their homes with open arms, and my friends included two exceptionally lovable people. A letter home noted on 9 May: 'The almost universal friendliness of people here is one of my deepest impressions'. My car deserved some of the credit for it provoked considerable mirth in a country keen on the latest models. This Englishman eccentrically attached to his antiquated Austin was commended by the Head Teacher at Fürth as an object lesson in non-conformity. There was little scope for stereotyping in a circle of acquaintance that included a generous Scotsman, a social democrat from the Sudetenland, a kindly war veteran, a Parisian who loved speaking German, a Hausfrau with an infectious sense of humour, and a musician who collected kites.

A further bonus was that the issue of military service had been resolved. My visions of police on the quay at Dover, waiting to pounce on defaulters, were laid to rest when I was notified that 'provided you remain in your present post until June 1st 1960, you will not be liable for call-up thereafter'. This gave me the green light to return to Cambridge. Early in June, Freddy Stopp wrote to assure me that a State Studentship was 'in the bag', although he was unaware of my intellectual reorientation. The focus had shifted from Baroque mystical poetry first to the biography of Arnolt Bronnen, then to the satire of Kurt Tucholsky and Karl Kraus.

CHAPTER SIX

City, Masks and Torch

'Of course, you will have to read every word Kraus wrote,' said Peter Stern, when we met at his home in Barton Road in October 1960. Given the limitations of a three-year research project, my idea had been to focus on Karl Kraus's most celebrated work, *Die letzten Tage der Menschheit*, a documentary drama of the First World War. After all, copies of his magazine *Die Fackel* (The Torch) were almost impossible to find. But there on Peter's shelf was a complete run, including the very first number of April 1899 with its eye-catching cover. Smiling at my astonishment, he explained that his father, a Czech diplomat, had been one of Kraus's great admirers. Forced into exile after the German occupation of Czechoslovakia, he had brought his set of the magazine with him. At the age of sixteen Peter too had fled abroad, reaching the Baltic coast in August 1939 just in time to catch the last boat to England. After being wounded while serving in a Czech airforce unit, Stern had studied in Cambridge, completing a doctorate on the aphorist Georg Christian Lichtenberg. His mentors included the historian Michael Oakeshott and the philosopher Ludwig Wittgenstein, whose view of language was partly inspired by *Die Fackel*. To be working on Kraus under Stern was a breath-taking prospect – 'taking up the torch' of a great tradition.

The Scrutiny of Satire

The decision to work on Kraus rather than Tucholsky had been taken during a summer job teaching English in Bournemouth. The informal atmosphere at the Anglo-Continental School enabled me to make friends among the students, including Ruth Stepischnigg, an elegant redhead from Vienna. After further reading and reflection. I concluded that Tucholsky was too journalistic – 'wielding a sharp pen, yet only inflicting pin-pricks'.

My growing enthusiasm for Kraus was recorded after working through his anti-Nazi polemic *Dritte Walpurgisnacht*: 'An impressive book; stylistically a tough nut; but just as you begin to despair he coins a phrase or slips in a pun to place his subject in an utterly illuminating light.' Kraus, I concluded, had the superior intelligence and biting humour that make the finest satire.

My appetite for the subject was intensified by authors with a taste for the grotesque like Schnitzler and Wedekind, who featured in my supervisions on modern German literature that autumn. Freddy Stopp was on leave, so he had assigned some teaching to research students, including my friend Terry Llewellyn, who was working on German mysticism. The bulk of the work was undertaken by a newly appointed Lector from Tübingen, Lothar Fietz, an expert on literary theory. As Caians we formed a triad, refining our ideas over drinks at Terry's lodgings while listening to recordings of his beloved Mahler. He also shared his passion for the plays of Harold Pinter, from which he could reproduce certain scenes verbatim, such as the dreams of the idealist who will conquer the world – once he has built his 'hut in the garden'.

The routine was punctuated by stimulating cultural events: the Brecht scholar Reinhold Grimm at the Research Colloquium; satirical reviews performed by amateur dramatic clubs; and speeches by politicians like the arch-conservative Enoch Powell, who debated economic policy at the Union with the Labour Party's Douglas Jay. It was awesome to watch Powell's razor-sharp intelligence slice through his adversary's woolly socialism. But emotional experience was still constrained by the overwhelmingly male ethos. In March a proposal to allow women to become members of the Cambridge Union Society failed to obtain the required two-thirds majority.

These were diversions from the study of Kraus, chronicled in my diary: 'Die Fackel Die Fackel Die Fackel Die Fackel – it's like a train churning along the line to Vienna, but progress seems terribly slow.' The routine was alleviated by trips to London to attend events organized by the German-Jewish refugee community, including a recital of Kraus writings by the actor Martin Miller, advertised in the *New Statesman*. Even more productive were the visits to Libris in Swiss Cottage, a rambling antiquarian bookshop run by the Suschitzky brothers, refugees from Vienna. In a locked cabinet Joseph Suschitzky kept signed editions of Kraus's books with handwritten dedications to his musical accompanist Mechtilde Lichnowsky. But I was more excited by the cardboard box discovered in a dusty corner, containing fragile copies of *Die Fackel* in their original bright-red covers, on sale for a song.

Having originals in my hands proved inspirational for my understanding of Kraus's satire. As I contemplated the cover design, it dawned on me that the rays from the Torch illuminating the silhouette of Vienna

Cover of Karl Kraus's
Die Fackel (1899)

are thrown forward in a pattern that suggests the boards of a stage. A
further sense of theatricality was conveyed by the grinning mask of
comedy and the goatish face of the satyr, proclaiming the intention
of comic and satirical stylization. These visual motifs generated fruitful
new ideas: the conception of Kraus as a frustrated actor, and the framing
of my argument under the heading City, Masks and Torch.

The study of satire involved a combination of critical strategies. Freddy
Stopp's lectures had alerted me to techniques such as the ironic encomium,
but Peter Stern guided my eye towards linguistic nuances. This was the
theme of his essay on The Dear Purchase, which included Kraus with
Kafka and Rilke among the modernists who deserved sustained attention.
Kraus's satire could thus be construed in terms of the existential crisis
explored in Eric Heller's eloquent study, *The Disinherited Mind*. These
approaches were underpinned by the study of social contexts, exemplified
by the scholarship of Walter Bruford, who was about to retire as Schroeder
Professor. During a dinner in his honour at St John's he delivered a moving
speech recalling the shattering impact of the First World War, as power
politics triumphed over Weimar humanism.

The historical context of *Die Fackel* was mapped by two outstanding
works: Wickham Steed's *The Habsburg Monarchy*, a political analysis
published on the eve of the First World War; and Carl Schorske's *Fin-de-*

siècle Vienna, a brilliant study of socio-cultural trends. Books on literary theory proved less helpful. Since satire inhabited a fringe area between didactic journalism and imaginative writing, literary scholars were reluctant to explore this disputed territory. The greatest disappointment was Gilbert Highet's *Anatomy of Satire*, which conceived satirical monologue in biographical terms. Even more sophisticated theorists like René Wellek and Austin Warren could not accommodate a documentary mode impelled by destructive animus. Among German critics, only Helmut Arntzen seemed prepared to acknowledge that satire could be creative.

However, help was available closer home. There were few formal links between Modern Languages and the Faculty of English, which were in adjacent buildings, but no one could ignore the controversial genius of F. R. Leavis. Although he had formally retired, his public lectures attracted large audiences and his books were frequently reprinted. Reading *Mass Civilization and Minority Culture, Culture and Environment* (co-authored with Denys Thompson) and *Education and the University* attuned me to a beguiling blend of intellectual radicalism and cultural conservatism. And his commentary on the *Lady Chatterley* trial developed into a critique of shallow liberalism with echoes of Kraus.

The affinity became even clearer when Leavis's critique of The Significance of C. P. Snow appeared in the *Spectator*. In his pamphlet *The Two Cultures and the Scientific Revolution* Snow had rebuked literary intellectuals for 'incomprehension of science'. For Leavis such assertions betrayed a portentous ignorance of the interactions between creative writing and modern civilization. There was no reason to suppose that he had heard of *Die Fackel*, but his writings helped to resolve my methodological difficulties. 'Swift is a great English writer,' Leavis observed in a passage from *The Common Pursuit* quoted in the introduction to my thesis. What we are concerned with, he continued, is 'an arrangement of words on the page and their effects – the emotions, attitudes and ideas that they organize.'

This reading strengthened my sense that it was counter-productive to approach satire through the biography of the author. But the focus would need to be extended so as to take account of historically significant polemic as well as timelessly imaginative satire. This perspective emerged as I was working my way through *Die Fackel* under the guidance of Peter Stern. A chance encounter in the Library led to an unforgettable afternoon spent with him and his family, including his father, the diplomat who had collected Kraus's writings. He was a fund of anecdotes and reflections on the tragedy of Czechoslovakia. During this tea party Sheila Stern, my supervisor's wife, quoted her husband as saying that mine was the best research project he'd ever encountered. This was welcome news, for Peter's judgements could be severe.

To be cooped up all day with Kraus could have become oppressive, but fortunately my lodgings were within walking distance of the Cam and the green belt that curves along its banks. We would meet for lunch at picturesque riverside pubs like the Granta or the Fort St George, and the river was also scene of Bump Races in the spring. The races were interrupted on 4 March 1961 by a real life satire – the sinking of the Ferry at Fen Ditton. Overloaded with spectators, the old tub swayed drunkenly as it took on water, plunging about fifty passengers into the river. From the bank this seemed hilarious, until we realized that some of them would have drowned, if students had not dived back in to rescue them. My interest in sailing was undiminished, and in April we set sail again – this time on the Norfolk Boards. The merry crew included my brother David, who had begun teaching after his discharge from the army, my younger brother Robert and his friend Johnny Horsler. Brought up on the stories of Arthur Ransome, we regarded sails as superior to engines, but it proved impossible to tack along narrow stretches of water without running aground. Further hazards were created by the numerous locks, bridges and weirs, but we enjoyed sleeping rough after celebrating our latest navigational feat at a pub on the towpath. This was the last holiday shared with David before he emigrated to Canada to continue his teaching career.

During the Summer Term I bought another car, an Austin dating from 1939, to enable me to travel to Vienna and pursue Kraus's ideas back to their source. My grant was unlikely to cover all the costs of a year in Austria, so I took a teaching job at the Bell School of English. Cambridge that summer seemed entrancing. One evening after a cloudburst a cluster of swans feeding on the river was caught in the setting sun. As the water was transformed by the reddening sky, the scene became connected in my mind with the news that the philosopher Bertrand Russell had been imprisoned after a demonstration by the Campaign for Nuclear Disarmament. My diary describes this as 'a shameful day for the England I love'.

In a more optimistic mood, four days later in Harwich, I watched my car being hoisted aboard the Channel ferry. It was exciting to be on the road again with the chance of visiting old friends, including the Glockzin family in Nuremberg and Hans Keith in Fürth. The evenings spent with Hans left my head buzzing with ideas – about Adenauer's politics (which he despised), the weekly magazine *Der Spiegel* (which kept him sane) and the cabaret songs of Georg Kreisler (which he adored). Travelling on through Passau, the Austin made good time to Vienna, a total of 1200 miles.

FIELDWORK IN VIENNA

My first move was to contact Ruth Stepischnigg, the girl befriended in Bournemouth. Calling at her home on the Kahlenberg, a hilltop location nestling in the Vienna Woods, I was greeted by her gorgeous cocker spaniel. Ruth had discovered a student hostel half-a-mile down the road at Sulzwiese belonging to a Catholic charity called Caritas. On the off-chance of finding a room for me, she had walked down and knocked on the nearest door. This proved to be the apartment of Dr Leopold Ungar, Director of Caritas, who explained that there was nothing available – they had been turning people away for weeks. Just as she was leaving, Ruth mentioned my interest in Kraus and was amazed by the transformation. It turned out that Leopold Ungar, as a Jewish student in the 1920s, had fallen under the satirist's spell. Indeed, it was Kraus's work that inspired him to enter the Church.

We drove down to meet Dr Ungar, a distinguished man in his forties. A small single room turned out to be free after all, and although the hostel was located several miles out of town, this was an offer that could not be refused. There was a tram service from Grinzing to the city centre, and the journey would be even quicker by car, though caution would be required on the hairpin bends. It didn't take long to complete the paperwork. The monthly rent of 1000 Austrian Schillings (roughly £14) provided a heated room with washbasin, together with breakfast and an evening meal. The hostel complex was scenically located on the edge of the Vienna Woods with delightful walks in all directions. Only later did I learn that it had been constructed during the war as a radar station. No one wanted to talk about Austria's Nazi past.

The following evening Dr Ungar invited me for a tumbler of whisky. As a young man he had attended over two hundred of Kraus's recitals, finding his performances of Shakespeare and Offenbach irresistible. To escape persecution after the annexation of Austria, Ungar had spent the war in England, studying the works of Saint Augustine. Returning to Vienna after 1945, he was given responsibility for the social reconstruction and international aid programmes of Caritas. Since he spoke fluent English, he was also Catholic Chaplain to the English-speaking community. During the war he had lost his library, but he still treasured original recordings of Kraus reading from his own work, including 'Das Ehrenkreuz', a satire on sexual hypocrisy, and 'Jugend', a lyrical recollection of childhood. We listened entranced to recordings that brought tears to my eyes. Taking up the torch in Vienna could hardly have started more auspiciously.

Work began in earnest the following Monday morning at the City Library. Here I was welcomed by the curator of the Kraus Collection, the kindly Paul Schick, who introduced me to the antiquated card catalogue. The collection left me with a feeling of delight and awe. It would take me the better part of a year just to work through the printed books and pamphlets, newspaper cuttings and court reports relating to Kraus's career. Later I was initiated into the mysteries of the manuscript collection, which had been moved to Switzerland for safety during the Nazi period and returned to Vienna after the war. Kraus's critical crusades needed to be correlated with the voluminous files of his lawyer, Dr Oskar Samek, which had also been taken abroad for safety in 1938.

The antiquarian bookshops provided a further resource, and I was delighted to acquire a first edition of *Die letzten Tage der Menschheit*. Copies of *Die Fackel* were harder to come by, although a bookshop by the Schottentor sold me eighty numbers. They dated from the final years of the Habsburg Empire and were stamped with the name of the original subscriber, Major Baron Lempruch. There was a mystery here: how could anti-establishment satire appeal to an aristocratic army officer? To acquire further copies of *Die Fackel*, I placed an advertisement in a magazine that elicited two replies. Dr Pranter, a lawyer with memories of his student days in England before the First World War, welcomed me to his apartment on the Michaelerplatz and presented me with a hundred numbers. And I was able to purchase another small collection from Frau Rütter, a retired graphic artist living in Sievering. It turned out that she was the heir of Lina Loos, the first wife of Kraus's architect friend Adolf Loos. Her house was a treasure trove of books and papers, including letters by another member of that circle, the bohemian poet Peter Altenberg.

My musical education would have been neglected but for a young flautist from England named Bill Tilden. After meeting at the Sulzwiese hostel we became firm friends, and he introduced me to a circle of aspiring musicians, including the pianist John Harrison and his family. We splashed out on tickets for Verdi's *Don Carlos* with Sena Jurinak, and also heard Dimitri Rostropovitch playing Dvořák's Cello Concerto, followed by a Shostakovitch concerto dedicated to Dimitri himself. Under Bill's guidance, my musical tastes were extended by further fine performances: Dvořák played by the Amadeus Quartet, Brahms at the Musikverein, César Franck at a recital by John Harrison, and a concert by the Amsterdam Concertgebouw, conducted by Pierre Monteux. The repertoire of the Opera was equally exciting, from Offenbach's captivating *Tales of Hoffmann* to Wagner's tempestuous *Flying Dutchman*.

Making friends with young Austrians proved more difficult – no one seemed to have heard of Kraus! The Caritas-Heim served as a residential finishing school for about twenty Austrian girls with little interest in research. A second building housed a dozen Hungarians who had fled after the 1956 revolt. Culturally, there was no common ground, although the Hungarians would invite me to join them for the occasional game of football. Visits to the Stepischniggs were also unrewarding, despite Ruth's kindness. Her father was a textile manufacturer with a passion for guns, and the walls of the villa were lined not with bookcases, but with hunting trophies.

There were invitations to a number of events at the British Embassy,

Combe-in-Teignhead (postcard dated 1943 showing the Rectory at the centre)

Dad's Army: The Home Guard at Combe, 1942, with Rev. John Timms (back row fourth from left)

Edward Timms (ET) aged five, convalescing on a tricycle

Holy Trinity Church, Buckfastleigh with (to the right) the Cabell Penthouse

Family group in the garden, 1944 (from left, back row): Brenda, Aunty Marion holding Christopher, Father; (front row): ET (hands in pockets), David, Robert, Mother

At Rock Preparatory School, June 1946 (back row, from left): Nicholas Coulton, Rosemary Bolton, ET, brother Robert

Buckfastleigh Vicarage viewed from the garden, framed by acacia trees

Under the acacia trees: Our parents in their prime

Congregational singing in Christ's Hospital Chapel (with the Brangwyn panels)

The Vicarage family in the mid-1950s (from left): Father, David, Edward, Mother, Helen, Robert, Christopher, Jonathan, Margaret, Simon

Summer holidays at Collery Farm: ET (left) with David, helping with the harvest

At Christ's Hospital: ET (right, in Grecian's gown) with Robert, Mother and Father

Gonville and Caius College in the snow, with the Gate of Honour in the foreground and the Gate of Knowledge centre

A gentle teacher: Francis Bennett in his rooms at Caius

Romantic Germany: Gila in 1959 by the ramparts of the Tiefburg in Heidelberg

Modern Nuremberg:
Changing trams at
the Plärrer

Vintage Austin: ET showing off his car to Trude Glockzin and her son Ernst

Critical heritage: Reading Kurt Tucholsky in Fürth with Dominique Tassell

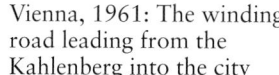

Vienna, 1961: The winding road leading from the Kahlenberg into the city

The Caritas Student Hostel at Sulzwiese (with ET in the garden)

ET in the Lothringerstrasse, standing under the Karl Kraus plaque

The Stalin monument in Prague, 1962

Making friends in Prague (from left): Peter Bartos, Blanca Bartosova, Mira Bartosova, ET, and American friend Bill Moore

A theoretical physicist from Turkey: Saime Göksu (autumn 1963)

Science with a smile: Brian Easlea (University of Sussex)

Showing German journalists the Sussex campus in April 1964 (from left): Herr
Joachim Schulz (deutsche presse agentur), ET, Frau Maria Stein (Stuttgarter
Zeitung), Dr Lothar Franz Labusch (Kölner Stadt-Anzeiger), Eva Schwarz (Sussex
student), Mr I. H. Hay (British Embassy in Bonn), Graf Fink von Finkenstein (Die
Welt), Herr Dankwart Reissenberger (Kölnische Rundschau)

'How eggstraordinary!' Joe
Townsend telling a joke

With Christine
in Marine
Square garden

Conversation over coffee: Farhad with Adelina at 5 Marine Square

Blanca on the balcony at 7
Marine Square

'Les amants' (photographed by Brian Easlea)

The Old Vienna Café,
Ovingdean

Istanbul night club:
Saime with Mehmet
Şenel

Middle East Technical University, Ankara

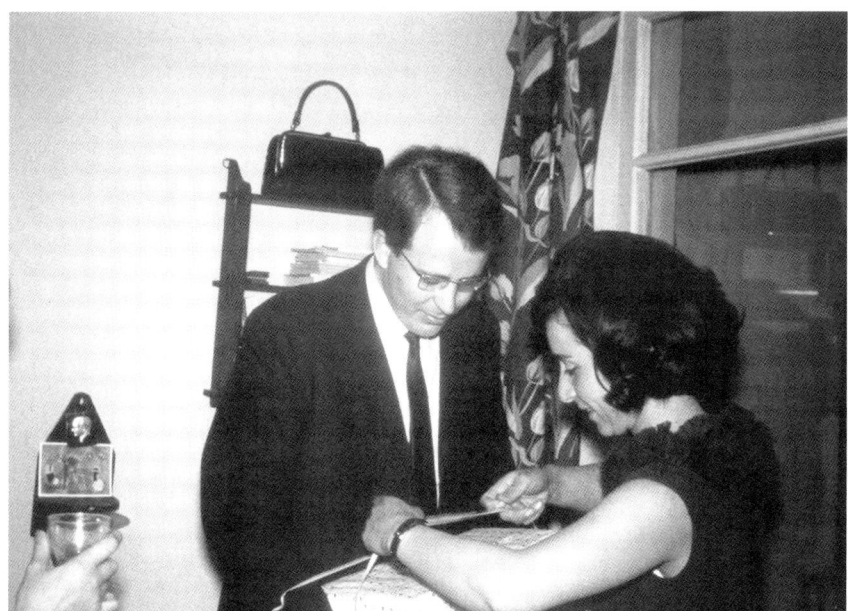

Engagement party in Ankara, April 1966: Opening presents with Saime

Garden House
Hotel,
Cambridge, with
Gavin Wraith
(right), Best Man
at the Wedding

Wedding group:
Mary Wraith,
Marion Axford,
Saime, ET, Joan
Timms

but the Christmas bazaar turned out to be a pretext for screening patriotic films. My closest social ties were with visiting American Catholics, pupils of Dr Ungar. They included Peter Devereaux, a student of theology who was considering the priesthood; Bill and Carolyn Moore, a married couple with a passion for the arts; and a young woman from Michigan named Shannon King, who had written a thesis on D. H. Lawrence. With Shannon, I would attend films and concerts, and over dinner with the Moores we would talk into the small hours about religion and politics. Hearing that I'd never accept military call-up, the hawkish Bill would hammer on the table as he denounced the Soviet threat, while Peter puffed reflectively at his pipe. The disarmament talks in Geneva had just collapsed, and in twelve months Bill might be serving in the Marines, while a conscientious objector like myself would doubtless be in Brixton Prison.

By Christmas the city was deep in snow and the temperature dropped to minus 20 centigrade. My car would never have remained on the road without friends to push the engine into life. With the help of Peter Devereaux, the car restarted in time for us to drive to Germany for the break. There I stayed in Erlangen with my friends the McLays, celebrating Hogmanay in a haze of Scottish hospitality. My companion during the February semester break was Bill Tilden, who invited me to drive with him to Alpbach in the Tyrol for a fortnight's skiing. By the end of our stay the snow was piled so high that a tractor was needed to haul our car on to the road. Back in Vienna, we were cheered by the festivities of Fasching. Hiring fancy dress was beyond my means so my friends dressed me as the Spirit of London, complete with bowler hat and a copy of *The Times*. It was good to meet fun-loving younger Austrians, but emotionally my life remained solitary.

That spring the focus of my studies shifted. Reading all 912 numbers of *Die Fackel* had made me sceptical towards all ideologies, for Kraus's satire could never be identified with any party line. His most devoted followers belonged to three competing factions. Leopold Ungar had found in Kraus's work the inspiration for a religious vocation, but a very different line was adopted by the Marxist aesthetician Ernst Fischer. He gave a compelling account of Kraus's theory of language at a lecture delivered to veteran communists at the Old Town Hall. Not long afterwards I met the editor of *Forum*, Friedrich Torberg, at his favourite coffee house. He too was a lifelong admirer of Kraus, with whom he had been friends in his youth. Now Torberg, after exile in California, had become a militant anti-communist (*Forum* was the Austrian equivalent of *Encounter*). Bustling into the Café Raimund, Torberg entertained me with anecdotes about conversations with Kraus thirty years earlier. Reminiscences in copies of *Forum* that he gave me provided glimpses of Kraus's personal charm, further highlighting the contradictions. If the satirist could inspire three such diverse figures, the secret must lie in a radicalism that defied conventional ideologies. Ernst Fischer put the matter well when he spoke of the 'loss of reality' caused by the distortions of the media. The key lay in Kraus's critique of the dehumanizing language of communications.

It was in libraries, theatres and coffee-houses that I learnt most during that year in Vienna. It would have been logical to register as a Visiting Student at the University, but the programme proved uninspiring. Moritz Enzinger's lectures on Austrian Literature between the World Wars sounded promising, but he avoided the political challenge by concentrating on Rilke's religious poetry. Kraus was clearly too subversive for a traditional academic. When I showed the programme to my mentor Leopold Ungar, he found little to recommend, apart from lectures by the maverick Catholic historian, Friedrich Heer. His course on European History of Ideas impressed me by its sympathetic approach to the theories of Marx and Engels, but Heer was marginalized by the university authorities, for he challenged the silence in which so many Austrians shrouded their Nazi past.

Disappointment with university lectures prompted me to sum up my feelings in one of my letters home:

> In 1934 the authoritarian Dollfuss government pruned all the left-wing elements from the staff; in 1938 the Germans removed all the Jews, most sincere Catholics and anyone of independent mind; and in 1945 the rest were sacked by the denazification measures, so that nowadays the only teachers are men who have never offended anybody and are never likely to do so.

The only truly enjoyable lecture was organized by the British Council and delivered by the solitary woman on the staff of the university's English Department. Speaking on P. G. Wodehouse's Use of Language, she had the audience in fits as she illustrated his extravagance of metaphor.

Theatre visits were facilitated by my Council of Europe student card, which entitled me to purchase a ticket one day before public booking began. The Burgtheater was thriving, for in Leopold Lindtberg, a director who had worked with Kraus, a great tradition was still alive. His staging of Goethe's *Egmont* made a strong emotional impact, dramatizing the struggle for the independence of the Netherlands through bold confrontations on a chessboard stage. More intimate productions were staged at the Akademietheater, including the erotic escapades of Schnitzler's *Anatol*. Further performances marked the centenary of Schnitzler's birth: Ernst Deutsch as the beleaguered Jewish doctor, explaining his position to Josef Meinrad in the culminating scene from *Professor Bernhardi*; Hans Moser and Johanna Matz in a scene from *Liebelei*; Paula Wessely reading excerpts from Schnitzler's stories; and Ernst Lothar paying tribute from the perspective of a veteran stage director. There was an aura of reconciliation as Deutsch and Lothar, Jews forced into exile in the 1930s, shared the stage with Moser and Wessely, stars of the Nazi era.

Lindtberg's stagecraft thrived on the work of Nestroy, the actor-dramatist whose satire Kraus found so inspiring. In the angular Josef Meinrad the Burgtheater had a comedian to revive the roles that Nestroy had made his own, from Weinberl, the frustrated shop assistant in *Einen Jux will er sich machen*, to the melancholy Herr von Lips in *Der Zerrissene*. The plays had trapdoors through which actors were plunged into unexpected depths. Equally enchanting was the performance by Hans Moser as the cobbler Pfrim in *Höllenangst*, Nestroy's satire on superstition. Moser's face was familiar from films of the 1930s, but his gift as a juggler with words generated tremors of profound unease.

Even more memorable was the premiere of a modern satirical masterpiece, *Der Herr Karl*, a worm's eye view of Austrian politics, written by Helmut Qualtinger and Carl Merz. Originally designed for television, this monologue was even more compelling on stage at the Kammerspiele. It was in this theatre that Nazi thugs had rioted against Schnitzler's *Reigen* forty years earlier, so the venue was well chosen. The curtain rose to reveal a larger-than-life Qualtinger discoursing about thirty years of modern history with the voice of Herr Karl, the toadying opportunist. Nothing could have been more subversive than his use of dialect to expose the devious twists of Austrian identity, from socialism through clericalism to fascism, from worshipping Hitler in 1938 to welcoming the Russians in 1945. The audience was scandalized by this all too plausible satire.

Further shockwaves were created by the American TV documentary *Our Man in Vienna*, which portrayed the Viennese as underworked, overfed and overgoverned. Watching this programme was one of the highlights of a day spent with Peter Devereaux at Dr Ungar's flat. After listening to recordings of Kraus reading from his own work, including the haunting anti-war poem 'Die Raben', we discovered that Ungar was himself a talented performer. He shared with us his own renditions of sketches by Peter Altenberg and ballads by Wedekind, as well as a sequence of Kraus texts culminating in the visionary epilogue to *Die letzten Tage der Menschheit*. While these magical experiences with an eyewitness from the 1930s refined my understanding of satire, the mystery of Kraus's lyrical impulse deepened.

A copy of his selected poems, acquired in March, included the celebration of a serene landscape with a lake and swans, entitled 'Wiese im Park', with the subtitle: Schloss Janowitz. The book by Werner Kraft, *Karl Kraus: Studien zu seinem Werk*, had identified Janowitz as a country estate in Bohemia belonging to the Nadherny family. Moreover, Kraft had revealed the secret of the satirist in love. For over twenty years Sidonie Nadherny, a cultivated woman with a passion for travel, had been the inspiration behind Kraus's most poignant poetry. It was time to extend my fieldwork into the Bohemian countryside, where the satirist had sought refuge from the stresses of life in Vienna.

The librarian Paul Schick, with the aid of an antiquated gazetteer, helped me to locate the village of Janowitz, just twenty miles south of Prague. On a bright May morning I set out in the car accompanied by Bill Tilden and Bill Moore. Schloss Janowitz proved a desolate spectacle, the entrance boarded up and the stonework in need of repair, but an elderly gentleman guided us through the wilderness to the point where the park touched the churchyard wall. There we found the graves of two of Sidonie's brothers, interred within the park as a gesture of natural piety. There were no swans on the lake, but it was not hard to recapture the elegiac mood of Kraus's poem. This expedition raised far more questions than it answered. I knew that Sidonie had fled to England after the communist takeover, but where were the hundreds of letters she had received from Kraus during their stormy relationship?

Our arrival in Prague coincided with a military parade to commemorate the liberation of the city by the Red Army in 1945. We watched the cavalcade of tanks and rockets on the Letna parade ground, photographing the gigantic statue of Stalin. What a contrast to the architectural dignity of Hradschin Castle, home of Rudolf II, that most cultivated of Renaissance rulers! Walking through the twisting streets we kept stumbling over residues of history. Here was the window through which the Habsburg envoys were thrown in 1618, precipitating the Thirty Years War. Around the corner was the Alchemist's Lane where Kafka took lodgings to escape his oppressive father.

Prague was replacing Heidelberg as city of my dreams, haunted by Blanca, the raven-haired girl encountered on Bethlehem Square two years earlier. This second meeting was the more magical for being so short, for we drove back to Vienna that same evening laden with presents. While I received a book of Czech poetry, the gifts we had brought from Vienna were more practical: make-up and movie magazines for Blanca, a raincoat for her brother Peter, an umbrella for their mother Mira. Amid the austerities of communism such goods appeared exotic. Writing home, I noted that the Czech economy was completely ruptured, with no fresh meat in the shops, long queues and dismal faces.

Back in Vienna our discussions were enlivened by visiting students from Germany. After arguing into the small hours in the wine bars of Grinzing, we would sober up by walking home as the sun rose over the Kahlenberg. At Easter, the sudden burgeoning of the beeches created a sense of festival, shared with Shannon on walks through the Vienna Woods; and Peter Devereaux encouraged me to develop my riding skills, cantering together through the Prater, where he stabled two fine horses. My car was running well, and we made numerous excursions, including an awe-inspiring afternoon visiting the monastery at Heiligenkreuz and delightful picnics at the Gänsehäusl, an open-air swimming-pool by the Danube.

My year in Austria ended with a holiday at Ehrwald in the Tyrol, shared by my mother, Aunty Marion and my brother Robert. It was difficult to convey to them my fascination with all things Austrian, but they thrived on the mountain walks. While they returned to England by coach, I drove home through Bavaria, stopping to visit friends and fulfil formal engagements. In Munich I was introduced to Heinrich Fischer, close friend of Karl Kraus and editor of his writings. This was followed by a visit to Erlangen, where Alan McLay arranged for me to deliver a trial lecture at the University. This resulted in the offer of a job as English Lector for the autumn of 1963, sending me back to Cambridge with my spirits renewed.

Irony and Tenderness

After selling my car, I took lodgings with the Mitchell family at 60 Grange Road, a short walk from the University Library. My room overlooked the garden in a house humming with life. My landlady Aileen Mitchell, a friend of Peter and Sheila Stern, would serve a hearty breakfast while keeping an eye on her teenage twins Jeremy and Julia, two cats, a Pekinese and a terrapin. Although I had little in common with those fun-loving creatures, I shared a bathroom with Julia, who would come wafting down the corridor in her nightgown. It was provocative to discover that she was helping herself from my magnum-size tube of toothpaste, squeezing it near the top in a way that distorted the shape. One evening, with the point of a pin, I inscribed 'Squeeze me here!' near the bottom of the tube. Her pert reply, equally neatly inscribed, was: 'You don't appeal'. Ah, well, after watching her zoom off in one of those trendy bubble-cars, it was back to the Library!

One afternoon among the bookstacks a flash of insight transformed my conception of the satirist. Earlier approaches to Kraus had insisted on the 'unity of man and work', but research in Vienna had revealed that this was untenable. Those who knew him best recalled that in private Kraus was a kindly and sociable person, qualitatively different from the implacable stance he assumed in *Die Fackel*. Moreover, his affair with Sidonie Nadherny revealed aspects of his character that had been concealed from his contemporaries. Given that Kraus reconstructed his public image to conceal those gentler traits, the only way to make sense was to distinguish the 'literary persona' of the satirist from the private identity of the author.

It was Carl Jung who gave new meaning to the word 'persona', traditionally used to denote characters in a play. Applying it to everyday life, he suggested that modern society requires us to conceal our emotions. But if public irony is not incompatible with private tenderness, how can the two be harmonized? Maynard Mack's essay on The Muse of Satire showed how the persona theory could be applied to eighteenth-century satirists like Alexander Pope, even when they appeared to be speaking in their own voice. Adapting these ideas to Kraus, I attributed his aggressive public stance to the existential urgency of his mission. Hence the paradox of the 'true mask', as defined by Walter Benjamin in an essay first published in 1931. In the figure of the satirist we have not the complexity of real life, but the stylized hero of a satirical drama. When I set out these ideas in a new introduction, Peter Stern found the argument so gripping that he read it (so he told me) standing up.

Once committed to persona theory, I found it haunting my own sense of self, as if ironic self-consciousness excluded me from emotional partic-ipation. Cambridge routines transformed life into a ritual. You were required to 'perform' at college functions and academic seminars, giving the impression that your thesis was almost complete even if you had barely sketched the parameters. But as research students our status was insecure, rubbing shoulders with an elite while aware that we might soon be un-employed. University appointments were scarce, and my friend Terry Llewellyn, while completing his doctorate, had taken a post as a school-teacher.

That autumn a vacancy arose at Bedford College, a women's branch of the University of London located in Regent's Park. Bedford had a good reputation, so I was pleased to be invited for interview. Asked which German-language critic had influenced me most, I mentioned Erich Heller's The Disinherited Mind. When Heller was ruled out (his book was published in English), my choice was Die Zerstörung der deutschen Literatur, Walter Muschg's analysis of the cultural impact of National Socialism. The discussion acquired such momentum that I was surprised not to be offered the job. Only later did I learn from Freddy Stopp, one of my referees, that he was asked by the Head of Department at Bedford whether I'd accept a more junior post as Tutor in German. He replied in the negative – without consulting me!

Hoping to keep me at Caius, Dr Stopp encouraged me to apply for a Research Fellowship. In a carefully worded application, dated 12 January 1963, I defined my aim: 'to rescue Karl Kraus from the neglect and misin-terpretation he has suffered at the hands of his critics and to establish more reliable criteria by which the much maligned genre of satire may be judged'. After stressing the need to distinguish the private life of the author from his satiric persona, I set out my reasons for regarding Kraus as the 'greatest modern satirist':

> A revolutionary in his social criticism, Kraus nevertheless defends the rights of the individual against the incursions of modernity. Out of this

tension emerges an art that illuminates the predicament of modern man in a society whose fate he no longer feels able to control.

Just as I was submitting this application, an Assistant Lectureship in German was advertised at the newly founded University of Sussex. So I rephrased my application, posted it off – and was again invited for interview.

On a bright winter's morning the Sussex campus buzzed with activity, as the students mingled with construction workers. Before the interview, there was just time to admire Falmer House, the new social centre. Construction of the Arts Building had barely begun, so the interview took place in a prefab. The questioning was led by Anthony Thorlby, head of the German group, and John Cruickshank, Professor of French, representing the School of European Studies. They tried to put me at ease by exploring a range of linguistic and literary questions while a third interviewer, the sociologist Helmut Pappe, listened in silence. As the focus shifted to Vienna, Dr Pappe suddenly asked: 'What do you think of Schnitzler's *Der Weg ins Freie?*' This shamed me into silence, for I had not yet read that classic account of the Austrian Jewish dilemma. Crestfallen, I returned to Cambridge.

The envelope that arrived from Sussex two days later felt so flimsy that it could only contain a rejection. Hence my amazement on reading the briefest of letters offering me the post of Assistant Lecturer in German with effect from 1 October 1963 at a salary of £900 per annum. Unsure how to respond, I sent a telegram to my father. Although he idealized the life of an Oxbridge don, he favoured the move to Sussex. Naturally, I also consulted my referees, knowing how much was owed to their support. While Freddy Stopp acknowledged the attractions of Sussex, Peter Stern quoted Schopenhauer's dictum that fundamental decisions are taken at an unconscious level – before we are aware of them. So the choice was made – I withdrew my Fellowship application and accepted the post at Sussex. The unconscious factor may have been my impression of Falmer House, for the building was teeming with glamorous young women.

Thrilled by this unexpected success, I began to relax. The Library Tea Room was the traditional meeting place for researchers in the humanities. Conversations with Gar Yates proved particularly fruitful (his research on Viennese popular theatre was to lead him to re-edit the plays of Nestroy). More theoretical issues were discussed with Paul Connerton, a postgraduate with a passion for Marxist aesthetics. Within weeks, our debates were overshadowed by the Cuban Missile Crisis, which brought the world to the brink of nuclear war. Scepticism about military propaganda led me to doubt Washington's claims about warheads threatening the American mainland, but President Kennedy held firm, Khrushchev backed down and the Soviet missiles were removed.

More sociable than the Library was the new Graduate Centre in West Road. This was created by Greta Burkill, wife of the Master of Peterhouse, a formidable woman who had led the campaign to help refugees from Nazism. Now Greta was breaking down the barriers that confined men and women to separate colleges, as well as organizing innovative lectures. Her first guest in autumn 1992 was Francis Crick, within days of the announcement that he and James Watson had been awarded the Nobel Prize for their discovery of the Double Helix. Further lecturers included F. R. Leavis and Nicholas Pevsner. Leavis excelled in polemical asides, delivered like an ant-eater casually knocking off an unsuspecting victim. Pevsner's lecture on cathedral sculpture traced the genealogy of figure carving from Chartres via Strasbourg (the Synagogue figure) to its climax at Naumburg, where the sculpture of Uta – as alive today as seven centuries ago – reminded me of Marlene Dietrich.

At the Graduate Centre I saw a young woman with auburn hair sitting alone. 'What are you working on?' was my predictable question. Her name was Christine Crow and she was studying the *Cahiers* of Paul Valéry, an author whose sceptical intelligence paralleled Kraus's satirical pessimism. Given complementary interests, we soon became friends. After lunch we would enjoy coffee on the terrace or croquet on the lawn, and in the evenings we might go to the theatre or attend the occasional Graduate Society dance. At her lodgings in Park Parade, Christine would share her passion for Berlioz, playing recordings of the Symphonie Fantastique to illustrate his programme music. Then we would stroll under the elms on Parker's Piece or through the Botanical Gardens. Christine related to certain trees as if they were personal friends, reciting their names with reverence. Visiting the hothouse plants, she introduced me to her favourite, *mimosa pudica*, whose tendrils recoil from the touch.

'Psychology never was your line,' she once remarked. With Christine, in some undefined way, I was out of my depth. Some of the plays we saw at the Arts Theatre, including Marlowe's *Edward II* and Genet's *The Maids*, explored extreme sexual practices. Perhaps, if I'd been more candid about my emotional encounters at Christ's Hospital, she might have shared her own experiences at a Girls Grammar School. Disdaining conventional ideas of intimacy, she would cite Valéry's definition of love as 'being alone together'. Sadly, I was hoping for more. My diaries expressed bewilderment about a woman with a rare blend of intellect and imagination, who seemed 'strangely detached – almost as gauche as I am'.

That winter the river froze all the way to Granchester, but as the snow thawed our conversation began to flow. Aware that my approach was one-sidedly satirical, I acknowledged Christine's ability to bridge the gap between scientific intelligence and artistic imagination. Why, she asked, should it be impossible to combine the spirit of 'géométrie' (analysis) with that of 'finesse' (intuition)? One evening in mid-June left me with the feeling that she was an 'almost entirely admirable person, who trails the gentlest clouds of glory and always has a fragment or two to spare'. Conscious of my tendency to make caustic remarks to disguise my insecurity, it was consoling to hear her say that 'the best personalities are a mixture of irony and tenderness'.

Despite moments of rapport, we were going separate ways. In May I left for three weeks in Vienna, staying with my friend Gar Yates and working in the Kraus Archive. Leopold Ungar brought me up-to-date on efforts to retrieve Kraus's letters to Sidonie Nadherny from their hiding-place in Czechoslovakia, and I was re-introduced to Friedrich Torberg, editor of *Forum*. So impressed was he by my ideas about the satirist's persona that he asked me to write them up as an article. 'What can *you* write about?' he asked, when Gar joined us at the Café Sacher. 'About everything,' Gar replied. 'That's not enough!' was Torberg's riposte. The spirit of the coffeehouse was thriving still, and I returned to my typewriter inspired. By mid-July I had completed two hundred pages, ready to be checked by Peter Stern.

Christine, too, was giving priority to research, setting off for a two-month visit to Paris. With her I had shared some of my finest hours, dancing on the lawn, disputing over coffee, and unravelling thousands of words. But my diary recorded a sense of resignation: 'She is a miraculous person, but it cannot be that the miracle is meant for me'. We were better at expressing feelings on paper. During the following months we exchanged dozens of letters and postcards, with literary interests serving as a bridge that sometimes felt like a barrier. The *mimosa pudica* cropped up again in an aphorism she cited from the *Cahiers*, where Valéry compared it with an oyster opening to reveal its secrets. 'Surely it should be a contrary motion?' Christine observed. My response was that Valéry was right. He saw 'not the gesture with which the *mimosa* shrinks from an immodest hand but the inexhaustible confidence in life with which it unfolds again into glorious openness'. This sparring became a coded form of courtship.

The Cambridge scene could hardly compete with Paris, apart from a summer Music Festival that included Britten's *Serenade for Solo, Horn and Strings* with the haunting refrain 'answer, echoes, answer'. In August the family celebrated Robert's wedding to Jill, daughter of Eric and Margaret Walker, my father's friends from student days. Seeing a younger brother happily married left an emotional void. While drifting away from the family, I had enjoyed Robert's company while he was studying at Queens. But it was hard to reconcile religious faith with satirical scepticism, and I was striking out in new directions. That summer a small legacy from our grandfather, Francis Axford, enabled me to acquire a new car, a Standard Companion designed for rugged terrain. My letters to Christine described the joys of exploring Dartmoor with its soaring rocks and secluded valleys, and I invited her to stay at the Vicarage after her return from France.

Throughout July Christine's letters cascaded with impressions of Paris. On 1st August she sent me eight foolscap pages, glowing with the stimuli received from the Conference of French Studies. Two days later there was a change of tone: 'This will not be a long or interesting letter,' she began. 'There is no point in telling you what has happened, so I won't try. Never mind! (Nothing has happened anyway, so don't imagine)'. The letter concluded with an apology: 'I'm sorry my plans for making resonances in other minds seem to be so abruptly at an end! The phenomenon was astonishing while it lasted!' The correspondence was becoming less a sharing of ideas than a grieving about difficulties of communication.

After Christine had returned to her home at Ashford in Kent, we spent a sunlit afternoon driving along the coast to view the Sussex campus. Early in October she was back at Cambridge busy teaching, but she found time to send me a poem dealing with communication in ironic form – 'irony being, of course, a check on sentiment'. Picturing an awkwardly intimate encounter, during which everyday objects like ashtrays fall to the floor in a shower of particles, the poem continues:

> Communication is a quality I do not share
> With the inanimate object,
> And one which I've yet to acquire.
> Though when I trip over the telephone wire,
> At least you will understand that!

Telephoning actually was tricky when you had to rely on a public call box, but we continued to write, and intermittently to meet, edgily attuned to the answering echoes.

CHAPTER SEVEN

Sussex in the Sixties

For observers with an international outlook Britain seemed politically overstretched and culturally undernourished. As children of the Welfare State we had much to be grateful for, from free orange juice to generous student grants. Emerging from the chrysalis of the early 1950s, we admired Winston Churchill as a larger-than-life Prime Minister who embodied the dream of Empire. But after he had retired to make way for Anthony Eden, the Suez fiasco revealed the remoteness of the ruling class from a changing world. When Eden was succeeded in January 1957 by another Tory grandee, Harold Macmillan, there was little prospect of renewal. To shake the country out of its lethargy would require radical readjustments, especially in education and the media.

'Top people take *The Times*' was the shamelessly elitist slogan of the leading daily paper. Its authority was scarcely questioned since copies of the more radical *Manchester Guardian* didn't reach the south of England until midday. The popular press was dominated by dinosaurs like Lord Beaverbrook and Lord Rothermere, while the liberal *News Chronicle* found it difficult to compete. Politicians were treated with deference, while television had barely begun to engage with current affairs. Public life was shaped by a coterie of conservative politicians and privileged mandarins, exercising their influence through the Church, the BBC and the Civil Service. This system of discreet authority became known as the Establishment, after the political analyst Henry Fairlie had identified the phenomenon in the *Spectator*.

SUBVERTING THE ESTABLISHMENT

Britain has never been short of cultural critics, but in the mid-1950s literary activity was becalmed. The tone was set by the high-minded T. S.

Eliot, whose prestige as a modernist poet now served Christian ends. Radical English writing had not recovered from the premature deaths of George Orwell and Dylan Thomas. The distinctive voice of Virginia Woolf had been silenced by her suicide, and E. M. Forster no longer published. The persecution of homosexuals had driven non-conformists underground, exposing them to blackmail and creating security risks. One of the consequences was the suicide of Britain's most brilliant code-breaker, the mathematician Alan Turing. And when the police set traps in public lavatories, they netted the leading Shakespearean actor, John Gielgud.

The aesthetic of the built environment was almost as depressing as English cuisine. Brash town planning led to the construction of monotonous tower blocks and soulless shopping centres, which even the occasional sculpture by Henry Moore could hardly relieve. Assumptions about innate intelligence shaped the education system, which used the eleven-plus exam to separate precociously gifted Grammar School children from the alleged dullards of the Secondary Modern system. Corporal punishment was widely used in schools, while the power of the state was embodied by the hangman's noose. In 1950 Timothy John Evans was hanged for killing his wife, a crime he did not commit. Three years later, a nineteen-year-old named Derek Bentley was sent to the gallows for the murder of a policeman, committed not by him but by his sixteen-year-old accomplice, Christopher Craig. Reports of this case provoked a campaign for the abolition of the death penalty, which intensified after a woman named Ruth Ellis was hanged for shooting her faithless lover.

Towards the end of the decade there were signs we were reaching a watershed. Fresh voices began to be heard, especially in popular music, through an emergent teenage culture of Teddy Boys and rock-n-roll. This provided a safety valve for youthful energies, but there was little scope for articulate dissent. At the Vicarage my parents subscribed to *Punch*, copies of which accumulated in the toilet; but there was nothing lavatorial about its humour for the editor, Malcolm Muggeridge, had a puritanical streak. It was permissible to make fun of foreigners and the lower orders, but the ruling class escaped largely unscathed. For many of us, the most popular humorist of the day – apart from the anarchic clowning of the Goons on radio – was Paul Jennings, who diverted readers of the *Observer* with his witty causeries. The equivalent in the theatre was the two-man show *At the Drop of a Hat*, performed by Michael Flanders and Donald Swann. On stage in the mid-1950s their lilting songs had sparkled with vivacious mischief, but in the more bracing climate of the early 1960s their jokes appeared passé. 'Delicate drawing-room entertainment,' I noted in my diary on 9 February 1963, 'rather disappointing'.

It was hardly surprising that British theatres were so tame. Since Victorian days they had been obliged to submit their scripts to the Lord

Chamberlain, who would delete passages deemed offensive. During the 1950s a generation of gifted actors, led by Laurence Olivier and Vivien Leigh, had been constrained by the paucity of contemporary plays. The system favoured those gentle social comedies ridiculed by Kenneth Tynan, the crusading critic of the *Observer*. The premiere of John Osborne's *Look Back in Anger* in May 1956 introduced a more abrasive tone, and women writers were also beginning to challenge the taboos about gender and sexuality. We enjoyed Shelagh Delaney's *A Taste of Honey*, the daring portrayal of a pregnant working-class teenager who is nurtured by a homosexual youth, after being abandoned by her black lover. But when Harold Pinter's more subtly subversive comedy *The Birthday Party* was staged in London in 1958, it was rubbished by most of the critics. Towards the end of the decade, however, the mood was beginning to change. The failure of the attempt to ban the unexpurgated *Lady Chatterley's Lover* exposed the absurdity of attempts to spoon-feed modern readers. This landmark judgment was reinforced by a liberalization of theatre and cinema censorship.

While I was wrestling in the library with Kraus and Swift, a new wave of satire emerged to challenge British complacency. Friday 25 October 1961 marked the launch of the magazine that was to drive *Punch* out of business, *Private Eye*. Within weeks this scurrilous rag had become a national sensation, adored by the growing student population, and within a year it was selling 35,000 copies. While its text seemed cobbled together in the heat of the moment, its cartoons – especially those by the delicately gifted Timothy Birdsall – were polished and incisive. The assault on conventional values was spearheaded by a group of obstreperous young men, including Richard Ingrams, Christopher Booker and William Rushton. Their polemics (like those of Kraus) repeatedly named names, provoking widely publicized libel actions that boosted circulation.

Equally astonishing was the impact of *Beyond the Fringe*, which opened that autumn in the West End after previews at the Edinburgh Festival. The audience could hardly believe their eyes as the show began with a skit mocking Harold Macmillan. This may have been the first time that a Prime Minister had been ridiculed on the London stage since Walpole was targeted in John Gay's *Beggar's Opera*. The stars of *Beyond the Fringe* were all Oxbridge graduates, but they addressed issues of national importance: the myth of heroic resistance against Hitler's Germany, the absurdity of civil defence against atomic bombs, the insecurity of ethnic minorities, even the Cold War rivalry with the Soviet Union. The show was driven by actors who combined acerbic wit with gawky body language: the aristocratic hauteur of Peter Cook, the dumpy despondency of Dudley Moore, the owlish solemnity of Alan Bennett, the angular intellectuality of Jonathan Miller. Sniffing cautiously under his armpit during an anguished monologue, Miller declared: 'I'm not a Jew – I'm

Jew-ish'. For highbrows there were allusions to Wittgenstein's language games.

Politically, these trends had been reinforced by the victory of John F. Kennedy in the American presidential election of autumn 1960. 'The torch has passed to a new generation,' he declared, using my favourite metaphor. British politicians were also canvassing new ideas. In a speech delivered in Cape Town, Harold Macmillan declared that a 'wind of change' was sweeping through Africa. His all-white audience was stunned to hear a British Prime Minister speaking in such radical terms, but Macmillan proved unexpectedly innovative. As Chancellor of the Exchequer he had defied the puritans by introducing a Premium Bonds scheme (with cash prizes) that proved surprisingly popular. Now he began to prepare Britain for a post-imperial role. Young men of my brother David's generation had done two years of National Service, but Macmillan surprised us by ending conscription, diverting resources to more professional armed forces.

The nanny state began to relax and allow us to enjoy ourselves. In July 1957, during one of his first speeches as Prime Minister, Macmillan had boldly claimed: 'Most of our people have never had it so good'. The intention was to highlight the affluence created by Tory economic policies, but his message was taken up by people pursuing more liberal life-styles. That same year the Wolfenden Report was published recommending that homosexual acts between consenting adults should no longer be a crime (it was several years before this reform was approved). At the beginning of the 1960s contraceptive pills became available on prescription for married women (for singles later in the decade). Women were beginning to control their fertility just as young men were released from the bondage of military service. This inspired a liberated youth culture enhanced by the colourful designs of Carnaby Street, by Beatles songs like 'I want to hold your hand' and by Philip Larkin's sardonic observation that sexual intercourse began 'in nineteen sixty-three'.

Conservative Britain was being upstaged by swinging London, and Macmillan's problem was how to control the energies he had helped to unleash. The first sign that he was losing his touch was the failure of his application to join the European Economic Community, blocked by De Gaulle in January 1963. There followed a seismic shift in relations between culture and politics. The satirists now made their breakthrough to prime-time television. We sat riveted to our screens as a group of subversives led by David Frost and Bernard Levin lampooned the Prime Minister and his Home Secretary, Reginald Maudling, in *That Was the Week That Was*. Graphics were provided by Timothy Birdsall, and each show ended with a song by Millicent Martin mocking events of the previous seven days. The programme was all the more shocking because it was screened by the BBC under its innovative Director General, Hugh Carleton Greene.

The tenor of British cinema was also changing with the release of more adult films, such as *Room at the Top* (1959), *The Angry Silence* (1960) and *Saturday Night and Sunday Morning* (1960). Hugh Greene took these developments in his stride. During the inter-war period he had worked as a political correspondent in Berlin, before becoming head of the German Service of the BBC. Where his predecessors had encouraged deference to authority, Greene gave television a cutting edge by promoting socially subversive drama and radical political commentary. *That Was the Week That Was* became the flagship of this new regime. The conduct of the Conservatives was feeding the satirists with unbelievably juicy morsels. Like Kraus, the editors of *Private Eye* and the cast of *That Was the Week* delighted in sexual scandals; but these stories related not to fin-de-siècle Vienna, but to a British government led by the party of family values.

The satire acquired a political impact when it targeted moral hypocrisy combined with military machismo – the ethos of the war in Vietnam. There was a surge of sympathy for the United States after President Kennedy was assassinated, and we admired Martin Luther King for his leadership of the non-violent campaign for civil rights. But attitudes cooled as the conflict in Vietnam escalated. Although British troops were not involved, the London press was fervently pro-American. But the study of Kraus prompted me to view this with increasing scepticism, and I began to chivvy leading newspapers with letters criticizing their coverage. After a Conservative by-election victory in the early 1960s, an editorial in *The Times* declared that the government was 'on the crest of a wave of popularity'. But I worked out that the percentage of votes obtained by the Conservatives was actually declining, so I wrote a letter to the editor citing my figures to prove it. This was duly printed under the heading: 'The Crest of a Breaking Wave'.

During my final year at Cambridge, I had begun to share these radical ideas with my brother Robert, who was working for a computer company in London. Although nurtured on P. G. Wodehouse our tastes were diverging, for I now preferred more acerbic humour. One spring evening he accompanied me to the Theatre Royal in Stratford, in the East End of London, to see *Oh What a Lovely War*, directed by Joan Littlewood. Nothing could have prepared us for the impact of her new show, which mobilized the popular songs of the First World War in order to mock military heroism – in a style that reminded me of Kraus:

A magnificent combination of drama and music: There's A Long Long Trail, sung straight, in the dark, while General Haigh in a spotlight explains how his soldiers are to fix bayonets and march and march and march until they reach Berlin; and Waltzing Matilda, two women talking, the song is heard and we watch an invisible troop of Aussies march by. 'Aren't they brown and handsome!' one of the women says, and then – as the song dies away – 'They're gone!'

My approach to satire was further enhanced by *The Naked Lunch*, the novel by William Burroughs published by the Olympia Press. Banned as pornographic in Britain, the book was posted to me by a friend from abroad and made a deep impression. This sent me back to my typewriter to insert motifs from *The Naked Lunch* into my chapter on The Language of Satire.

We hardly needed Burroughs to remind us of the connections between sex and satire. In March 1963, after a court case at the Old Bailey, John Profumo, the Minister of War, made a statement in the House of Commons denying that there was any impropriety in his relationship with Christine Keeler, a model who had mysteriously disappeared. In previous decades the peccadilloes of politicians might have been handled with discretion, but the easing of censorship created a more bracing climate, joyously exploited by the satirists. Rumours began that Miss Keeler had also slept with a Soviet diplomat, the naval attaché Eugene Ivanov, and three months later Profumo was forced to resign after admitting that he had lied to Parliament. The truth was disclosed by a fashionable osteopath

Macmillian's Roman Orgy (detail from a cartoon by Timothy Birdsall, 1964)

named Stephen Ward, who confirmed that Profumo and Keeler had met at his flat, and the scandal escalated when Ward was charged with living off immoral earnings. Worse was to follow on 31 July, the final day of the trial, when Stephen Ward was found to have taken an overdose of sleeping pills (he died three days later).

The trial lifted the lid on a salacious underworld where the rich and famous consorted with call girls and drug addicts at Ward's country cottage. This was located at Cliveden on the estate of Lord Astor, owner of the highly regarded Sunday *Observer*. Timothy Birdsall responded with a full-page spread showing a recumbent Prime Minister presiding over a Roman orgy.

For the artist's admirers this image epitomized the decline of the British Empire. We were stunned to read a few weeks later that Birdsall had died of leukaemia.

Although Macmillan conducted himself with dignity, he had clearly lost his touch. That autumn he was censured by the Denning Report for failing to act more decisively in the Profumo affair. Falling ill in October, he resigned as Prime Minister, to be replaced by Lord Douglas Home, an aristocrat so obscure that he was nicknamed the Faceless Earl. There were astonishing parallels with the scandals of the declining Habsburg Empire, also governed by bumbling aristocrats. Then it was the Balkan Wars that presaged disaster, now Vietnam. The fall of Macmillian marked a watershed, not only politically. For at Sussex, where my teaching duties had just begun, the map of Higher Education was being redrawn.

A New Landscape of Learning

It was a bold move to create a university at Brighton for the town had a reputation. This seaside resort with its pleasure domes, race tracks and dirty week-ends had been strictly off-limits during my schooldays, and we had to pretend we were going to Rottingdean, a tranquil village on the edge of town. We would then squander our pocket-money on antiquated peepshows on Brighton pier. Slip a penny in the slot and you could watch puppets jerkily enacting scenes like the Haunted House, the Miser's Dream, or the Beheading of Mary Queen of Scots. Brighton was incorrigibly vulgar and there was a sexual frisson in the air, even if you were only buying ice-cream. 'This will put lead in your pencil!' the vendor exclaimed during one of our visits, thrusting a luscious cornet into my hand. The image of the town was hardly improved by the film of *Brighton Rock*, a version of Graham Greene's novel that highlighted its seedy glamour.

An earlier scheme for a University College at Brighton had been scuppered by the First World War. There was already a Technical College, serving the needs of the region, and the proposal was not reactivated until the 1950s, when a Joint Committee was set up by the local authorities. The high post-war birth rate, the so-called 'bulge', meant there would be an increasing demand for student places in the 1960s, and affluence was raising educational expectations. The Committee seized the opportunity to update their proposals, and this time their efforts were rewarded. The state-funded University Grants Committee, chaired by Sir Keith Murray, had started a programme of expansion that envisaged seven new universities, and in February 1958 the government announced that £60 million would be allocated to new construction, including £1.5 million for a University College of Sussex. Suddenly, everything was in flux. Expansion was to be combined with autonomy, so plans for a university college were set aside in favour of a self-governing institution. The Committee designed an innovative non-departmental structure, John Fulton was appointed as Vice Chancellor and Basil Spence as architect. The University of Sussex received its Royal Charter in August 1961 and the first students arrived just two months later.

It was brilliant timing to launch a new university at the dawn of the 1960s. For too long access to higher education – especially for women – had been limited by the exclusiveness of Oxford and Cambridge. The University of London had pioneered external degrees and become the first British university to award degrees to women. But the civic universities of the Victorian period, founded in centres like Manchester and Leeds, had struggled to establish their credentials in the face of academic prejudice and financial constraints. Similar difficulties were faced by the red-brick universities constructed between the wars. Worthy municipal projects, they tended to replicate established practices rather than introduce radical reforms. Even the first post-war foundation, the University College of North Staffordshire at Keele, made a limited impact, despite its attempts to combine Natural Science with the Humanities.

At Sussex, educational innovation coincided with a new political climate that questioned established hierarchies and encouraged student participation. A further asset was the location. Less than sixty miles south of London, it attracted metropolitan talent while benefiting from the facilities of a seaside resort. Moreover, Brighton Borough Council provided a magnificent two-hundred acre site between the villages of Stanmer and Falmer, formerly the estate of the Earls of Chichester. Situated just north of the main road from Brighton to Lewes, it could be also accessed on foot from Falmer Railway Station.

Rising towards the South Downs through a valley abounding in mature trees, the undulating parkland provided scope for an elegant campus. Basil Spence recognized that there was no call for tower blocks constructed from pre-cast concrete. Instead, he took his cue from the solitary building that already existed, a barn with gables constructed of mellow brick and knapped flint. The site called for a vernacular style, clustering low-rise

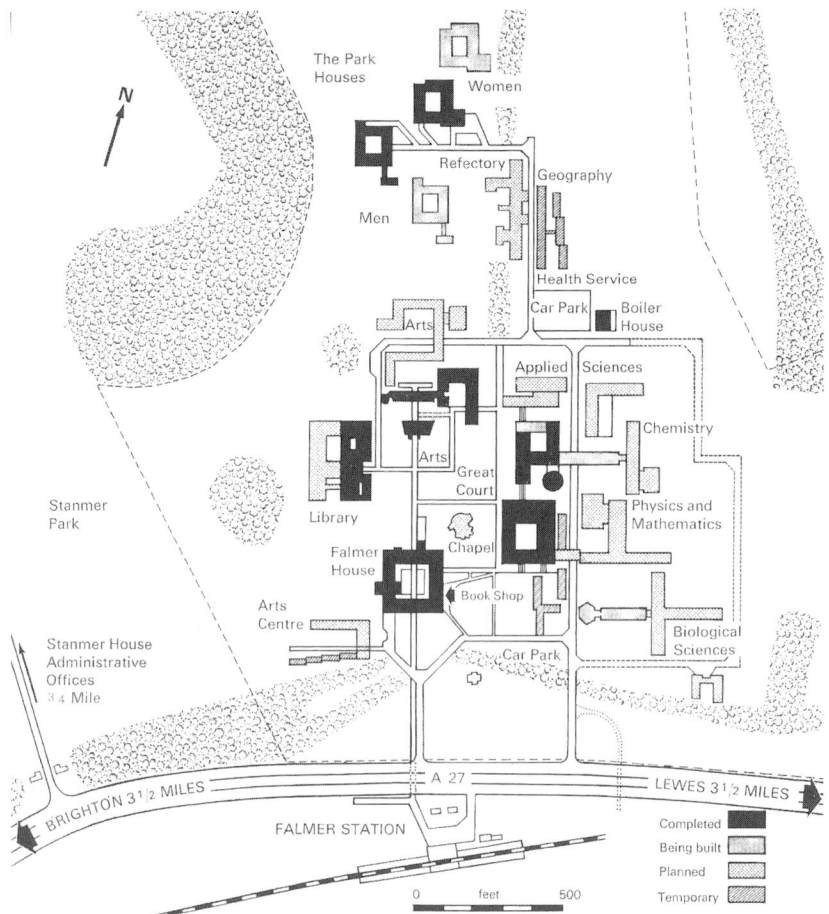

The Park Houses

Women

Refectory

Geography

Men

Health Service

Car Park

Boiler House

Arts

Applied

Sciences

Chemistry

Arts

Great Court

Stanmer Park

Library

Physics and Mathematics

Falmer House

Chapel

Arts Centre

Book Shop

Stanmer House
Administrative
Offices
3 4 Mile

Car Park

Biological Sciences

BRIGHTON 3 1/2 MILES

A 27

LEWES 3 1/2 MILES

FALMER STATION

Completed
Being built
Planned
Temporary

0   feet   500

University of Sussex campus plan (1964)

buildings around a central concourse with a series of inter-connected courtyards. No building was to be higher than the stately trees, while the precise shade of bricks was chosen with special care – a russet brown that harmonized with the woods and fields. The monumentality required by a project on this scale was achieved by combining pillars of brick with elegant concrete arches that echoed the rhythm of Roman colonnades.

The first students were taught in temporary quarters in town, while construction got under way. Landladies accustomed to providing Bed & Breakfast for week-end trippers had to adjust to the needs of students. 'I found them *reading* in their bedrooms!' one complained. By the time the generation of 1963 arrived, the buildings forming the core of Spence's design were complete.

Walking due north from the railway station, we were welcomed by the lofty arches of Falmer House, the social heart of the university. Immediately beyond was the main concourse, with the Physics Building to the east and the Library to the west. The campus resembled an Oxbridge College in an undulating landscape. The intimate scale of the buildings fostered a sense of community, and Spence designed low-slung armchairs to create a feeling of informality. At my office, in the Arts Building that crowned the design to the north, the door-handle was still waiting to be fixed. With mud on our boots we felt the thrill of pioneers.

Sussex enjoyed unprecedented freedom. The new colleges of the past had taught the syllabus of the University of London, which examined their students and awarded their degrees. Leicester, Hull, Exeter and Southampton had all passed through a period of tutelage before achieving full university status. But this centralized system had outlived its usefulness in a rapidly changing world, and Sussex was authorized to design its own courses and award its own degrees. The impact was liberating, not least in my own field of German studies. There was no requirement to master the intricacies of Old High German and trawl through centuries of literary history. Instead, students were faced by challenging texts within a new discipline entitled Critical Reading. This was elucidated by the Dean of European Studies, Professor Martin Wight, a fatherly figure with an unexpected gentleness of manner. 'You will be expected to teach beyond the familiar frontiers,' he explained. The focus during the autumn term would be on European Tragedy and Fiction. Starting with Homer's *Odyssey*, small tutorial groups would study seminal texts like *Oedipus Rex*, *King Lear* and *Hedda Gabler*. Only later would works in German come into the picture.

By mid-September I had settled into a furnished room in a quiet suburb on the road to the university. Several days were spent on the seashore, reading a translation of the *Odyssey* as the waves lapped the breakwater. Having been baffled by Greek at school, was I now expected to become an authority on Homer? 'Sounds like one of those American Great Books programmes,' remarked a sceptical Cambridge friend. Teaching in the United States had indeed influenced the founding fathers – not only Martin Wight but also David Daiches, Dean of English and American Studies, and Asa Briggs, Dean of Social Studies. This triumvirate created a programme that combined the modern seminar system with the personal rapport of Oxbridge tradition.

Newly appointed staff learnt that everything depended on context. No subject was to be studied in isolation from its social and intellectual concomitants. The strategy was to avoid academic introversion by creating open and inclusive Schools. Where departmental structures confined students to a restricted curriculum, the Schools at Sussex would encourage a dialogue between different disciplines. In European Studies, students would take three interconnected courses for their prelims: Critical Reading (focused on literary texts), Language and Values (probing philosophical problems), and Introduction to History (questioning methodologies). This grounding would enable them to tackle more advanced combinations in later years together with wide-ranging 'contextuals' such as Marxism and Existentialism.

Asa Briggs had just published a monumental study of *Victorian Cities* and his energy was formidable. More quietly incisive was the feline David Daiches, who articulated the strategy of making literary studies fundamental to the curriculum. When he was a student at Edinburgh before the war, a command of Anglo-Saxon had been required for honours English, just as Old High German was compulsory for linguists. That approach had favoured survey courses offering second-hand information about literary developments rather than direct experience of imaginative writing. Later, at the University of Chicago, Daiches had sampled New Criticism, which insisted on close analysis of individual works. Finally, at Cambridge, he had been influenced by F. R. Leavis, the impassioned advocate of Practical Criticism.

All this proved inspirational for Sussex. The practice of teaching literary history, using lectures to convey information about books, was replaced by seminars that encouraged students to become pro-active, taking turns to present papers to the group. The approach was to be comparative, for the careful study of a good translation was surely better than ignoring key texts in unfamiliar languages. Since the list of books for in-depth study had to be limited, there was a commitment to quality: intellectually rigorous works that enriched the mind. But texts alone were not enough. Literature, Daiches argued, explores the human condition, but under circumstances that are continuously changing – hence the importance of context. This radical idealism chimed with my own outlook – testing out the idea of literature as a criticism of life, while avoiding Leavisite dogmatism. The curriculum also incorporated good practices from other quarters, including one of the strongest features of Cambridge Modern Languages, the linking of literature with thought and history. But at Sussex joint seminars would be conducted by teachers from different disciplines. What appealed to me most was the openness towards Europe. Brighton's proximity to the continent would encourage a unified focus, linking the study of a foreign language with our broader European heritage.

The most remarkable innovation was the Modern European Mind, a course originated by Daiches in English and American Studies. Colleagues contributed across a plurality of subjects: literature, philosophy and the history of ideas, psychology and even theology. For lecturers in English, the central issue was the response to modern industrial democracy from the late nineteenth-century onwards – from Ruskin and Morris to Joyce and Lawrence. For those in the European School, the key lay with the concept of 'alienation', as formulated by Hegel and Marx and fictionalized by Kafka and Camus. The course was framed by lectures from different disciplines, staged at noon in the Physics Lecture Theatre. Staff and students would pack the auditorium, with the debates spilling over into the refectory over lunch. Dickens's model of learning from experience was elucidated by Daiches in a lecture on *David Copperfield*, while Sybil Oldfield elucidated the feminism of Virginia Woolf, as epitomized by *Mrs Dalloway*. Larry Lerner explored Joseph Conrad's disturbing vision in *The Heart of Darkness*, while Peter France and Robin Milner-Gulland shared their passion for French and Russian poetry.

The prominence of German within the Modern European Mind was due to Anthony Thorlby, Reader in Comparative Literature. In his previous post at Swansea, he had fallen under the spell of the charismatic Erich Heller, whose *Disinherited Mind* highlighted the significance of Nietzsche and Spengler, Kafka, Rilke and Kraus. It was Thorlby, a warm-hearted mentor, who took me under his wing as a fledgling member of the German group. Our efforts were enhanced by the appointment of a German lector, Ladislaus (Laci) Löb, who had gained his doctorate at the Zurich. The three of us would meet every week to discuss German idioms, compiling examples for our students in preparation for their Year Abroad. And at Laci's suggestion I began checking entries for Langenscheidt's German–English dictionary.

Tony Thorlby possessed exceptional imaginative flair. As a student remarked after one of his poetry tutorials: 'We started with a jumble of words and ended with a revelation.' It was difficult to repress a pang of envy – would I ever acquire such finesse? One of our discussions dealt with *Die Leiden des jungen Werthers*, Goethe's epistolary novel. The hyper-sensitive hero falls for the motherly Charlotte Buff, only to discover that she is already engaged to the extroverted Albert. Driven to distraction by unrequited love, Werther ends his life with a revolver. He must have forgotten that, well before his first encounter with Charlotte, he had already been warned that she was betrothed. 'I fear,' Charlotte says to Werther, 'that it is only the impossibility of possessing me that makes the impulse so irresistible.' This hints at an unconscious dimension that links Goethe with Freud.

A similar spirit informed the approach to modernism. Under Thorlby's guidance textual engagement became an intellectual adventure. 'Our students arrive as well-adjusted sixth-formers,' he observed, 'and we alienate them!' This was said in jest for no one was more concerned with the university's pastoral responsibilities (each student had a Personal Tutor). But teaching was certainly designed to challenge middle-class complacency. Where Marx had diagnosed the alienating effect of capitalism, the Modern European Mind explored the concept of alienation through further permutations from Dostoevsky's *Notes from Underground* and Kierkegaard's existential questioning to Kafka's isolated heroes and Camus's absurdist outsiders.

As editor of the *Penguin Guide to European Literature*, Thorlby was to share these findings with a wider world. But the Europe explored at Sussex was not only a continent of the mind. All those majoring in our School were expected to spend their third year studying abroad, and on their return they would write dissertations about contemporary France or Germany. Sussex extended the frontiers of education to include Berlin and Paris, Milan and Moscow. 'Students are to become explorers,' Asa Briggs insisted. The metaphor of a 'new map of learning' figured prominently in his public statements, including his contribution to *The Idea of a New University: An Experiment at Sussex*, published in 1964 under the editorship of David Daiches. The result was an intellectual landscape designed for adventurous spirits. New teaching methods were vigorously canvassed by an American colleague who questioned the value of tutorials, advocating distance learning through television. Despite advance publicity about trendy lecturers debating Marx, Nietzsche and Freud, there was no identifiable Sussex type. My own upbringing was decidedly unadventurous compared with the hazards experienced by my closest colleagues.

Daiches had made some inspired appointments, including a young Oxford graduate named Gabriel Josipovici. Since Gabriel's office was close to mine, we were soon deep in conversation. Here was a lecturer in English with a passion for Rabelais who impressed me through his exotic origins and literary sophistication. Born in France of Jewish parents from Egypt, he had survived the Nazi occupation as a child by hiding with his mother in a village in the Massif Central. He spent his youth back in Egypt with the extended family, before travelling to England to complete his education. When he invited me to his home in Rottingdean to meet his American wife and his mother, the poet Sacha Rabinovitch, there was a sense of incongruity – intellectual brilliance ensconced in a cosy bungalow.

Two more friends had grown up under the shadow of the swastika. Although born in London, the historian John Röhl spent his early years in Nazi-occupied Europe with his German father and English mother. When he started school in his father's home town of Forst on the River Neisse, Russian shells and Allied bombs were falling all around. John spent the immediate post-war period amid the rubble of Frankfurt-am-Main, followed by two years in a children's home in Switzerland. He was almost nine by the time he resettled in Manchester with his mother and her other children. Despite these upheavals, John was proud of his dual heritage, which suited him admirably for the interdisciplinary ethos of Sussex. Committed to empirical research, he had a command of German archives that made him a leader in the field marked out by this first book, *Germany without Bismarck*.

The extreme case was provided by Laci Löb, the German lector. At first rather shy, he gradually opened windows on the past, sharing his extra-ordinary experiences. Born of Jewish parents in Hungarian-speaking Romania, he had endured the antisemitic persecution of the fascist period, which intensified after the Germans occupied Hungary in March 1944 and Eichmann began to organize mass deportations to Auschwitz. His mother had died young, and he had no brothers or sisters, so at the age of eleven he found himself alone in Budapest with his father. Their escape was due to his father's exceptional resourcefulness. As the situation in Budapest became increasingly perilous, they secured places on the train to freedom organized by a Zionist named Reszö Kasztner, after hard bargaining with Eichmann. This succeeded in bringing over 1700 Jewish refugees via Belsen to safety in Switzerland.

There was a chasm between my sheltered upbringing and the turbu-lence of the continent. Protected by the English Channel, we had been schooled in an optimistic view of history that highlighted the values of democracy and the welfare state. But the Europe of those years was battle-ground of ideologies and ethnicities, shaped by Hitler and Stalin and haunted by camps and gulags. European Studies had a dark underside, but the gap was bridged by the apocalyptic satire of Karl Kraus.

ON THE CREST OF THE WAVE

Sussex was conceived as a small university with the student population rising to about one thousand within five years, but this strategy was trans-formed in autumn 1963 by the Robbins Report. The government accepted the recommendations of a committee chaired by Lionel Robbins, a polit-ical economist with international experience, that there should be further expansion of student numbers to meet the demands of a changing world. So John Fulton informed the assembled staff that Sussex would grow far more rapidly than originally planned. The Report, based on statistics compiled by Claus Moser of the London School of Economics, made generous provision for both lecturers' salaries and student grants, while staff–student ratios would allow time for both teaching and research. The tide was turning towards a policy of inclusiveness and we were riding the crest of the wave.

Credit for this far-sighted policy was due to the Conservative govern-ment, but the Tories were under pressure from a reinvigorated Labour Party, led by Harold Wilson. When Wilson appeared at a meeting on the Sussex campus in December 1963, he received rapturous welcome. The Tories had been in power for over a dozen years, and it was time for change. The General Election the following autumn provided Labour with their chance, especially after the scandals that caused Harold

Macmillan to be replaced by Alec Douglas-Home. As the campaign gained momentum it became clear that Labour might win Brighton Kemptown. The county of Sussex was traditionally true blue, and if the election had been held during vacation the Conservatives would doubtless have held the seat. But the lodging houses were now swarming with students, many of them on the electoral register.

As Election Day approached my friends were out canvassing for Labour, and after the polls closed we stayed up all night watching the results on television. It proved to be one of the closest contests on record. Not until the following day was Harold Wilson able to claim victory – by a margin of four seats out of a total of more than six hundred. The breakthrough came, after several recounts, when the Kemptown result was announced: the Labour candidate, a Trade Unionist named Dennis Hobden, had scraped home by seven votes (out of 50,000 cast). That night there were student parties all over Brighton, each group claiming that *their* votes had tipped the balance. Recalling my letter to *The Times* about the Tories being 'on the crest of a breaking wave', I felt strangely elated. The tide had turned in favour of both political and educational reform.

Amid the excitement of those first months at Sussex, it was difficult to focus on research. There were eleven first-year students taking my Critical Reading course, mostly taught in pairs. The format was familiar to me from Cambridge, but the students were refreshingly diverse. While one student came from an elite boarding school, another was a rough diamond from the East End of London. Testing out the Sussex innovations on such a varied group could prove frustrating: 'seems baffled, essay haywire', was my comment after teaching one student for the first time. The Fiction texts left students foundering as we surfed from Homer to Goethe, from Jane Austen to Heinrich von Kleist. Far more successful was the sequence on Tragedy, framed by the theories of Aristotle and Hegel, Erich Heller and George Steiner. Here our course was charted far more clearly: from *Oedipus Rex* through *King Lear* to *Hedda Gabler*, from *Iphigenie auf Tauris* through *Wallenstein* to *Mutter Courage*. A coherent conception of the tragic emerged with significant variations: fated for Sophocles, self-inflicted in Shakespeare, avoided by Goethe, gendered by Ibsen, politicized by Brecht.

The Goethe course, taught to second-year German Majors, took us into deeper waters. The focus was on the sceptical imagination of the author of whom Matthew Arnold wrote: 'Goethe puts the standard, once for all, inside every man instead of outside him'. When told that a certain idea has gone unchallenged for a thousand years, Goethe answers: 'But *is* it so? Is it so to *me*?' Examples were chosen from the whole range of his poetry, from early love lyrics to the late philosophical poetry, while *Egmont* and *Faust* were the key texts for his evolution as a dramatist. Even by Cambridge standards, this would have been a testing course. A series of discussions with a student who delighted in generalizations left us both equally frustrated. 'If you can't understand what I'm trying to say,' he exclaimed, 'you might as well stop being my tutor!' Against the name of another student there is a gap in my notes followed by the word: 'RUSTI-CATED!' Temporarily excluded for some misdemeanour, he still managed to complete his vacation project on Goethe.

The Translation class for second-year students was a further challenge. Working with complex German texts, we transformed a routine linguistic exercise into a form of practical criticism, showing how the speculative mode favoured by German intellectuals resisted the idiom of English empiricism. Passages chosen included Walter Benjamin's reflections on the life of students, Hans Magnus Enzensberger's critique of the conscious-ness industry, Walter Muschg's diagnosis of the paradoxes of western culture, and Walter Jens's analysis of the disappearance of the hero from modern fiction. The ensuing cross-cultural debates were enriched by the presence of a German native speaker named Thomas Elsässer.

My duties during the spring term included interviewing new applicants. The University Central Council for Admissions, created by Keith Murray, forwarded to us the well-designed forms completed by sixth-form students, and we invited the most promising to Sussex. The task of assessing their suitability was eased by the wisdom of two more senior lecturers in French, Cecil Jenkins and Beynon John. If my approach was unduly serious, they would lighten the mood with jocular comments. We were looking for students with a good linguistic grounding and an apti-tude for literary studies. A note dated 24 February records my impression of Sandra D, an applicant from a southern Grammar School: 'A convert from Science to the Arts, who only took up German two years ago and has the convert's boundless enthusiasm. But this goes with a delightful lucidity and an admirable discipline of mind. She should make the world of Sussex'. Not all applicants inspired such glowing reports, but it was clear that we were attracting gifted students with inquiring minds.

At the end of my second term the annual conference of University Teachers of German took place at the University of Reading. This included a discussion of teaching strategies, during which James Macfarland, an expert on modernism, was invited to speak about European Studies at East Anglia, another 1960s foundation. Macfarland felt that it was too early to assess the new developments, but Sussex had boosted my self-esteem. So I took the floor, eulogizing the interdisciplinary approach as an alter-native to the narrowness of traditional departments. My eloquence reflected a critique of established practices already prepared for publication.

My Cambridge mentor Freddy Stopp, Editor of the *Modern Language Review*, had asked me to review the first two volumes of *German Men of Letters: Literary Essays*, edited by Alex Nathan This invited comparisons with English Men of Letters, a celebrated monograph series. German literature, Nathan's title implied, had authors of comparable stature, but this approach ignored the fracturing of the German cultural tradition. The essays struck me as little more than descriptive accounts of a writer's life and works, prompting the following conclusion: 'There are traces of a provincialism that indicates the equivocal position in which German Studies at British universities now find themselves: autonomous and yet, in their departmental isolation, scarcely fully viable.' This was provocative, but Freddy Stopp supported me and the review was duly published.

The innovations at Sussex were attracting media attention, with students complaining that the television crews were distracting them from their reading. One of my tasks, in April 1964, was to take a group of German journalists on a tour of the campus and sing the praises of the Sussex system. It was difficult to find German equivalents for the new terminology of contextuals and interdisciplinarity, but our visitors were certainly impressed. A carefully staged photograph, with my right arm boldly pointing towards new horizons, shows us with our backs to the colonnaded façade of the Physics Building. This photo is a historical curiosity, for that view no longer exists. We are standing near the site earmarked in Spence's master plan for the construction of a chapel.

The controversy about the chapel shows that there were tensions among the pioneers. John Fulton deserves credit for his readiness to experiment, but the motto he chose was biblical: 'Be still and know', a phrase derived from the Psalms implying belief in God. For radicals like the philosopher Patrick Corbett the idea of a chapel at the heart of a modern university seemed preposterous. When a staff meeting was convened on 3 June to debate the issue, I noted the divergent opinions. The philosopher Ted Honderich, supported by the political scientist Jack Lively, spoke out against the proposed chapel. However, members of the English Literature group, including Angus Ross and Tony Nuttall, tended to be in favour. The most eloquent speaker was Stephen Medcalf, advocate of the Christian humanism that reverberated in the writings of his favourite authors, T. S. Eliot and William Golding. The debate was moderated by the emollient John Cruickshank, Professor of French, who explained that the proposed building would be funded by a private donation, which we could hardly refuse. So the focus shifted to the question where the building would be sited and how it should be designated. As a compromise, it was proposed that the University Council should resite the chapel outside the main court. This was approved by 40 votes to 18. My sympathies were with the modernizers, but in the event the University found another solution. The building was located in the great court, as originally planned, but it was renamed the Meeting House.

This proved to be one of Spence's most imaginative buildings, divided into a secular space on the ground floor and a consecrated chapel above. Visually, it was also an ingenious compromise, blending traditional and innovative motifs. Echoing the rotundity of the oast houses which are such a feature of the English landscape, he created a circular brick building with concrete arches and a conical roof reaching towards the sky. While the spacious windows on the ground floor open invitingly towards the Downs, light is filtered into the chapel through opaque panels set within a beehive pattern of concrete slabs. A tapestry by John Piper illustrating a passage from Isaiah enhances the sacramental mood.

As the end of the academic year approached, I obtained leave to spend a week in Vienna and attend the world premiere of *Die letzten Tage der Menschheit*. This sprawling collage of documentary and visionary scenes, completed in 1922, had for decades been regarded as unperformable. But this production was orchestrated by gifted professionals who had worked with Kraus in the 1930s: his literary executor Heinrich Fischer and the theatre director Leopold Lindtberg. Before catching my plane, I wrote to the editors of *Encounter* offering to report on this event. Three years earlier, when approached with a similar proposal, they had replied that Kraus was 'too marginal'. This time they simply failed to reply, but there was a more encouraging response from *The Times*.

Vienna provided a whirlwind of new impressions. Delayed by a thunderstorm, it was almost midnight on 12 June when we took off from Heathrow, the scintillating propellers of the four-engined Viscount looking like saucers of steel. A stop-over in Munich meant that dawn was already breaking as we descended towards the Danube. By 5 a.m. the airport bus had deposited us at the Southern Railway Station, too early for breakfast. So I strolled down Prince Eugene Street to the block in Lothringer Strasse where – exactly twenty-eight years earlier – Kraus had breathed his last. The inscription was still just legible: 'In this house the writer Karl Kraus lived from February 1912 until 12 June 1936, the day of his death.'

It was at the theatre on the Naschmarkt, where Mozart's *Magic Flute* was first performed, that *Die letzten Tage* was staged, but the resources of a traditional theatre could hardly accommodate Kraus's sprawling masterpiece. The play had to be reduced to about one-sixth of its original length, losing the turbulent crowd scenes that convey war euphoria, as well as the apocalyptic visions that accompany the final cataclysm. While short satirical scenes were performed with compelling power, the cumulative effect was less than convincing. Seated in the Café Schwarzenberg after the show, I composed my review, finding it hard to hide my disappointment. 'Any abridgement will weaken the impact of the play,' I wrote, 'but this production has emasculated it.' Despite these strictures, I paid tribute to Peter Lühr's performance of the role of the satirist. And my review placed Kraus's work in a wider context:

Vienna 1900: in this reactionary city the breakthrough to the twentieth century was made, to the century that has written music in the manner of Schoenberg, built houses after the designs of Adolf Loos, philosophized with Wittgenstein, explored its unconscious with Freud and conducted its catastrophic politics in accordance with the apocalyptic visions of Karl Kraus.

Putting five closely written pages in the post, I expected them to be cut for publication. But on 22 June the complete review appeared in *The Times* with the by-line 'From Our Special Correspondent'.

Back in Brighton, it was high time to complete my dissertation. The more closely I studied Kraus's writings, the more compelling his prophecies became. In the pages of *Die Fackel* the impending apocalypse was revealed through a scrutiny of everyday life, from the nationalistic strife of the Habsburg Empire to the military imperialism of the German Reich, from the trenches of the Western Front to the Nazi concentration camps. My task was to integrate these political dimensions with Kraus's linguistic subtlety. Mapping out the introduction of my thesis, I observed: 'So much of *Die Fackel* takes a referential and even directly documentary form that it is impossible to discuss his work as if it belonged entirely to some autonomous world of the imagination.' Literary criticism was complemented by political analysis, as contacts with historians like John Röhl counteracted the bias of my Cambridge years.

The review in *The Times* might have compromised the cordial relations with Heinrich Fischer which I had enjoyed since first contacting him in June 1962. But he accepted my invitation give a talk at Sussex, and a few months later we welcomed him on campus. Students listened enthralled as our visitor described how in 1928 he had collaborated with Brecht in Berlin on the first production of *The Threepenny Opera*. Fischer became even more eloquent when he recalled his friendship with Kraus, reciting a selection of his texts in both English and German. These included an excerpt from *Dritte Walpurgisnacht*, the polemic against the Third Reich which Kraus composed in 1933 – but then withheld from publication. Over dinner, Tony Thorlby questioned his claim that the satirist had been right to leave his anti-Nazi polemic unpublished. 'Publish and be damned!' was Thorlby's principle. But in the mid-1930s, as Fischer recalled, Kraus feared there would be reprisals against defenceless Jews in the German Reich, if his anti-Nazi polemic appeared.

Fischer's visit was hosted by a thriving German Society, which also invited Martin Esslin to speak on Brecht. Lectures by distinguished visitors attracted large audiences, and Sussex was creating such a stir that a series on modern history by Hugh Trevor-Roper was televised by the BBC. Other speakers included Raymond Williams on Tragedy and Revolution, and Christopher Hill on Literature and Society in Seventeenth-Century

England. Talks by Sussex colleagues also proved inspiring, especially when they intersected with my own research. In January 1965 the mercurial Peter Burke spoke on the concept of Culture, showing how Cicero's *cultura animi* evolved into one of the defining concepts of modern anthropology.

My teaching was confined to tutorials and seminars with few opportunities to acquire lecturing skills. The chance finally arrived when I was asked to contribute to the Modern European Mind. My lecture on Culture and Catastrophe dealt with the prophetic work of the German Expressionists and the cataclysm of the First World War. This provided the framework for my most compelling theme, the visions of the apocalyptic satirist. Now all that remained was to weld that wealth of ideas into the doctoral dissertation that would complete my apprenticeship – providing I kept focused amid the distractions of Brighton.

Breakthroughs in Brighton

If the intellectual map was clearly drawn, there was no guidebook for the emotions. The bookshops of Brighton were not strong on psychology, and it was easy to lose your way in the maze of twisting lanes, shady bars and sleazy nightclubs. 'How can you find happiness,' I wondered, 'in a place notorious for hedonism?' An answer was provided by the erudite Stephen Medcalf, who advised me to buy *Brighton: Old Ocean's Bauble*, an illustrated history by Edmund Gilbert. This traces the transformation of the decaying fishing port of Brighthelmston into an elegant Regency town, explaining its reputation for both dissipation and refreshment. The growth of the resort was due not simply to the Prince Regent, who entertained his mistresses amid the splendours of the Royal Pavilion. Far more significant was the discovery of the medicinal properties of sea water, which earned Brighton its popularity as a health resort.

The history of Brighton demonstrates the power of ideas. The breakthrough began with the publication in 1750 of a *Dissertation on the Use of Sea Water in the Diseases of the Glands* by a local doctor named Richard Russell. The 'singular healthfulness' of the town was stressed by another medical man, Dr A. Relhan, in his *Short History of Brighthelmston, with Remarks on its Air and an Analysis of its Waters*. These theories caused people to flock to the coast, and the population doubled in two decades. 'The air is pure as pure can be, / and such an aspect of the sea!' wrote a local poet. The result was a revolution in town planning. Fishing villages tended to huddle with their backs to the sea, sheltering from the storms, but the outlook was transformed by the idea that breezes are beneficial. The Regency façades of the new terraces and crescents were turned towards the Channel, absorbing light through large sash-windows with elegant balconies. The air resounded with the cries of herring-gulls as they swooped across the skyline and feasted in rock-pools. Other resorts also benefitted, as Gilbert's study showed, but Brighton enjoyed multiple advantages. It was a mere fifty miles from London and had a lengthy south-facing coastline awaiting development. Moreover, the chalk hills that encircle the town – the South Downs – formed a natural amphitheatre for the drama that was about to unfold.

Despite these wide horizons, my first term at Sussex left a sense of frustration. There were surprisingly few young women among the teaching staff, and a diary note in December 1963 records my mood 'hovering on the brink of friendships' but liable to 'attacks of lethargy'. Feeling too old to mix with students, I envied the family life that sustained my married colleagues – and could hardly wait to renew contact with Christine from Cambridge. We met in London towards the end of December and spent the afternoon viewing a Goya exhibition at the Royal Academy. Confronted by grotesque lithographs and inscrutable portraits, she took everything in her stride. How I admired her 'wholeness' – another way of saying how incomplete I felt in myself.

TALKING TO STRANGERS

My New Year's resolution was to overcome my reticence. As children we were told 'Don't talk to strangers!' while at Cambridge it was regarded as bad form to speak to someone casually encountered – you waited to be introduced, usually by your surname. But with Christine I had broken the ice, so why not take similar risks at Sussex?

'Hello,' I said to the young man standing next to me in the lunch queue. 'What's your name?'

'Hi,' he replied, 'I'm Brian Easlea and I'm teaching theoretical physics'.

We soon struck up a friendship, for Sussex had an Arts–Science scheme that promoted interdisciplinary dialogue with courses on the Impact of Science taught by lecturers from both sides of the divide.

Brian struck me as a man of the world, for he had already taught in Denmark and the United States. As a full lecturer he could afford to rent an apartment at 7 Marine Square, a Regency development on the seafront. By contrast with opulent schemes like Lewes Crescent, Marine Square encouraged a sense of community. Set back from the coast road by a crescent-shaped approach, all the neatly designed terrace houses overlook the secluded garden. Brian's flat had one of those wrought-iron balconies that are such a feature of Brighton, and there I would join him over coffee, drinking in the spectacular view and debating the claims of science. Advances in the study of subatomic particles gave young Sussex physicists a sense of mission, but they accepted me as a sparring partner, ready to question the political consequences. The idea that society could transformed by science was making headlines after Harold Wilson's speech setting out his vision of a 'new Britain' – forged in the white heat of

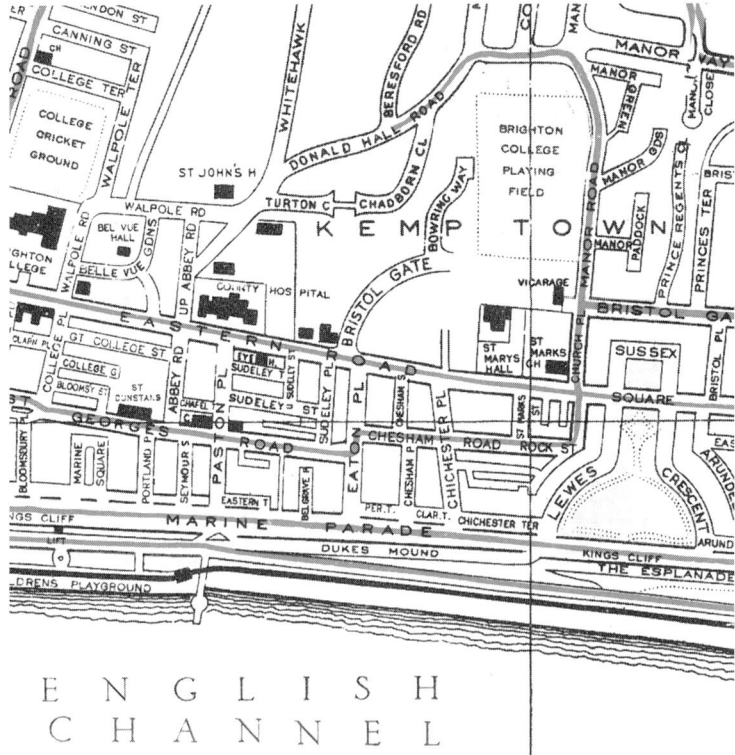

E N G L I S H
C H A N N E L

Plan of Kemp Town in the 1960s from Marine Square to Lewes Crescent

modern technology. Citing Kraus's critique of the machine running out of control, I took a very different line, holding the scientific community responsible for the nuclear arms race.

The location of Marine Square, a sheltered enclave at the heart of Kemp Town, made it a perfect meeting place.

There was a sensuous quality about the seafront architecture - was there a correlation between balconies and bikinis? Opposite the square was an antiquated public lift on which you could descend to the beach for an evening stroll or a ride on Volks electric railway along to Black Rock swimming pool. At weekends our discussions might spill out into the garden, sloping gently towards the sea. Clustering on the lawn, we debated whether we could avoid the dangers described in *Brighter than a Thousand Suns*, Robert Jungk's critique of nuclear weapons. Or would we regress into a savagery, as suggested by William Golding's *Lord of the Flies*, another cult book? The mathematician Gavin Wraith, who also lived on the square, took a sceptical view of our phobias – his passion was for English folktales and Indian music. Towards evening he would revive us with a tray of drinks, descending into the garden like one of Arthur Rackham's benevolent goblins. Although there were thirty houses on the square, few people used the garden, neatly tended by the Borough Council. Were they inhibited by some unwritten 'Keep off the Grass'? The lace curtains twitched as elderly residents peeped out to see what was happening.

There was a palpable gap between the new generation pursuing radical ideas and a retired population nostalgic for the glories of Empire. Sitting on a bench overlooking the sea one afternoon, I heard two retired colonial ladies pouring out their grievances:

> 'Young people have no consideration nowadays. If I slammed a door when I was a girl, my mother made me go back and shut it again and again and again until I closed it properly.'
>
> 'People have no sense of discipline. When I met a girl with tight jeans the other day, I said: "Don't you know what modesty means?" She said: "No, what does it mean?" When I meet someone like that, I speak my mind.'
>
> 'They have too much money these days, they don't know what to do with it.'
>
> 'All that raving about love. It's not love, it's filth!'
>
> 'We didn't have anything like that in my day. If I did anything wrong, I was beaten, and then I never did it again.'
>
> 'How long have you been back in England?'
>
> 'Since 1956, but I've been out there again three times. They haven't got orderly minds like the English. There's no discipline. When we were there, things were kept in order. But now everything's falling apart. They just aren't ready for self-government.'

So impressive was the flow of platitudes that I recorded them in my notebook, adding my own comments:

> Of course there is some truth in what they say: Africans may be immature for self-government, and it is unfair for a lovely girl to flaunt her desirability. One can't help being sorry for these walking assemblages of meagre clichés. And yet hopeful that we, remembering in old age the abandon of our youth, will be more tolerant.

While our elders were grieving over a long-lost past, we were saving the world by pursuing liberated relationships within an international framework.

Even in the Arts my colleagues were remarkably multicultural. It was a surprise to discover how few of the English faculty were of English origin. David Daiches was the son of an Edinburgh rabbi whose mother tongue was Yiddish, while Angus Ross spoke with a strong Scottish brogue. Other lecturers in English included Larry Lerner from South Africa, Sybil Oldfield from New Zealand, Gabriel Josipovici from Egypt and Gamini Salgado from Ceylon. The scientists were even more diverse. Gavin Wraith could trace his mother's line back to the Jewish community in Istanbul, while Brian's circle included Costas Costanados from Greece and Farhad Faisal from Pakistan, as well as two Turkish postgraduates, Cengiz Yalçın and Saime Göksu. It was strange to find an oriental woman specializing in elementary particles, especially as Saime was strikingly beautiful.

Although there were few black faces to be seen on the streets of Brighton, the resort was unmistakably cosmopolitan. This was a challenge for an Englishman brought up to believe that foreigners should be kept in their place. The French might be envied for their cuisine, the Germans for their music, but non-Christian cultures were beyond the pale. In church we would pray at Easter for protection against 'Turks, infidels and heretics', and there were residues from books read in childhood. The *Children's Encyclopedia* had informed us about exotic colonial peoples, but there was no hint that they would ever migrate to Britain. Why had we been taught so little about our multicultural heritage? Accounts of British involvement with slavery claimed credit for Wilberforce's campaign to abolish the slave trade while ignoring the plantation owners who pocketed the profits. In short, we had been fed a Whig view of history which left me struggling to slough off my parochial upbringing.

At first this left me on the margins, reluctant to form attachments. It seemed safer to socialize with young professionals at the Coffee Pot, an informal club that held weekly meetings at the Royal Pavilion. This venue seemed at odds with a pedestrian programme of wine tastings and lectures on local history, but my spirits rose when the club announced an excursion to Goodwood Races. Horse-racing had been one of my hobbies, and Glorious Goodwood was a highlight of the racing calendar. Our coach was halfway there before it dawned on me that we were heading for the Motor Racing circuit. An afternoon of screeching tyres and petrol fumes made it clear that this was not my scene. The one person to catch my eye was a slim young schoolteacher named Marina, but our exchanges were uninspired. 'No thank you, I'm sweet enough already,' she would say when offered sugar with her coffee. We continued to meet, getting sunburnt by the sea, without venturing in too deep.

Emotionally we still had everything to learn. Fortunately Brian Easlea was a born teacher – not only of science. His bookshelves included volumes on sex education, and he explained that love-making, for me a distant dream, formed a normal part of adult life. For a libertarian socialist there was nothing wrong about saying to a woman you met at a party: 'Shall we spend the night together?' This struck me as so casual – easy come, easy go, but it was not hard to imagine Brian making conquests, given his engaging personality. The lovelight would come into his eyes when he spoke of the dark-eyed beauty from Brazil who had inspired him to produce some of his best scientific work. He took it upon himself to educate his friends, lending Saime a book about human reproduction when he discovered how little she knew. Intrigued by my lack of experience, he introduced me to her as a typical inhibited Englishman.

On the Sussex campus it was certainly distracting to see glamorous creatures reclining on low-slung chairs in their skimpy mini-skirts or tight-fitting jeans. During a seminar on Kant, I made the mistake of pronouncing the philosopher's name in the German way, a Freudian slip that caused considerable merriment. My insecurity was obvious one afternoon at Brian's flat, when two young women joined us for coffee and I felt provoked into throwing a book at one of them – a flimsy paperback that reflected my fragility. The gap in years may have been small, but I found it hard to relate to the intensely emotional Beatles songs blaring out from student parties. My taste had scarcely advanced beyond the tinkling lyrics of *Salad Days*, but Brian's favourite, *Another Side of Bob Dylan*, contained tracks that shunted feelings in radically new directions. As an internationalist, he loved the sound of other languages, playing us a Brazilian folk opera, plangent settings of poems by George Seferis and poignant Russian ballads. Gradually, I began to shake off my shyness, although there were still dismal evenings eating fish-and-chips alone.

Brighton was the scene of a new youth culture, as rival gangs of Mods and Rockers converged on Marine Parade. These confrontations were dramatized by tribal modes of transport: dainty Lambrettas versus hunky Harley Davidsons. My Standard Companion could hardly compete, but it was large enough for several friends to squeeze inside. Social life improved as the lengthening days prompted excursions into the country. Next to me might be Marina, picked up after school, but there was room in the back for Saime and another visiting Turkish scientist named Serap. Driving was a pleasure when there was so little traffic on the roads that curved across the downs. One evening Saime, in the seat behind me, amused everyone by snipping off a lock of my hair. During the Easter break she moved from her lodgings into a spacious basement flat in Russell Crescent, a Regency villa near the station. This location, combined with her personal charm, made her flat a magnet, especially as she rented a television in order to improve her English. There was parking at the nearby pub, so I would sometimes stay for a drink after dropping her home. My own digs in the suburbs felt isolated by comparison, so I began to look for a place in town.

The academic year ended with a barbecue and dance, to which I invited Christine from Cambridge, booking a room for her at the Downs Hotel. This coincided with a visit from my parents, who were pleased to see me with such a well-groomed woman. When the breeze caught a wisp of hair as we walked along the sea front, I brushed it from her forehead, only for her to shrink from the friendly gesture. During the dance she seemed completely self-sufficient, an observation I shared with her in a letter. 'I am not quite sure what you are implying,' she replied. 'I hope that what is meant to be the art of relevance does not seem like egocentricity.' Her gifts were exceptional, but our cerebral rapport left my desire unanswered. 'After Christine,' I asked myself in my diary, 'does life begin again? Sunshine, beach, bathers, Karl Kraus! Where does it lead?'

THE ATTRACTION OF OPPOSITES

The scene changed dramatically when Brian left for a conference in Paris, followed by a holiday in Yugoslavia. With characteristic generosity he gave me the keys to his flat so that I could live for a month in Marine Square. When I drove him to Newhaven to catch the ferry, Gavin and Saime came too. On the way home we stopped for tea in the garden of the Old Vienna Café in Ovingdean, the ramshackle home of an eccentric Austrian named Mrs Brown. This was one of our favourite haunts, nestling in the foothills of the South Downs only a few hundred yards from the sea. It did not remotely resemble the elegant coffee-houses of Vienna, and the food could be dire. But it was early summer and there was freshly stewed rhubarb, a dish that reminded Saime of her childhood. As I sprawled on the lawn, she began to feed me succulent spoonfuls while Gavin watched in astonishment.

We had often bumped into each other in the Falmer House refectory, but I'd kept my distance from this dark-haired beauty, assuming she was Brian's girl. Before leaving Turkey, she had been warned about meeting unattached males. If they ask you round for a coffee, she was told, this means they want to make love. On her first day at Sussex she had met Brian in the Physics Building. 'Why not come round for a coffee tonight?' he said. Determined to be on her guard, Saime discovered in reality that all he wanted was to show off his coffee percolator, the latest Scandinavian design. With Brian away, she and I began to meet more often, drinking coffee at the Lorelei Café in the Old Steine. On fine afternoons we might spend a couple of hours on the beach, soaking up the sunshine. As we relaxed, her bathing costume revealed a diagonal scar on her back. This took us into deeper waters as I coaxed her into telling her story.

As the daughter of a large family in Ankara, she had been obliged to work full-time while studying for her degree. The arduous conditions caused her, like so many of her generation, to catch to tuberculosis during her final year. For two years she languished in a sanatorium near Istanbul, where it was hoped that fresh air would cure her. What helped her most were the friendships with other patients, including a handsome young cartographer named Haldun. Returning to Ankara to visit her family, she met another sufferer named Rüştü, who had heard that the Red Crescent offered funds to enable TB sufferers to travel to Germany for surgery. Saime was able to join him, after the Ankara Physics Department gave her a compassionate grant.

Arriving in Munich after an arduous train journey, they received a mixed reception. Rüştü's infection was so advanced that it was too late to operate, while her life was on a knife-edge: German surgeons removed half a lung. Saime's back story gave our friendship an unexpected depth. Lying on Brighton beach, she also recalled her convalescence at Garmisch, where she was nursed by cheerful nuns. She risked her life for a second time when walking in winter sunshine. With only the most basic grasp of German, she misread the signs and found herself as darkness fell not on the intended path to nearby Partnach Alm, but climbing the snowy trail to Partnach Klamm. She was fortunate, when she reached the summit, to see the lights of a tavern, where she could rest before returning to the anxiously waiting nuns.

This blend of fragility and fortitude left me strangely moved. After returning home a less determined woman might have opted for the life of

---

Having found the type of possible couplings and the form factors for the "black vertices", the diagrams we now have to evaluate in order to calculate "d_p" are those shown in figures 5 and 6.

First, we write the matrix elements with scalar coupling for the "black vertex", in diagrams 5a and b; and add these two; we find:

$$M_{fi} = -B \int u(p') \left[G \overset{*}{\gamma_5}(\gamma_\mu k_\mu + m) - G(\gamma_\mu k_\mu + m)\gamma_5 \right] u(p) \cdot \frac{(p+p'-2k)_\nu \, d^4k \; \overset{\nu}{\epsilon}(p'-p)}{(k^2-m^2)((p-k)^2-\mu^2)((p-k)^2-\mu^2)}$$

where

$$B = \sqrt{2} \; g \, f(m^2)e = \sqrt{2} \; g \, f'(m^2)\alpha \, Ae \; ; \quad \mu = \pi\text{-meson mass}$$

$f'(m^2)$, α, A, g are defined in the previous chapter.

Excerpt from a dissertation on the Electric Dipole Moment (by Saime Göksu, 1965) an invalid, but Saime was strengthened by her ordeal. Within a year she had completed her course at Ankara University, taken a Masters degree in Theoretical Physics, joined the staff of the newly founded Middle East Technical University, and won a NATO scholarship to study in England. Her subject, Elementary Particles, could not have been further from my own. How could a specialist in German satire converse with a woman whose ideas were expressed in equations?

The answer lay with an attraction of opposites that inspired an Arts–Science scheme of our own invention. Newton's laws of attraction sounded familiar, but when Saime began to talk about Maxwell's equations I was out of my depth. However, dialectical thinking suggested that contradictions needn't be counterproductive. Worlds apart, we were drawn together by delicate skeins. While I as a boy was pursuing butterflies along Devon lanes, she as a girl had been cultivating silkworms in Anatolia.

Saime drew me out of my insularity, for I now had someone to care for. My concern for her well-being increased when I learnt that she was scheduled for a kidney-stone operation in the autumn. My first move was to dissuade her from smoking and encourage her to enjoy fresh air. We would walk for hours on the Downs seeing only the occasional windmill. Walking enriched our talking, and a strange intimacy arose as our eyes were drawn to the horizon. Imperceptibly, we found ourselves 'walking out', our spirits lifted by the springy turf and scudding clouds. Saime, an intensely sociable person who had made new friends at a summer school, was invited to Oxford for a few days, leaving me alone with my typewriter. On her return we headed for the hills, walking from Devil's Dyke towards Poynings. Suddenly I heard myself saying 'I missed you!' There was an audible silence – and we walked a dozen steps before she replied 'I missed you, too'. It was the pause I heard. Did she say it merely to avoid hurting my feelings?

Walking led to dancing for the bar on Devil's Dyke ran a disco for late-night revellers. Wearing a shimmering turquoise dress, Saime would be the star of the evening, swaying to the rhythm of Blue Suede Shoes or Stranger on the Shore. On sunny afternoons, as our closeness increased, a favourite meeting place was the beach by Banjo Groyne, a few minutes from Marine Square. Although Saime had not yet learnt to swim, she was unfazed by the chilly waters, and we had towels to cover us both if there was a sudden breeze. The lift carried us back to the comfort of Brian's flat, where I would brew tea while she was changing. It took so long for her lustrous hair to dry that sometimes I'd rest on the bed beside her, separated from her mirror image by her back arching above me. Was it that her arms grew tired, or did my hands reach towards her? Once we started to kiss, there was no going back.

'You never take notes in a love affair,' according to a dictum by Robert

Frost noted in my diary the previous year. So overwhelming were my feelings that the pages for the summer of sixty-four remained blank as my desire explored a foreign tongue. It was Saime who recorded in her diary on 3 August (in German) 'Erste Küsse', and she was soon teaching me terms of endearment that took my breath away. As we struggled to find a common language, Kafka saved the day. Learning of my literary interests, Saime recalled her visits to the German library in Ankara after her return from Munich. There she had come across Kafka's Letter to his Father with its portrait of an oppressive parent. She too had an authoritarian father, liable to fits of rage, so she decided to translate it into Turkish.

I could now introduce Saime to colleagues as a translator of Kafka. Her father, for all his faults, had the progressive outlook of a health officer, and for the first time I heard about the achievements of Kemal Atatürk, who had created a republic out of the remnants of the Ottoman Empire. More puzzling was Saime's account of the military coup of May 1960, which had deposed Prime Minister Adnan Menderes. She had joined student protests against an oppressive government, defying the riot police. Amazingly, the army had sided with the students, arrested Menderes, impeached him and executed him for abusing his powers. Led by a reformist general, the Army Council introduced a new constitution that guaranteed freedom of speech, and for the first time a Marxist group, the Turkish Workers Party, won seats in parliament. Saime's political analysis left me confused, but I had visions of a heroic young woman helping to bring down a tyrannical regime.

It was exhilarating to encounter a living culture embodied in a lovely person, but visits to Russell Crescent could be frustrating, for Saime's flat was thronged with friends. The most intimate was Adelina, a student nurse from Catalonia in whom she confided. Politically, too, there was much to discuss for Spanish fascism threw a long shadow and Adelina's family had suffered under General Franco. Saime was sharing her flat with Serap, a colleague from Ankara who envied her new-found freedom. 'You are living a more liberated life,' Serap said, 'than you ever did before and ever will again.' The place had a bohemian feel, for the bath-tub was next to the hot-water geyser in the kitchen. Sizzling aromas would blend with the fragrance of soap bubbles, while Saime and Adelina were preparing an omelette on the stove. Only later did I learn that they had joked together about which of them would be kissed first.

Brighton created a climate of liberation. 'The Single Girls: Free and young and far from home' was the slogan used on an *Evening Standard* poster to publicize an article by Maureen Cleave, a friend of the Beatles. Seeing the poster one evening on a news-stand in Western Road, I added it to my archive. The image appealed through its indeterminacy, suggesting there was all to play for. What were young women to do with their new-found freedom? American feminism, epitomized by Betty Friedan's *The*

Feminine Mystique, had yet to make an impact in Britain, and we scarcely questioned traditional gender roles. The Brighton scene of the 1960s was captured by Colin Spencer's portrayal of footloose youngsters in *Anarchists in Love*. 'They are on the side of the angels in their celebration of love and in the anarchic rejection of the stifling ties of family and convention,' the *Times Literary Supplement* observed (FIGURE: *Anarchists in Love*). We could identify with that.

While the pier provided traditional entertainment, Brighton was reinventing itself as a centre for alternative life styles. Some people spent their days getting high on cannabis. 'If you can remember the sixties,' they say, 'you weren't there!' But we were so enraptured that we scarcely needed further stimulants.

For several weeks Saime and I kept our feelings secret, finding excuses to slip away to Le Bistro, a Kemp Town restaurant noted for coq au vin. After an evening gazing at each other across the table, Saime caused a pang of jealousy by remarking that I reminded her of Haldun, her friend in Ankara. A further dilemma arose at the Four Aces, an intimate dive in the Laines – the bohemian quarter with cottages dating from the old fishing village. During a discussion of birthdays Saime mentioned that she was

Anarchists in Love
(popular paperback, 1965)

twenty-nine. This was a shock. I'd assumed she was several years younger, but couldn't help being impressed: a person so honest about her age should prove trustworthy in other ways. When Brian returned from abroad to reclaim his flat, another became available at number 27 on the opposite side of Marine Square. Saime helped me move in, displaying impressive domestic skills. Noticing my happiness, Brian guessed I was in love – with reticent Serap rather than vivacious Saime! When he realized that his best friends were an item, he captured our mood in a snapshot taken in the garden of Marine Square, adding the teasing title 'Les amants'.

We shared a passion for the theatre, making trips to London to see Marlene Dietrich at the Queen's Theatre and John Osborne's *A Patriot for Me* at the Royal Court. We also loved the Brighton Theatre Royal, which staged pre-London runs. With a self-contained flat, I could now invite Saime to stay overnight, so on 15 August, while planning a visit to the theatre, I suggested she should to come back after the show. My delight when she consented was tempered by panic at being hopelessly inexperienced. Fortunately, an illustrated guide entitled *An ABZ of Love* caught my eye in the window of a shop in Duke Street, discreetly named Hygienic Supplies. This translation from the Danish original by Inge and Sten Hegeler was expensive, but I couldn't wait. That afternoon was spent absorbing a reassuring blend of practical guidance and emotional insight. There was clearly nothing to be feared about sleeping with someone you love, as long as you respect their feelings.

Collecting Saime from Russell Crescent, I drove her to the theatre to see *Season of Goodwill*, a comedy about growing old gracefully. 'Are you sure you want to come home with me?' I asked after the show. She was, and it changed our lives. In the following weeks I learnt more about a woman's feelings than in the previous twenty years. Exploring our own variant on the alphabet of love, we discovered the delights of sensuous touch, but the breathtaking learning curve plunged us into turmoil, as we reflected on the longer-term implications. The odds were against us, for Saime was a scientist with a career ahead of her in Turkey. Fortunately, her supervisor Gabriel Barton arranged for her grant to be extended so that she could complete her dissertation. We thus had twelve more months together before the decisions had to be made.

Saime settled into a new flat at 5 Marine Square, just across the garden from mine. It was good for each of us to have our own space, especially as she was expecting a visit from her sister Yeter, on the way to Sweden for a postgraduate course. Even when there were visitors, we could slip discreetly across the square or withdraw if we needed to nurse bruised feelings. Much as we valued the group dynamics of Marine Square, they also caused complications. In addition to Brian and Gavin, the Turkish physicist Cengiz Yalçın lived in the square with his wife Semin and their baby daughter, renting a flat two storeys above Saime. But Saime wished to conceal our feelings from Turkish friends, fearing that rumours would filter back to Ankara and upset her parents.

I would return to my desk convinced that Kraus was right to see sensuous experience as a source of creativity. The challenge was to balance work and pleasure: 'If one of these has to suffer, I don't hesitate for a moment,' I wrote to Saime on 17 October, 'after all, I have forty years to write books'. Saime was in hospital for treatment that required a full anaesthetic. On the eve of the operation, she recalled her earlier brush with death: 'Don't be sad; think at least you have given me the happiest time in all my life,' she wrote, before explaining how to contact her family in an emergency. She was helped through the post-operative trauma by a combination of pain-killers and poetry, prompting me to quote Goethe's definition of love as 'Glück ohne Ruh' – 'joy unconfined'.

Life would have been less exciting had we had lived in Lewes, for there was little scope for anarchy behind its prim Georgian façades. But Lewes holds a special place in the history of fanaticism, for it was there in the reign of Queen Mary that Protestant martyrs were burnt at the stake, providing a pretext for extravagant Guy Fawkes Day celebrations. That autumn we were invited to a party by our friend John Myerscough, whose rooms overlooked the torchlight parade. Amid a spectacular firework display, the revellers burnt the effigy of a modern villain, Lord Beeching, the chairman of British Railways who was demonized for closing unprofitable branch lines. Myerscough, a social historian, recalled that originally it was the construction of the railways that had been condemned – for desecrating the countryside! The parade left me with queasy feelings, for that throng marching through the night awoke echoes of the hysteria of Nazism.

'The Torch' – 'Die Fackel' – Karl Kraus! I should have been at my desk, but there were too many distractions. Social events were far more enjoyable now that Saime was included. Tony Thorlby and his Welsh wife Jill welcomed us to their home in Seaford, while John Röhl invited us to Kingston near Lewis to meet his wife Rosemarie. Brian's circle was enlivened by the arrival of Giuseppi Martelli, an urbane Italian physicist with a wealth of stories. Through chance encounters in a Brighton pub we made friends with Joe Townsend, a journalist proud of his Irish-Jewish heritage, and Chuck Engelman, a cheery schoolteacher from Ghana. Fish-and-chips became a thing of the past as our gastronomic horizons expanded. Semin introduced me to Barbunya Pilaki, a blend of red beans, chopped carrots and onions which looked like Heinz baked beans – but tasted delicious. We also frequented a restaurant in the Laines run by a Greek Cypriot couple who made Saime especially welcome. Less than a decade earlier there had been anti-Greek riots in Istanbul, but the taste of kebabs and dolmas confirmed how much Greeks and Turks have in common.

There had been no Greeks in Malatya, the Anatolian town where Saime had spent her childhood, but she did recall tensions with the Armenian community. Growing up in the 1940s, she heard from her grandmother how rumours that the Armenians were planning to attack a mosque had caused Muslims to take action in self-defence. Listening to this story, I was surprised by the suggestion that it was the Armenians who were to blame for the conflicts. But it was understandable that, for Saime and her sisters, the Armenian quarter was off limits. At school she had become friends with an Armenian girl named Anne Özkaragöz. One afternoon, without telling her parents, she accompanied Anne home. They had a great time playing in the Armenian family's garden, but as the evening drew in Saime began to wonder how she would ever find her way back. Then she heard her grandmother's voice calling her name. Back home she was punished by having her arms tied to a hook on the wall and left there in disgrace, until a kindly uncle set her free.

This story brought home to me two of Saime's distinctive qualities: her readiness to break rules if she thought them wrong, and her gift for making friends from different backgrounds. No wonder she thrived in Brighton with its cultural diversity, including the clandestine homosexual community. But the town was also a hotbed of right-wing nationalists, and in a bookshop at the bottom of Duke Street I found a much-thumbed German edition of *Mein Kampf*. Worse still, our friend Joe Townsend, with his striking black beard, was taunted when out walking out with a blonde Scandinavian girl. As a journalist, he was planning to write a feature about the British National Party, whose leader John Tyndall lived in Hove. So Joe persuaded us to infiltrate one of their meetings, held in a grand Regency building overlooking the sea. The meeting was held in sumptuous rooms with statuettes of blackamoors deferentially bearing trays of delicacies – lesser breeds who knew their place. Once our cover was rumbled we were out on the street, but this episode was an ominous sign of the times.

Right-wingers in the Conservative Party were agitating against coloured immigration, so we welcomed the Labour government's reforms. Saime, who had joined the Party on arrival at Sussex, was among the canvassers for that knife-edge Labour victory in Kemp Town. Fortress Britain was crumbling, and we were learning to celebrate diversity. Socialists were to be disappointed by the policies of the Wilson government, which held power until 1970. Promises of radical change remained largely unfulfilled, as the economy was blown off course, but there were welcome social reforms, starting with the abolition of the death penalty. When the government pushed through the Sexual Offences Bill, homosexual acts between consenting adults ceased to be a crime. This was a crucial breakthrough – the era of police entrapment was over and people who had been stigmatized could now display their preferences with impunity.

In December 1964 Saime joined the family at Buckfastleigh for Christmas. Aware that my parents would be shocked by the idea of marrying someone from a Muslim country, I drove down to Devon a few days in advance to prepare the ground. But no words could have done justice to the apparition that alighted from the train at Newton Abbott. Saime had kitted herself out in a figure-flattering suede coat with tiger-skin patterned lapels. With her bouffant hairstyle and amber necklace, she looked every inch the femme fatale. However, she impressed everyone with her intelligence and charm, dutifully attending church on Christmas Day. This did not prevent her from bearding Father in his den and questioning him about Christian belief. From then on he would omit the prayer for protection against Turks, infidels and heretics – out of respect for Saime.

We headed back for Brighton, taking the picturesque country road over the Wiltshire Downs. It began to snow as we started our ascent, but Saime was thrilled by the glistening landscape. Soon we were halted by a line of snowbound cars, unable to climb a treacherous slope. Revving too fast, they skidded and slithered to a halt, so one by one they abandoned the struggle and turned back towards lower ground. Suddenly I noticed that the way ahead was no longer blocked by cars. Gently accelerating, we surged forward, breasted the slope and descended towards the outskirts of Southampton. There we booked into a hotel, treated ourselves to dinner and dived into a voluptuous double bed. Over breakfast we learnt that stranded motorists had spent the night sleeping rough in makeshift rescue centres.

In Brighton a letter awaited me from Christine, who had spent the autumn researching in Paris. The strain of her studies had prompted her to return home to convalesce with her family in Kent. Driving across to Ashford, I spent an afternoon walking with her in the woods. 'Thank you,' she wrote on 3 January, 'for such patient listening.' The disclosure that my life had taken a new turn stimulated more general reflections about the 'rewarding fact that the utterly individual tone of every human contact prevents its confusion with others; and that the initial ambivalences of love and friendship always do work out clearly in the end.' There were several further meetings, both at Ashford and in London, and Christine soon recovered, but our dialogue left a residue of strangeness.

Saime and I were haunted by a more fundamental ambivalence. We knew we were destined to go separate ways, but there were moments when this scarcely mattered. When Brian first introduced me as an inhibited Englishman, the thought had flashed across her mind: 'Should I ever marry, it will be him'. Recalling how we kept bumping into each other at the refectory, she confessed that this was not entirely fortuitous. Watching from a window in Falmer House, she would wait for her lunch until she saw me walk across from the Arts Building, contriving for us to meet. She had eyes and chose me. She also explained that heart-stopping silence on Devil's Dyke. At home in Turkey, she and her friend Haldun had never been open about their feelings. But here, between the downs and the sea, she had taken a deep breath and opted for honesty.

SHIFTING SANDS

One afternoon Brian took me aside. 'I must warn you, Ted,' he gently observed, 'that your feelings are bound to fade.'

'Nonsense,' I replied, 'you are underestimating the attraction of opposites! That's what makes Saime so appealing.' I was thinking of Goethe's novel *Elective Affinities*, in which contrasting personalities are drawn together by forces over which they have no control.

'Goethe's science is completely outdated,' he replied. 'In the realm of sub-atomic particles, everything is unstable.'

'But think of the Downs and the sea,' I objected. 'They complement each other perfectly!'

There could hardly have been a worse analogy. Coastal towns are continuously threatened by erosion, and Brighton was no exception. On our favourite walk along the undercliff to Ovingdean, we had to scramble over lumps of chalk dislodged by tide, wind and rain, while at high water the waves crashed over the coast road. The cliff was crumbling and there was no bedrock to be seen – only swirling tides and shifting sands. Our forebodings intensified after watching Fellini's *La Strada* at the Duke of York's cinema. The most compelling scenes are set on the mournful beaches of a bleak post-war Italy. The simple-minded Gelsomina (played by Giulietta Masina) clings to the hope that every pebble must have a purpose, but Zampano the strongman (Anthony Quinn) ends the film alone with nothing but a handful of sand. Wasn't there some middle way?

Marine Square formed the oasis where we could shelter from the storms and share our stories with a wider circle. Students would come to my flat for play-readings led by our friend Laci Löb, who had a passion for German theatre. For Laci it was the writings of Büchner that proved most compelling, especially his tragedy *Danton's Death*. 'What is it in us,' Danton asks in a famous scene, 'that lies, whores, steals and murders?' Were our lives at the mercy of irrational drives? Or was it the irrepressible energy of youth, bubbling up in Brighton? Laci too was in love, and that autumn I attended his wedding to Jill, an elegant young woman with whom he set up house in Shoreham. Together we organized an excursion to London to see Peter Brook's production of *The Assassination of Jean-Paul Marat* by Peter Weiss with a star-studded cast: Ian Richardson as Marat, Patrick Magee as Sade, and Glenda Jackson as Charlotte Corday.

The innovative stage technique, enhanced by the songs of Adrian Mitchell, transformed the Aldwych Theatre into a madhouse.

We made several trips to East Anglia to visit the families of our closest friends, staying overnight in Norwich with Brian Easlea and his family. Stopping off in Cambridge, we visited Gavin's mother, Mary Wraith, whose tiny house in City Road was a treasury of illustrated books. As a young woman she had studied English at Birmingham University, before marrying a businessman and settling in the Lake District to bring up their two sons. Divorce led her to move to Cambridge where she pursued a wide range of interests, including working for the Samaritans. Given her openness towards foreign cultures, she took a special interest in Saime. In Brighton we had failed to engage with the genteel ladies on the promenade, but here in Cambridge was an experienced woman from whose wisdom we could learn.

As a courtesy, I called on my former tutor Freddy Stopp and his wife Elisabeth at their home in Drosier Road. In a recent letter he had encouraged me to apply for one of the two Assistant Lectureships in German advertised at Cambridge. Life at Sussex was so rewarding, I replied, that it was far too early for a move; but over tea at Drosier Road my resolution faltered under the influence of my mentor and his wife. Unbeknown to me, the Stopps had been contacted by my father, who idealized the Oxbridge system and felt that Sussex offered undesirable distractions. Couldn't they persuade me to apply for Cambridge? Reluctantly I conceded that there was no harm in applying (it seemed inconceivable that a person without a doctorate would be appointed). For Saime, as we drove home, this felt like a betrayal: 'Aren't you being untrue to yourself?'

Back in Brighton we spent every spare moment together, exploring the countryside in my car. While I was encouraging her to develop practical skills like driving and swimming, Saime was initiating me into the richness of Turkish culture and the conflicts it caused. She had followed her father in becoming a resolutely secular person with communist sympathies. On the wall of her Marine Square flat she pasted a poem clipped from a newspaper, entitled 'Bugün Pazar' (Today is Sunday). The theme was deceptively simple: a prisoner allowed outside on a Sunday morning feels exhilarated by the sunshine. The verses were by Nazım Hikmet, a communist poet sentenced by the Turkish authorities to twenty-three years on trumped-up charges. Saime shared Hikmet's vision of a classless society, and she was determined to return to Ankara and train a new generation of Turkish scientists. The terms of her scholarship committed her to teaching for four years at Middle East Technical University. Was she to abandon her career for an uncertain future in a foreign land? Difficulties of adjustment provoked all-night discussions, resolved – if we were lucky – by break of day. After one dispute Saime declared that our relationship was over and retired to her flat, where she pruned the rose bush on her balcony. But after taking out her feelings on the hapless plant she consented to see me again.

There were other visitors to Marine Square who incurred her wrath. One day Saime felt provoked by Joe Townsend, a warm-hearted rogue with a taste for glamorous girls. He and Brian were standing beneath her window admiring Gavin's latest acquisition, a Lotus sports car. After watching the drooling males from her balcony, Saime threw an egg at Joe's invitingly bald pate, spattering the group with fluid. 'What a wonderful yolke!' Joe exclaimed, and for days our conversation was peppered with phrases like 'Here's something eggstraordinary!' Honour was satisfied when Joe finally offered to shake hands with Saime – and squeezed an egg into her palm. Fed by the mulch of friendship, our intimacy thrived. Chuck would provide the music and Brian the beer, while Saime welcomed Joe's latest girlfriend, Seija from Finland. The English were a minority at our cosmopolitan parties. Through Joe we also met an artist named Stina, who made a poignant line drawing of Saime, bringing out the sadness behind those sparkling eyes. A further pleasure was provided by the folk clubs we visited with Margareta, a gifted singer from Germany. We'd enjoy cheekily suggestive songs like 'I put my finger in the woodpecker's hole', but the mood changed when Margareta took the floor to sing 'Plaisir d'amour'. Ribaldry blended with romance in the repertoire of love.

Brilliant sunshine brought other visitors to Brighton: my brother Christopher, a student at Oxford, my sister Margaret, studying medicine at King's College London, and my brother Simon in his Christ's Hospital uniform. Blanca Bartosova arrived from Prague, thrilled to visit England for the first time. Having grown up under a claustrophobic form of communism, she relished the wide horizons of Marine Square. Amid these distractions there was little time for typing. Three hundred pages of my thesis existed in first draft by mid-July, but the final version had only reached page twenty-five. After the library closed, Aquarius would take over as we headed for the sea. While others battled the waves, Saime said, my strokes caressed them as if afraid to hurt their feelings. For someone longing to be manly it was a surprise to be admired for gentleness.

Intrigued by the work of Freud, we talked through our dreams, and if there were emotional lows, we were buoyed by a circle of friends. A diary entry of August 1965 describes a day 'typical of my life over the past year':

> At 9 a.m. Saime came across the square to wake me (her sister Yeter still being asleep). As I struggled out of the sea of dreams, we almost drowned. After breakfast I worked on my thesis, then drove to the university for lunch. Delayed by a chat with Stephen Medcalf – about Cambridge, Oxford and their buildings – I worked on entries for Langenscheidt's dictionary. Around 5 p.m. Saime, Yeter, Gavin and I made for the beach below Marine Square. The sea was enticing, and I swam out till the others

quite lost sight of me. In such calm water, you could breaststroke up the sunpath for ever. After such exercise our supper – omelette, Turkish olive salad, potatoes, Danish lager, bananas and ice cream, black Polish bread with cheese – was a veritable feast.

In such company, *Langenscheidt* could hardly compete. I was not destined to become a lexicographer.

Earlier that summer, to my intense surprise, I had been invited for an interview at Cambridge together with my friend Terry Llewellyn. Quizzed by a panel that included Leonard Forster and Dennis Green, I was cocky enough – knowing that monologue lectures were the norm – to ask whether I'd be able to introduce seminars. We were both appointed, and within twenty-four hours I'd survived the further ordeal of being vetted at High Table in Caius. So I returned to Brighton with both an Assistant Lectureship and a College Fellowship in my pocket. Although I felt guilty about abandoning my students, the German group was strengthened by new appointments, so things were left in good hands.

Sussex without Saime would never have been the same. There were some colleagues who had succeeded in bridging the cultural gulf that we were finding difficult. My mentor Tony Thorlby cited the example of David Daiches, the foremost English scholar of the day, whom he described as 'a wise old Jew'. Taken aback by this comment, I was referred to the memoir in which Daiches recalled his orthodox Jewish childhood in Edinburgh under the title *Two Worlds*. Daiches claimed to feel equally at home in both Scottish and Jewish cultures. But he conceded that 'marrying out' had strained relations with his parents, prompting him to spend a dozen years in the United States.

Would we be capable of similar adjustments? As we watched the Last Night of the Proms on television in the seclusion of Saime's flat, we were surprised by the surge of feeling after the final Sea Shanties, reaching out more urgently as we drifted apart. 'Even at times of greatest intimacy,' I reflected in my diary, 'we both accept the test of separation.' Shortly before her departure, Saime received the final instalment of her grant and splashed out on a tweed skirt and jacket with an eye-catching chequered waistcoat. A further windfall resulted from injuries she had suffered in a car accident eighteen months earlier. After consulting a solicitor in the Old Steine, she was awarded £1500 in compensation – well over a year's salary. 'As to the money,' I noted in my diary, 'I would like her to invest £1000 of it in England, in case we decide next summer to marry – it would help towards buying a house.' But Saime felt that having a car in Ankara would enhance her independence, so she ordered a brand new Volkswagen, sky-blue with silver trimmings.

The Marine Square community was dissolving, for Brian had already left to spend two years teaching in Brazil. Joe Townsend consoled us by throwing a farewell party, cramming our friends into his flat. 'Saime has been the centre of everything,' Gavin sadly observed. The party took place on that fateful September evening when she was due to catch her plane from Heathrow. Leaving the party early, we drove off heavily loaded with her luggage for Ankara and mine for Cambridge. A final embrace at the airport left us both in tears. Too tired to complete my journey, I parked by the roadside and dozed off in the car. At daybreak I drove on to Cambridge, stopping for a snack before settling into my college room and falling asleep. It was dark by the time I awoke. A glance at my watch showed that it was 6 o'clock – I must have slept all day! So I phoned the only person who knew about Saime, our friend Mary Wraith. Startled, she confirmed she was at home. As I drove across town, the horizon lightened. It was the blue hour, between night and day, and the earth was turning. Drained by my journey, I had slept for twenty hours – so it was time for breakfast. 'Don't let Saime slip away,' Mary urged, 'pin her down!'

Across the Divide

Could the élan of Brighton be recaptured amid the Fens? Back at Caius, there were few visible signs of change. The main concession to modernity was the new building in West Road, named after William Harvey, the medical pioneer. Harvey Court lacked the charm of Spence's campus at Sussex, for the architect had made no attempt to harmonize his angular block with the flowing gardens and mature trees. However, the design broke with Caius tradition by having no gates – and hence no restrictive gate hours. Students and their guests were treated as adults, free to come and go as they pleased. My fellowship entitled me to a self-contained bachelor flat, which made it easy to settle in, consoling myself for Saime's absence by hanging the sketch by Stina on the wall. My rooms were a short walk from the University Library and the new Modern Languages Faculty, so this enclave of modernity proved more convenient than the inward-looking Old Courts. But even there a new spirit was stirring, epitomized by Joseph Needham, the man who loved China.

COLLEGE POLITICS

A four-course dinner was served every evening at Caius High Table and the claret flowed during dessert. This was a mixed experience for a person with international interests, for most of the Fellows appeared absorbed in their own affairs. However, if you were lucky enough to sit next to Needham, you would be drawn into a wider world. It was enthralling to hear what had prompted him to give up his original calling as a biochemist and become the world's most accomplished sinologist. During the 1930s his laboratory had attracted a group of young researchers from China, one of whom – a woman named Lu Gwei-djen – had kindled his passion for all things Chinese. After the Japanese army had occupied large tracts of mainland China, Churchill's government sent supplies through India to the beleaguered Chiang Kai-shek. By this date Needham had mastered Mandarin, so he was sent on a mission to organize aid for Chinese universities. Between 1943 and 1946 he travelled to the remotest regions, making extraordinary discoveries that were to inspire his pioneering research. He also met Zhou Enlai, one of the leaders of the communist movement, which Needham passionately supported. The publication in 1954 of the first volume of his *Science and Civilization in China* marked a revolution in the history of ideas, and by the early 1960s three further magisterial volumes had followed.

Two stories heard at High Table were so striking that I shared them in my letters to Saime. When I asked one evening about the rare books he had discovered, Needham replied that during his mission to China he had bought a whole collection from a bookseller and flown them to England. Taking a closer look, he discovered a volume marked 'Royal Library. Only copy in existence'. It must have been stolen, and the bookseller, unable to dispose of such a compromising item in any other way, had slipped it in with this collection. 'I have still got the book,' he said, 'and in my will I have left it to the National Library in Peking'.

The second story heard at High Table was recounted by a visiting scholar from a Catholic university in the United States. Travelling through Turkey a few years earlier, he was treated at a US Army hospital after a car accident. The doctor, a fellow Catholic, mentioned that there was a Capuchin monastery with a valuable library, located near their base in the vicinity of Trebizond (Trabzon). Back in the US, my colleague reported the incident to the President of his university. 'There must be some interesting material in that library,' said the President. 'See if you can buy it for our university'. So he returned to the monastery, accompanied by a scholar from Rome, and selected five hundred volumes. When he asked how much to pay, the answer was: 'You can have them for nothing, if you help us to get a further five hundred volumes out of Turkey and back to Rome.'

It was feared that the Turkish authorities, who had given refuge in the eighteenth century to monks fleeing with their library from persecution in Russia, would ban the export of the books. 'You can guess what happened next,' my table companion continued. 'The US Airforce flew five hundred books to the States and five hundred to Rome – and everyone was happy.' Since this infringed Turkish law, I asked whether he had any moral scruples. At that moment the waiter intervened with a dish of vegetables, so our visitor could recover his composure. 'You mean, did the Capuchins have any moral scruples?' he replied. 'Well, the books belonged to them and were of no use to the Turkish government. They would simply have tried to extract money from Italy and the US, before issuing an export licence.' Reporting this episode to Saime, I distanced myself from modish anti-Americanism; but the story was worth recording as an example of western arrogance towards non-Christian cultures. 'You can see,' my letter concluded, 'why I was so impressed by Needham's attitude, which is rooted in respect.'

Such conversations were unusual in having international implications, for it was domestic politics that generated most excitement. Plotting to overthrow the Master was a college tradition. Four centuries earlier our second founder, John Caius, during his final years as Master, had been denounced by puritanical Fellows for hoarding forbidden vestments. With the connivance of the Vice-Chancellor, the rebels ransacked the Master's lodgings and burnt books and vestments which they regarded as Popish trumpery. While those events formed part of college folklore, an equally bitter conflict had erupted in the 1950s between young bloods, mostly under forty, and the old guard who controlled the College Council, chaired by the Master, Sir James Chadwick. For all his fame as a physicist, Chadwick was no match for the conspirators. By coordinating their votes at College Council elections, the rebels ejected several of their seniors from key positions. This became known as the Peasants' Revolt, probably named after one of its instigators, the economist Peter Bauer (in German his surname means 'peasant'). Things became so fractious that Chadwick resigned, to be replaced by another eminent physicist, Sir Nevill Mott.

Those events had lasting consequences. They whetted the appetite of the next generation of conspirators, who now began to intrigue against Mott, regarded by some as remote and autocratic. Within weeks of our induction in autumn 1965, newly elected Fellows were taken aside by the reformers and advised to vote for specific candidates for the College Council, including one known to be at odds with the Master. Since there were seven new Fellows, including a precocious young astrophysicist named Stephen Hawking, our votes really counted. Three reform-minded candidates were duly elected, led by my colleague Grahame Castor, Director of Studies in Modern Languages. Shortly afterwards the Master, feeling increasingly isolated, announced that he would resign the following summer.

The Fellows of Caius traditionally elect the college's most distinguished member as Master, and during preliminary discussions two outstanding candidates emerged, polarizing opinion. In the blue corner was Michael Oakeshott, a Life Fellow who held a chair at the London School of Economics. Through publications such as *Rationalism in Politics* and *Why I am a Conservative* Oakeshott had made his reputation as one of the most brilliant political philosophers of the day. But in the red corner was Joseph Needham, a man who – despite his erudition – was regarded by many as politically unsound. 'Don't people realize that he's a communist?' asked my supervisor Peter Stern, when I consulted him. 'Needham disgraced himself during the Korean War by falsely accusing the United States of using bacteriological weapons.' He obviously favoured

Oakeshott, who had been one of his teachers.

In a traditional college the conservatives would have won the day, but at Caius younger Fellows taking over as tutors and directors of studies. Oakeshott certainly had his supporters in the conservative camp, but being based in London he was unfamiliar to younger Fellows, while we met Needham almost every day. Even those appalled by his politics found him personally approachable as well intellectually inspiring. Effortlessly bridging the gulf between the arts and sciences, he was bringing together two civilizations that had been estranged for thousands of years. Moreover Needham was a quintessential college man, a practising Christian dedicated to the traditions of Edmund Gonville and John Caius. These qualities enabled him to garner support across the ideological divide, so he emerged from the preliminary straw polls as the clear front runner. By mid-December the race was over. The news may have startled the wider world, but there was rejoicing among the younger Fellows when Joseph Needham was pre-elected as Master, to take over in autumn 1966.

Writing to Saime, I made no attempt to conceal my delight at this turn of events. Of course, there was still an influential conservative faction among the Fellows, but the tide was turning towards reform, with a marked shift in attitudes to teaching. For scientists like Nevill Mott, it was work in the laboratories that mattered (his research was to earn him a Nobel Prize for Physics). But in the humanities everything depended on the quality of college tutorials, known in Cambridge as supervisions. In earlier days these had been gentlemanly affairs. Lounging in an easy chair, the tutor would listen as the student read out his essay, making occasional erudite comments. With an exceptionally gifted teacher, such as Francis Bennett, the exchanges might be inspirational, but too often both students and their supervisors had an easy ride. But at Caius the modernizers were gaining ground, led initially by my mentor Freddy Stopp, the reforming Senior Tutor who had implemented arrangements at Harvey Court, discarding archaic restrictions. One of Needham's first actions was to approve the appointment of a new Senior Tutor with even more liberal credentials, my colleague Graham Castor. This meant that – within twelve months of becoming a Fellow – I was appointed Director of Studies in Modern Languages.

Supervisors like Stopp and Castor set exacting standards. Under the new dispensation students were required to hand in carefully researched essays several days in advance, so their work could be rigorously assessed and they could receive systematic feedback. This made increasing demands on the supervisors, and there were those who mourned the leisurely ethos of earlier days. The pace of life was quickening, and my first two terms were a race to keep up with the demands of the job, combining college supervisions with university lectures and language classes. Everything had to be prepared from scratch, with additional hours spent reading new texts and marking written work. Teaching at Sussex had been less pressurized and enlivened by a more informal social climate. Cambridge, by contrast, clothed personal contacts in academic rituals.

Caius was an exclusively male college, and among the forty or fifty students in my language classes and supervision groups there was not a single woman. Worse still, my colleagues seemed to think this was normal. Many of them were passionately wedded to the patriarchal system, and when I hazarded that first-year students might feel intimidated, one of the younger Fellows retorted: 'Exactly! That's how they *should* feel!' Socially, my position was both privileged and constricted, rubbing shoulders with eminent colleagues while lacking intimate friends. My confidante from the early 1960s, Christine Crow, had moved to Scotland to take up an appointment at St Andrews. When she visited Cambridge in December, she was so self-absorbed that we scarcely communicated. Fortunately the Modern Language students included Bill Tilden, my friend from Vienna, now a choral exhibitioner at Selwyn, while his fiancée Jill was studying art history in the tradition of Ernst Gombrich, so we enjoyed lively exchanges. However, my own work on Kraus was languishing, for I was struggling to find time for research amid the piles of scripts to be marked.

There was a warm welcome from the Head of the German Department, Leonard Forster. He and his Swiss wife Jeanne were extremely hospitable, but formidable figures from student days like Dennis Green were now my colleagues, requiring brisk readjustments. My closest ally was the genial Terry Llewellyn, now living in a university flat with his wife Lisa and their first son. He had completed his doctorate on German Mystical Poetry, but found it challenging to combine teaching with parenthood. As Assistant Lecturers we were under pressure to perform, for the appointment was untenured, and at the end of five years we might find ourselves out of a job.

My duties would have been even more demanding but for Edmund Stegmaier, the Caius German Lector, who also had rooms in Harvey Court. While I introduced him to the satire of Karl Kraus, he shared with me his passion for the religious philosopher Martin Buber, author of *Ich und Du* (I and Thou). Intense personal relationships, Buber argued, formed the path to a mystical union with the divine. Although Buber's thought was rooted in Judaism, this was an idea likely to appeal to anyone touched by the transformative power of love. Another colleague based in Harvey Court was the historian Norman Stone, who joined me in my room for supper one evening before a college wine party. His subject was the Austro-Hungarian Army, and he had conducted research in Budapest while I was working in Vienna, so there was a lively exchange of ideas. If Norman's manner seemed dogmatic, it had the merit of directness. 'Are you getting married soon?' he asked, noticing the sketch on my wall.

I loved the sadness that Stina had drawn out of Saime's eyes and the

'Saime: with lots o' love' (pencil drawing by Stina, 1965)

stoical tilt of her lips, so this prompted me to share my longing.

EMOTIONAL LIFELINES

My thoughts were always in Ankara, nourished by a stream of letters, often running to a dozen pages. Since boarding-school I had treasured letters from home, especially the circulars which Father typed week by week, using carbons to send copies to eight children. Saime's written English was rather sketchy, so it scarcely seemed likely that letters would bridge the divide. But telephoning was almost impossible, since the international switchboards were notoriously unreliable, so the postal system became our lifeline. A letter mailed from Ankara would reach Cambridge within forty-eight hours and it was agony if a week passed without news. For the letters were resonant with dreams and desires, recalling those 'most glorious moments when the spirit of love suddenly swept over us', as I wrote on 19 February 1966. These introspective moods were balanced by the practical demands of teaching. Lecturing on Heine's lyric poetry was a special pleasure, enabling me to chart the shifts from romantic irony to the uniquely spirited late verses composed to while away sleepless nights.

Christmas at Buckfastleigh provided a welcome break, enlivened by a visit from my brother David, now teaching in Toronto. He particularly enjoyed a book of humorous stories about Nasreddin Hodja, the wise fool of Turkish folklore, received from Saime as a family present. During intimate conversations David, now divorced after a precipitate early marriage, counselled caution about sexual commitments, sharing ideas over tumblers of whisky. Father went further: 'Who would be so foolish as to sacrifice the privileges of Oxbridge to the claims of marriage?' But the experiences at Brighton had taught me that the rewards of research are a poor substitute for personal intimacy.

Meanwhile Saime was making more radical readjustments. When she arrived home after the long flight, she found 'a poor sheep waiting to be sacrificed' – a thank-offering for her safe return. None of her relatives was religious, which made the situation even more incongruous, and she now felt almost a stranger in her own family, sharing a bedroom with her Aunt Melahat. The only person she could confide in was her sister Saliha, an employee at the state Customs Office. With the younger Göksu children she played a more parental role, supporting Emel's efforts to train as an actress and helping the two boys, Maksut and Kemal, with their homework.

In Brighton Saime had become accustomed to such spontaneous friendships that social life in Ankara seemed strange. At Middle East Technical University (METU), an English-language institution founded with American support, she initially had only one close friend, an experimental physicist named Tuncay Incesu. However, she was welcomed back by Professor Erdal Inönü, who asked her to teach the General Physics course to first-year students (three groups of fifty). Even problem-solving on the blackboard could be stimulating with such a charismatic teacher. 'After the first class, they didn't want to go,' she wrote in her idiosyncratic English. 'They surrendered me asking unnecessary questions.'

Such colourful vignettes formed high points in Saime's letters, contrasting the stresses of life in Turkey with the fulfilment enjoyed in England. She divided her time between teaching and politics. After the coup that had ousted the government of Adnan Menderes, METU was founded as a driving force in the programme of westernization pursued by the reforming governments of the early 1960s. The aim was to create an educated elite to counteract the residues of Ottoman bureaucracy and Islamic superstition. International funding made it possible to hire teachers from Europe and the United States, creating a lively mix among the academic staff, and the new venture attracted highly motivated students. That autumn Saime joined her colleagues on an excursion to

Adana to celebrate a festival. But the patriotic chorus on the coach appealed to her far less than the lyrics of the left-wing Turkish folksinger Ruhi Su. She was shocked by conditions in the countryside: families living in mud-built huts and young women swathed from head to toe. In discussions with colleagues she usually found herself in a minority as she challenged both the self-styled intellectuals and the sycophantic Ankara girls in their entourage. When the coach reached Iskenderun on the Syrian border, the girls rushed to buy fashionable clothes smuggled from Lebanon, while Saime shared a dish of pilaf with a peasant family she had befriended.

The primitive conditions in the countryside found a parallel in the shanty towns springing up on the fringes of Turkish cities. A loophole in the law allowed poor families to build a makeshift home on waste land, provided it was completed within a single night. Her uncle Abdullah had constructed one of these 'night-built houses' (gecekondular) on the outskirts of Ankara, and when Saime visited this primitive two-room dwelling, she heard the whole story: how a friend had distracted the night watchman while workmates helped Abdullah to construct the bare walls, improvise a roof, and move his wife and children in before dawn. The work was completed before sunrise and once the family were inside, the police were not permitted to pull it down.

Through her contacts with left-wing groups, Saime became immersed in politics. During the General Election shortly after her return to Ankara she pinned her hopes on the fledgling Turkish Workers Party (TIP), while her family supported the Republican Peoples Party (RPP), the Kemalist faction led by Ismet Inönü. All were disappointed when Süleyman Demirel's conservative Justice Party won a clear majority, while TIP scraped only 15 seats. This was a setback for the Kemalist principles of state planning, since Demirel favoured private enterprise. When Çetin Altan, a TIP member of parliament for Istanbul, spoke out for the socialist alternative, he was ridiculed. Saime's socialism was based on the evidence of her own eyes. At a meeting in an Ankara cinema in November to mark the anniversary of Atatürk's death, she was struck by the sickly appearance of the boy sitting next to her, who had followed the crowd into the auditorium. It turned out that he was hoping to see a free film. As they began to chat, she discovered that he came from an impoverished village in the Çorum district, with no school and no doctor. The boy couldn't read or write, having been taught only to recite the Koran. Realizing that he needed medical care, she took him to the emergency service of Red Crescent.

Saime supported the proposal that remote rural populations should be resettled in larger villages so that they could receive education and health care. This, she noted in a further letter, might involve an element of compulsion, but hadn't Atatürk used force to expedite his reforms?

However, the Justice Party denounced such radical proposals, associated in their minds with the Soviet programme of collectivization. Indeed, the anti-communist legislation meant that supporters of TIP risked arrest if they were too outspoken. A clause in the Turkish Criminal Code prohibited activities designed to establish the domination of one class over another, which could include the publication of Marxist literature. For a new generation of students this made the forbidden fruit all the more attractive.

Two issues dominated foreign affairs, Cyprus and Vietnam, intensifying the hostility towards the United States. American policy on Cyprus was seen as favouring the Greeks, and there was outrage when it was revealed that plans to intervene on behalf of the beleaguered Turkish minority had been blocked by President Johnson. Among students at METU, the brutality of the American offensive against the Vietcong provoked mass demonstrations. Saime can hardly have been impressed by my comments in a letter of 3 December 1965. Although sympathizing with colleagues opposed to the Vietnam War, I argued that student protests were unlikely to influence the hard line taken by the US. 'Since American resources are in effect unlimited,' I concluded, 'the Vietcong are bound to fail.'

Another issue addressed in Saime's letters was the gender divide. 'I hate hypocracy' she wrote – a mis-spelling that suggested a whole system of deceit. Supposedly emancipated women turned out to be obsessed with finding a husband, but male ambivalence towards the fairer sex was encapsulated in verses by Nazım Hikmet, which Saime translated for me:

We steal her and take her to the mountains.
We kill other human beings for her sake.
We go to prison for life for her sake.
Her place at the table comes after the oxen.

That month Saime's life took a new turn, as she travelled to Istanbul to collect her Volkswagen, cleared at last through customs. There she spent an evening with the artist Mehmet Şenel, another close friend from their days in the sanatorium. 'No Turkish man would be happy with you,' Mehmet observed. 'They prefer pussycat-like girls, for they can't cope with an active and assertive woman.' Sensitive to gender politics, Mehmet felt that no other girl was worth a 'fingernail' of Saime. But he was contemplating marriage with one of his students, a young woman from a wealthy family. Would she approve?

The photo Saime sent me, showing her with Mehmet in a nightclub, provoked a spate of reflections:

You look wonderful – such character in your eyes and mouth, such beautiful hair. The expression on your face (and even the cigarette in your hand) tells me so much. Both you and Mehmet have faces full of seriousness and at the same time filled with sorrow. The difference is: Mehmet looks more resigned and passive – his face says: 'There is no cure for my sadness', whereas your face is full of movement and vitality – your face says: 'Yes, life is hard, but we can still make something of it.'

There were no macho males among Saime's friends from the sanatorium. Their illness had engendered an unusual sensitivity, expressed in Mehmet's artwork, the poems of Ali Püsküllüoğlu, and the letters that Haldun exchanged with her during a relationship that was to last a lifetime. Growing up in a family of females, she appreciated the company of young men with whom she could discuss politics and ideas.

By this date Saime had acquired a circle of new friends. Through Tuncay she was introduced to Çetin Bey, a manufacturer of illuminated signs whose workshop provided a city-centre meeting place. On campus she joined the Socialist Club, making friends with its student secretary, Bekir Harputluoğlu. A further ally was the diminutive Cem Çakmak, Lecturer in Administrative Science, who invited her to attend socialist discussion groups and contribute to their magazine. Together with colleagues, Cem published an open letter criticizing Turkish foreign policy, especially support for the war in Vietnam. This earned them a public rebuke from Prime Minister Demirel. My letter describing how the Capuchin Library was smuggled out of Turkey by the US Airforce prompted Saime to write an article criticizing the conduct of the country's so-called allies. She arranged for this to appear in Yön, the influential socialist journal edited by Ilhan Selçuk. It was a sensation, she told me, for it prompted the government to monitor the movements of American ships, suspected of spiriting further treasures out of the country.

The first months of 1966 were dominated by the saga of Saime's Volkswagen, driven back to Ankara with Tuncay as chauffeur. Although she had not yet passed her driving test, a provisional licence allowed her to practise, providing she had a qualified driver with her. But Saime's motto, quoted to me on 29 December, was: 'Whatever I do is against the conventions.' As soon as the car was licensed and insured, she was on the road, even if there was no qualified driver to accompany her. This was courting trouble, as the temperature in Ankara dropped to minus 20 centigrade. One icy afternoon in February she was involved in an accident, and although physically unhurt, she faced prosecution. Her letters gave the impression that she wouldn't have minded spending a night in jail, but her friends organized a cover-up, and thanks to a good lawyer she was acquitted.

'I want to draw the real picture of the society, so that you can imagine me and yourself in it,' Saime had written in November. This affair left me bemused. On paper there were clearly defined procedures operated by the courts, but in practice there were ways of getting around the regulations by pulling strings. Public affairs unfolded on different planes, one formal, the other pragmatic. The westernizing principles of Kemalism had been grafted on to an oriental culture, and the mismatch between the two created unexpected escape routes. 'You cannot imagine how we solve our problems,' Saime wrote in mid-February, 'through friends of friends, or by beating, cheating and shouting.' Politically, the consequences were problematic. The republic defined itself as a secular state despite its overwhelmingly Islamic population, but Demirel was adept at playing the religious card. Saime hated the exploitation of religion for political purposes. After an outbreak of cholera in the Middle East, the logical thing would have been to restrict travel on grounds of public health, discouraging Turkish Muslims from going to Mecca. When the government shrank from these precautionary measures, she was incensed by the subordination of public health to religious ritual.

Having lost contact with Haldun, there was no one in her circle with an inside knowledge of Islam. One of the few references to the subject in Saime's letters related to a play in which her sister Emel was acting, 'Blowing Out The Candle' ('Mum Söndü'). This focused on the superstitious practices of Islamic sects, including pilgrimages to the shrines of prophets. The most memorable scene enacted the Festival of Candles, an event which – for this Mevlevi sect – permitted men and women to worship together in a brightly lit room. The celebration reached a climax when the candles were suddenly extinguished. According to this tendentious scenario, what followed under cover of darkness was a festival of carnal union, as a result of which several women became pregnant without knowing who had fathered their child.

During March the political tensions escalated, as the Justice Party tried to silence its critics. Violence erupted in parliament, and leading socialists were arrested, including the novelist Yaşar Kemal and the folksinger Ruhi Su. Saime was even more shocked by the arrest of Bekir Harputluoğlu, secretary of the socialist club. 'McCarthyism in Turkey is getting worse,' she wrote, enclosing a photo of Bekir being frogmarched through the streets. Was the country irreconcilably split between socialists and reactionaries? It was time to find out for myself.

THRESHOLD ENERGY

Desperately missing Saime, I poured out my heart in letters, while her replies showed that she was finding separation equally testing. As a token of trust, I had lent her my diaries, and as she read entries from the spring of 1963, she was surprised by the allusions to other women – Gila, Blanca and Christine. 'I'm sure you never forgot their birthdays,' she wrote with some asperity, when her own birthday passed without any greeting. My gift to her arrived several days late: a sovereign featuring Saint George slaying the Dragon. 'On one side a respectable profile,' I explained, 'on the other a hero willing to risk anything for you.' My impatience was increased by an encounter with the physicist Farhad Faisal, who was attending seminars in Cambridge. Together we resumed the dialogue of our Sussex days, as he took me to task for my lethargy. 'What's stopping you from flying to Ankara?' he asked, just as the term was ending. But I felt obliged to give priority to my dissertation, so I wrote to Saime on 15 March saying I'd devote the next four weeks to Kraus.

Two days later my resolution was shaken by a letter that crossed in the post. Saime faced a difficult choice: whether to accept Erdal Inönü's offer of a grant to enable her to complete her doctorate in Trieste. This would have left our relationship in limbo. Fortunately I had arranged a further meeting with Farhad in the Kenco Coffee Shop near the bus station. Perched on plastic chairs we discussed my dilemma, which reminded me of Kafka's 'Before the Law'. In that fable a man from the country wishes to gain access to the Law, only to find the entrance guarded by a powerful gatekeeper, who forbids him to enter. So the man dutifully waits for many long years, only to discover – on his dying day – that the gate was intended for him. Kafka's paradox had perplexed literary critics for decades, so I hardly expected a solution from a physicist, but Farhad's response was incisive. Listening as much to my tone as to the tale itself, he sensed that the gatekeeper represented the constraints that were keeping us apart. Surely the solution lay with quantum mechanics. Particles, he explained, interact through fields of attraction and resistance, only fusing when the electrodes acquire the necessary 'threshold energy'. Surely, the same principle should apply to human relations.

This was the moment when the Sussex Arts–Science scheme paid dividends, transforming my self-awareness. Back at my rooms I re-read Kafka's fable in my battered edition of his collected stories, embellished by one of the author's angular drawings. Responding to the admonitory power of Kafka's images, I decided to cross the threshold. Saime had said that from 19–26 March she would be attending a conference on Particle Physics in Istanbul, staying with her group at the Çınar Hotel. For the first time in my life I had four hundred pounds in my bank account – easily enough for an air ticket. On the spur of the moment I booked a flight to Istanbul, sending a telegram to the hotel to announce my impending arrival.

Walking through the twilight towards the airport terminal, I glimpsed two figures waving from the spectators' gallery – Saime and Mehmet. Her beauty radiated through the glass doors as the customs checked my luggage. Mehmet was on good terms with the hotel staff, so that evening an extra bed was carried into Saime's room, crossing the foyer before the eyes of her astonished colleagues. This time there would be no secrets – we were resolved to get married. It only remained to settle the Bride Price, the sum paid by the suitor to the girl's family as recompense for the costs of raising her. That night Mehmet graciously accepted a symbolic silver coin.

Crossing the Bosphorus by ferry, we caught the overnight train, sharing a swaying couchette as we ascended towards Ankara. Thinking that Saime's family would be expecting me, I was in for a surprise. She hadn't even confided in her sister Saliha, let alone her parents. Her mother, Ismet, seemed apprehensive when we arrived for a late breakfast, but that evening her father, Ibrahim, insisted on throwing a party. Now was the moment to confront the gatekeeper. As the drinks began to flow, I tried to explain in my halting Turkish that I loved Saime. 'But we all love Saime!' he replied. It took some time for the message to get through, for convention required that a family friend should initiate the engagement. So we arranged for Saime's parents to receive a visit from Ali, the poet, who had agreed to petition for her hand. Ali was so shy that several hours of small-talk passed before he could bring himself to say: 'We all know why I am here.' We hardly expected Saime's father, a Kemalist with communist sympathies, to welcome the alliance, for he knew too much about the crimes of the British Empire. But something in my manner reminded him of the gentleness of his wife, so – despite his regret that Saime would no longer be working in Turkey – he consented.

Saime was surrounded by innumerable admirers – how could I be the one to carry her off? As we chose our wedding rings, the words of a popular song, suitably adapted, reverberated in my mind: The ring on my finger is Saime give me, Saime alone until morning. The next priority, for a young couple on the threshold of marriage, was to visit Atatürk's Mausoleum and view the exhibition chronicling his career. This represented threshold energy on a grand scale. In 1920 the Turkish hero had defied the Sultan, escaping by boat from Istanbul to set up his headquarters in Anatolia. During the ensuing War of Independence, his forces defeated the invading Greek army and expelled the imperialist powers that were intent on carving up the country. Small wonder that there were monuments to his memory in every town in Turkey, for the country had been transformed by his reforms.

Saime had to negotiate a period of leave to enable her to accompany me back to England, but the obstacles melted in her path. No one could have been more understanding than Erdal Inönü, who granted her leave to continue her scientific training in Cambridge. Our plan to get married in Ankara was frustrated when we learnt that it would take six weeks to obtain the necessary papers. Otherwise, everything went like a dream, and within a couple of weeks we were celebrating our Engagement Party at her parents' flat. Her father made an impassioned speech about international reconciliation, ending with dire warnings about what he'd do if I made his daughter unhappy. The Volkswagen was sold before we left and most of the proceeds were presented to Saime's parents to help them buy their flat. So there was a Bride Price, after all, paid by the bride herself.

On 16 April, a week after landing in England, we were married in Cambridge with our friend Mary Wraith acting as Saime's chaperone. If her family had been astonished by the speed of events, the wedding came as an even greater shock for my parents, who were dismayed to learn that we were planning a secular ceremony. Aunty Marion was more open-minded, but even she wrote that 'your sudden romantic flight surpassed anything I had imagined'. After I had phoned from Cambridge to confirm the date of the wedding, Father replied: 'Mother seems a little sad that you have decided on a register office,' adding in his own hand 'unless followed by a religious ceremony.' There was scarcely a hint that he thought the marriage unwise, apart from the precipitation. But many years later my brother Jonathan revealed that this wedding had caused the greatest family row ever witnessed. Our parents had just decided *not* to attend when Marion announced that she was certainly going, at which the sparks began to fly. In the event, Mother, Marion and my sister Margaret travelled to Cambridge together, while Jonathan stayed at home with Father. Writing to congratulate us on our wedding day, Jonathan alluded to the turmoil in coded terms, as if it formed one of the farcical plots of P. G. Wodehouse:

> Recent events have left me rather breathless. Bertie Wooster would have sailed to Turkey to escape Aunt Agatha, rather than flown to a future wife. Wodehouse would have arranged the wedding differently, too, with the bride marrying someone else, who is kidnapped by a third party just before the act, leaving the way clear for the passing hero, hot in pursuit of an eighteenth-century cow-creamer, to step into the vacant space in the registry office.

At Shire Hall that day there almost was a vacant space at the registry office. Driving to the ceremony with my mother, I took the wrong turning in Jesus Lane and we found ourselves stranded on the banks of the Cam. As the bride waited the best man, Gavin Wraith, gallantly offered to step into my shoes. The ceremony was more solemn than we expected, involving lifelong vows. As we sat down for the wedding breakfast at the Garden House Hotel, we would have been thirteen around the table, had not our good angel Farhad Faisal arrived to complete the circle.

Our honeymoon was the more delightful for being delayed. That summer we joined a house-party organized by Mary Wraith at a rambling estate overlooking Lake Windermere. While she, her son Gavin and a group of other friends stayed in the spacious bungalow, Saime and I had a tiny garden pavilion to ourselves. We could slip down to the water for a swim before breakfast or spend an afternoon rowing on the lake, before joining the party for a communal supper. Marriage was experienced, not as a union between solitary individuals, but as the core of ever-widening relationships.

The following year we enjoyed a second honeymoon in Turkey. As we explored the remoter regions of Anatolia, I was struck by the contrast between city and countryside. While Islamic tradition required the wearing of the veil, the emancipated young women with whom we holidayed at Erdek on the Sea of Marmara relaxed in bikinis. And as we explored the cliff-top paths, guided by local lads, we came upon an ancient plane tree reputed to have magical powers. It was festooned with scraps of fabric, inscribed with prayers (I secretly wished for children).

We had to forget the bikinis when we visited the tobacco-growing region around Aydin in the south-west. There we saw women swathed from head to toe, working in the fields with their babies slung on their backs, while the landowners, including Saime's uncle Halil Goral, operated the irrigation system. Camels were a common sight, tractors a rarity. We were also introduced to a cousin named Muharem Amca, a burly farmer with a house overlooking the sea. We were nervous when we heard that he had served ten years for shooting one of his wife's admirers, but he welcomed us with quantities of fish and raki. Later he showed us the moon rising over the sea with a grandiose gesture, like a spectacle laid on for our benefit, and recited poems of his own composition. It seemed idyllic, but driving back we saw lanterns flickering in the fields. Tobacco is best picked at night when the leaves are cool and moist, and the peasants were working while the landowners serenaded the moon.

There was no way of bridging the socio-economic divide. Back in Ankara with Saime's parents, I reflected on the contradictions embodied in Atatürk's Mausoleum, which could be seen from their balcony. It was Turkey's tragedy that only a man as ruthless as Atatürk could enforce much needed reforms. Being necessarily hard in politics, he could not set an example of gentleness in private life. But an alternative vision was offered by a slim volume of poetry. In April 1968, to mark our second wedding anniversary, Saime presented me with the *Selected Poems* of Nazım Hikmet, translated by Taner Baybars. Repeatedly imprisoned for his communist writings, Hikmet explored the conflicts of the twentieth century as incisively as any political analyst. His poems blend love with politics, national pride with the critique of imperialism. For Hikmet, the Kemalist reforms did not go far enough. The injustices of the capitalist system called for more radical remedies.

CHAPTER TEN

Cultural Revolutions

Cambridge was reassuringly calm and by January 1968 my dissertation was complete. Reading Kraus with English eyes, I drew from his writings a defiant hope, citing Matthew Arnold. 'We have not won our political battles,' Arnold writes in *Culture and Anarchy*, 'but we have told silently upon the mind of the country and kept up our communications with the future.' Just as I was starting to revise my work for publication we were overtaken by events. Unrest in the universities was increasing, led by students at Berkeley California. They drew their inspiration from the Civil Rights movement, but the assassination of Martin Luther King exposed the hollowness of the American dream. The failure of the US Government to put its house in order was compounded by its policies overseas. Fear of Soviet expansion led the Pentagon to support dictatorial regimes, and the CIA was implicated in the capture and execution of the Latin American revolutionary Ernesto (Che) Guevara. Meanwhile in Vietnam, American conscripts were wiping out whole villages suspected of harbouring communists. But in January 1968 the Vietcong launched their Tet Offensive, exposing the fault lines of US strategy. Even in Britain the media were becoming more critical, with reports on prime-time television that stoked public outrage. On 17 March Saime and I joined a massive anti-war demonstration outside the US embassy in Grosvenor Square.

SELF-REFLECTION AND THE STUDENT REVOLT

In European universities, too, there was growing unrest. Why was Washington supporting the Greek junta, which had seized power in April 1967? As socialists we supported the reforms of Aleksander Dubček in Czechoslovakia and were horrified when the tanks rolled into Prague in August 1968. Sympathy for friends behind the Iron Curtain prompted us to undertake a tour of Central Europe the following summer to see things for ourselves. Our impressions of the German Democratic Republic were rather favourable, and in Weimar we made friends with a school-teacher and her family who had clearly made their peace with the regime. However, a visit to Prague left us under no illusion about the miseries of Soviet domination. Although we were by no means blind to the crimes of communism, our primary concern was with the failings of western democracy. With governments on both sides of the Iron Curtain deeply compromised, who would be the agents of renewal?

For a few breathless months we seemed to have found the answer – the international student movement. Historians tend to foreground the Paris events of May 1968, but for me the starting pistol had been fired the previous year in West Berlin. Students were demonstrating against the Shah of Iran as an agent of American policy in the Middle East, and as the protests ran out of control, a young Christian pacifist named Benno Ohnesorg was gunned down by the police. His death was rendered more poignant by the resonance of his name, which translates as 'without a care'. We *did* care, and there was a wave of international sympathy accompanied by further demonstrations.

In Germany there was a dramatic generational divide. The Federal Republic was envied for its social market economy, but prosperity had been achieved at a cost – a failure to acknowledge the crimes of fascism and bring those responsible to justice. A wall of silence separated parents from their children, for many of those in leading positions were concealing the fascist enthusiasms of their youth. Although the Frankfurt Auschwitz Trials of 1964–5 had exposed the system of slave labour and genocide, former Nazis remained in denial. This resulted in an unresolved national trauma, documented by Alexander and Margarete Mitscherlich in their study *Die Unfähigkeit zu trauern* (The Inability to Mourn). The older generation were unable to reconcile the crimes of Nazism with the memory of the leader they had loved. Now there was a spectacular return of the repressed, as the young reacted against the complacent materialism of their authoritarian elders.

These historically grounded developments seemed to me more instructive than the meteoric events in France. The protests at the new university in Nanterre began as localized disputes, but when the demonstrations spread to the Sorbonne, the police overreacted, provoking a wave of sympathy with the students. Led by Daniel Cohn-Bendit, the militants showed energy and imagination, forming alliances with industrial workers who felt exploited and underpaid. Within weeks the protests escalated into a mass movement that challenged the authority of President De Gaulle and his prime minister, Georges Pompidou. By mid-May 1968, the streets of Paris were the scene of pitched battles between baton-wielding riot police and students building barricades, while strikers in the industrial suburbs were paralyzing production.

It was riveting to watch the televised scenes from Paris. When a national strike disrupted essential public services, including hospitals, railways and television programmes, De Gaulle panicked, taking flight to a French military base in south-west Germany. Confronted by students chanting revolutionary slogans on the streets and workers occupying their factories, the ruling class appeared to have lost control. Those at the vortex of the Paris events felt they were experiencing a momentous transformation, but to sceptical observers they seemed rebels without a cause, for the solidarity generated by dreams of a classless society soon evaporated. Lacking a unifying political theory, the leftist factions made a virtue of spontaneity, but slogans like 'imagination takes power' owed more to the exuberance of youth than to any tangible objective. There were only tenuous links between student activism and the old-style communism of the French trade unions. While industrial workers wanted wage awards to raise their standard of living, students from middle-class backgrounds were challenging the whole culture of consumerism. At the end of May the Gaullists organized a massive counter-demonstration, flooding the streets of Paris with their supporters, and De Gaulle reclaimed the initiative by calling a general election. Within a few weeks the strikes had been contained through shrewd political concessions and generous wage awards. The communists claimed credit for these successes, but if the left hoped to make significant gains in the elections on 30 June, they were rapidly disabused. The results confirmed the primacy of the party politics, returning the Gaullists to power. Educationally, the most enduring achievement was the creation of a new university at Vincennes, set up in response to long-standing grievances.

The conflicts in Germany proved harder to contain. The grand coalition between the Christian Democrats and the Social Democrats, formed in December 1966 under the arch-conservative Kurt Georg Kiesinger, was stifling debate in the Bundestag, leading to the emergence of an extra-parliamentary opposition. As a young man Kiesinger had joined the Nazi Party, which provoked protests from authors like Karl Jaspers and Heinrich Böll, as well as student leaders. Former Nazis were now called to account by a younger generation which discovered that German institutions rested on flawed foundations. The universities, like the churches, had deeply compromised themselves in the Nazi period, and higher education remained autocratic even in the supposedly egalitarian Federal Republic. There were violent demonstrations during the late 1960s in many university towns, led by the Socialist Students Federation. Theirs was an alternative Marxism, driven by a pervasive sense of the oppressiveness of capitalism and the ideological distortions of the Cold War. It was hard to keep track of the proliferation of anarchist groups, although my friend Hans Keith, who had joined us at Caius as a Lector, published a hair-raising account of their excesses in the *Cambridge Review*.

The issues came into focus through the stance of two key figures – the rebellious Rudi Dutschke and the reflective Jürgen Habermas. Having grown up in East Germany as a member of the student Christian movement, Dutschke was well aware of the failings of communism. His research focused on the emancipatory potential of early Marxism, as interpreted by Georg Lukács. Now, at the Free University in Berlin, Dutschke identified parliamentary democracy as the agent of oppressive authority. This challenge might have been contained, had the older generation come up with honest answers and enlightened reforms. Instead, there was a crack-down on student militancy, which provoked further confrontations. Readers of *Der Spiegel* could follow developments week-by-week. The death of Ohnesorg had polarized opinion, and on 10 July 1967 Dutschke set out his programme in an interview: the 'politicization of the university' in order to expose an authoritarian system. His position was again highlighted on 4 March 1968 in a wide-ranging report entitled 'Revolution in Germany'. Disruptive activity at universities, the weakest link in the system, was in his view the first step towards a more fundamental transformation. However, Dutschke was opposed to violence. In a democratic society the assassination of leading politicians would be self-defeating, for they were interchangeable 'character masks'. This concept, derived from *Das Kapital*, defined them merely as ciphers in a system of production that would continue unaffected by their loss.

During the Easter 1968 demonstrations against emergency legislation there were clashes with the police, leading in Munich to two fatalities. As the students continued their protests, the popular *Bild Zeitung*, owned by Axel Springer, began to demonize Rudi Dutschke. This stoked a climate of hysteria, and in April 1968 Dutschke was shot in the head by a maverick anti-communist, narrowly escaping with his life. The man who pulled the trigger was a loner named Josef Bachmann, who had a passion for pictures of Hitler, but for Heinrich Böll and Günther Grass the right-wing press was mainly to blame. During the ensuing panic, intensified by the news from Paris, it was difficult to keep a cool head, but it seemed to me that Jürgen Habermas struck the best balance. For a number of years he had campaigned for university reform and he welcomed the protests that followed the death of Ohnesorg while warning against the use of force. Borrowing from Max Weber's sociology of knowledge, he defined the essential task as self-reflection, which he contrasted with irrational activism. Both teachers and students should reflect more critically on their role in the production of knowledge. Habermas set out his position most clearly in the *Frankfurter Rundschau* on 5 June 1968 under the title 'Die Scheinrevolution und ihre Kinder' (The Phoney Revolution and its Children). While praising the students for developing imaginative forms of protest, he condemned those who believed they were leading a revolution.

Habermas brought a philosophically schooled intelligence to bear on contemporary problems. His background, as a follower of the Frankfurt School, led him to place student agitation in a constructive perspective. His articles and speeches linked proposals for reform with searching reflections on the German past. Collected and published early in 1969 under the title *Protestbewegung und Hochschulreform* (Protest Movement and University Reform), they stimulated me to reflect on my own function. While the consensus at Cambridge was that we should introduce our students to canonical literature, the turmoil prompted me to develop a course on Political Thought, connecting the philosophy of Hegel and Marx with the dynamics of the modern world. Even more topical was a course on Culture and Society in Germany since 1945, which discussed Theodor Adorno and Herbert Marcuse, Jürgen Habermas, Ralph Dahrendorf and Hans Magnus Enzensberger. This included a topic on the Critical University, designed to encourage students to reflect on their own position, with a reading list that included Dutschke's *Rebellion der Studenten*.

REVERBERATIONS IN CAMBRIDGE

While American protests were fuelled by the fear of being drafted, student militancy in Britain was more restrained. Herbert Marcuse, the theoretician of the student revolt, defined western democracy as a system of repressive toleration. Recognizing the element of truth of this dictum, we welcomed a home-grown cultural revolution that was reducing the authority of the state. The ending of conscription meant that our lives were no longer at the mercy of sadistic sergeant-majors. This was followed by a raft of legislation promoted by the reforming Home Secretary, Roy Jenkins. Under the Labour government of 1966–70 capital punishment was abolished, homosexuality decriminalized, abortion liberalized, theatre censorship ended, divorce procedures simplified and immigration controls relaxed. The Race Relations Act banned discrimination in key areas of public life, while a pioneering Disabled Persons Bill was piloted through Parliament by Alfred Morris, Labour member for Manchester Wythenshawe.

In this liberal climate British students felt less inclined than their confrères to take to the barricades – the sectarian violence in Northern Ireland showed that armed struggle provoked a backlash. The Labour government may have left economic problems unresolved, bringing few benefits to manual workers in declining industries; but there were palpable gains for graduates from the thriving new universities and art colleges. By contrast with the impersonal campuses on the continent, our students, supported by generous grants, enjoyed a tutorial system that gave individual access to their teachers, while the outreach of higher education was extended by the success of another Labour Party pipedream, the launching of the Open University.

Saime and I had left-wing sympathies, but instead of joining the Socialist Society we created a more intimate forum, holding an Open House every Friday evening during Full Term, when students were encouraged to drop in for a drink. Saime would be the centre of attention, radiating warmth and wisdom, while I poured the beer. Unlike other colleagues in their thirties, we were not distracted by the demands of children. Moreover, our terrace house in Hertford Street was a short walk from the city centre, making it easy to drop in on impulse. The formula worked so well that our Open House continued intermittently for seven years.

On a good evening, a cluster of precocious talents would cram our tiny front room. The philosophically inclined Nicholas Boyle would arrive from Magdalene with his quicksilver friend Colin Imber. While Paul Connerton held forth on Marxist aesthetics, Margot Waddell would respond with a defence of Victorian poetry. Richard Overy might arrive, flushed from scoring at football, only to find his success interpreted by Naomi Segal in Freudian terms. Listening intently would be the lanky John Nicholson, eager to pick up ideas for his subversive broadsheet, *THE 1/- PAPER*. As Peter Hutchinson sang the praises of Newcastle Brown Ale, Leslie Hill would insist on the superiority of Yorkshire Bitter. Origins proved as varied as ideas: Raphael Salkie might recall his childhood on a kibbutz, Miguel Bodea his schooldays in Brazil. It was fascinating to observe the flow of ideas, not least for graduate students like Hugh Salvesen and John Halliday, who were studying the creative alliances of Karl Kraus.

If there was a lull in the conversation, we might ask what career they had in mind. Predicting professions became a parlour game: not tinker, tailor, soldier, sailor, but historian, sociologist, diplomat, analyst. An increasingly mobile world made career paths unpredictable. Did someone already dream of becoming biographer of Goethe, chronicler of the international labour movement, professor of linguistics, or director of a London research institute? Could one predict the future psychoanalyst, historian of Nazi Germany, headmaster of a Scottish academy, or ambassador to Peru? Who would be drawn to French modernism, who to the literature of the German Democratic Republic, who to the history of the Ottoman navy, who to the theory of social memory? The common factor was an interest in way-out ideas, generated by the counter-culture.

In Cambridge the concept of cultural revolution was being redefined by Raymond Williams. His assessment of Matthew Arnold, in *Culture and*

Society 1780–1950, highlighted the interactions between cultural advance and social reform, while his take on Marxism in the sequel, *The Long Revolution*, outlined a gradualist alternative, foregrounding the role of communications within a 'deeper cultural revolution'. My own task was to reconcile English gradualism with German dialectics. My first foray into this field was an article on University Studies and Critical Consciousness published in November 1969 in *Granta*, a student magazine that attracted contributions from contemporaries like Clive James, David Hare and Jeremy Prynne. Reviewing a cluster of publications about university politics, I asked whether intellectual rigour could be squared with revolutionary activism, Max Weber with Rosa Luxemburg. The student revolt challenged politically illiterate thinking, using issues like the visit of the Shah of Iran to Berlin to refute the fairy-tale images of the Middle East purveyed by the right-wing press. I then contrasted the stance of the militants with that of their most discriminating critic:

> For Habermas, the critical functions of the university take gradual forms, since they depend on a scientific rigour which cannot be sacrificed to propagandistic aims. For the more radical German left, the situation, seen as one of political repression at home and economic exploitation in the third world, demands the development of a politically activist university.

Drawing an analogy with Arnold's *Culture and Anarchy*, I concluded that it was no longer possible to ignore the contrast between the intellectual pursuits of the universities and the crushing impoverishment of the third world.

My tone became more urgent in an article entitled Intellectuals and Mandarins, published in *Granta* the following February. Citing Noam Chomsky's critique of imperialism, *American Power and the New Mandarins*, I launched a tirade against the failure of the British government to condemn American atrocities in Vietnam, such as the My Lai massacre. They were not an aberration, I insisted, but formed part of the 'general pattern of American strategy'. This claim was backed by quotations from Chomsky, stigmatizing the brutality of the war and condemning its sycophantic supporters. The new mandarin, he declared, 'is not a breast-beating superpatriot who wants America to rule the world, but a scholarly and reasonable man'. Such people are the 'terror of our age' because they justify atrocities in the language of liberalism. When they claim that the United States is defending the 'open society', they mean 'a society which remains open to American economic penetration and political control'. Against this, I set Chomsky's model of intellectual responsibility: 'For a privileged minority, democracy provides the leisure, the facilities and the training to seek the truth lying behind the veil of distortion and misrepresentation, ideology and class interest, through which the events of current history are presented to us.' In England too, I concluded, the call must not go unheard.

None of this would have sounded remarkable at one of the new universities, where radical attitudes were widely shared. Students at Essex defied their Vice-Chancellor as they struggled to create their own form of Free University, while at Sussex too there were serious disruptions. We were kept informed by our friend Brian Easlea, whose teaching now focused on the political impact of the sciences, highlighting their complicity with various forms of oppression. He was surprised to find that my ideas had also taken a radical turn. 'You promised to be faithful to Saime,' he said, 'and you've fallen in love with Rosa Luxemburg!'

Cambridge remained relatively immune to student radicalism. The university was fortunate in having Sir Eric Ashby as Vice Chancellor during the years 1967–69. Ashby was an even-handed administrator as well as a pioneering environmental scientist. He conceded the case for greater student participation in *Masters and Scholars: Reflections on the Rights and Responsibilities of Students* (1970), calling attention to the moral vacuum at the heart of modern education. The university can teach you to build a cathedral or an atomic bomb, he observed, but it doesn't tell you which to choose! This phrase imprinted itself on my mind, for Cambridge colleagues were working on the military applications of lasers.

A further restraining influence was the college system, which frustrated the emergence of a militant student union. At Caius, under Needham's leadership, joint committees were created to give students a greater say in college affairs. However, things were less peaceful in the Old Schools, seat of the University Administration. In January 1969 a group of students occupied the East Room in solidarity with protestors at the London School of Economics (LSE). This attracted support from the economist Joan Robinson, who improvised a seminar on political spontaneity. The sit-in fizzled out after a couple of days, partly due to resolute action by Charles Goodhart, the Proctor nominated by Caius. Having spent several years in a prisoner-of-war camp, he had the stamina to outlast any student occupation, spending two nights sleeping on a bench with his head resting on University Regulations. Events at the LSE had more serious consequences as two lecturers were dismissed for supporting the occupations, Robin Blackburn and Nicholas Bateson. The campaign for their reinstatement was supported by a petition signed by 67 members of the Tawney Group in Cambridge, an informal association of socialist academics. My name appeared alongside those of left-wingers like Elias Bredsdorff and Raymond Williams when the petition was published on 25 April in *THE 1/- PAPER*.

The following year Cambridge witnessed a riot provoked by the military dictatorship in Athens. In February 1970, in an effort to repair its tarnished image, the Greek National Tourist Office sponsored a Greek Week in Cambridge, culminating in a dinner at the Garden House Hotel. To mark this event, the *Cambridge Evening News* produced an eight-page advertising supplement publicizing holidays in Greece. Given the brutal treatment of political prisoners, this was seen as a shameless provocation. Students were also incensed by the support given to the Junta by the Master of Jesus College, Denis Page, Regius Professor of Greek. On Friday 13 February, as the guests were settling down to dinner, about five hundred demonstrators gathered outside the hotel, thronging the narrow approaches and spilling out into the garden. The demo was to be addressed by Marcus Dragoumis, an exiled Greek parliamentarian, but the loudspeaker set up in a college room overlooking the hotel was cut off. The mood of the demonstrators changed when someone inside the hotel began drenching them with a hosepipe. Windows were smashed and several people injured including Goodhart, who was patrolling in proctorial robes. A peaceful demo had turned into an unholy riot, which was only brought to an end when police reinforcements arrived.

That week-end the conservative press had a field day. 'Into a Cambridge hotel where diners are quietly enjoying Greek food storms a destructive mob of student demonstrators,' wrote the *Sunday Express*, going on to draw the political conclusions: 'What is the Government doing to stop them? Roll on the day when the angry electorate throws it out – and a Tory administration gets down to the urgent and vital job of restoring Law and Order.' Law and order were restored with a vengeance when the case came to court in June. This time the role of the Proctors was more controversial. Having rubbed shoulders with student leaders during the peaceful occupation of the Old Schools, Dr Goodhart knew many of them by name. Now he and the Senior Proctor, Dr Fairest, identified those they saw as ringleaders. A total of nineteen demonstrators, including members of the Socialist Society, were charged with riotous assembly. In some cases the evidence was so flimsy that the jury decided to acquit, but eight students were sent to prison for up to eighteen months.

Addressing those convicted, Mr Justice Melford Stevenson said the sentences would have been heavier, had they not been exposed to the 'evil influence of some senior members of the University'. It was not simply unruly students who were stigmatized. The sentences were upheld by the Appeal Court, which declared that 'any person who actively encouraged or promoted an unlawful assembly, whether by words, signs or actions, was guilty of an offence'. Thus even non-violent participation in a demonstration could constitute a crime. Although we were abroad at the time, Saime and I sensed that the affair had been inflated by hostile journalists and vindictive judges. Among those imprisoned was our Brazilian friend

Miguel Bodea, but Raymond Williams visited the prison to coach him through his exams. Melford Stevenson had ordered that Miguel should be deported on release, but a petition was organized on his behalf and the Appeal Court quashed the deportation order.

Cambridge reverted to its habitual calm, which had its compensations. Seeking a haven in which to recover from his injuries, Rudi Dutschke applied for admission as a graduate student. The German student leader, who had been allowed into Britain for medical treatment by a Labour Home Secretary, now proposed to write a thesis on theories of revolution. His studies were supported by a Swiss foundation, and he had given an undertaking not to engage in political activity. While Rudi, his American wife Gretchen and their two small children lived in a London commune, their Marxism took a new turn. That 'the educators themselves have to be educated' became a hands-on involvement with his son Hosea and his baby daughter Polly.

At the same time Dutschke was finalizing his research proposal on Georg Lukács. At Oxford, he met a sceptical response, but in Cambridge he was received more favourably. After his proposal was approved by Raymond Williams and Joan Robinson, he was befriended by a Fellow of King's College named Bob Young. Once accepted, there was a chance that

"Off you go laddie – you promised to keep out of politics and here you are in the middle of a great row again!"

Rudi Dutschke being expelled by Reginald Maudling (cartoon by Garland, 1970)

Dutschke's health could be stabilized by means of regular medication and a rewarding research project. But just as the family were settling into their flat at Clare Hall, they were plunged into further controversy.

In July 1970, against all predictions, Harold Wilson's Labour government had been defeated at the general election. There was a late swing towards the Conservatives in the Midlands, attributed by some commentators to the appeal of Enoch Powell's anti-immigration stance, and unease about the student revolt may have tipped the balance. Flushed by their unexpected victory, Edward Heath's incoming Tory administration decided to teach those students a lesson, so Home Secretary Reginald Maudling announced that Dutschke would be deported. This provoked a passionate debate, mostly critical of the government. *The Times* led the way with an editorial describing the Home Secretary's action as 'timorous, insular and morally wrong'. The cartoonists also had a field-day, mocking Maudling for creating the political upheaval he claimed to be preventing. 'Off you go laddie – you promised to keep out of politics and here you are in the middle of a great row again!' was the caption of a cartoon by Garland in the *Daily Telegraph* of 17 September.

Since there was no suggestion that national security was threatened, the letters that filled the correspondence columns constituted a defence of intellectual freedom. Unlike the manoeuvres of the Home Office, the admissions procedures at Cambridge had been scrupulous. Dutschke had been interviewed, his testimonials assessed and his published writings scrutinized before his application was approved by the Board of Graduate Studies. While the academic case was convincing, the political objections to Dutschke's presence were so dubious that Maudling became a laughing stock. His first move, in a letter to the Labour MP Michael Foot, was to claim that it was 'wrong in principle that people who come to this country should do so on the basis that they refrain from any activities which are lawful for the ordinary citizen'. In plain English, this meant that Dutschke was to be deported because the conditions imposed on him were unfair. But when Dutschke appealed, Maudling suddenly claimed that Dutschke did threaten national security, after all. The appeal proceedings would therefore have to be held in secret. Before such a tribunal, Dutschke had no chance, for the evidence to justify his expulsion was not disclosed. Among the protests by Cambridge academics was one that put the issue plainly:

> As university teachers we are concerned to preserve the necessary freedom to take part in the study and discussion and expression of opinion on all matters, political and otherwise, however controversial. We further regard it as part of our duties to examine all opinions and to encourage our students to do so, even and perhaps especially when we disagree with them.

This statement appeared in the *Cambridge Review* on 29 January 1971. It was gratifying to find my Head of Department, Leonard Forster, among the signatories.

That term my course on Theories of Culture and Society in Germany was due to be repeated. Dutschke was still in Cambridge, having been granted a temporary extension to enable him to find another haven, so I wrote to Clare Hall inviting him to participate. When we met at the Modern Languages Faculty, Dutschke impressed us by his engaging personality and intellectual sophistication. After I had outlined his conception of a 'critical university', the man himself took the floor. Speaking in German, he gave a lucid exposition of his own position of 'reflektierter Aktivismus', midway between the extremes of pure 'Selbstreflexion', devoid of political purpose, and unconsidered 'Aktivismus', designed to cause disruption. In the past, he conceded, he had allowed himself illusions about what could be achieved. Now he was committed to what, adapting a phrase from Chairman Mao, he called 'the long march through the institutions'. He looked hopefully towards the founding of new left-wing universities, such as that at Bremen. And the change of government in Germany – Willy Brandt had taken over as Chancellor in October 1969 at the head of a centre-left coalition – gave him grounds for cautious optimism.

The students attending my course could hardly have asked for a clearer exposition. They included Miguel Bodea, now released from prison, who was researching the Labour movement in Brazil. But even Miguel was baffled when Dutschke concluded his presentation by invoking the dialectic of Master and Servant ('Herr und Knecht') from Hegel's *Phenomenology of Spirit*. Applying this paradigm to Habermas, he suggested that the sociologist was 'following the path of the Master, not the far more complicated path of the Servant'. At one level this was clear enough, implying that intellectuals should identify with the oppressed. But Dutschke lost his audience by repeatedly invoking the concept of 'Verfügung' to elucidate the dualism. What did this really mean? The decrees imposed from above by the ruling class, or the empowerment from below of those who are oppressed? We reached the end of the seminar with mysteries still to be resolved.

Dutschke represented a humanistic form of Marxism with Hegelian undertones. His concept of the 'long march' chimed with my own efforts to reconcile dialectics with gradualism. After leaving Britain he found sanctuary at the University of Aarhus, but the gunshot wounds had left him susceptible to epileptic fits, which were to cause his premature death. From his detached position in Denmark, Dutschke continued to contribute to German cultural politics, sympathizing with the burgeoning Green movement, but the younger generation of German radicals lacked his wisdom. A militant faction was emerging that saw only one way to destabilize the capitalist system – political assassination.

BETWEEN EAST AND WEST

Even more unstable was the situation in the other region that claimed my loyalty – republican Turkey. From autumn 1969 onwards Saime spent a year teaching at Middle East Technical University, so when Cambridge granted me six months of study leave, I decided to join her. This was a calculated risk, for my appointment as an Assistant Lecturer was to end in September 1970, after which I might be unemployed. Prospects would have improved if I'd spent my leave in the University Library, but the opportunity to study Turkish developments at first hand was too good to miss. Discussing political theory in Cambridge would be child's play compared with teaching students caught up in the conflict between Islam and modernity.

Between East and West is the title of one of Nazım Hikmet's most challenging poems. During the train journey via Vienna my imagination travelled from the decaying Ottoman Empire through to the poet's dreams of social equality and emotional liberation. Even in translation the sweep of his imagination was impressive:

'Opium!
Submission!
Kismet!
Latticework, caravanserai
fountains . . .
women with henna-stained noses
working their looms with their feet.
In the wind, green-turbaned imams
        calling people to prayer;'
This is the Orient the French poet sees.

The poet in question is Pierre Loti, castigated for romanticizing the Orient. Against those seductive images Hikmet sets the brutal realities of life in Anatolia, 'the land where hunger itself / perishes with famine!'

Hikmet's poetry comes as a shock for those who picture the Islamic world through the lens of orientalism. The book that had coloured my image of the East was the *Rubayiat of Omar Khayyam* in Fitzgerald's haunting translation: 'A flask of Wine, a Book of Verse – and Thou / beside me singing in the Wilderness.' Saime's beauty had fulfilled that dream, but her mind was that of a modernizer. Where the *Rubayiat* ends on a fatalistic note, Hikmet celebrates the forthcoming liberation of the East. His admirers included Ibrahim Balaban, who had shared a cell with the poet in Bursa Prison. It was Hikmet who had inspired the untutored peasant boy to take up painting, and now Balaban was one of the most successful Turkish artists. It was thus with great excitement that I learnt from Saime, when she met me at Sirkeci Station, that Balaban had opened a new exhibition.

The following day our friend Mehmet Şenel, now an assistant at the Academy of Arts, introduced us to Balaban and showed us around the exhibition, which included a sequence of paintings of oxen harnessed to the plough. At one level, as the artist explained, these pictures dramatized the backwardness of Turkish agriculture and the oppression of the rural population. But the most eye-catching painting depicted a yoke of oxen struggling in opposite directions, hinting to my eyes at something more archetypal – the eternal Yin and Yang. There could hardly have been a more expressive symbol for our excitement at being reunited, and we longed to purchase the picture. This would have been impossible, given Saime's modest salary, had Balaban not agreed to accept payment in monthly instalments. As a socialist he preferred to sell to us, rather than to wealthy collectors.

Within a few weeks Saime and I had found a flat in a quiet suburb of Ankara. From our balcony we could watch cows grazing on open fields where crumbling cottages resisted the encroaching city. Balaban's painting took pride of place on the wall of the lounge, while in the study we hung a poster depicting a flaming torch and inscribed with Hikmet's incandescent lines: 'If we don't burn, / How will the darkness turn to light?' Duly inspired, I set up my typewriter, but it was not easy to concentrate on *Die Fackel* when the flaming torch on the wall proclaimed more urgent priorities.

Driving together to Middle East Technical University, we were soon aware of the tensions. What impressed me most was the number of women studying scientific subjects, and it was fascinating to visit the laboratory where Saime's sister Yeter was setting up equipment for the radio-carbon dating of archaeological materials. Progress was being made towards removing gender barriers and creating a more egalitarian society. The programme of Westernization included rights for woman, public ownership of major industries, social equality, organized trade unions and secularized education. The alternative as depicted by the modernizers was darkest reaction: the regression to a nation of feudal landlords, superstitious Imams and ignorant peasants, with unschooled women confined to domestic roles.

There were political posters everywhere and mass meetings in the main lecture theatres, but the student revolt in Turkey had a distinctive trajectory. Activists drew inspiration from that dramatic moment in April 1960 when a young man named Turan Emeksiz was shot dead by the security forces outside the gates of the University of Istanbul. That incident had helped to provoke the military coup of 27 May which deposed Adnan Menderes, sentenced him and two of his ministers to death, and introduced a more liberal constitution. The success of the protests after the

shooting of Emeksiz created the impression that society could be transformed by student militants, but by 1970 the conflicts on campus had
become far more ideological. Student activism was split three ways. The
Marxists, who followed the international model for student protest, found
themselves confronted by both Nationalists and Islamists, and the ensuing
battles involved guns and kidnappings.

That spring, Saime and I were taken on a tour of Parliament by her
uncle, Halil Goral, a Senator for the Republican People's Party. Although
impressed by the elegantly functional building, we sensed the instability
of the party system. Each of the main factions had a charismatic leader.
The veteran statesman Ismet Inönü had recently retired as chairman of the
Republican Peoples Party, to be succeeded by the more radical Bülent
Ecevit, a poet as well as a politician. Ecevit's principal adversary was the
Prime Minister, Süleyman Demirel, chairman of the Justice Party. Further
to the right was Necmettin Erbakan, leader of the Islamist Salvation Party,
while on the far right Alpaslan Türkeş, a former army officer, led the
proto-fascist National Party. These were men with formidable energy, but
their dogmatic convictions led to bitter confrontations, including fistfights
in the debating chamber.

Later that year we had a political encounter across the generations.
To one of our parties we had invited Saime's head of department, Erdal
Inönü. Invited back, we were astonished to find his father Ismet Inönü
sitting quietly in a corner. This frail figure embodied seventy years of
Turkish history. After serving as an officer in the Ottoman army during
the First World War, he had become Atatürk's second-in-command during the war of independence. Once the invading armies had been driven
out of Anatolia, it was Ismet who represented Turkey at the Lausanne
Conference of 1923. Later, as President during the Second World War,
his policy of cautious neutrality saved the country from disaster.
Although now in his eighties, he impressed us by his knowledge of
current affairs, including a shrewd assessment of Edward Heath's Conservative Party.

Ismet Inönü was exceptional in bringing the wisdom of past to bear on
the challenges of the future. The problem for younger politicians was the
lack of a shared public memory. Modern Turks lived in denial of their
multicultural heritage, but as we explored Anatolia we discovered traces
of dispersed minorities and sunken civilizations. The Hittite fortifications
at Boğazkale were even more impressive than the ruins of Troy. At Ephesus
we found ancient Roman libraries and early Christian churches standing
side by side, as the cult of Aphrodite merged with that of the Virgin Mary.
Travelling with Saime's parents to visit relatives near Silifke, the town
where she was born, we stumbled on a row of beautifully carved wooden
houses. These, we were told, had once housed a community of Armenians.
Most extraordinary of all were the cave dwellings of Cappadocia, where

Greek monks had carved chapels into the soft volcanic rock. The colourful frescoes depicting biblical scenes had survived since the tenth century, for the inhabitants of that region had been largely Greek until the exchange of populations in 1923.

From discussions with friends from Paris we had heard about the dilemma of another minority – the Kurdish population of the East. The Kurdish language was not taught in schools, for Kemalist ideology defined everyone born within the national boundaries as a Turk. Full of curiosity, we set out on an expedition to the Kurdish region of Van, in the company of our American friends Arthur and Judy Snoke. Our first stop was Malatya, the town in eastern Anatolia where Saime had spent her childhood. Her family home had disappeared, but we were fascinated to find the water-mill still working, grinding corn just as it had thirty years earlier when she was driving a horse-drawn cart. Before we could continue our journey, Judy went down with appendicitis and had to be rushed to hospital. She soon recovered after delicate keyhole surgery, but we never reached the Kurdish region.

I longed to learn more about the expulsion of the Greeks, the oppression of the Kurds and the massacre of the Armenians, but for most people these problems did not exist – or had never even occurred! No wonder it was proving difficult to construct a national narrative both coherent and inclusive. Sharing Saime's commitment to modernization, I was sensitive to the lure of the past. Modern trucks were thundering along the highways, but in villages without electricity you could still hear the voice of the muezzin calling the faithful to prayer. It wasn't only my feelings that were divided, for the whole country was caught between extremes. Should women be scientists working with chemicals in the lab or peasants fetching water the well?

Students might well have benefited from seminars on their own history. Instead, I was invited to teach European history of ideas, based on *The Western Intellectual Tradition* by J. Bronowski and Bruce Mazlish. We began with the Reformation and the Scientific Revolution, adding topics on Marx, Darwin and Nietzsche, Freud, the Socialist International and the rise of Nazism. This option attracted over thirty students, mostly engineers, to a class that evolved into a cross-cultural dialogue. The topic they found most difficult was the impact of Martin Luther, for Islam had never known a modernizing movement comparable to the Reformation. 'Is it like the schism between Sunnis and Shiites?' they asked. But that age-old dispute over the heritage of the Prophet lacked the modernizing dynamic that made Luther into a catalyst for social change. 'Now I understand why the Islamic nations stagnated,' one of the brightest students observed. After assessing their written work, I noted in my diary (3 August 1970):

They know more about Robert Owen, Adam Smith, Johann Kepler, Copernicus, Hobbes and Locke than I myself did six months ago! And what they know is worth knowing: principles of empirical scientific method, Luther's challenge to intellectual authority, the theory of the economic and social value of capitalist self-interest, critique of the said theory (by Marx) and the revision of that critique. I was lucky to teach such able students. They were lucky to be taught by someone who can suggest ways to digest their favourite stimulant, Marxism.

The militants on all sides were against the prevailing system, denouncing Demirel for policies that favoured entrepreneurs, and it was scary to sit among a vast audience chanting revolutionary songs, for the hysteria threatened to run out of control.

Among Saime's colleagues there were heated debates about the role of universities in the forthcoming struggle. The Turkish Constitution of 1961 was under threat, and one week-end we were urged to join a demonstration. 'Of course I support the Constitution,' observed a liberal colleague. 'Do I need to demonstrate to prove it?' The situation was seen more clearly by outsiders like the American sociologist Ned Levine. After surveying the social attitudes of students, he was surprised to find that the majority thought of themselves first and foremost as Turks, rather than Muslims. This contrasted with a survey of rural-to-urban migrants, the majority of whom considered themselves Muslims. Levine's research also identified certain similarities among his respondents, regardless of their politics. Most were first-generation city-dwellers, and there was a cultural divide between them and their parents. Moreover, group solidarity took precedence over individual opinion. This led to a form of tribal warfare in which defeating the enemy counted more than achieving specific reforms.

Democracy was indeed in danger as the conflict escalated, but we were no longer in Ankara when the crisis erupted. By the spring of 1971 the Demirel government was losing its grip as the streets became a battleground. The leader of the leftists was a student named Deniz Gezmiş, responsible for the kidnapping of four American servicemen. After releasing the hostages, Gezmiş was captured together with two comrades, Yusuf Aslan and Hüseyin Inan. These disturbances led the High Command to intervene, ousting Demirel's government and installing an administration of technocrats. Initially, some left-wingers were delighted, since they regarded the army as the guardian of Kemalist principles. But the killing of an Israeli diplomat in May provoked harsher measures, and marshal law was introduced.

The trial of Deniz Gezmiş attracted international attention. In October he and his comrades were sentenced to death under Article 146 of the Turkish Criminal Code for attempting to overthrow the constitutional order. Fearing that the death penalty would lead to a further escalation of violence, I drafted a letter to *The Times*, appealing for clemency. Such a letter, signed by Cambridge academics, might possibly tip the balance, and Joseph Needham was the first to sign, placing his name near the bottom of the page so as to leave space for other signatories. At his suggestion I phoned another left-winger, the economist Maurice Dobb, who signed next to Needham. His advice was that, between Timms at the top and Needham and Dobb at the bottom, the signatures of at least half-a-dozen further colleagues were needed to make an optimal impact. The letter would be ignored if it appeared to be merely the initiative of communist sympathizers. Sadly, I failed to obtain any further signatures, so the letter remained in my drawer, and Turkish justice took its course. On 6 May 1972 the three young men were hanged.

These tragic events could hardly have been foreseen during the summer of 1970, when we were still teaching in Ankara. For several months our own future hung in the balance as we waited to hear from Cambridge whether I would be promoted to a full Lectureship. The backlash after the Garden House affair seemed likely to work against me, and my Caius colleague Grahame Castor wrote to explain that my upgrading had indeed run into difficulties. Not until the end of July did the long-awaited letter arrive – with the offer of a further three-year appointment. As a foreigner working in Turkey, my position would never be secure, whereas Cambridge offered the prospect of tenure. So the decision was not hard to take, even though my feelings, as reflected in my diary, were decidedly mixed:

> So I am to go back to my 'luxury trade' with its self-contradictions. But let us – good Marxists that we are – note that educational needs will vary with socio-economic conditions. Turkey certainly needs engineers, doctors, technologists – throw in three hours a week on the history of ideas and they have an education for their world. But England needs administrators, managers, businessmen with a degree of intellectual and imaginative culture.

Turkey had advanced the process of self-reflection. Had we remained in Ankara, my role would have been that of a traditionalist in a modern institution, but in Cambridge I'd be seen as a rebel.

CHAPTER ELEVEN

Cambridge Transformed

In my student days Cambridge was a sleepy provincial town with a university soaked in tradition. On graduating in June 1959, I chose as one of my prizes *The Historical Monuments in the City of Cambridge*, published earlier that year. Two beautifully illustrated volumes portrayed a community in a time-warp. The Victorians had built with prodigious energy, tearing down old houses to make way for grandiose neo-gothic blocks and courtyards designed like chateaux, such as the Waterhouse building at Caius. There followed a period of inertia punctured by two world wars. Academic privileges solidified into a cocoon, and for more than a generation there was little visible change despite interventions by Royal Commissions. The colleges were still clasped within the arm of the river, as they had been in pre-modern times. If there had to be a new building, it would usually be made to look old, like the mock-Tudor court at Queens. Caius was exceptional in choosing a contemporary design for its 1930s development on the Market Square. Apart from the University Library, funded by a grant from the Rockefeller Foundation, there was scarcely any academic development west of the Cam. Only a couple of colleges had residential blocks on the left bank, which consisted of gardens and playing fields, the Victorian foundations of Newnham and Selwyn, and houses for married dons.

Original work can of course be done in ancient buildings. It was in a four-hundred-year-old wing of Caius Court that Joseph Needham composed *Science and Civilization in China*, while Wittgenstein wrote the *Philosophical Investigations* in Victorian rooms at Trinity. Even scientific research may flourish in cramped quarters: it was in the Old Cavendish that James Watson and Francis Crick discovered the structure of DNA. But more modern facilities were now needed, in the arts as well as the sciences, if Cambridge was to hold its own. The administrative structure was equally outdated, for there was a lack of leadership at the centre. By comparison with other universities, the Vice-Chancellorship carried little weight, for this was a short-term and largely ceremonial position, filled by a succession of Heads of Houses.

In these reflections, from the perspective of a junior lecturer, the word Cambridge denotes not the city but the university. On paper, it was a participatory democracy, with each of the thousand-odd senior members who constituted Regent House entitled to vote on any controversial proposal. This protected us from autocratic decision-making by a centralized administration, but at times the system inhibited reform. For new measures required majority support, and it was easy for a mischievous minority to organize a 'non placet' – the ten signatures required to call a ballot. A resourceful campaign could then bring out the backwoodsmen and block the proposed reform. For fundamental changes, such as amending statutes to allow the admission of women to the dominant all-male colleges, a two-thirds majority was required, so conservative votes carried twice the weight of those of the reformers. How could such obstacles be overcome? The answer lay with the reformist energies and financial investments of the following decades, which drove a strenuous but ultimately successful campaign for modernization. By the end of the 1980s Cambridge had undergone a startling transformation.

New Wine in Old Bottles

'Port or claret?' During the 1970s the Fellows of Caius dined in style, barely touched by a world in turmoil. A group portrait by Paul Gopal-Chowdhury shows them seated at desert with Joseph Needham, the most distinguished scholar of his generation, profiled in the right foreground. The candle-lit ritual has a timeless quality. There might be repression in the Soviet bloc, pitched battles on American campuses, ethnic conflict in Cyprus, apartheid in South Africa, and reverberations from the war in Vietnam, but resident dons enjoyed a cloistered life. Cambridge, as the historian Christopher Brooke has observed, is a strange mixture of cosmopolitan breadth and extreme parochialism. Did anyone notice the slogan FREE NELSON MANDELA daubed on the wall of Darwin College, which caught my eye on the way to lectures? Scrub as they might, the cleaners never completely erased the haunting words.

Cambridge actually seemed less cosmopolitan than Sussex, but we had a circle of friends from the Indian sub-continent with artistic and musical interests. Through our friend Mary Wraith we met Jamal Islam, a theoretical physicist from Bengal whose wife Soraya was studying Ottoman costume. Even more riveting were the conversations with the art historian Partha Mitter, whose pioneering study of European attitudes towards Indian painting and sculpture appeared under the title *Much Maligned*

Monsters. From his wife Swasti, an agricultural economist who was to become a specialist on women's employment in the third world, we learnt that the Sanskrit origins of her name denoted good luck (a meaning tragically distorted by the Nazis). For Saime these friendships had a special value, given the predominance in Cambridge of a white Anglo-Saxon protestant ethos. For me the gain was political, for our Indian friends challenged the myth of Britain's 'civilizing' mission. Draconian policies during the final years of the Raj were to blame for the great famine of 1943 and the massacres that accompanied partition.

At Caius, left-wingers like the cultural theorist Paul Connerton and the social historian Vic Gatrell formed a minority. Other socialist friends included the Canadian physicist Mick Brown, an expert on dislocations, and his American Jewish wife, the anthropologist Susan Drucker. Among those who sported the badge of the Campaign for Nuclear Disarmament was the astrophysicist Stephen Hawking, whom we would visit at his house in Little Saint Mary's Lane, a stone's throw from the Department of Theoretical Physics. His illness made it difficult for him to speak at meetings, but he was making astonishing advances in cosmology, clarifying the behaviour of 'black holes', the singularities caused by gravitational collapse.

Fortunately the college was led by men of vision. The physicist Nevill Mott played a leading role in the Pugwash movement, promoting dialogue with scientists from the Soviet Union. Recognizing, as Cavendish Professor, the limitations of the old buildings, he launched the plan for extensive modern laboratories on a green-field site to the west of the Cam. When Mott retired, he was praised by his successor Brian Pippard for promoting younger scientists: 'Who would have thought that under such a mighty oak so many saplings could grow!'

Mott's successor Joseph Needham had an even more remarkable range. As Master he was committed to reforming the college while preserving precious traditions. 'Can you pour new wine into old bottles?' he asked in June 1972. 'My firm belief is that you can'. The new vintages he had in mind were the women who were denied entry to Caius by college statute. Among those in favour was my mentor Freddy Stopp, who as Senior Tutor had compiled a feasibility study on co-residence. Over dinner, Freddy reminded me that women had been studying at Cambridge since the establishment of Girton and Newnham in the 1870s. A dozen years later the governing body of the university agreed to admit women to university examinations, although they were not permitted to claim their degrees. This injustice prompted the university set up a Syndicate, which reported in favour of degrees for women. 'You might have expected that young men would welcome this move,' Freddy continued. 'Not a bit of it!' Over-educated women were seen as a threat, and two thousand students signed a petition against the admission of women, while less than three hundred were in favour. When the issue was put to senior members in 1897, students picketed the Senate House and the proposal was defeated by a large margin.

'Of course,' I said, as the discussion continued over dessert, 'the suffrage movement changed everything.' After the First World War women had won the right to vote in parliamentary elections, so when were they allowed to take their degrees? The answer was provided by another modernizer, the historian Neil McKendrick. 'Not until 1948,' he replied, 'decades after London and Oxford.' This was hard to believe – why was Cambridge so tardy? An answer could be found in the guide to academic politics by Francis Cornford, *Microcosmographia Academica*, published in 1908. Originally intended as a satire, this pamphlet defined the sources of academic inertia, especially the tactics used by the 'non placets' to block reforms. The most cogent concept was the Principle of Unripe Time. However strong the case for change, the right moment never quite arrives, for it is always better to be on the Safe Side. According to Cornford, the fundamental motive for procrastination is fear, especially 'fear of females' and 'fear of giving yourself away'.

The great exception was Joseph Needham, the most warm-hearted of scholars. One of his reforms was to instigate Domestic Evenings, at which female guests were welcome, and after lunch he would serve coffee in the Master's Lodge so that he could chat with younger colleagues and their wives. He had a soft spot for Saime, not least because of her combination of scientific interests and left-wing convictions.

'As a scientist, how do you combine Christian faith with communism?' she asked.

'Religion is a belief system,' he replied, 'while science provides rational explanations and communism offers hope for the future. Together, the three may help us to create a better world.'

We also discussed the impact of modern technology. 'Read Theodor Roszak's *The Making of a Counter-Culture*,' he advised. 'Here you have a call for greater reverence for Nature, such as the Chinese had, as opposed to the domination of Nature propagated in the West.'

Needham's essays of the 1930s impressed me by their optimistic tone. 'Was that whistling in the dark,' I asked, 'or grounded in a philosophy of history?'

'I sometimes wonder,' he replied, 'considering they were written when Hitler was coming to power. But my view of history was influenced by my evolutionary observations as a biologist.' He gave us an inscribed copy of *History is on our Side*, the collection of essays in which his outlook is defined.

With Needham you could discuss anything – from Taoist sexual practices to the origins of Morris dancing. Effortlessly, he bridged the gap between the sciences and the arts, and his personal life was as multicultural as his mind. Life at the Lodge was shared with Dorothy (née Moyle), his English wife, and Lu Gwei-Djen, his Chinese collaborator. With Dorothy during the 1930s he had promoted 'Brighter Biochemistry' – the title of the magazine they produced while publishing outstanding work on embryology. With Lu Gwei-Djen he was adding further volumes to his monumental *History of Science and Civilization in China*.

Needham was mortified to discover was how difficult a Fellows Meeting could be when sixty intelligent men were crammed around one table. Had the discussion of the refurbishment of the kitchens been recorded, it would have competed with any surrealist drama. And nothing could compare with the eloquence of Jeremy Prynne, a poet with a passion for words. Topics like the need for a larger library certainly deserved sustained attention – for years this problem appeared intractable. However, domestic issues claimed a disproportionate amount of time. Should four courses (followed by desert) be served at High Table, or should it be three? Which shrubs should be chosen to replace the wilting conifers in Tree Court? An over-elaborate plan aroused the wrath of the Professor of Latin, Charles Brink, one of those German-Jewish refugees who enriched Cambridge life. Born in Berlin in 1907 as Karl Oskar Levy, he spoke with the inimitable authority of Germanic scholarship. 'This is not a replanting scheme,' he declared. 'This is a programme of afforestation!'

Meetings became more fractious when we debated the proposal closest to Needham's heart: the admission of women. The most opinionated would hold forth at greatest length, while the majority silently gnashed their teeth. The biologist Charles Goodhart led the opposition. 'Women's brains,' he insisted, 'are smaller than men's.' Their primary duty was procreation, for the gene pool would be depleted if intelligent women wrote books instead of having babies. When statistics were cited to prove women's academic abilities, Goodhart shifted his ground. 'It's not that women have no brains,' he said, 'it's that they have no balls.' Lacking the alpha-male drive for competitive success, they were less likely to obtain the coveted First Class degrees. These ideas were echoed by conservative colleagues in the humanities. 'When I'm marking an essay by a woman,' another opponent claimed, 'I can always tell. They wrap the subject up in woolly prose without ever coming to the point.' There were old fogeys in most colleges whose attitudes could be laughed away, but it was disturbing to find their views replicated among younger Fellows. The consequences could be extremely depressing. In April 1967 the German lector Edmund Stegmaier shared with me his sense of malaise, and the issue became more acute when he was succeeded by a young woman from Heidelberg named Christiane Reitter.

During a series of hotly contested meetings the tactics of resistance were refined by resident Fellows like Peter Tranchell, a noted musician. Women's voices would unbalance the Chapel Choir, he claimed. To obtain the blocking third they needed, Goodhart and his allies rallied other groups: Boat Club buffs who anticipated a dearth of beefy oarsmen, and scientists who feared that female applicants would tend towards the humanities, undermining physics and chemistry. Nevill Mott spoke against reform on the grounds that investments in equipment would be less productive if women reduced the numbers in the hard sciences. Despite Needham's leadership, proposals for their admission were blocked on two occasions, and when he retired it proved difficult to find an equally forward-looking successor. Fellows traditionally elect an outstanding scientist or scholar, and a small group favoured Francis Crick. But when Crick was unwilling to stand, the choice fell on William Wade, Professor of English Law at Oxford. Since Wade made it clear that he was opposed to statute change, the cause of women seemed to be lost.

If there was no hope of making history, at least it could be recorded. As editor of *The Caian*, the college magazine, I began to publish interviews with academic luminaries, including Needham and Wade. There were giants in those days. Rudolph Peters recalled his exploits as a Medical Officer during the First World War, before describing the discoveries about vitamins that won him fame as a biochemist. The biologist Vincent Wigglesworth gave a vivid account of the expedition he led through the jungles of West Africa to study sleeping sickness and malaria. The economist Peter Bauer clarified his involvement with the so-called Peasants Revolt, as well as his controversial views on overseas aid. And the numismatist Philip Grierson recalled the mystery of the forty gold coins, discovered among the remains of a longship in a burial mound at Sutton Hoo. After a meeting of the Society of Antiquaries, it suddenly occurred to him that longships with twenty oars required a crew of forty. Surely the coins must be payments for ghostly oarsmen, ferrying an honoured warrior into the other world.

The interviews seeded a gift for oral history that was to bear fruit in the future. Further articles appeared in the *Cambridge Review*, until the departure of the editor, Iain Wright, put an end to my contributions. Wright was succeeded by John Casey, the most articulate of the Caius conservatives. In theory, the review was to revert to the tradition of reporting on university life and letters, publishing sermons as in bygone years. But in practice Casey used his position to propagate an idiosyncratic brand of right-wing libertarianism. When the Labour Government introduced the Race Relations Act of 1976, prohibiting speech or writing likely to stir up racial hatred, this was denounced (in an unsigned editorial) as a repressive measure that would inhibit politicians like Enoch Powell from warning against coloured immigration. 'Why should people not be free to stir up hatred?' the editorial asked. 'We are well provided with laws protecting public order.' A longer article on Antiracialism argued that English patriotism was threatened by the forces of 'modern charlatanism':

media-liberalism, the movement for sexual freedom, and the myths of feminism.

The proposals to admit women to Caius provoked a further editorial in December 1977 entitled The Tyranny of Fashion. It alleged that an attempt was being made to suppress the male colleges, led by 'educational totalitarians'. This prompted me to reply that it would be better to attack those who have obstructed women's education in Cambridge for the past hundred years. Conservatives at Caius were counting on the new Master, Bill Wade, to consolidate their position. An article in *Times Higher Education* the previous year had associated Wade with a Conservative Philosophy Group, whose aim was to check the intellectual dominance of the left; but in dealing with a lawyer, you have to read the small print. During my interview with Wade, I asked him about co-education. 'Although my instincts are conservative,' he replied, 'I think that the maintenance of the highest possible academic standards overrides everything else.' With other colleges changing their statutes, Wade feared that Caius might no longer attract the brightest applicants, so he surprised us by announcing that he would vote for the admission of women. This tipped the balance in favour of reform, and in January 1978 Saime and I threw a party to celebrate a historic victory, dancing on the grave of the old order to the rhythms of *Nightflight to Venus*. Once the statutes were amended, a group of thirty women students were admitted to Caius, the first in the college's six-hundred-year history.

THE CHALLENGE OF DIALECTICS

'The reason why academic disputes are so bitter,' they say, 'is that the stakes are so low.' But such battles are worth fighting when they bring palpable benefits in the form of vibrant communities, stimulating courses and innovative research. Cambridge was a classic example of a ritualistic society, but attitudes were changing and student unrest continued to act as a catalyst. In February 1972, after a protest meeting at the Faculty of Economics, students again occupied the Old Schools. In response to the sit-in, the university set up an inquiry chaired by Lord Devlin, a retired judge. His Report recommended student representation on university bodies, together with a centrally-funded Student Union, but these cautious reforms left the structure of governance unchanged. When challenged on these issues, one of my senior colleagues replied: 'We are already working at the frontiers of knowledge.' To me those frontiers seemed far too circumscribed. Surely received ideas, sustained by archaic regulations, should be measured against challenging developments from aboard.

The authors featured in my lectures, from Hegel and Heine to Max Weber and Bert Brecht, illustrated the power of dialectical thinking. In

Edmund Wilson's classic study of the origins of communism, *To the Finland Station*, the energizing effect of dialectics is attributed not to some impersonal law of history, but to the recurring insurgence of the young against repressive social structures: 'an organic development out of the past, for which the reactionary forces have themselves in their way been preparing'. Initiated by Hegel and elaborated by Marx, dialectical theory was reformulated by the Frankfurt School, notably Theodor Adorno and Walter Benjamin. My articles in the *Cambridge Review*, at the time when it was still under Wright's editorship, had set out the case for this counterculture. In Adorno's Dialectics (November 1970), I argued that the key concepts of dialectical thinking are 'treated as undesirable aliens, upon whom a deportation order is likely to be clapped, the moment they show signs of gaining a foothold this side of the channel'. A translation of Adorno's *Prisms* prompted the following reflections: 'The failures of intellectual and political honesty associated with dialectics are so well known that it is salutary to be reminded of the opposite: the tyranny of empiricism, the myopia of exact scholarship, the criminal complacency of common sense'. Empiricism tends to 'freeze reality into static categories', while dialectics keep alive 'the idea of potentiality'.

A few days later I was confronted by Peter Stern, waving a copy of the offending article. 'How much of this is Adorno,' he asked 'and how much is Timms?' Feeling that my attitude was equivocal, he used the *Cambridge Review* to publish a rejoinder: a review of Walter Benjamin's *Illuminations*, translated by Harry Zohn. Stern acknowledged the 'ghostly poetic justice' that intellectual life in Germany is dominated by the Jewish Marxist outcasts of yesteryear: Adorno, Horkheimer, Marcuse, Bloch, Benjamin and Lukács. One can see why Benjamin is all the rage with our votaries of 'relevance', he added, with reference to his famous Theses in the Philosophy of History. Stern analysed the 'acrobatics' of Benjamin's style – the 'condensations, snooty syntax and idiosyncratic use of abstractions'. This was followed by cruder comments on Adorno. 'A brief history of Benjamin's writings,' Stern declared, 'shows us the beauty of the dialectical process to which he and his more "committed" friends so frequently refer us.' The despair that drove Benjamin to suicide in 1940 is associated with Adorno's decision to 'turn down some of his best essays', while the credit given to Adorno for publishing Benjamin's writings in the 1950s demonstrates his 'superior command of the dialectical method'.

This coded rebuke raised the question whether Adorno really was to blame for his friend's suicide. My reply was published in the next *Cambridge Review*. Stern, I complained, seems to regard 'dialectical' as a synonym for 'disreputable'. Adorno actually accepted for publication several of Benjamin's best essays, and only one manuscript was sent back for revision. Moreover the letters showed that Benjamin and Adorno enjoyed an intellectually productive friendship. Of course, there were differences of opinion, but this was what makes their correspondence so illuminating – 'a clarification of ideas through critical dialogue ("dialectic" in the best sense)'. In a further letter to the *Cambridge Review*, Stern conceded that Adorno had only rejected one Benjamin manuscript. The sting in the tail of his letter related to the word dialectical. What Stern found disreputable was 'the habit of justifying every defection and dishonesty, every contradiction and every obscurity by calling it "dialectical" as long as it occurs on the left'.

This controversy made me more cautious in my next article in the *Cambridge Review* on Benjamin and Brecht (March 1973). This focused on Benjamin's writings about the Epic Theatre, translated by Anna Bostock and published by New Left Books under the title *Understanding Brecht*. A key text in this collection is the lecture on The Author as Producer, in which Benjamin argues that art subverts not only the values of bourgeois culture, but the rules by which it operates. He recalled one of Brecht's remarks while playing chess in Danish exile. 'We really ought to work out a new game,' Brecht said. 'A game in which the moves do not always stay the same; where the function of each piece changes after it has stood on the same square for a while'. For me, this anecdote epitomized the aims of those Marxist intellectuals. Their contribution, I concluded, 'lies in changing the rules of the game'. By contrast with the austerely cerebral Adorno, I found Benjamin's reflections – especially on archetypes – far more rewarding. But I was mystified by his attempt to link the materialist perspectives of Marxism with the Talmud. For the first time I was explicitly confronted by the Judaic element in German-Jewish thinking.

The antipode to Peter Stern was the medievalist Dennis Green. There was no doubting Green's devotion to scholarship and some colleagues found him a genial table-companion, but to me his attitude seemed prickly. The forum for our encounters was the Modern Languages Faculty Board, to which I was co-opted in January 1974. Introducing reforms required the support of like-minded colleagues such as Anthony Close, Lecturer in Spanish, and Ann Duncan, who taught French at Newnham. Discussions tended to be led by Lloyd Austin, Professor of French, who revered the literary canon. He could usually count on the support of the Professor of Italian, the Dante scholar Umberto Limentani, and the Professor of Slavonic Languages, Lucian Lewitter. Confronted by this phalanx, our spirits might have failed had tensions not been eased by an urbane chairman, the Hispanist Theodore Boorman. He would sometimes arrive in riding gear, ready with a gentle touch of the whip.

The Board met around a magnificent oval table in the Old Schools. There were approximately twenty members, so it was sometimes possible to push through changes by majority vote. A small group became known as Young Turks, determined to revive a somnolent institution. Why waste time on trivia such as the Comma Hunt, so memorably described by

Cornford? Should the title of exam papers be 'Literature, Thought, and History' or 'Literature, Thought and History'? There were eloquent arguments on both sides before the single-comma faction won the day, but we also debated matters of substance. One aim was to ensure that existing rules were properly applied. University Ordinances contained nuggets of information that could be turned to our advantage. Traditionally, after taking their Tripos exams, students were placed in a Class without receiving any feedback about individual subjects. This seemed counterproductive. Averaging of marks might place a student in the lower division of Class II when some of his papers were First Class, while others bordered on failure.

'Wouldn't it be better to give students their full spread of marks,' I asked, 'especially at the end of their first year, so that they are aware of their weaknesses and can work to improve them?'

'That is prohibited by University Ordinances,' declared a senior colleague. It was feared that there might be challenges to the percentage marks used to convey intellectual quality. But at this point Ann Duncan read out the text of the relevant Ordinance, which stated that Tripos marks *could* be disclosed to candidates under conditions to be determined by the Faculty Board. This raised the hackles of Dennis Green and other opponents of liberalization. Claiming that the debate was taking too much time, Green insisted that a fifteen-minute guillotine be imposed on discussion. This enabled him, watch in hand, to interrupt me in full flow, and the issue had to be deferred. But we turned this delay to our advantage by collecting information about developments in other arts faculties. As a result, a reform was approved that disclosed to students the grade for each of their papers.

There was a shift in the balance of power in 1979 when Leonard Forster retired. As Head of Department he had run a happy ship, welcoming us to working lunches at Selwyn College, so a great deal depended on the choice of successor. Wishing to sound out opinion in the department, the chairman of the electors, Sir Harry Hinsley, invited me to dine at St John's. In commenting on the leading candidates, I tried to be even-handed, but my plaudits were reserved for Peter Stern. His lectures and publications were inspirational, I explained, combining the subtlety of Lichtenberg and the rigour of Wittgenstein; and his reputation had been enhanced by *Hitler, the Fuehrer and the People* (1975), an incisive study of National Socialism. Since Hinsley was an authority on the Second World War, he would surely find this persuasive. There was a short pause before he replied: 'Yes, he *is* an *intellectual*'. Only afterwards did it dawn on me that intellectual could imply 'too clever by half'.

When the electors met three weeks later, they chose Dennis Green. Realizing that this would cause ructions in the department, Leonard Forster took me aside. Wouldn't it be possible for me to act as a peace-maker, following the example of my predecessor at Caius, Francis Bennett? Even if I had possessed Francis's saintly qualities, it is unlikely that Professor Green would have responded. His first move was to scrap the convivial working lunches. Instead, we were summoned to departmental meetings in a cramped classroom at 9 o'clock on Saturday mornings. Of course, there were faults on both sides. Green was a stickler for punctuality so I would arrive late to irk him. One outburst was so brusque that a senior colleague, the lexicographer Trevor Jones, offered a whispered explanation: 'Something terrible happened to him in a tank.' Green had served in the Royal Armoured Corps and taken part in the Normandy landings.

It was hard to match such a seasoned campaigner, but our skirmishes continued. One of the duties of the Faculty Board was the award of doctorates. We received reports from examiners, together with their recommendations, and adjudicated on success or failure. The aim was to maintain high standards while allowing unsuccessful candidates a fair chance to resubmit their dissertations. The flaw in the system lay in the confidentiality of the reports, which were often outspoken and sometimes contradictory. Only excerpts were released to the candidates and their supervisors, who tended to feel that essential information was being withheld. How could they improve if they were left in the dark about the most damaging criticisms? One reason for the reluctance to release full reports was the fear of legal action, but withholding information from candidates could result in grave injustice. Careers were at risk if they failed their Doctorate or were awarded only a Master's degree. Being a research supervisor as well as a member of the Board, I saw the issue from both sides, arguing for the greatest possible transparency.

Acute difficulties arose when the dissertation of one of my own students was referred back. As a member of the Board I was expected to remain silent about undisclosed sections in the reports, while as supervisor it was my duty to give the candidate the fullest possible guidance. This was a contradiction that could not be harmoniously resolved, for my sympathies lay with the student, even if it meant bending the rules. Incensed by what he saw as a breach of confidence, Green summoned me to his office. Never again, he declared, would I be appointed as a research supervisor. My response was to call his bluff. Writing to the Board of Graduate Studies, which had overall responsibility for doctorates, I offered to resign from postgraduate supervision, since my competence was questioned. My strongest card was my cohort of doctoral students, for the resignation of a supervisor so much in demand would cause reverberations. Who would take over topics like the Theatre of Hofmannsthal (researched by the musically gifted Sally McMullen) or Kraus's Influence on Walter Benjamin (the theme envisaged by Christopher Thornhill)? Anxious to avoid a showdown, the Graduate Board put pressure on

Dennis Green, and during a further tetchy interview he retracted his allegations.

Relaxing the rules made the system more transparent. Shortly after this episode the Faculty Board accepted students as co-opted members – one graduate representative and two undergraduates. Another breakthrough was a pilot scheme for course evaluations. Students attending specific lectures were asked to complete a questionnaire. Was there a clear lecture plan? How helpful was the reading list? Was time allowed for discussion? The tables were turned as students provided their teachers with an incentive to improve. But Cambridge, despite these changes, was scarcely an open society. In myself, as well as others, I sensed a reluctance to reveal thoughts and feelings that might compromise you at a college meeting or promotions committee. No wonder Cornford identified the primary factor in academic politics as 'fear of giving yourself away'. In Cambridge, according to his most devastating observation, there was a lack of 'sincere dishonesty'.

CIRCLES OF CREATIVITY

My impulse was to explore alternative spaces both at home and abroad. During the early years of our marriage Saime had one foot in Cambridge, the other in Ankara. While giving courses on Physics at Middle East Technical University, she was becoming intrigued by the impact of science on Turkish society. She was also influenced by pioneering feminist publications like Simone de Beauvoir's *The Second Sex*. My own interests embraced the psychology of childhood, as interpreted by Erik Erikson and Wilhelm Reich. Although our life was enriched by an expanding circle of friends, we had no children (medical tests suggested we were unlikely to have any of our own). Saime claimed she lacked the patience to be a good mother – as the second oldest of seven siblings she had done enough parenting during her childhood! However, my instincts were aroused by children in need, as indicated by a diary note of August 1967 about an incident in Turkey:

> Last night on the coach from Erdek the father of two gorgeous little girls began slapping his five-year-old daughter to stop her crying, while the girl's classically beautiful Turkish mother hid her face in shame. She seemed ashamed – not of her brutal husband – but of having tired and frightened children.

Children are cherished in Turkey, but fathers are disciplinarians. When we visited our Ankara friends, Semra (whom Saime knew from the sanatorium) and Yılmaz Gümüşbaş (who wrote for the liberal *Cumhuriet*), we discovered that bedtime stories were unknown to their children, Barış and Irmak. Years later, Irmak recalled how thrilled they were when I read them *The Princess and the Pea*, while Saime used newly invented Blu-Tack to suspend mobile decorations from the ceiling.

Saime was aware of my longing for children, so in the spring of 1974 she took me to visit the Children's Home in Keçiören. During one of her teaching stints in Ankara a television programme about the need for foster parents had prompted her to contact the Adoption Agency. A heart-rending scene awaited us at the rambling building. Each ward was crammed with a dozen metal cots, to which infants were confined for most of the day. At feeding time a bottle of formula milk would be placed in their mouths, and twenty minutes later the bottles would be collected, regardless of how much had been ingested. Some babies were so weak they could hardly move. One foundling had been abandoned on 9 November 1973 in the courtyard of the great mosque at Düzce. His estimated age at the time was one month, so he was given the name Ilkay (First Month). His weight at six months was that of a one-week-old baby and he seemed unlikely to survive. Captivated by his quirky smile, we applied to become his parents.

We were fortunate in being interviewed at the Agency by a sympathetic young woman named Öznur, but her more conservative colleague, Rezan Hanım, raised questions of principle. Should a foreigner be permitted to adopt a Muslim child? My Turkish left me floundering while the debates raged around me, but I kept a diary entitled Quest for a Son. Success would have been impossible without a circle of friends, especially Saime's sister Yeter, now married to the American sociologist Ned Levine. We were also assisted by Iffet Renda, a lecturer in nursing, and by an enterprising lawyer. Iffet assured us that Ilkay was a healthy child, underweight from lack of nourishment. Travelling to the children's home every day, I would feed him for an hour, while Saime battled with bureaucracy. After two weeks of uncertainty, the drama reached its climax. Our application was approved, Ilkay consented with gleeful smiles, and he was delivered into our arms.

The following week I flew to England for the new Cambridge term, leaving Saime to look after Ilkay with the aid of Yeter and Ned. Other members of the Göksu family rallied round, including Saime's mother and her brother Maksut, who was courting a fellow student named Miray. Given the family's left-wing views, it was ironic to discover that Miray was the daughter of Kenan Evren, Commander-in-Chief of the Turkish armed forces. Ilkay's health remained precarious, and the emergency hospital visits described in Saime's letters were heart-rending. Only after my return to Ankara in June did our son feel safe in my arms, wrapped in a beautifully crocheted shawl. Mindful of the story of Joseph and his coat of many colours, we named him Yusuf. Once he had been added to Saime's

Cambridge Contrasts: The modernist building (right), designed for Caius in the 1930s by Murray Easton, forms a foil to the adjacent town houses, the gothic windows of Great St Mary's (foreground), and the Waterhouse Building in the background.

Fellows of Caius at Dessert, from a painting by Paul Gopal-Chowdhury, showing (from left) Noel Malcolm, John Casey, Peter Bayley, Mark Birkinshaw (behind), Stephen Hawking, Neil Mckendrick (standing), Iain Macpherson (presiding), Sir Vincent Wigglesworth, Nicola Nichols, Robin Holloway (standing), Peter Tranchell, Richard le Page, and Joseph Needham. In the background (left) Mr Quintana, the butler, and Mr Healey, the deputy butler.

(Above) On Hunstanton beach: Daphne (right) pursued by her friend Sophie Shotton (centre)

(Left) What a handful! Saime holding Yusuf

Family group at Metcalfe Road with (from left) Saime, Daphne, Yusuf and Sebastian (photographed by Paul Christie)

With Saime during a party in Madingley Hall

Celebrating the International Year of the Child, 1979: ET as Nasreddin Hodja with Saime as his donkey

Brothers reunited:
Robert Timms (left)
from Melbourne
with Owen Young
from Gothenburg

Joan Timms at 90,
surprised by her
portrait, painted by
John Chaltas from a
photograph (Saime is
just visible on the
left, Christopher on
the right)

The renewal of
marriage vows:
Receiving a sprig of
Honesty from
Saime, witnessed by
Elaine Brown and
Peter Tamplin

The German Democratic Republic: Every Effort for the Consolidation of Workers' and Peasants' Power!

Life behind the Curtain (by an underground photographer)

Free German Youth
(by an underground
photographer)

When the Wall came
down: Collage of
political headlines
from autumn1989

University of Sussex:
A view of the
Meeting House (from
a prospectus of the
1990s)

Brighton: With Jakov
Lind and Silke Hassler
on the balcony at The
Cliff

Help from Stella Rock
with research on
Russian sources

Launching
*Romantic
Communist*:
Saime with
Haldun in
Ankara

Don't Attack
Iraq! – Saime
(foreground
second from
right) on the
anti-war
demonstration in
London

At Belsize Square
Synagogue:
Ralph Emanuel
(left) with Max
Kochmann

Lewis Goodman with Diana Franklin

Arthur Oppenheimer with Andrea Hammel

Lori Gemeiner with Theo Marx

With Lord Attenborough at the inauguration of the German-Jewish Centre archive in Sussex University Library

Chana Moshenska (holding
Celia) during a visit to 4 The
Cliff

Julius Carlebach
with his wife Myrna
in the garden at The
Cliff

Ulrike
Walton-
Jordan with
Henri
Soussan
(centre) and
David
Groiser

(Left) Max Kochmann with Hilde (after receiving his honorary doctorate at Sussex)

(Below) Researching the German-Jewish Dilemma: A selection of conference programmes

In Vienna with Saime for the award of the State Prize for History of the Social Sciences

At Buckingham Palace in 2005 with Daphne Leff, Diana Franklin and Jamie Leff

From *Unreal City* to *Austrian Exodus*: A selection of co-edited publications

At the Austrian Cultural
Forum in London with the
editors of Austrian Studies
(from left): Ritchie Robertson,
Robert Vilain and Judith
Beniston

Admiring a Festschrift: *Austrian Satire and Other Essays*

Ralph Emanuel (right) at the
Brighton Dome, being awarded
an honorary doctorate by the
new Sussex Chancellor Sanjeev
Bhaskar (January 2010)

Christian Wiese (centre), Director of the German-Jewish Centre, chairing a conference at Sussex

Deborah Schultz, co-author of *Pictorial Narrative in the Nazi Period*

passport, the way should have been clear for our return to England. But on 15 July the Cyprus problem, rumbling intermittently for years, erupted into armed conflict, as Greek officers staged a coup and the junta in Athens attempted to annex the island. The sky buzzed with military aircraft as Turkey responded by occupying northern Cyprus. The success of this operation, which resulted in the partition of the island, won popularity for Ecevit's government, while the Greek junta was disgraced and overthrown.

We paid a further visit to Ankara in March 1976. Our first port of call was the Adoption Agency, where we learned that the Children's Home in Keçiören had been closed, after an epidemic that cost several lives. We were all the more eager to adopt a second child when we visited the new premises, accompanied by Yusuf, now a lively toddler. This time we were introduced to a six-month-old girl named Banu, also a foundling, abandoned outside a block of flats in Ankara. She was in a feeble state, perhaps due to an injury at birth, but we felt that Banu would have a better life in England, even if she proved to be disabled. This time everything went smoothly, and within three weeks we had a daughter. Recalling the legend of the girl who blossomed into a tree, we named her Daphne.

Family life was transformed as we moved to a semi-detached house with a large garden within cycling distance of the city centre. Even on a lecturer's modest salary there was no difficulty in obtaining a mortgage from the Cambridge Building Society. With its six bedrooms this house evolved into a family-centred community, shared with colourful characters like the poet Peter Singer and Duska Novakovic, a language student from Croatia who helped with childcare. It was no surprise when they decided to get married, and their daughter Sophie became one of Daphne's playmates. Family celebrations, especially at Christmas, were shared with our closest friends, Mick and Susan Brown and their three children. To keep track of the comings and goings we instituted a visitor's book, which evolved into a house journal.

A further advance from the building society enabled us to buy a cottage near the coast at Snettisham. Seaside holidays are such an English institution that we couldn't wait to start building sandcastles, before cycling home for bedtime stories. The summer holidays opened our eyes to the beauty of the Norfolk countryside and put us in touch with a community of carpenters and potters, sculptors and painters, including Trevor Tennant and Dorothy Annan, elderly artists living with their four-year-old great-nephew Sebastian, whom they had adopted. Canoeing together on the lagoon at Holme-next-the Sea, Yusuf and Sebbie became close friends.

Parenting proved emotionally liberating, for I was a hands-on father, coping cheerfully with tantrums, wet beds and soiled nappies, and devising creative ways of coaxing toddlers to have a good breakfast. As the kids grew older, what larks we had! We spent untold hours playing trains and spaceships on the living-room floor, building a tree-house in the garden, and enjoying cricket and tennis in the fields beyond our house. Saime, who had resigned her lectureship in Ankara, would hold the fort at home while I was at work. She now had the chance to extend her polit- ical activities in the Labour Party and the Campaign for Nuclear Disarmament. Encouraged by Joseph Needham, she was also collecting information for a project on science and society in Turkey.

During the day Saime would take the children with their friends to enjoy outdoor activities at swimming pools or adventure playgrounds. But being a full-time mother sometimes proved wearisome, and by the evening – surrounded by cries of 'I want my Daddy!' – she could hardly wait for my return. After the success of *ET*, the Spielberg film about an extrater- restrial visitor, I would pick up the phone in college to hear a plaintive voice saying 'ET come home!' The struggle to settle the children was enlivened by bedtime reading, including old favourites like Lewis Carroll, Arthur Ransome and Conan Doyle. When the children clamoured to sleep in our double-bed, we developed a game called Reichenbach Falls, wrestling like Holmes with Moriarty until someone tumbled over the brink.

Could academic productivity be combined with the pram in the hall? 'Having children could delay your book on Kraus by a dozen years,' said our friend Brian Easlea during a visit from Sussex. Concentrated solitude had been needed to complete his first book, *Liberation and the Aims of Science*. Parenting was becoming a political issue – not only for a new generation of militant feminists. We made contact with a pressure group known as NAG, the Nursery Action Group. Other universities, including Sussex, had opened creches for the benefit of students and staff, so why not Cambridge? In June 1975, after a series of petitions had been ignored, NAG occupied the Senate House, armed with babies. As the chamber resounded with the clamour of children, the Vice-Chancellor backed down, and the Council of Senate agreed to set up a working party to discuss the feasibility of a university nursery. On 13 November the first meeting was front-paged in the *One Shilling Paper*. 'Equality of opportu- nity,' it argued, 'is meaningless as long as nothing is done to free women from the burden of child care.' But by the time the working party reported, the pressure had eased and the Council shelved its proposals.

Fortunately, there were other avenues. Early in 1978 Newnham College offered the use of a house in Wordsworth Grove, if funding could be raised from wealthier colleges. So proposals were drafted for a Joint Colleges Nursery, and Saime and I hosted a meeting at which it was decided to set up a Limited Company. My commitment to child develop- ment prompted me to join the Management Committee, acquiring a flair for financial planning. There were endless meetings with the bursar of Newnham, Dorothy Hahn, who checked every detail of our market research. 'How much have you budgeted for providing toddlers with an apple a day?' she asked. To enable young mothers to continue with their studies, we planned to provide places for babies, which scandalized the advocates of breast-feeding and maternal bonding. We also had to outsmart conservatives determined to block any project emanating from a student occupation.

Although seen as subversives, we were in truth respectable rebels. Several of our committee were to become professors and one – Joanna Womack – was later appointed Treasurer of the University of Cambridge. Entrusted with a budget of several hundred millions, she must have looked back benignly on our efforts to squeeze out of the coffers a paltry five thousand pounds. We could never have succeeded without the generosity of a member of the original working party, Mrs Hill, who donated start-up funding. Finally, in September 1980, the Joint Colleges Nursery opened its doors – and thirty years later it is still thriving.

The 1970s tend to be seen as a dismal decade of political strife and economic decline, but the advances in women's education heralded a quiet revolution. The new opportunities, combined with reliable child care and family planning, meant that women would increasingly qualify as doctors or lawyers, teachers, translators or psychotherapists. However, other initiatives were less successful. My impatience with the pace of change was shared by a friend from undergraduate days, George Hughes. After attending business school, he set up highly profitable firms manufacturing coaches and promoting innovative cattle-breeding, which earned him the Queen's Award for Industry. While we were proud of our semi in the suburbs, he owned a stately home in rolling parkland – Hampton Court Castle in Herefordshire. Over lunch at Caius, George unfolded his plans to the Master, now Sir William Wade. It was time that Cambridge had a business school like Harvard, and given the right conditions he was prepared to fund the launch. This was the period when the Thatcher government was imposing stringent economies, so we expected a positive response. However, Wade felt that business studies had no place at a university dedicated to intellectual excellence. Dismayed by this response, George withdrew his offer, and Cambridge had to wait a further decade for its business school.

Time for research was reduced by my administrative and family commitments. Short review articles remained my forte, especially in the *Times Literary Supplement*. The main focus was on Austrian Jewish themes, including Wittgenstein's Vienna, Karl Kraus's letters and Arthur Schnitzler's diaries. The mission of the *TLS* was to make sophisticated scholarship accessible in a condensed and rigorous style. Using weary epithets like 'shedding new light' tended to raise editorial hackles. The message was clear: avoid clichés like the plague! There was a mystique about a journal which in those days published articles anonymously. We knew that T. S. Eliot and Virginia Woolf had been frequent contributors, and we could sometimes guess the authorship of articles by George Steiner or Erich Heller. For me, Steiner and Heller were inspiring for they way they connected culture with politics, and I was not surprised that they had found Cambridge constraining. 'Why does Steiner keep droning on about concentration camps?' I recall a colleague from the English Faculty complaining. But Steiner's lectures had opened my eyes to new dimensions of experience.

My most original work dealt with turn-of-the-century Vienna. The invitation to give a lecture at the University of East Anglia in February 1978 provided the ideal opportunity to present my findings, for its staff

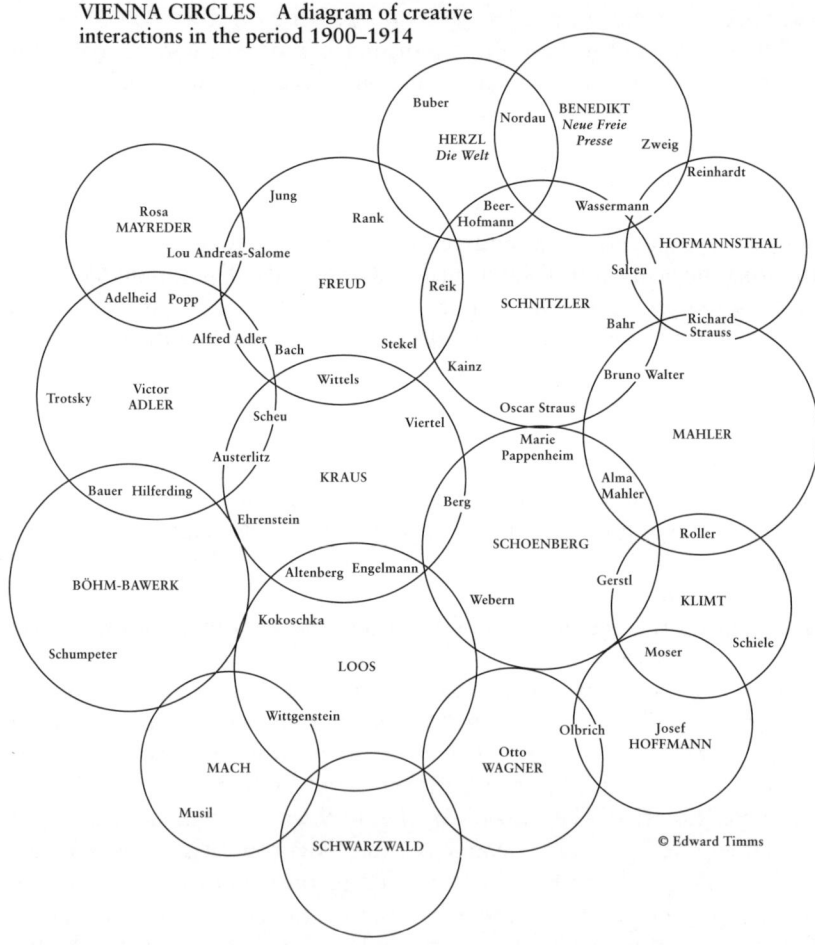

VIENNA CIRCLES A diagram of creative interactions in the period 1900–1914

© Edward Timms

included the Austrian specialists Cedric Williams and W. G. (Max) Sebald. The great strength of the Viennese modernism, I suggested, lay in its internal organization. By analogy with the Vienna Circle of logical positivists, the whole structure of avant-garde culture could be pictured as a condensed system of micro-circuits. This idea was illustrated by a diagram of 'Creative Interactions in Vienna around 1910', incorporating fifteen intersecting circles, each of them centred on a dominant personality: from Victor Adler and Rosa Mayreder through Freud, Kraus and Adolf Loos to Schoenberg, Mahler and Klimt.

Each figure was surrounded by a group of disciples, and the crucial feature was that the circles intersected, ensuring a rapid circulation of ideas. This model of creative cross-fertilization helped to explain the contribution to twentieth-century civilization which made the Vienna of Freud and Herzl, Schoenberg and Wittgenstein so renowned. For all its simplifications, this model of creativity was well received, since it illustrated the interaction between different disciplines that was such a feature of late Habsburg Austria. One member of the audience was so impressed that he made a sketch of the speaker, incorporating the circles drawn on the blackboard.

This model of collaboration had parallels in Cambridge, where university societies catered for every interest. 'What about founding a Turkish Society?' Saime suggested in autumn 1978. Remembering the isolation that had frustrated efforts to save Deniz Gezmiş from the gallows, I readily agreed. Within a few weeks we had assembled an enthusiastic team, including Susan Skilliter, a specialist on Ottoman diplomacy, Sinan Bayraktaroğlu, the Turkish Lector, and his wife Arın. The founding meeting was held on 26 January 1979, when David Tongue of the *Financial Times* spoke about Turkey and the West. We also staged a musical evening with Laurence Picken at his rooms in Jesus College, where he demonstrated his unique collection of oriental instruments. Next came a moving poetry recital by Nermin Menemencioğlu, who recalled the meeting with Nazım Hikmet in 1935 which inspired her passion for his work. Our commitment to multiculturalism led us to stage a show for the International Year of the Child in a working-class district near our home. In addition to folk dancing, we performed scenes from the life of Nasreddin Hodja, the wise fool of Anatolian folklore. While I played the bumbling Hodja and Arın played his long-suffering Wife, Saime stole the show in a costume with floppy ears as the Donkey who outwits her master.

Aware of the fragility of Turkish democracy, we hosted a lecture by Niyazi Berkes, author of *The Development of Secularism in Turkey*. This brilliant raconteur borrowed from Aladdin's Cave his symbol for Turkish governance: a bulbous jar topped by a tiny lid. Despite centuries of modernization under the Ottomans, the Young Turks and the Kemalists, the structure (he argued) remained essentially top-down: an elite imposing decrees upon a vast unruly nation. The majority of the population remained resistant to westernizing reforms designed by the governing class. These warnings proved timely for in Turkish cities the street-battles were intensifying. The disturbances became so extreme that in September 1980 the army, led by Kenan Evren, staged a coup and suspended democratic institutions.

By this date Saime's sister Yeter had remarried and was teaching physics at the University of Adana with her second husband Hakkı Ögelman, Dean of the Science Faculty. But in May 1981 she was arrested as one of the leaders of a left-wing women's group. Daily letters and occasional visits from her husband helped her endure the rigours of prison. With the aid of Amnesty International, we campaigned for her to be released together with others wrongfully imprisoned, and that autumn we visited her in prison. She was keeping up her spirits by writing poetry and giving lessons to fellow prisoners. From Professor Erdal Inönü she had received the message: 'Creative people do not cease to be creative under difficult conditions.' This gave her the courage to write up a scientific experiment carried out before her arrest. This paper on thermoluminiscence was so original that on 18 March 1982 it was published in *Nature* with a note in which Yeter thanked her fellow prisoners for their friendship and her husband for easing the 'agony of life in prison'. After seven months in prison she was released, but the relief was short lived for her younger brother Kemal, editor of a left-wing magazine, was also arrested. This occurred just as their brother Maksut was about to marry Miray, daughter of General Evren.

The military regime brought stability at grievous cost. Thousands of young people were imprisoned, hundreds tortured – and more than twenty-five executed. Evren revived authoritarian Kemalism, appealing to Turkish nationalism while hounding the intelligentsia. When fellow university teachers were dismissed, Saime's friend Haldun Özen and his wife Ülkü were also caught up in the witch-hunt. Haldun resigned from his lectureship at the University of Trebizond in protest against the dismissal of fellow teachers, including the Rector of the University, while Ülkü also felt compelled to resign from her position as librarian. Life for Haldun, Ülkü and their two small children had been full of hope a couple of years earlier when we visited them for a shared family holiday, enjoying the beauty of the Black Sea region. Now they had to re-establish themselves in Ankara, becoming active in non-governmental organizations and Human Rights campaigns.

After a referendum in 1982 approving an authoritarian constitution and confirming him as Head of State, Evren was invited to London by the British government, led by Margaret Thatcher. In addition to being entertained by the Queen, President Evren spent a day at Cambridge, provoking vociferous protests. These events split the University Turkish Society, some of whom supported the military regime. Saime and I lost a further friend when Yahya Tezel, who had studied at Cambridge, was delegated to recruit British academics to take over the jobs of Turkish lecturers who had been victimized. Through the Association of University Teachers we warned colleagues about his controversial mission. The real need, as indicated by an article published in *Nature* on 18 March, was to provide support for refugees.

Yeter's ordeal reawakened our interest in the most celebrated Turkish prisoner to remain creative behind bars. 'Why,' I complained to Saime, 'is there no decent biography of Nazım Hikmet?' It was hard to find any literature in English about this gifted and courageous poet. Like Yeter, he had responded to incarceration by providing tuition for other inmates – in painting, philosophy and current affairs. Bursa Prison had evolved during the 1940s into an informal Marxist academy with Hikmet as presiding genius. So Saime and I decided to pool our talents and write an article on Poetry and Politics in Kemalist Turkey. Having given up her scientific interests, she began research in Turkish archives, while I was moving into comparative literature.

This was facilitated by developments in the Modern Languages Faculty, where we had won approval for a new special subject – Avant-Garde Movements in Europe 1900–1939. Focusing on a period of revolutionary turmoil, this course compared the achievements or German Expressionists, French Surrealists, Russian Constructivists, Italian Futurists and English Modernists. We bridged the gap between lectures and supervisions by means of collaborative seminars attended by a dozen colleagues, including several sophisticated feminists. The project also lured senior scholars out of retirement, including the cultural theorist Raymond Williams, the surrealist poet Hugh Sykes-Davies, and the communist Margot Heinemann. Even Jacques Derrida came to Cambridge, at the invitation of my friend David Kelley, to give a lecture on Kafka. And our focus was further extended to include experimental film-makers.

The Avant-Garde course, which ran for over fifteen years, became a benchmark for interdisciplinary studies. The seminars, conducted in congenial college rooms like the Caius Senior Parlour, encouraged a critical approach to visual culture, building on the insights of John Berger's *Ways of Seeing*. And under the guidance of the art historian Frank Whitford, students began to grasp the complexity of the dialogue between poets and painters. Our Film Seminar took over the Arts Cinema on Wednesday mornings to screen classics like Lang's *Metropolis* and Eisenstein's *Battleship Potemkin*. This collaborative project proved so successful that we decided to publish. The first two volumes, co-edited with David Kelley and Peter Collier, appeared with Manchester University Press: *Unreal City: Urban Experience in Modern European Literature and*

Art (1985) and *Visions and Blueprints: Avant-Garde Culture and Radical Politics in the Early Twentieth-Century* (1988). At Saime's suggestion we included in the second volume our article on Poetry and Politics in Kemalist Turkey.

It was not only the Modern Languages curriculum that was changing. Cambridge was transformed as other subjects updated their courses, student numbers increased and new staff were appointed. There were significant readjustments in relations between colleges and faculties, between the privileges of dons and the needs of students. After the publication in 1989 of a further report on university governance, conducted by Sir Douglas Wass, a more professional Vice Chancellor was appointed and limits were placed on the power of the 'non-placets'. Although the Regent House retained its authority, some of the flaws satirized by Cornford were remedied at last. Moreover proposals for a business school, which had earlier fallen on deaf ears, were implemented when funds were provided by the Judge family to refurbish the old Addenbrookes hospital in Trumpington Street. Some of these reforms took years to complete, but the expansion achieved within two decades was truly remarkable.

During the 1980s there had been severe pressure on funding for universities, but Cambridge, buttressed by its endowments, weathered the storm better than most. At Sussex a scheme of early retirement had to be introduced to cope with the curbs imposed by the Conservative government. At Oxford the crisis was reflected in the famous Congregation of January 1985, when the University voted by a margin of two to one to deny Margaret Thatcher an honorary degree. But at Cambridge we kept our heads down and got on with the job. The success of this strategy is reflected in figures quoted by my Caius colleague Christopher Brooke, historian of the University of Cambridge. Between 1970 and 1990 the number of academic staff increased by 60 per cent (from 938 to 1,527), while student numbers rose from 10,500 to over 13,000. Thus the staff–student ratio improved while the creation of new colleges meant that additional numbers could be absorbed without any loss of cohesion.

For Cambridge those were vintage years, and even at Caius the curmudgeons were silenced. Academically and socially, the co-educational college flourished, while the Boat Club miraculously revived. After decades in the doldrums, the oarsmen responded to feminine charms by racing to the Head of the River, while the newly fledged oarswomen also excelled. When Neil McKendrick was elected Master, Caius launched an ambitious appeal for funds. Impressed by the new spirit in a college that cherished its traditions, the alumni responded with exceptional generosity, making it possible to construct a new residential block in West Road. Caius also succeeded in purchasing from the university the magnificent Cockerell Library – the finest neo-classical building in Cambridge, adjacent to our old courts. The refurbishment of the library, masterminded by

Jeremy Prynne, enhanced the college's status as a centre of excellence. Giants like Joseph Needham had passed away, but his vision of new wine in old bottles was fulfilled, and the most distinguished Fellows were still making waves. Stephen Hawking's *Short History of Time* had become an international bestseller. Reviewing these developments in 2003, McKendrick delivered a veritable encomium. Caius was the fourth oldest college, the third largest and the second most intellectually distinguished – but for all-round achievement it aspired to be the best!

CHAPTER TWELVE

German Developments and Austrian Alternatives

Keeping track of events in Germany was part of my task. For almost twenty years the Federal Republic was haunted by urban terrorists. Their practical aims were hard to gauge, but they were fiercely anti-capitalist and anti-American. In May 1972 three US soldiers were killed by a terrorist bomb planted at their base in Heidelberg. The threat appeared to have been contained when leading members of the Red Army Faction were arrested and put on trial, including Andreas Baader, Ulrike Meinhof, Gudrun Ensslin and Jan-Carl Raspe. But tighter security measures created a climate of repression, especially for left-wing sympathizers. There were hunger strikes in the high-security prisons, and in May 1976 Meinhof hanged herself in her cell. The terrorist campaign reached its climax the following year. On 7 April 1977 the Public Prosecutor, Siegfried Buback, was assassinated together with his driver. Three months later the Director of the Dresden Bank, Jürgen Ponto, suffered the same fate. Tensions increased in September when Hanns-Martin Schleyer, Head of the Employers Association, was taken hostage by members of the RAF in an effort to free their comrades. The government refused to budge and on 18 October, after a tense stand-off, Schleyer was killed by his captors. The following day Baader, Raspe and Ensslin committed suicide in their cells.

It was difficult to make sense of this dismal spectacle, but in the aftermath of the crisis the German Academic Exchange Service staged a conference on Literature and Society in the Federal Republic. That December, in an idyllic setting overlooking the Rhine, I joined thirty-five participants from a dozen countries in discussing recent developments. My report in the *Times Literary Supplement* (27 January 1978) portrayed leading German authors as the dissenting conscience of their age. A wave of repression in communist East Germany had forced independent spirits like Wolf Biermann into exile. Even in the Federal Republic, Heinrich Böll was denounced for attempting to understand the psychology of terrorism. The conference helped to put these events into context. A conservative spokesman claimed that dissident voices merely dramatized conflicts dreamt up on the fringes of a society that was 'doing very nicely thank you and has no need of public moralists'. But to others it seemed that the self-confidence of the Federal Republic concealed conflicts and insecurities which the wave of terrorism was bringing into the open. My conclusion was that literary developments reflected fundamental trends. 'In Germany,' I observed, 'the works of individual authors tend to be seen as fragments of a dialectically evolving collective consciousness' – a crisis of identity construed in Hegelian terms.

HEGEL, HEINE AND THE DIVIDED SELF

No one interested in dialectical thinking could ignore Hegel. His ideas claimed a central place in my lectures on German Philosophy of History, which ranged from the enlightened ideals of Lessing to the cyclical visions of Spengler. Seminars on German Philosophy, taught jointly with Nicholas Boyle, also enabled me to refine my understanding of Kant. The problem for Enlightenment thinkers like Kant and Lessing was how to reconcile the education of the human race with the realities of war and suffering. Herder's answer was that while cultures decay, they can be seen as rungs on an ascending ladder. His empathic and pluralistic vision in *Another Philosophy of History for the Education of Humanity* proved especially thought-provoking. 'Feel your way into everything!' he proclaimed.

For Lessing and Herder, suffering was a regrettable by-product of human activity, but Hegel took the bolder step of placing conflict at the centre of his system. His concept of Reason in History hinged on the idea that 'negation' yields gains – the dialectical contradictions that drive events towards reconciliation. The multifarious processes of 'Aufhebung' (Sublation) eliminate primitive residues, preserve valuable potentials and raise the outcome to a higher plane. Although the process can be seen as rational, nothing great is achieved without passion, especially the clash between competing nations. The individual 'Volksgeist', which Herder had celebrated for its intrinsic value, is subordinated to the historical process.

Hegel's *Phenomenology of Spirit* became the subject of closer scrutiny. A key chapter deals with the 'self-estranged spirit' – the dissatisfaction with things as they are that motivates human activity. Taking this idea as a reference point, I traced this dialectical conception of 'development' ('Entwicklung') through its multiple manifestations in German literature and philosophy. There were parallels with the striving for self-fulfilment in Goethe's *Faust* (as Walter Kaufmann pointed out in an influential study of Hegel). A similar idea of self-development underlies the 'Bildungsroman', that characteristically German conception of the novel that can be traced from Goethe to Thomas Mann. In this tradition the social determinants of character, which we associate with European realism, tend to be subordinated to a more intellectualized ethos of self-discovery, epitomized by *Der Zauberberg* (The Magic Mountain).

For German cultural historians this concept of development proved so seductive that they created the multi-volume publication *Deusche Literatur in Entwicklungsreihen* (German Literature in Developmental Sequences). This approach integrated Hegel's forward-moving dynamic with Herder's insistence that 'every culture has its centre of happiness in itself'. Each sequence is documented in a distinctively coloured binding, from Reformation, Baroque, Enlightenment, Classicism and Romanticism through to Political Poetry – over a hundred volumes in all. It was inspiring to use the set in the College Library that had belonged to Francis Bennett, a humanist in the Herder tradition. But how were those cultural riches to be harmonized with the sense that the political development of modern Germany was fundamentally flawed? Colleagues in the History Faculty like Geoffrey Eley were debating the so-called 'Sonderweg' – the 'wrong turning' that German society must have taken to evolve into a dictatorship.

Politically, Hegel's legacy was certainly problematic. German nationalists saw him as the philosopher of the nation state who provided a rationale for power politics, while left-wing Hegelians construed dialectic in revolutionary terms. Instead of states of consciousness, Marx identified economic production, technological innovation and class conflict as the driving forces. In his *Economic and Philosophical Manuscripts* Marx endows Hegel's concept of self-estrangement a more subversive momentum, going on to claim in the *Communist Manifesto* that only revolutionary action can overcome the alienating effects of capitalism and liberate us from our chains. 'In its rational form the dialectic is a scandal and abomination to the bourgeoisie,' Marx concluded in his afterword to *Das Kapital*, 'because it regards every historical form as a state of flux and is in essence critical and revolutionary.'

Fundamental to this dialectical drive is the idea of the divided self. This motif is even more explicit in the writings of Heine, whose poetry had haunted me since my schooldays. Now it was his political writings that claimed my attention. Having attended Hegel's lectures as a student in Berlin, Heine too tended to think in dualistic categories, contrasting thought with feeling, spirituality with sensuality, Nazarene and Hellene, Church with Synagogue, Germany with France. But unlike Hegel, he doubted whether the conflicts could ever be resolved, linking the ideological tensions to divisions within his own personality and endowing the idea of the divided self with exemplary force. 'Zerrissenheit' (inner discord) became the leitmotif of his poetry and prose. No sensitive person can claim that his heart has remained whole, he wrote in 1830, for the world is torn apart and the global rift runs through the heart of the poet.

While Hegel's tortuous prose proved a struggle, Heine endowed abstractions with an exuberant energy. Sampling the humour of *Die Harzreise*, students were delighted by his vision of Saul Ascher, the philosopher who insists on the primacy of Reason – even for a ghost! Dualisms generated memorable images, especially in the final years when Heine was trapped by a paralyzing disease. He pictured himself as the prodigal son who had herded swine with the Hegelians and explored the dizziest paths of dialectic. If only he could find his way back to the faith of his fathers! Intellectually he was too alert to gloss over the contradictions, while politically he foresaw the direst consequences, especially Teutomania, the revival of aggressive nationalism envisaged in his *History of Religion and Philosophy in Germany*. In his political testament, the preface to *Lutezia*, he identified two great antagonists: the communists, speaking with the voice of logic, and the nationalists – the voice of hatred. While fearing the first, he must admit that 'all men have the right to eat'. Against the second, the false patriots, he has fought all his life. 'Out of hatred for the nationalists,' he concludes, 'I could almost fall in love with the communists.'

It was not only Heine who was haunted by dualisms. The divided self forms a leitmotif from the Romantics to the Expressionists, from E. T. A. Hoffmann and Theodor Storm to Hermann Hesse and Thomas Mann. In German poets of the early twentieth century it took apocalyptic form. After the Hegelian cult of the state had triumphed in the German Reich, the notion of the divided self resurfaced in anguished forms. Sensitive spirits responded to the pressures of an authoritarian society with images of impending destruction. The most eloquent of the poets was Georg Heym, who expressed this apocalyptic vision in compellingly taut stanzas. Even more fascinating were the condensed quatrains of his eccentric friend Jakob van Hoddis, which envisaged an incongruous End of the World in which everything is falling apart: hats fly off heads, the seas are rising, dams no longer hold, trains drop off bridges – and almost everybody has a cold. First published in 1911, this became a cult poem, expressing a sensibility bombarded by incomprehensible stimuli.

The careers of both Heym and van Hoddis were cruelly curtailed. Heym was drowned in 1912 while skating on a frozen lake near Berlin, and two years later van Hoddis was confined by his family to an asylum for the insane. The work that helped me make sense of their visions was *Zerbrochene Formen* by Karl Ludwig Schneider, a scholar persecuted by the Nazis. But I also drew on one of the cult books of the 1970s, R. D. Laing's *The Divided Self*. Laing interpreted the disconnected utterances of schizophrenic patients as poetry. Eccentricity was to be understood not as mental illness, but as protest against an oppressive society. While avoiding Laing's simplistic opposition between 'true' and 'false' self, I linked these ideas to the case of Jakob van Hoddis. His divided identity had led him to change his name, originally Davidsohn. The anagram transposed a Jewish name into something more cosmopolitan. Once again, the global rift ran through the heart of a poet.

It was chilling to recall that the Nazis, seeing van Hoddis as a degenerate Jew, deported him to his death. These themes prompted me to reflect on the possibility of decentring the Hegelian model of historical development. Shouldn't it be reassessed it from the perspective of the excluded other – the exiled Heine or the eccentric van Hoddis? The evolution of the German nation state had clearly become entangled with anti-Jewish discrimination long before the Hitler period, as was clear from another of my sources, Hans Kohn's *The Mind of Germany*. Thus a new focus began to emerge from the preoccupation with dialectics – a course on the Tragedy of the German-Speaking Jews, analysing the antisemitic myths that drove so many into exile.

Can lives be divided without suffering disintegration? This was not merely a theoretical question, for there was an existential undertone to my teaching. To find an answer my attention segued from German developments towards Austrian alternatives – from linear evolution towards plural self-expression. Psychologically, the focal point was Sigmund Freud, but in literary terms it was Robert Musil, another author forced into exile by the Nazis. Musil explored plural states of consciousness with unparalleled subtlety, first in the story *Confusions of Young Törless* and then in his novel, *The Man without Qualities*. What appealed to me was the idea of living simultaneously on several planes, balancing the sense of reality (Wirklichkeitssinn) with a highly developed sense of possibility (Möglichkeitssinn). For years, my dreams had been haunted by unanswered questions. What if I had lived in exile, sharing life with Gila – the girl from Heidelberg who had attracted me as a student? Towards the end of the 1970s, out of the blue, she contacted me again and we resumed our correspondence. When she visited us in Cambridge, Saime was able to form her own impression of the person who had caused such heartbreak, now a married woman with three children.

What surprised me was the intensity of the relationship that ensued – a revival of feelings left in limbo when we parted in 1960. Trips abroad to attend conferences provided the opportunity for further shared experiences, for the torch I was carrying had been smouldering for twenty years. With Gila I lived wholly in German, feeling at home in what had once been the language of the enemy. Captivated by her melodious voice and mischievous smile, I was drawn into the symbolic realms she created with such artistry. Sometimes a letter would arrive decorated with women and

Letter from Germany (1982), decorated with symbolic figures

stars, birds and trees (FIGURE: Letter from Germany), which I would interpret in Jungian terms, casting her as my anima in a drama of rejuvenation.

To inhabit parallel universes, each with its own rewards, left me feeling
doubly blessed, although my priority lay with Saime and the children.
Family life in Cambridge flowed on with its invigorating eddies,
augmented in June 1983 when Saime and I became guardians of twelve-
year-old Sebastian Tennant. This fulfilled the wishes of our recently
deceased artist friends from Norfolk, Dorothy and Trevor. We now had
three children with divergent temperaments. Academically, too, there was
a rich harvest. The book on Kraus was ready for publication at last, and
I was planning a project on psychoanalysis.

BEYOND MARX AND FREUD

When my term as editor of *The Caian* came to an end, the College Council
offered me wine to the value of £250 as a token of appreciation. My incli-
nation was to spend the sum on books. My first idea was the English
edition of the Collected Works of Marx and Engels, published in thirty
volumes by Lawrence and Wishart. For political theorists this was an
invaluable resource, but in practical terms the communist experiments
were approaching their limits. The Soviet Union had little to offer during
the stasis of the Brezhnev era, while China remained a mystery. A few days
later I discovered an unexpected treasure in a second-hand bookshop: the
Complete Psychological Writings of Sigmund Freud, published in twenty-
four volumes by the Hogarth Press. How evocative the titles seemed
in James Strachey's translation – *The Interpretation of Dreams*, *The*

Psychopathology of Everyday Life, Studies in the Theory of Sexuality, Civilization and its Discontents. Intellectually and emotionally, this was my world. Never before had I spent such a large sum on books, but soon the whole set was at my office in Caius, nestling against notebooks recording my own dreams and desires.

The shift towards Freud was something that Saime and I shared, for we were learning the lessons of family life. The staff at Milton Road Primary school found our children a handful, especially headstrong Yusuf. After taking advice, we contacted the Family Therapy department in Brookside: 'Can you please sort this child out for us?' To our surprise, they recommended family therapy. For several years we attended regular sessions with Yusuf and Daphne, led by a skilled psychiatrist and funded by the National Health Service, after we agreed to be observed for training purposes through a one-way mirror. We soon realized that difficulties attributed to a single child involved us all. 'Daphne,' the psychiatrist would ask, 'how do you think Yusuf reacts when Saime feels upset by Ted coming home late?' This must have been a regular occurrence for one of our houseguests, Jesus Delgado from Spain, captured the incongruous family scene in a watercolour.

Family therapy offered salutary lessons. One on occasion the psychiatrist, after consulting the observers behind the mirror, summed up the session with the words: 'Ted seems like a lodger in his own home'.

Family scene at Metcalfe Road (by Jesus R. Delgado, 1980)

The interest in psychology was intensified by a personal tragedy. With her husband Peter, our friend Duska had moved with their daughter Sophie to a small house in Histon, a few miles north of Cambridge. We remained close friends, and Duska would share her troubled feelings with Saime, especially after she and Peter separated. She exerted a calming influence on our children and on several occasions she moved back into our house, looking after all three kids while we took a break. In March 1980 Duska and Sophie came to keep Yusuf and Daphne company while we enjoyed a week's holiday. Everything went well, but during our absence she pasted a page from the *Guardian* into the visitor's book: an article by Polly Toynbee about serious depression in mothers of small children. If she was sounding the alarm, we were too busy to notice.

Duska's interest in photography was encouraged by Nicholas, a gifted young photojournalist who helped her to create a darkroom in her garden shed. When relations with Nick became difficult, Duska stayed with us for several nights over New Year 1981–82. She visited us again on Friday 15 January while Sophie was staying with Peter. Returning to Histon for the night, she hanged herself in the darkroom. 'Life suddenly doesn't seem worth it any more,' she wrote in her farewell note. 'Constant worries about money, no relationship, being stuck in the house, no hope of a better world.' We were in tears as we attended the funeral. Tributes were led by John Brackenbury, a teacher who knew her well. 'Suppose a fair woman,' he began, quoting from the devotional writings of Thomas Traherne. 'Some have seen the beauties of heaven in such a person. They loved her not too much but upon false causes. They love a creature for sparkling eyes and curled hair, lily breasts and ruddy cheeks: which they should love more for being God's Image.' Even for those without faith, the words were unbearably moving. We had loved Duska but failed to listen, or rather listened but failed to hear.

How could we plumb such depths of sorrow? The shock of Duska's suicide led us to join a self-help psychotherapy group known as Re-evaluation Co-counselling. Founded in Seattle by an inspired teacher named Harvey Jackins, this movement identified oppressive patterns formed in childhood, exacerbated by the pressures of capitalist society, as the source of depression and despair. For Saime, this was the start of a second career helping others through psychodynamic counselling, for which she proved exceptionally gifted. For me, it reinforced a more theoretical interest in Freud's writings as a means of understanding both creative and destructive drives. Freud and the Literary Imagination proved a productive lecture topic leading to the publication of articles on authors influenced by psychoanalysis, including Schnitzler, Kafka and Hesse. And Carl Jung's study of Four Archetypes helped to elucidate the aesthetic of the dream.

My mentor Peter Stern was intrigued to see me discarding the claims of socialism – only to succumb to the equally unscientific appeal of psychoanalysis. During the 1970s, when I was sketching my first lectures on Freud and Jung, I also had to contend with the scepticism of my father. He and my mother enjoyed visiting us in Cambridge. Dining in college, he would reminisce about his university days. Oxford theology in the 1920s must have been rather progressive, for he had taken an optional course on Freud, Jung and Adler. 'They all reached different conclusions,' he declared over dessert, 'so they must all have been wrong.' Given my father's scepticism, it was surprising to learn that he had benefited from psychotherapy. His spiritual advisor, Mother explained during an intimate conversation, was a former army chaplain who had been trained to counsel shell-shocked soldiers. The depression which Father experienced in his early fifties had become most acute one winter's day when he was conducting a funeral. He almost fainted after hearing voices in the church-yard, turning so pale that the undertaker remarked to the verger: 'Whatever came over your vicar? He looked whiter than the corpse!' When Father recalled this experience during a counselling session, his therapist suddenly asked: 'What was the name of the person who was being buried?' My father's answer was: 'Knight, Jane Knight'. At that moment it felt as if the top of his head was lifted off. For the name Knight, my mother explained, released a memory that had been dormant for forty years. As a child of ten or twelve, Father had felt terrified when taken to see the corpse of his grandfather, also named Knight – Edward Knight. That conversation marked the moment when recovery began.

Hearing about this episode reinforced my interest in Freud. Whatever its logical flaws, psychotherapy yielded astonishing insights into repressed memories, while family counselling sessions helped us through the middle years of marriage. Saime and I drew sustenance from works of popular psychology, talking things through for hours while upstairs we could hear Yusuf playing his favourite Pete Townshend record, Teachers, Leave the Kids Alone. We enjoyed the witty dialogues between Robin Skynner and John Cleese in *Families and How to Survive Them*, while Gail Sheehy's *Passages: Predictable Crises of Adult Life* alerted us to the shifting balances of a long-term relationship. A further favourite was *Knots* by R. D. Laing, which helped us sort out emotional tangles. Strong-minded Saime, sensing my indecisiveness, added a further twist: 'I want you to do what *you* want to do, not what *I* want you to do!'

While I was dreaming of synthesis between Marx and Freud, political activists were supporting the struggle of the coalminers against the Thatcher government. 'We are striking to protect our industry,' declared the National Union of Coalminers, after the announcement in March 1984 that twenty unprofitable pits would be closed in order to reduce state subsidies. During the following months striking miners in the north of England had to endure such arduous conditions that left-wing sympa-thizers raised donations to support them. Saime travelled to Yorkshire with a group from Cambridge, and in September we welcomed to our home a miner's family from Blidworth, giving them a week's break from the increasingly bitter confrontations. Massive police deployments were used to protect strike-breakers, and Union leaders were demonized by the Tory press, using Margaret Thatcher's slogans about 'mob rule' and the 'enemy within'. By March 1985 she had achieved her aim of breaking Trade Union power and reducing coal-mining to the status of a marginal industry.

My Marxism remained on a theoretical plane. The term 'Charaktermaske' had been coined by Marx to designate the oppressive socio-economic identities imposed by the capitalist division of labour. For Max Weber this became the iron cage of an alienating work ethic, while Bert Brecht was inspired to deconstruct traditional models of dramatic character on stage. For Wilhelm Reich the idea evolved into the character armour of emotional defence mechanisms, and there were further linkages with Jung's persona theory and Kraus's exploration of the masks of satire. These concerns prompted me to devise lectures on Intellectual Antecedents to Twentieth-Century Literature, ranging from Marx's theory of alienation to Freud on repression. I wanted to go beyond Marx and Freud, exploring their influence on a generation of innovative thinkers from Ernst Bloch to Herbert Marcuse. Utopian socialism was experiencing a revival through Bloch's *Das Prinzip Hoffnung* (The Principle of Hope). Captivated by his idea of anticipatory consciousness, I too was determined to keep open dreams of the future.

The interest in psychoanalysis acquired a more scholarly grounding through research on Sigmund Freud's library, located at the Freud Museum in Hampstead. The Curator, David Newlands, generously allowed me to explore the thousands of volumes which Freud brought to London in 1938, when he and his family found refuge from Nazi-occupied Vienna. Together we planned a conference to explore the consequences of Freud's arrival in London, held – at the Museum in Hampstead and at the Germanic Institute in Bloomsbury – in 1986. The thrill of sitting on the famous couch was intensified when we met veteran analysts from central Europe, including Ernst Federn, Frederick Wyatt and Walter Toman, as well as cultural historians like Sander Gilman, Riccardo Steiner and Uwe Henrik Peters.

Freud appealed to me, not because his theories were scientifically proven, but because they stimulated such a range of insights into the human condition. It was quite a feat to bring together orthodox analysts like Pearl King and Andrew Paskauskas, feminists like Naomi Segal and Theresa Brennan, and so outspoken an opponent of psychoanalysis as the anthropologist Ernst Gellner. A further highlight was the paper on attachment theory by John Bowlby, author of *Child Care and the Growth of Love*, a controversial study of the separation anxiety experienced by infants deprived of maternal love. A tape recorder was at hand to capture the richly orchestrated medley, from Bowlby's plummy upper-class English to the incisively central European timbre of Gellner. With contributors of such distinction, it was easy to find a publisher. This collection, including my paper on Freud's Library and his Private Reading, appeared under the title *Freud in Exile: Psychoanalysis and its Vicissitudes*, co-edited with Naomi Segal.

HABSBURG AUGURIES AND LEGACIES

These interests prompted me to join the international conference circuit. By contrast with the routines of the Cambridge German Department, the symposiums sponsored by the Austrian Cultural Institute in London felt doubly rewarding. The event to mark the fiftieth anniversary of the death of Hofmannsthal, held in March 1979 at Bedford College in Regent's Park, marked a turning point. Several of the speakers were familiar to me including Michael Hamburger, poet and translator, and it was a delight to meet Eda Sagarra, Professor of German at Trinity College Dublin. But who was that large man bustling around in the background, helping even the shyest participant to feel at home? Peter Stern referred to him as 'the Baron', and one could well believe it, for he had a seigniorial panache. 'Let me have details of your travelling expenses,' he said, pulling out a bulging wallet as he introduced himself: 'Dr Bernhard Stillfried, Director of the Austrian Institute'.

The allusion to aristocracy was not merely a joke. Until the collapse of the Austro-Hungarian Empire put an end to titles of nobility, Bernhard's father had been Alfons Freiherr von Stillfried und Rathenitz, while his grandfather Raimund had been Court Photographer to Emperor Franz Joseph. Dr Stillfried continued the family tradition in the field of cultural politics, encouraging young academics to reassess the Hapsburg legacy. Convinced that Vienna had been the cultural capital of the early twentieth century, he was equally passionate about life on the margins of the Empire – from Czernowitz to Trieste, Innsbruck to Prague. It was hardly surprising that my interest in Kraus and Freud appealed to him. Before long we were on informal 'Du'-terms and Bernhard was inviting me out to supper with Ira, his charming wife.

Bernhard transformed the horizons of colleagues with an Austrian bent by supporting a series of symposiums, so-called because of their informal style and nourishing refreshments. In 1984 the focus was on Karl Kraus at the Germanic Institute in Russell Square, where Peter Stern had become Director, and the proceedings were co-edited with an Austrian colleague, Sigurd Paul Scheichl. This was the period when Margaret Thatcher's government was curbing the power of trade unions and imposing stringent reforms on universities. Her ascendancy was increased by a swathe of support in the press from the high-minded *Times* to the populist *Sun*, both owned by an Australian media mogul named Rupert Murdoch. During those difficult years Bernhard's ebullience lifted our spirits, while Ira was equally life-affirming. 'Viewed from the future,' she sagely remarked over supper, 'we are living *now* in the good old days'. Such insights helped to maintain a sense of proportion.

The highlight of this period was the long delayed publication of my study of Karl Kraus. Originally the book was to be entitled *The Satirical Masquerade*, concentrating on Kraus's critique of duplicity, but the focus on masquerade faded in the final years before the Great War as his tone became increasingly pessimistic. The inner disintegration of the Habsburg Empire provided him with abundant auguries of disaster. 'Apokalypse' was the title of the visionary essay of 1908 in which he identified Kaiser Wilhelm II as an apocalyptic horseman with power to take peace from the earth. This vision acquired more menacing implications as he transformed the newly invented airship into 'the great dragon' which dominates the War in Heaven sequence in Revelations, chapter 12. Peace on earth, he felt, was threatened by unprecedented horrors from above. For Kraus this foreshadowed the aerial bombardments of the Great War. Experience, his spokesman the Grumbler observes in *The Last Days of Mankind*, should have taught the perpetrators of 'murder from the air' that 'although their intention is to hit an arsenal, they must unavoidably hit a bedroom instead, and in place of a munitions factory, a girls school'.

My new title *Apocalyptic Satirist* formed an arc across seventy years of military conflict. Flushed with success in the Falklands War of 1982, Margaret Thatcher joined President Reagan's in putting pressure on the Soviet Union by means of NATO's 'twin-track' strategy, involving the deployment of Cruise missiles in the Home Counties. For the Campaign for Nuclear Disarmament this was a dangerous escalation of the arms race, and as the first missile-bearing transporters arrived at Greenham Common in Berkshire, the base was surrounded by tens of thousands of protestors. Saime intensified her activities in this field, and we both visited the Women's Peace Camp at Greenham, as well as attending demonstrations at NATO bases in East Anglia. The threat of a nuclear conflagration was becoming so pervasive that ten-year-old Yusuf dug a fall-out shelter in our garden with the help of Daphne and their friends – a play activity that soothed real fears.

Confident there would be readers for a book to be entitled *Karl Kraus – Apocalyptic Satirist: Culture and Catastrophe in Habsburg Vienna*, I started looking for a publisher. The book was rejected by Weidenfeld & Nicolson: a polite letter, signed by Robert Baldock, suggested that it was more suited to a university press. Cambridge University Press would have accepted it, provided the typescript was extended to cover the inter-war period – and then reduced to half its length! This request would have reduced me to despair, had not another letter arrived by the same post – from Robert Baldock. He had moved to the London office of Yale University Press and wondered how the Kraus book was doing. Within days we were closeted at his office in Bedford Square, where Robert accepted my bulky manuscript and guided me through the referral process. Yale delegated a copyeditor named Catherine Carver to go through the typescript with me line by line, and the beautifully produced volume was then published to great acclaim. 'An essential and prophetic voice,' wrote Tom Phillips on 9 October 1986 in the *Independent*, a paper just launched in an effort to raise journalistic standards. There was special interest in the critique of links between the press, the military, politics and big business. 'Kraus is becoming *the* writer for the age of Ronald Reagan and Rupert Murdoch,' commented Neal Ascherson in the *Observer*. And the *New York Review of Books* featured an extended article by D. J. Enright, who nominated *Apocalyptic Satirist* as one of his Books of the Year.

My commitment to Austrian studies had been strengthened by the arrival from Oxford of the Kafka scholar Ritchie Robertson. Our first encounter in October 1983 was at a London seminar organized by Peter Stern. Arriving late, I heard a young man holding forth in a strong Scottish accent about Kafka's interest in Zionism. There is not a single reference to the Jewish question in Kafka's stories and novels, so this seemed strange. 'Kafka took such pains to transpose his dilemmas into universal images,' remarked a colleague. 'Why translate them back into narrowly Jewish terms?' This echoed my own reaction, but my views soon changed. After Ritchie had settled into his teaching duties at Downing College, we began to meet for convivial lunches, and it became clear that there was much to be learnt from his searchingly contextual approach.

Ritchie's support made it possible to launch the Austrian Study Group in October 1985. Although unable to offer a fee, we attracted a stimulating range of speakers, some sponsored by the Austrian Institute. They included Wendelin Schmidt-Dengler and Alfred Doppler from Austria, Mark Anderson, Sander Gilman and Joseph Peter Strelka from the States, as well as Cambridge scholars like Steven Beller and Derek Beales. Topics ranged from the Enlightenment to the feminist narratives of Ingeborg Bachmann, but there was a concentration on the creative ferment of turn-of-the-century Vienna, including the paintings of Oskar Kokoschka and the music of Richard Strauss. More specifically, the focus was on Jewish authors: Altenberg and Schnitzler, Kafka and Kraus, Manes Sperber and Hermann Broch. This led logically to the theme of exile. Early in December 1989 two speakers from the Austrian National Library described efforts to trace the literary estates for writers forced to flee abroad by the Nazis. The flavour of these seminars was captured by my colleague Elisabeth Stopp, who had grown up in Vienna. 'I've been meaning to write & express enthusiasm about the last Austrian group meeting,' she wrote, 'good talks, splendid exhibits, a warm and friendly atmosphere.' Enclosed was a generous cheque – 'a Christmas present to Austrian Studies'.

The most challenging topic was the poetry of Paul Celan, a Holocaust survivor who wrote hermetic verse. The room at Caius was crowded on 13 March 1987 when this most elusive of poets was introduced by Amy Colin from Washington State University in Seattle. Celan's haunting poem 'Death is a Master from Germany' was already widely known, but the focus of the lecture was on 'Huhediblu', a more cryptic response to the Holocaust that infringes syntactic and phonetic conventions. The speaker impressed us all through her intellectual energy and cultural range. Born of Jewish parents in communist Romania, Amy had been educated in Düsseldorf before completing her doctorate at Yale. She embodied the tragic brilliance of the Habsburg legacy, bringing to life the pluralistic culture of Bukovina, shared by Austrians and Romanians, Germans and Jews, until nationalistic frenzies swept everything away. Meeting Amy intensified the attraction of Austrian Jewish studies, and I arranged for her to stay at Caius so she could work undisturbed on her Celan book *Holograms of Darkness*. The title was inspired by a display of holograms that we viewed together, combining surface brilliance with an illusion of depth that caused my head to spin.

The Austrian Study Group was acquiring such momentum that Ritchie Robertson and I decided to launch a journal. We were encouraged not only by Amy Colin, with whom I began a lively correspondence, but also by Bernhard Stillfried, who was returning to Vienna to take up a position as Sektionschef in the Foreign Ministry (we hosted a farewell party for him at Caius). Our Advisory Board included W. G. Sebald, who had recently published a fine book on Austrian literature entitled *Die Beschreibung des Unglücks* (The Description of Unhappiness). Where Sebald dwelt on the theme of melancholy, our aim was to explore more dynamic links between culture and politics. In Martin Spencer, our contact at Manchester University Press, we found an enthusiastic publisher. Martin was taking over as Director of Edinburgh University Press and decided to launch the project from there. The production of a quarterly journal was beyond our resources, so after extensive consultations we decided that *Austrian Studies* should be an annual publication with each volume organized around a specific theme, supplemented by book reviews. Volume 1, *Vienna 1900*, was launched in June 1990, followed by a second volume on *The Austrian Enlightenment*.

By this time Ritchie Robertson had returned to Oxford, but our partnership continued to prosper. Further jointly edited volumes included *Psychoanalysis in its Cultural Context* and *The Habsburg Legacy*. What impressed us most was the international range of scholarship in the field. While Austrian academics sometimes appeared reluctant to dig into their own past, outstanding work was being done by the French critic Jacques Le Rider, the Canadian book historian Murray Hall, my Exeter-based colleague W. E. Yates, the Prague Kraus scholar Kurt Krolop, the editor of Kraus's writings Christian Wagenknecht in Göttingen, and Friedrich Pfäfflin in Marbach, editor of Kraus's letters. Moreover, some of the most successful Austrian Studies conferences were hosted by Gerald Stieg in Paris, John Warren in Oxford and Gilbert Carr in Dublin.

Clearly, there was no single Habsburg legacy but a plurality of perspectives. Kraus's satire held a central position, but it was increasingly balanced by the affirmative vision of Joseph Roth. In autumn 1989 we staged an exhibition in the Faculty Library documenting the career of this Jewish author from his birth on the eastern frontier of the Habsburg Empire to his death in French exile. The pluralism of old Austria, so eloquently evoked by Roth, provided an antidote to the authoritarian German Reich. Of course, the Habsburg Empire was also plagued by nationalism and antisemitism, but the Josephinist ideal of toleration lived on – and deserved to be commemorated.

When the Conference of University Teachers of German met in Cambridge in 1990, I spoke on National Memory and the Austrian Idea. German theories of history, my research suggested, were dominated by myths of national destiny, based on the unity of the 'Volk'. Inspired by Hegel, ideologists like Paul Lagarde campaigned for the union of all German-speaking peoples and a Europe governed from Berlin. The stumbling block was the Habsburg Empire. Drawing on the writings of Friedrich Schlegel and Frantisek Palacky, I argued that the multinational idea was all the more significant because it challenged the Germanic vision of a 'Mitteleuropa' purged of Slavs and Jews. Clearly, this could not be the last word on such a controversial subject, but it defined an agenda relevant to our own day. The concept of Europe as a federation of states sharing a common patrimony could hardly have been more topical, as the walls dividing East and West came tumbling down.

CHAPTER THIRTEEN

The Writing on the Wall

In December 1989 Saime and I staged a New Year's Eve party complete with belly dancers and bagpipes. To record the events of that momentous year, we created a wall newspaper with headlines like Gorbachev's Gamble and 'We are one nation!' (Helmut Kohl). As we worked on this collage, lines from Heine were going through my head – the ballad about Belshazzar's Feast, set to music by Schubert:

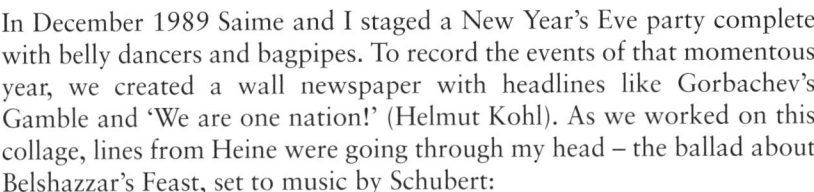

Die Mitternacht zog näher schon.	The midnight hour was drawing on.
In stiller Ruh lag Babylon . . .	silent and still lay Babylon . . .
Und sieh, und sieh, an weisser Wand	Behold, upon the wall of white
Da kam's hervor wie Menschenhand . . .	a spectral hand began to write . . .
Magier kamen, doch keiner verstand	The fiery writing on the wall
Zu deuten die Flammenschrift an der Wand.	held the magicians in its thrall.
Belsazar wurde in selbiger Nacht	That night ended Belshazzar's reign:
Von seinen Knechten umgebracht.	by his own minions he was slain.

In Heine's poem, as in the Book of Daniel, the tyrant is punished for sacrilege, but now a whole political system had been weighed in the balance and found wanting. The writing was on the wall for the Soviet bloc as the nations of Eastern Europe claimed their freedom. By a strange coincidence the Berlin Wall was breached on 9 November, a red letter day in the German political calendar. The same date had marked the collapse of

Imperial Germany in 1918 and the Kristallnacht pogrom of 1938.

Freedom was not an abstraction for our family. We could never forget the ordeal of Saime's sister Yeter, whose spirit was unconfined by prison walls. One of her poems marked the moment when a pregnant fellow prisoner felt a stirring in her womb, offering hope for a better world: 'Kick, baby, kick – and open the door / to your mother's most beautiful days.' After her release Yeter, who had lost her job, escaped from Turkey with her husband Hakkı, finding new employment with scientific institutes near Munich. Now she was celebrating with us in Cambridge. We hoped there would be a peace dividend after the ending of the Cold War, but there was also a fear that the collapse of East European communism would undermine efforts to create a more egalitarian society in the West.

SHADOWS FROM THE PAST

For me, the challenge was to connect all these events, casting back with Kraus to the catastrophe of the Great War and using testimonies from the 1930s to explore the reverberations of communism and fascism. This involved refining my listening skills and compiling oral history narratives of endurance and survival. Partly, this was an attempt to repay personal debts. My former Tutor Freddy Stopp had suffered a stroke, which left his speech impaired (his wife Elisabeth thought that his health had been damaged by his war service in Italy). He still appreciated visitors, so over tea at their home in Drosier Road we would converse through a mixture of words and sign language. When Freddy died, my tribute in *The Caian* praised his seminars as a scholarly initiation, adding that 'students initially alarmed by his erudition were soon won over by his humanity'.

A further volume of Austrian Studies was planned on the experiences of refugees from National Socialism, for the symposiums in London had brought us into contact with survivors who had compelling stories to tell. The principal speaker at the launch of *Karl Kraus – Apocalyptic Satirist* was Johann Wolfgang Bruegel, a Social Democrat from Prague, who recalled the controversies of the 1930s as if they had occurred yesterday. The Libris bookshop in Swiss Cottage provided further links with the refugee community. Saturday mornings were sociable occasions at 38a Boundary Road, for the owner Joseph Suschitzky would reward regular customers with tea or coffee as they inspected new acquisitions. The habitués included a book-lover named Ernst Pories, who worshipped the shades of Karl Kraus. It was not long before we were sitting in his flat just off the North Circular Road, trading quotations. As a schoolboy in Vienna he had witnessed the destruction of Austria. When the Germans marched in, his parents felt obliged to destroy their copies of *Die Fackel*, fearing they would be incriminating. So dedicated was Pories to the Kraus tradition that he succeeded, after fleeing to Britain, in reassembling a complete set of the magazine. By profession, he was a technical translator, but he also had a gift for deciphering Kraus's almost illegible manuscripts. When I brought photocopies back from research in Vienna, he would make impeccable transcripts.

A more riveting story was told by a Holocaust survivor named Eric Walters-Kohn, whose reminiscences extended from the legacy of Metternich to the tyranny of Hitler. When we first met at the Austrian Institute in June 1988, he startled me by reciting a poem heard from Kraus's lips fifty years earlier, 'Libido' – a skit on psychoanalysis. During the following years we had an intensive correspondence punctuated by further meetings and phone calls. 'People do not understand the *emotional* effects of the Holocaust,' he said, 'I cannot forget it for a single day.' Like other refugees, Eric was living a double life – as a businessman in modern Britain and a memorialist of old Austria. In his eighties he was still running Eric Walters Ltd, Manufacturers of Uniforms and Fashion Blouses, proudly taking me on a tour of the workshop in Kimberley Road. But what he valued most was my appreciation of his writings, especially the family memoirs that he was longing to see in print. 'You are one of the few people who tries to understand these things,' he said.

Excerpts had already appeared in print describing his ordeals in the Dachau and Buchenwald concentration camps, followed by anecdotes about service in the British army. Eric was haunted by personal tragedies – the death of his parents during the Holocaust and the loss of his fiancée. But the most evocative chapters in his memoirs dealt with Koritschan (Korycany), the rural paradise in Moravia where he had spent summer holidays during the final years before the First World War. He was continuously revisiting the region in his imagination, even though the heroes of his youth had passed away. Proudly, he showed me his drawings of local characters, done from memory: Bozena Foretek his Catholic governess, Dr Erbmann the family physician, Ignaz Deutsch the grocer, Suslik the watchmaker, and Commander Kotzmann of the voluntary fire brigade. To me they sounded like characters from a folktale, but for Eric they recalled the paradise of antediluvian Austria. He was also full of praise for the Metternich family, whose estate was at Koritschan. Prince Clemens Metternich, he explained, had planted beech woods to source the bentwood furniture manufactured by Thonet Brothers, Huguenots settled in Moravia.

Eric's typescript was shared with Cambridge friends, including Elisabeth Stopp. To our astonishment she revealed that her mother, born Marie Vcelak, had worked for Thonet in Vienna before the Great War. 'For about a year,' she explained in a letter to Eric, 'Marie was sent to Koritschan, where they needed a secretary who knew Czech as well as German. She had a very happy time there, loving to walk in the woods which you describe, learning the folksongs which she later sang to us as children.' In about 1906 she was transferred to London, where she met – and later married – Elisabeth's father, director of Thonet's English branch. Sadly, such associations carried no weight with publishers, but perhaps we could find space in Austrian Studies. Ritchie Robertson was intrigued by Eric's spirited writings and drawings, but it would have required a major effort to prepare them for publication. So the sylvan idyll of Koritschan, counterpoint to the horrors of Buchenwald, remained unpublished (a copy was deposited at the Jewish Museum in London).

A further discovery was the collection of David Joseph Bach, an Austrian Social Democrat whose name was familiar to me from *Die Fackel*. As Director of the socialist Arts Centre in Vienna, Bach held a key position in the cultural life of the First Republic. When he celebrated his fiftieth birthday, he was presented with a casket containing original artistic works and manuscripts by leading painters, composers and writers, including Kraus and Schnitzler, Kokoschka and Schoenberg. When Bach was forced into exile by the annexation of Austria, he was allowed to take the collection with him, since the Nazis regarded it as valueless. The casket, together with several hundred books from Bach's library, was now in the possession of his great-nephew, an English doctor named Philip Marriott, who had trained at Caius. With the College Librarian, Jeremy Prynne, I paid a visit to Dr Marriott's home in Harlow to view the collection. After further consultations, the books found a home in Cambridge University Library while the artistic treasures were destined for Caius.

These narratives of survival prompted me to take out the tape recorder I'd used for interviews at Caius. My next subject was Ilse Hellman, an émigré psychoanalyst who had attended our Freud symposium in London. Long afternoons were spent at her apartment in South Kensington, recording episodes from family history. Born of Jewish parents, she had been brought up in Vienna as a Catholic and was now a devout Anglican. In the early 1920s her father, a friend of Hugo von Hofmannsthal, had helped to launch the Salzburg Festival. She herself had trained with Charlotte Bühler as a child psychologist, before finding refuge from the Nazis in London. During the war she had worked with Anna Freud at the Hampstead Nursery, before becoming an independent analyst specializing in longitudinal studies. Life history, even when supported by written sources, raised intriguing questions. 'Switch off the tape recorder,' said Ilse at a crucial point. 'I'd rather not record my answer to your question about my family's attitude towards Eastern Jews.' As a psychoanalyst her mission was to relieve traumatic memories, but she preferred to gloss over the tensions between her acculturated family and the orthodox Jews who had fled from the impoverished eastern provinces.

Hearing of this interest in oral history, my father agreed to record his early memories, talking for hours with the recorder on our kitchen table.

His reminiscences included a vivid account of his student days. 'How was it that after training for the Methodist ministry,' I asked, 'you were ordained as an Anglican?' He brushed the question aside, insisting there was no real difference between the denominations. His reason for serving the same parish for so long was that communities needed 'stationary men' who could draw on a wealth of experience. Seniority on the County Council had even earned him the rank of Alderman, a title deriving from Anglo-Saxon England.

Two years after this interview Father fell seriously ill. He and Mother had moved into a smaller house at Buckfastleigh, but the Vicarage was still available for family gatherings, including a grand reunion in summer 1979. By that date all my siblings were married with children of their own. Father, who was determined to die in harness, continued to take services until he was hospitalized in January 1981 with terminal cancer. At his funeral in February the church was thronged by the parishioners he had served so well. Mother showed great fortitude while all around were weeping. But later that year we were astonished to learn a secret which our parents had kept from us for almost fifty years.

Sorting through papers from a locked drawer, my brother Christopher, acting as executor, discovered letters that explained the break with Methodism. The young John Timms had owned a motorbike, invaluable for travelling to remote Cornish villages as a probationer for the ministry. He would also collect his girlfriend Janie Axford from Collery for the occasional spin in the countryside. The night they spent together at a hotel returned to haunt them, for they were spotted by a senior Methodist, who reported them. The result was that Father was hauled before the local Synod and accused of an 'infringement of discipline'. The matter was referred a national committee in July 1931, when the Methodist Conference met in Birmingham. Given his ability, Father had eloquent supporters, including members of the Cornish Synod, but the decision went against him.

Now we understood why Father had become an Anglican, taking a tutorial post at St Stephen's House while completing his second degree at Oxford. However, we were unprepared for a further revelation. In September 1931 Janie Axford became pregnant. This was the era of the Marie Stopes sexual advice clinics, but for Christian parents there was no question of an abortion. On 6 February 1932 they were quietly married in Oxford, and on 14 June their first son Owen was born. In that same London hospital a married woman named Mrs Young was recovering from an operation that left her infertile, so an adoption was arranged. Mother was persuaded to give up her child so that her husband could be ordained – there was no place for them in the Church with a son conceived out of wedlock. It was only after the adoption that they were able to make a new start under the patronage of the Bishop of London. Father was still based in Oxford in August 1933 when my sister Helen was born, and two months later he was ordained at St Paul's Cathedral. Mother later told me that not a day had passed without her thinking of Owen, while Father, too, was pursued by shadows from the past.

In that period respectability was prized above all things, especially when it was hard won. After the truth was revealed, my feelings were mixed. On the one hand our parents' powers of recovery were impressive. Surmounting their ordeals, they had gone on to lead constructive lives and raise a large family. But the social code proved so inhibiting that they rejected their son for a second time when he succeeded in tracing them. At first they returned Owen's letters unopened, and when he finally appeared on their doorstep they still concealed his existence. The most they could manage was to meet him surreptitiously in Dorset, denying him access to the rest of the family. How often had Mother told us the parable of the Lost Sheep, Father the story of the Prodigal Son! But they were unable to rejoice when that which had been lost was found.

In the innumerable circulars received from my father there was no hint of the meetings with Owen that had taken place during the last dozen years of his life. After his death Mother struggled to come to terms with having borne nine children. Would it be possible for the whole family to meet in a spirit of acceptance? Owen was married and living in Sweden, David in Canada, Robert in Australia – all with families of their own. The year 1987 marked a watershed. It was Mother's eightieth birthday in April, followed by my fiftieth in June, so we invited the whole clan to Cambridge. Miraculously, all nine siblings came, mostly accompanied by spouses and children. Those meeting Owen for the first time were astonished by the physical resemblance and similarity of character, including the passion for reading. Much as Owen appreciated the love of his adoptive parents, the only book in their home, as he recalled, was *Scouting for Boys*. An innate hunger for knowledge had prompted him to spend many hours visiting a relative and devouring the books on the shelves.

Once the family had gathered at our house, we spent an afternoon sharing memories. We had pulled down so many dividing walls that there was ample space in our extended living-room for thirty people. It proved a fraught occasion, especially for Mother (now Grandma Joan) and for Owen. He had to listen in silence while we recalled the joys of a Vicarage childhood, from which he had been excluded. His own – symbolic – contribution was to recite a narrative poem about the inexplicable disappearance of three lighthouse keepers, Flannan Isle. Things became more relaxed when we organized an inter-generational football match in the field beyond our garden. The gathering concluded with a dinner in the Senior Parlour at Caius. There were mixed feelings as the party ended, reflected in our Visitor's Book. 'Four days ago it seemed an impossible family jigsaw,' wrote David, who had come from Toronto with his elder son, 'but we are not really an impossible family, are we?'

PAPERING OVER THE CRACKS

Compulsive hoarders sometimes wonder whether they should have trained as archivists. In addition to the family records, papers were piling up in college documenting my international contacts, both personal and professional. The letters from Gila in Germany, all addressed to Caius, already filled a large drawer. Like my father I was guarding a secret that could not be shared with the family. It was hardly a new discovery that truth is elusive. Historians should spend their time copying from each other, the waspish A. J. P. Taylor once suggested. They are bound to get it wrong when they cite original documents! During the 1980s scepticism about objective truth reached a new peak, driven by post-modernism, but my research left little time for theorizing. The Kraus Archives had revealed that the idea of unity of man and work rested on a fallacy. The satirist might affirm the connection between 'word and being', but his private letters reflected dimensions of experience erased from the public record. This enabled me to solve the conundrum represented by copies of *Die Fackel* stamped with the name of Major Baron Lempruch. How could anti-establishment satire have appealed to an aristocratic military man? The answer lay with letters which showed that Kraus was on cordial terms with officers in the imperial army. Initially his opposition to war had rested on conservative foundations.

A further mystery surrounded his triangular relationship with the physician Fritz Wittels, a member of Freud's circle, and the actress Irma Karczewska. The first volume of *Apocalyptic Satirist* suggested that she and Kraus had a 'short-lived love affair' and that Wittels, who was another of Irma's admirers, became 'extremely jealous'. It turned out that the story was more complex. The quest for Karczewska involved long conversations with the woman who knew most about the Kraus Archive, Sophie Schick. Sitting in a coffeehouse near the Vienna City Library, she held me enthralled by her reminiscences. Like her late husband, the librarian Paul Schick, she was a Holocaust survivor. When serving in the resistance in Vichy France, she had passed as a Polish woman, before slipping across the border into Switzerland. My tape recorder was in Cambridge, but I made copious notes – about Kraus's private experiences as well as her own. Apparently, she possessed a cache of documents and photographs, including Irma's diary, which provided a key to that relationship; but the details were too sensitive to be revealed.

Giving priority to research in Austria did not mean ignoring German affairs. A thaw in relations with the German Democratic Republic (the

GDR) enabled me to attend a summer school in 1983 at Weimar, the small town in Thuringia where Goethe spent most of his life. Four years earlier, during our tour of communist countries, Saime and I had already visited the town. As we approached, we had taken a wrong turning – and found ourselves on the road to the Buchenwald concentration camp. Soon we were visiting the memorial museum, created by the East German government to document the crimes of fascism. We continued our journey in reflective mood, visiting Goethe's house that same afternoon. Would it ever be possible to square Weimar humanism with the horrors of National Socialism? Feeling exhausted, we rested by the fountain, and Saime began to refresh herself from water bubbling from the spout. 'Nicht trinken! Nicht trinken!' cried a voice, and a middle-aged woman bustled up, warning us that the water might be polluted. She introduced herself as Susannah Lawrentz, a schoolteacher from a neighbouring town. In a few moments we were such good friends that she invited us to supper with her family – her husband, who was already retired, and her youngest daughter Sabine. This had provided the chance to form a first impression of 'real socialism'.

The primary focus of the Weimar summer school was on language and literature: we were introduced to the holdings of the Brecht Archive and allowed to handle first editions by Goethe and Schiller. It was a delight to visit the modest dwelling where Johann Gottfried Herder had lived with his wife Caroline, more homely than Goethe's classicizing residence. In addition to excursions to nearby towns like Martin Luther's Wittenberg, there were excellent lectures on current affairs. Speaking on East German economic problems, a professor from Jena named Ursula Gabler was astonishingly frank about low levels of productivity and an over-dependence on imports, not only from the Soviet Union. The trade deficit was forcing the country to negotiate credits from West Germany, while the burden of foreign debt was increased by high interest rates – part of President Reagan's strategy for putting pressure on communism.

Among my priorities was the desire to learn more about the peace movement. The official position was presented by the President of the state-sponsored Peace Council, who defended compulsory military service including the fortifying of the Berlin Wall as a bastion against fascism. All the more reason to contact groups associated with the Evangelical Church, whose values were closer to my own. We were allowed considerable freedom of movement, enabling me to renew acquaintance with the Lawrentz family and make delightful new friends. No doubt our movements were monitored by State Security (the Stasi), but this did not feel inhibiting. People were open in their criticisms, especially about the lack of freedom to travel, but also proud of what had been achieved: the educational opportunities, job security and social equality, especially for women. Among the younger generation who steered clear of the cadres of the Free German Youth and frequented the cafés, there was stronger sense of frustration. They found a sympathetic hearing from a bearded Englishman keen to understand life behind the curtain. Whole afternoons were spent in conversation with people half my age, and there was a lively arts scene, including an underground photographer who produced images of East German life normally hidden from view.

Bulging notebooks accompanied me on the return journey via Frankfurt-am-Main. Looking through the window of the railway carriage, I was struck by the contrasts between East and West. The Federal Republic was visibly thriving now that urban terrorism had been contained (thoughtful critics of capitalism were joining the Green Party). But the GDR was caught in double bind, dominated politically by Moscow and economically by the West. In short, socialism was far from fulfilling the Marxist scenario. The publicity leaflets handed out during our course might claim that the GDR was the most stable and successful country in the Soviet bloc, but I sensed that the communist regime was papering over the cracks.

The weeks in Weimar prompted a fresh approach to teaching. My colleague Peter Hutchinson, author of *Literary Presentations of Divided Germany*, kept us in touch with trends behind the Berlin Wall by inviting East German authors to give readings in Cambridge, including Stefan Heym and Reiner Kunze. And I had already lectured on the satirical ballads of Wolf Biermann, whose outspoken performances led to his expulsion from the GDR. While Biermann's songs were sardonic, a more subtle commentary on life under socialism was provided by Christa Wolf. Her writings prompted me to design lectures on the theme of War and Peace as viewed from each side of the Iron Curtain – by Christa Wolf and Heinrich Böll.

The lectures on Böll focused on his critiques of social deprivation, military conflict and political propaganda – from *Und der Zug war pünktlich* (*The Train was Punctual*) to *Die verlorene Ehre der Katharina Blum* (*The Lost Honour of Katharina Blum*). The essential question is set out in the subtitle to *Katharina Blum*: How violence originates and where it can lead. Böll's commitment to 'Trümmerliteratur', the unsparing description of life among the ruins after the destruction caused by Allied bombers, provided my opening theme. But his social realism acquires religious undertones in *The Train was Punctual*, a gripping account of the feelings of young conscripts as they travel towards death on the Eastern Front. Böll's troubled hero recalls the Good Friday prayer, which he loves for its inclusiveness. To illustrate the power of this passage, I quoted the wording from the Anglican Book of Common Prayer: 'Have mercy upon all Jews, Turks, Infidels, and Heretics, and fetch them home, blessed Lord, to thy flock.' Böll's anthem for doomed German youth becomes a kadish for the Eastern Jews.

His later work hints at continuities between the repression of the Nazi era and the demonization of left-wing dissidents and their sympathizers by the conservative press of the 1970s. This is the theme of *Katharina Blum*, a novel that was compellingly filmed. An antidote to this climate of repression is provided by the gestures of human solidarity so poignantly expressed in his shorter fiction, especially *Und sagte kein einziges Wort* (*And Never Said a Word*). In this understated novel, set in the squalid urban landscape of post-war Germany, alternate chapters are narrated by a young couple, Käte and Fred, as they struggle to repair a marriage that is on the rocks. Narrative sympathy lies with the young woman. One of the lessons Böll had learnt from the war, as he put it in an interview, was the absurdity of traditional models of 'manliness'.

For Christa Wolf there is a similar emphasis on gender roles and the tensions between the personal and the political. The jacket design of her first novel *Der geteilte Himmel* (Divided Heaven) graphically evokes the idea of a divided self (FIGURE: Cover of Christa Wolf's *Der geteilte Himmel*).

The impression – not simply of a person but of a planet in eclipse - is

Cover of Christa Wolf's *Der geteilte Himmel* (1968)

borne out by the story of Rita, a young woman injured working in a factory cooperative. Through a montage of flashbacks in hospital, Rita reflects on the sacrifices required to create an egalitarian society, mourning the loss of the boyfriend who has fled to the West. What might have been a simple boy-meets-girl dramatizes the unbridgeable gap between two political systems. Wolf's feminism becomes more explicit in *Cassandra*, which sets the struggle between the sexes within the framework of the Trojan War. The fundamental male impulse, the novel suggests, is to dominate and destroy, for war is being waged for a 'phantom'.

The topicality of these themes became almost unbearable when I repeated the lectures in the spring of 1991. By that date the division of Germany had been overcome, but there was little prospect of a peaceful world. For the Gulf War, precipitated by Saddam Hussein's occupation of Kuwait, was reaching its grisly climax as American airpower pulverized a bomb shelter in Baghdad. My lectures were always illustrated by textual excerpts, and this time the hand-outs included front-page reports about the bomb-shelter atrocity from two British newspapers. *The Times* of 14 February printed an eye-witness account by their correspondent Marie Colvin, describing the overwhelming grief as corpses were pulled out of the ruins. Four of the bodies she saw were those of small children, and from under a green plaid blanket protruded the blood-stained face of a woman. The *Sun* reported on the same day:

> Saddam Hussein tried to trick the world yesterday by saying hundreds of women and children died in a bomb attack on an 'air raid shelter'. He cunningly arranged TV scenes designed to shock and appal. Allied intelligence reports showed the bunker was a military communications command post.

This demonstrated the overkill of macho politics and tabloid journalism, so effectively critiqued in *Cassandra* and *Katharina Blum*. That lecture course (my last in Cambridge) marked a growing crisis in the Middle East and a seismic shift in the global balance of power.

WHEN THE WALLS CAME DOWN

Around the year 1990 everything changed as the Soviet empire collapsed. Gorbachev was the Joshua who sounded the trumpet by abandoning the Brehznev Doctrine of armed intervention in satellite states. The collapse of the German Democratic Republic took everyone by surprise, although I was aware of the economic weakness that made the state dependent on loans from the West. In the summer of 1989 the situation was changing not only in the GDR, but also in neighbouring Czechoslovakia and

Hungary. A reformist government in Budapest began to remove the barbed wire dividing Hungary from Austria. As a result, hundreds of East Germans began streaming across the border into the West. A further factor was the attitude of the Evangelical Church. It was certainly not a force comparable to the Catholic Church in Poland, but by autumn 1989 people attending the Monday evening services in Leipzig were in open confrontation with the regime. The ensuing street demonstrations provided an object lesson in non-violent political mobilization. There were armed troops in Leipzig ready to suppress the demonstrations, but Honecker held his fire, and the protests acquired such momentum that they swept the state away.

No one anticipated that abandoning the Brezhnev Doctrine would bring the Eastern bloc tumbling down, but when the Wall was breached I did at least know more about the two Germanys than members of the British government. There was hardly time to celebrate the breaching of the Berlin Wall before people started worrying about the dangers of unification. Would this open the floodgates, they wondered in Warsaw and Prague, to claims for the restitution of Germany's lost territories? In London, too, members of the government, including the Prime Minister, took fright at the spectre of an all-powerful German state. 'We beat the Germans twice,' said Margaret Thatcher, 'and now they're back.' In one sense she was right: for almost a century British policy had been shaped by Anglo-German rivalries. However, there was little evidence to support the assumptions about 'German national character' which made her oppose reunification.

It was important that those working for greater understanding should argue their case. The most astute commentator was Timothy Garton Ash, an Oxford academic whose articles about Eastern Europe proved exceptionally far sighted. Ash was one of the historians invited by the Prime Minister to Chequers in March 1990 for a seminar on the question: How dangerous are the Germans? Fortunately, the historians supported the more constructive line of the Foreign Office. My own take on events had already appeared in the *Independent* under the title The Writing on the Wall, accompanied by a striking illustration.

This recalled how authors like Wolf Biermann and Christa Wolf placed Berlin 'at the cultural interface, where East and West meet in creative confrontation'. For writers on both sides of the border, the Wall was a monument not simply to the failures of communism but to the far more terrible Nazi tyranny that preceded it. In November no one imagined that Berlin would again become the capital of a united Germany. But my article ended with a quotation from Gottfried Benn, who had witnessed the destruction of the city in the Second World War: 'When the walls come tumbling down / The very rubble will resound / Defying destiny.'

The political events had educational consequences. On 27 March 1990

THE INDEPENDENT   Monday 13 November 1989

…t breach, **Edward Timms** considers the impact of the Berlin Wall on the German literary imagination

The writing on the wall

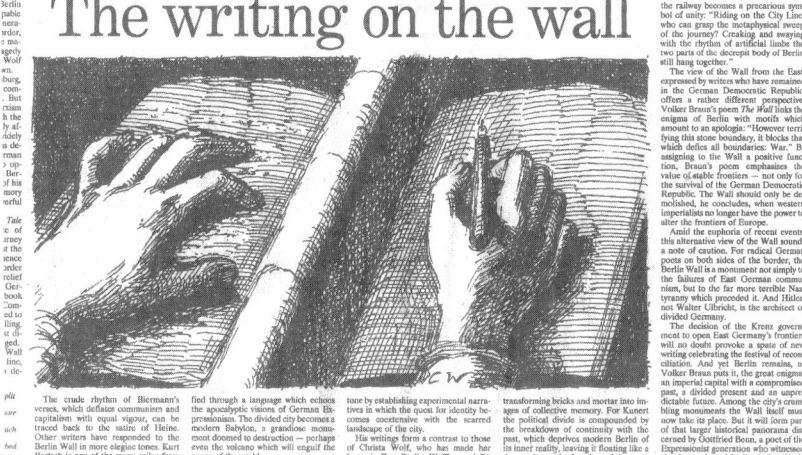

with West. For Kunert, as for Biermann, the railway becomes a precarious symbol of unity: "Riding on the City Line, who can grasp the metaphysical sweep of the journey? Creaking and swaying with the rhythm of artificial limbs the two parts of the decrepit body of Berlin still hang together."

The view of the Wall from the East, expressed by writers who have remained in the German Democratic Republic, offers a rather different perspective. Volker Braun's poem *The Wall* links the enigma of Berlin with motifs which amount to an apologia: "However terrifying this stone boundary, it blocks that which defies all boundaries: War." By assigning to the Wall a positive function, Braun's poem emphasises the value of stable frontiers — not only for the survival of the German Democratic Republic. The Wall should only be demolished, he concludes, when western imperialists no longer have the power to alter the frontiers of Europe.

Amid the euphoria of recent events, this alternative view of the Wall sounds a note of caution. For radical German poets on both sides of the border, the Berlin Wall is a monument not simply to the failures of East German communism, but to the far more terrible Nazi tyranny which preceded it. And Hitler, not Walter Ulbricht, is the architect of divided Germany.

The decision of the Krenz government to open East Germany's frontiers will no doubt provoke a spate of new writing celebrating the festival of reconciliation. And yet Berlin remains, as Volker Braun puts it, the great enigma: an imperial capital with a compromised past, a divided present and an unpredictable future. Among the city's crumbling monuments the Wall itself must now take its place. But it will form part of that larger historical panorama discerned by Gottfried Benn, a poet of the Expressionist generation who witnessed the destruction of Berlin during World War II. It is in Benn's poetry that the Wall finds its most eloquent epitaph:

The crude rhythm of Biermann's verses, which deflates communism and capitalism with equal vigour, can be traced back to the satire of Heine. Other writers have responded to the Berlin Wall in more elegiac tones. Kurt Bartsch is one of the many exiles from the East who have chosen to make their home in West Berlin. Their work is in-…

…fied through a language which echoes the apocalyptic visions of German Expressionism. The divided city becomes a modern Babylon, a grandiose monument doomed to destruction — perhaps even the volcano which will engulf the peace of the world.

At the same time these writers through their very presence have helped…

…tone by establishing experimental narratives in which the quest for identity becomes coextensive with the scarred landscape of the city.

His writings form a contrast to those of Christa Wolf, who has made her home in East Berlin. Wolf's novel *Divided Heaven* explores the traumatic effect of the building of the Berlin Wall…

…transforming bricks and mortar into images of collective memory. For Kunert the political divide is compounded by the breakdown of continuity with the past, which deprives modern Berlin of its inner reality, leaving it floating like a dream city on the frontiers of time.

It is not the bright lights of the Kurfürstendamm which feature most…

The Writing on the Wall (article in the *Independent*, 13 November 1989)

the University of Sussex advertised for a new Professor of German. When the advert appeared in the *Guardian*, I showed it to Saime with the words: 'That's got my name on it!' In addition to the surge of happy memories, I felt that Sussex would offer scope for innovation. We visited the campus and had long conversations with our old friend Laci Löb, now Reader in German. He warned us that we were likely to feel frustrated by the financial constraints and administrative pressures, so different from the 1960s. Moreover, there was a risk of upsetting the balance in the German department, which was just emerging from a period of tension. On reflection, it seemed advisable to remain in Cambridge, although here too life had its frustrations.

The previous year I had applied for both the Taylor Chair of German in Oxford and the Cambridge Schröder Professorship. Oxford appointed T. J. Reed, author of a fine study of Thomas Mann, while in Cambridge the lot fell on Roger Paulin, an expert on Romanticism. It was disappointing to find my own claims passed over, but there were compensations. The Avant-Garde seminar continued to flourish and there were gratifying developments in Austrian Studies. In summer 1990 we staged an exhibition at the Faculty Library on Biedermeier in Austria, illustrating both the homely domestic designs and the subtly understated modes artistic and literary expression, such as Raimund's comedies and Schubert's Lieder. However, the political activists of the 1840s had used

Biedermeier as a term of contempt for the parochial attitudes of the previous generation. 'Isn't there too much Biedermeier about life in Cambridge?' I wondered. Academic routines and cosy domestic evenings – was that really enough?

After listening to my conference lecture on The Austrian Idea, a colleague from the North of England had complimented me on 'growing old gracefully'. In reality, I was in a trough. By this date I had shaved off my beard, already streaked with grey, but nothing was achieved by this gesture of rejuvenation. Saime, as a practising counsellor, provided invaluable guidance, and I was attending a men's support group consisting of colleagues in their middle years. We shared our frustrations with unwonted frankness under the guidance of an experienced facilitator.

In autumn 1990 I was offered a lifeline. The phone rang in my office at Caius, connecting me with Margaret McGowan, the Sussex Pro-Vice-Chancellor. She explained that they had not yet succeeded in filling the vacant Chair of German. Would I be interested? Flattered, I travelled to Brighton and lunched with the appointments committee. It was explained that although they had great respect for Dr Löb, the search was for someone with wider European interests. My approach to cultural politics and comparative literature would make me ideal for the job.

I was sorely tempted, but Saime and the children were reluctant to move. It would be hard to say goodbye to friends like Susan and Mick Brown and their family, with whom we had shared so many Christmas celebrations and Norfolk holidays (they had now bought our cottage in Snettisham). And cherished research projects would have to be left behind. Chris Thornhill's comparison of Kraus and Benjamin was almost complete, but Sally McMullen's study of Hofmannsthal had been interrupted by the birth of her two daughters.

Brighton would be bracing, but could I cope with the change? For weeks we agonized, phoning other Sussex friends for advice. 'You'll be miserable,' some voices said. 'It's not the liberated Sussex of the sixties.' But others, including Gabriel Josipovici and John Röhl, suggested there would be opportunities to pioneer new courses. To resolve the dilemma, I wrote to Margaret McGowan setting out a series of questions. They amounted to twelve points in all, recalling the diplomatic note sent from Vienna to Belgrade in 1914. The Austrians deliberately included in their ultimatum certain points that could not possibly be met, so that they would have an excuse to break off relations with Serbia. If my letter had a similar aim, I had reckoned without McGowan's diplomatic skills. She sent a most persuasive reply, offering a constructive response to each of my twelve points.

Obtaining Saime's consent proved more difficult. She was on the point of leaving for Moscow to spend a week working on Nazım Hikmet's papers in the Lenin Library. On her return the debate continued.

'I want to be the Big Chief,' I said, echoing my childhood passion for Red Indians.

'If like your father you are having a mid-life crisis,' Saime replied, 'you won't solve it by running away.'

The men's support group provided encouragement, and we revisited the Family Therapy Centre to ease the burden of decision-making. Of our children, Yusuf was most open to change. At the age of seventeen he was ready to strike out on his own by renting a bed-sit in Mill Road and taking his Advanced Level exams at Anglia Polytechnic. 'If they move to Brighton,' the psychiatrist asked him, 'how long do you think it will take Saime to make new friends?' His answer was 'five minutes!'

We paid one more visit to Sussex on a dark December day, talking to Alasdair Smith, newly appointed as Dean of European Studies, and Mick Burton, Director of the University Counselling Service. 'Might Saime be able to find work as a counsellor?' we asked. Burton could make no promises, although he was generally encouraging, and we had a lively conversation about Freud. Before we left, there was just time for coffee in the European School common room, shared in democratic Sussex style by students and staff. The place was a tip, with pools of coffee on the tables and garbage strewn over the floor. Who would give up Cambridge for such squalor? Saime clearly thought moving a mistake, and I respected her judgment. At breakfast the following morning the decision was taken to stay in Cambridge, so I phoned Sussex from my college room. A secretary answered: Professor McGowan was in a meeting, could I phone again in the afternoon?

When I phoned Saime to explain the delay, she suggested we should meet for lunch. For two hours we talked things through again. 'Feel the fear and do it all the same!' was the message of one of the books she had given me to read. Now she sensed my depression at having to say 'No'. Our conversation with Mick Burton came back into her mind. 'You know Freud's advice about taking difficult decisions,' Mick had said. 'Spin a coin, and if it comes down the wrong way, do the opposite!' Actually, it took three spins before the coin came down the way I wanted, so I could sprint to college to phone my acceptance. Shortly afterwards I received a letter from the Vice-Chancellor, Sir Leslie Fielding, confirming my appointment.

This red-letter day was followed barely a week later by what Saime in her diary described as one of the blackest in her life. Shortly after the deal with Sussex was agreed, she came across a letter in Gila's handwriting referring to happy days in Vienna. Since I had never mentioned our rendezvous in Vienna, she felt betrayed. Even though she was aware of our continuing contacts, she had not realized how frequent and intimate they had been. Spending time with Gila was a way of keeping my finger on the pulse of events in Germany. Now I had to admit that those meetings had set my own pulses racing. Further questions were raised by the fact that her letter was signed 'Pandora'. This term of endearment derived from my research on Kraus and his friend Frank Wedekind, author of *Pandora's Box*, a pioneering drama of transgressive desire. 'We really *did* play Pandora's Box,' the satirist wrote to his friend, alluding to an actress whose favours they had shared. *Apocalyptic Satirist* was dedicated to Saime, who had supported me unstintingly, but the Preface also acknowledged the help of other friends, crediting Gila with many stimulating conversations. It ended with a cryptic double tribute: 'My interest in Kraus was originally inspired by his revival of the myth of Pandora. But my research would never have been completed if it had not been sustained by the patience of Penelope.'

Now there was no escape into mythology. I was weighed in the balance and found wanting – wanting more than our marriage vows allowed. There was no way of justifying my breach of trust, but long heart-to-heart talks helped to clarify why I had acted on feelings arising from a first love. By this date meetings with Gila had become so infrequent that they constituted no threat to our marriage. The explanations involved both straight talking and serious walking. We communicated best on treks through the countryside, as we had in courting days – across Grantchester Meadows or along the towpath towards Fen Ditton. During a walk on Royston Downs I likened my relationship with Gila to the way a solitary tree on the horizon may act as an emotional landmark, guiding me along my path. Our conversations were enriched by co-counselling, structured to encourage one partner to listen in attentive silence while the other expresses painful emotions. We confided in our teenage children, who understood the need to work towards a resolution. Further guidance was provided by a relationship therapist. Working through difficult feelings, we reached a new understanding that strengthened our emotional bond. After each session we would spend a further hour at a restaurant by the river, renewing our intimacy over chablis and tiramisu.

Three months later we were ready to renew our marriage vows. On 27 April 1991 we welcomed a hundred friends and relatives to a ceremony at Finella, a college house in the gardens on West Road. The guests included the Master of Caius, Peter Gray, and his wife Barbara. Several friends made the journey from Brighton including Gavin Wraith and Joe Townsend. For Joe there were additional causes for celebration, for the likeable rogue from the 1960s was about to become Mayor of Brighton. Joe was on the committee for the Nelson Mandela Scholarship, set up at Sussex after the leader of the African National Congress was sentenced to life imprisonment. By enabling young blacks to study in England, the scholarship made significant contribution to the campaign against apartheid. In South Africa, too, the walls were tumbling down, for in February 1990 Nelson Mandela was released from Robben Island. We were awed by his steadfastness of purpose, for he had spent twenty-seven years in prison – half my lifetime! This heralded the end of white domination and the start of the movement for truth and reconciliation.

Our recommitment was a multi-faith ceremony conducted by an Anglican priest, the Reverend Peter Tamplin, also a therapist. The readings incorporated lines from Khalil Gibran's *The Prophet*: 'Stand together, but not too close together: / For the oak tree and the cypress grow not in each other's shadow.' Further lines paid tribute to our children: 'You may give them your love but not your thoughts, / For their souls dwell in the house of tomorrow.' Only our closest friends sensed the difficulties we had been through, as we celebrated twenty-five years of marriage. The moment of truth was captured in a photograph showing Saime giving me a sprig of Honesty, a plant that does not flower every year. For us, too, truth was the key to reconciliation, and we were ready to move on.

CHAPTER FOURTEEN

Sussex at the Turn of the Century

'Welcome back after a short absence of twenty-seven years!' said Alasdair Smith, Dean of European Studies, at the School Meeting in January 1992. At Sussex surprisingly little had changed. My office was in the original Arts Building, and from the window I could see Falmer House, the social centre where Saime and I had met almost thirty years earlier. Other buildings had been completed according to plan, including the Meeting House and the Arts Centre. Among a bevy of younger colleagues at that first meeting were stalwarts from the pioneering days like Robin Milner-Gulland and Beryl Williams, Stephen Medcalf and Gabriel Josipovici. It was Gabriel who had suggested my name to the appointments committee, so he was delighted to see me back, while the historian John Röhl welcomed the prospect of strengthening German at Sussex. Colleagues with cognate interests included William Outhwaite, author of a critical introduction to Habermas.

European Studies had roughly sixty teaching staff responsible for a thousand students, including a third-year cohort studying abroad. This ratio encouraged a creative rapport with individual students, especially for Personal Tutors responsible for their welfare. The School felt like an extended family with teachers and support staff on first name terms. Tony Thorlby had retired, but I was again working closely with Laci Löb, and the German group included younger talents like Margarete Kohlenbach, a literary scholar with philosophical interests. Language teaching was led by the Swiss Brigitte Diplock in conjunction with a lector from Berlin named Anne Vonderstein. After classes we would meet for a convivial lunch at the Arts Centre, followed on fine days by a stroll through Stanmer Woods.

My impression was that the original interdisciplinary vision had stood the test of time. Students and staff were still grouped in Schools, preserving an intimacy of scale amid rapid expansion. Moreover, there was a flourishing new School of Cognitive and Computing Sciences, led by Margaret Boden, an authority on Artificial Intelligence. The campus was creeping up the hillside towards the Downs, and a new Refectory Building had been constructed incorporating a bookshop, but the integrity of Spence's design had survived: low-rise buildings constructed of russet brick relieved by flowing arches, grouped around a tree-lined concourse with footpaths leading in all directions. A university originally conceived for five hundred students was now approaching the ten thousand mark, with the balance tipping towards the humanities as the recruitment of science students proved increasingly difficult. Among friends from the 1960s Gavin Wraith was still teaching mathematics, although Brian Easlea had taken early retirement. However, the Arts–Science scheme, to which both had made significant contributions, continued to enlarge the horizons of Sussex scientists.

CONTINUITIES AND CRISES

My aim was to enjoy the best of both worlds. During the week I lived in a handsome mock-Tudor house on the way to the Sussex campus, which we had purchased with a bridging loan; but we had not yet sold our house in Metcalfe Road, where Saime remained with the children until the end of the academic year. So I would drive back to Cambridge at week-ends, literally a commuter, emotionally a time traveller. During that first term the weeks flew by in a surge of activity, but after Easter my feelings took a plunge. The university's most hideous secret had been hidden from me: the Annual Planning of Teaching (APT). This sounded innocent enough, for clearly duties should be shared among colleagues, but no one had told me about the fiendishly complex system operated in the humanities at Sussex. Statisticians insisted that one hour's teaching of a class of eight students earned the university only 0.75 of the income attributable to a class of twelve, while the rates also fluctuated between Schools. Students from English and American Studies were worth 'more' because they had no language classes to attend, so the fee income was divided between fewer classes. These differences might have been ironed out through collegial give-and-take, but the aim was mathematical precision.

This approach dehumanized the language of education. Instead of discussing students and courses, the APT required us to use the jargon of FTEs (full time enrolments) and TGWs (teaching work units). Acronyms have their uses as long as their organizational algebra does not displace common sense, but we were bombarded with barely legible computer print-outs that combined the worst features of the capitalist and the communist systems. On the one hand there was a Thatcherite method of budgeting that required the exact prediction of monetary flows for every activity; on the other a Stachanovite insistence on the fulfilment of work norms that monitored the productivity of every staff member. I bought myself a calculator and began to have sleepless nights, for the figures wouldn't add up.

The number majoring in German was not large, and language students devoted half their time to contextual subjects. My duties included language classes for German Minors, students of History or Economics who were preparing for a year abroad. Equipping them to become citizens of Europe was a part of our mission, but this was hard to achieve with a textbook weighted towards grammar. There was a need for more stimulating teaching materials, so we devised a series in the target language entitled 'Deutschland, heute und gestern', exploring both history and current affairs. These classes highlighted regional traditions (including those of Austria and Switzerland) that have survived centuries of turmoil, a rewarding project that made additional demands on my time.

My quandary coincided with a larger crisis. Sir Leslie Fielding was due to retire as Vice-Chancellor, but the committee set up by Council to choose his successor was divided. The choice lay between an outstanding scientist and a senior civil servant with contacts in Whitehall. On 17 December 1991 a leaked report in the *Independent* named Sir Clive Whitmore as the favoured candidate. However, some committee members were resisting the pressure to appoint the former Permanent Secretary of the Ministry of Defence. On 20 March 1992 the *Higher Education Supplement* devoted a full page to the dispute, reporting 'an extraordinary saga of intrigue and counter-intrigue'. This localized power struggle, they suggested, reflected an unresolved debate about who should govern British universities and how the governors should be chosen. The Jarratt Report of 1985 had stressed the need to make universities more accountable: the traditional academic vice-chancellor should be replaced by a chief executive with managerial expertise.

The issues at Sussex were not quite so clear cut, as a member of the appointments committee confided. The chairman of the Council, a retired admiral, was certainly campaigning for a non-academic, but other committee members were open minded. After the decisive interviews the majority supported Gordon Conway, an ecologist who had taught at the University of California before setting up the Centre for Environmental Technology at Imperial College London. Attempts to question his credentials failed when it became clear that Conway had also served on the Royal Commission on Environmental Pollution and spent four years administering grants on the Indian subcontinent on behalf of the Ford Foundation. Given this blend of scientific and managerial experience, I was delighted by his appointment.

As this controversy reached its climax, I was still commuting between Brighton and Cambridge, and the pressure began to tell. So I started therapy sessions in Lewes on Friday afternoons before the journey home. Since guilt towards Saime was one source of distress, the therapist suggested that to make amends I should give priority to our biography of Nazım Hikmet, a poet who understood separation. The therapist also suspected that Sussex was restimulating the misery experienced when packed off to boarding school at the age of nine. Lying on the couch, I was overcome by memories of my father, who had died ten years earlier. That summer, by a strange coincidence, the church he had served for almost forty years, Holy Trinity Buckfastleigh, was destroyed by an arson attack. Although the roof burnt out, the walls and the tower remained forming a picturesque ruin, symbolic of my troubled heritage.

The sleepless nights continued. A book on Time Management which Saime gave me contained a section on Prioritizing your Pending Tray – but where was my pending tray? My desk was strewn with papers and my feelings were equally chaotic. The climax came during the journey home on Friday 3 June, my fifty-fifth birthday. Exhaustion forced me to leave the motorway about ten miles south of Cambridge and rest by the road-side. Once home, I had to pretend to be cheerful while hunting for presents hidden around the house. 'Must we leave Cambridge?' I moaned, but Saime was resolute: 'We are selling our house and moving!' And so we did – in July 1992. By that date the summer term was over and the stress was easing. Even the Planning of Teaching proved manageable. Under the twelve-point plan agreed with Margaret McGowan we now had a new colleague, Anita Bunyan, who took over some of the language teaching. This made it possible to concentrate on a task that excited me far more – seminar planning for the Modern European Mind.

At one of our first meetings, Alasdair Smith had asked me to take over as convenor of this course, which attracted students from both European and English & American Studies.

'It was Tony Thorlby's baby,' he began, 'and thrived under the care of Gillian Rose, but recently the course has fallen into disrepair. It is vital to the intellectual structure of our School and needs firm leadership'.

When the Modern European Mind was launched in 1961, it had seemed challengingly contemporary, for some of the key figures were still alive – the surrealists Dali and Breton, the existentialists Sartre and Beauvoir, and the modernists Eliot and Auden. Now the perspective had changed. Early twentieth-century Modernism could be seen as a distinc-tive movement that had flourished for fifty years, starting around 1910 when (as Virginia Woolf remarked) 'everything changed'. So I called a tutors meeting and we updated the course, casting back to pioneering figures like Baudelaire but also making links with more recent trends like structuralism and postmodernism.

By the beginning of the new academic year the pressure was easing. We had spent summer afternoons swimming with our teenage children and making new friends, including Kate Springford, a therapist married to a colleague in French studies named George Craig. While dining at their home in Lewes, I mentioned how stressful those early months had been. 'Aha,' said Kate, 'Hopson's Curve!' To illustrate this concept, she produced a diagram entitled 'The predictable crises of transitional experiences'.

Counselling clients in managerial positions had familiarized her with this model, designed by the psychologist Barrie Hopson: elation followed by doubt and despair, gradually modulating into acceptance of change. 'You see,' Kate said, 'what you've been going through is quite normal.' It certainly did not feel normal at the time.

Designing innovative courses proved a tonic. The revitalized Modern European Mind, including topics like Literature & Psychoanalysis and Modernism in the Arts, was proving exceptionally popular. However, the approach to German literature through periods like the Age of Classicism struck me as pedestrian, so I drafted two fresh proposals: German-Jewish Culture and Politics, and Anglo-German Intellectual Relations. The Anglo-German project would have focused on the influential achievements of poets like Goethe and Heine and philosophers such as Herder, Hegel and Nietzsche. This would have involved a review of concepts that have shaped western thinking from 'Bildung' and 'Wissenschaft' through

SEVEN-PHASE MODEL OF STAGES ACCOMPANYING TRANSITION (Adapted from Hopson, 1981)

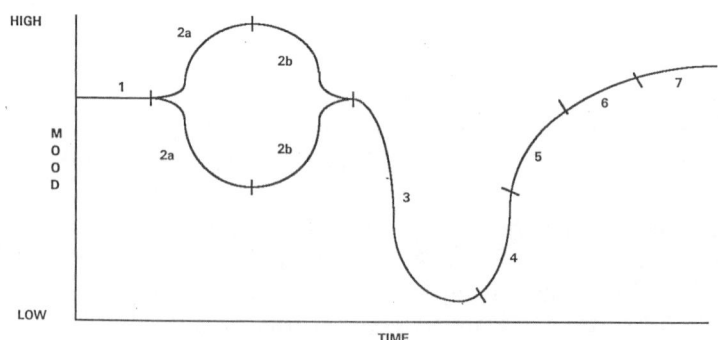

1 Immobilisation

2 Reaction
   a) Elation of Despair   b) Minimisation

3 Self-doubt (depression, anger, apathy)

4 Letting go of past – point at which change begins to be accepted, coming to terms with the change

5 Testing out new behaviours

6 Search for meaning – looking back and trying to understand meaning of transition

7 Internalisation

Predictable Crises of Transitional Experience (by Barrie Hopson, 1981)

'Dialektik' and 'Entfremdung' to 'das Unheimliche'. To encourage students to reflect on their own position, there would have been a module on the idea of the university, so influentially redefined by Wilhelm von Humboldt.

It was the Jewish option that appealed to colleagues whose judgment carried most weight, Laci Löb, John Röhl and Gabriel Josipovici. All three had indelible memories of their childhood in Nazi-occupied Europe, a factor that may have inhibited them from making the academic case themselves. The challenge was to explain how such a civilized nation as the Germans had succumbed to barbarism, charting the trajectory from the ideals of the Enlightenment to the atrocities of the Holocaust. To modify the crude perpetrator–victim model of German–Jewish relations, we would highlight the role of Jews as catalysts for European civilization. Their innovative achievements attracted envy, as I'd noted in a *Jewish Quarterly* article of autumn 1990:

> Jewish entrepreneurs built the railroads, financed the coalmines, set up pilsner beer production, pioneered sugar-refining, developed the iron and steel industries, controlled the leading banks and newspapers, and were prominent in the leather goods, furniture, clothing and food-processing trades.

Tragically, I concluded, this provoked such resentment in both Germany and Austria that the Jews became the victims of their success.

Before introducing the new course we circulated other universities to ensure we were not duplicating work already done elsewhere. Literary authors of Jewish origin like Heine and Kafka were certainly receiving attention, but there was no dedicated course of the type we proposed. This prompted me to write to the *Times Literary Supplement* setting out the case for change. Back came a message from the editor, Ferdinand Mount, asking me to expand my ideas for their Commentary column. Published on 4 June 1993 in a Jewish Studies number, this article noted that – in contrast to the United States – German-Jewish studies scarcely featured at British universities, even though Britain, in proportion to its size, had received more refugees from Nazi Germany than any other country. After noting that scholars like Peter Pulzer and Siegbert Prawer had made outstanding individual contributions, the article became more polemical:

> To insist on the centrality of Exile and Holocaust studies has been regarded as bad form in certain circles, as George Steiner found to his cost in Cambridge. Even the activities of the Wiener Library and the Leo Baeck Institute have not decisively affected the agenda of British universities.

To place research in this field on a firmer institutional footing, I concluded, it was time to set up a centre for German-Jewish studies at a British university.

Jewish specialists were understandably sceptical: how could a parson's son with no grounding in Judaism have such chutzpah? And why base the centre in Brighton, where there was only a relatively small community? 'You must speak to Arthur Oppenheimer!' I was told by two colleagues, the historian Bob Benewick and Raphael Salkie, a lecturer in Linguistics at the University of Brighton. Arthur, they explained, was an executive at American Express who was taking early retirement. As the son of a German-Jewish businessman who had fled to Britain, he would be keen to reclaim his heritage. They were right: Arthur's personal ebullience and professional judgement proved inspirational. He put us in touch with friends in London, notably Diana Franklin, and it was she who introduced me to Max and Hilde Kochmann. We now had supporters in London to back our local initiative.

Meeting Hilde, as indicated in the opening chapter, awoke barely conscious memories of that primal Hilda, the Jewish refugee who had nurtured me during infancy. Haunted by the past, my aim was to create a programme for the future – for a post-imperial Britain that was struggling with its own heritage of racial prejudice. This could only be achieved with the help of allies equally committed, especially Diana Franklin, whose motivation was also shaped by early memories. Her father Gerald Loewi, born in Nuremberg in 1922, had fled to England as a teenager to escape persecution. His exceptional gifts had enabled him to become one of Britain's leading immunologists, but he never came to terms with the loss of his German roots. Our project would contextualize this kind of personal tragedy, helping the families of survivors to reclaim their heritage.

GERMAN-JEWISH DILEMMAS

Diana Franklin began to travel down to the university once a week to support our work, while Arthur Oppenheimer kept us focused on 'deliverables', including a series of public events. In April 1994 my inaugural lecture on Goethe and the Wandering Jew was publicized by an eye-catching poster.

The figure of Ahasverus ('Der ewige Jude') entered German literature around 1600 as a symbol of piety and repentance. It its original form, I explained, the legend emphasized the links between Christianity and Judaism. After witnessing the crucifixion, Ahasverus was destined to wander over the face of the earth until the Day of Judgment. The young Goethe was fascinated by the legend. Defying the prejudices of his day, he

The Wandering Jew (poster,
April 1994)

Ahasverus, the Wandering Jew (from a German print of 1618)

University of Sussex Professorial Lecture

THE WANDERING JEW:
A Leitmotif in German Literature and Politics
EDWARD TIMMS
Professor of German

made a point of visiting the ghetto in Frankfurt and participating in the
Feast of Tabernacles. But by the late nineteenth century the figure of
the Wandering Jew had become associated with problems of migration
and assimilation, and it was later ruthlessly exploited by Nazi propaganda. One consequence was that Britain became the home of thousands
of refugees, but decades after the defeat of Hitler the agitators were still
at work, giving a further impulse to our German-Jewish project:

> The mission of the Centre will not only be historical, but also contem-
> porary and critical. For racial prejudice constitutes a continuing political
> danger, as recently published antisemitic leaflets show, and German-
> Jewish studies may serve as a model for understanding the problems of
> other multi-ethnic societies.

This point was illustrated by a German pamphlet, *Remer-Depesche*,
published – to the astonishment of my audience – in Brighton in January
1994. This neo-Nazi propaganda sheet, named after a right-wing general,

was produced by the so-called British Historical Society. Holocaust denial was banned in Germany, but the authors were exploiting the liberality of English law to distribute hate mail. Their aim was to convince the world that the Jews had tried to destroy the Germans, not the other way round; and that accepted accounts of the Holocaust were a fraud, since there were no gas chambers at Auschwitz. The challenge, I concluded, was to expose the consequences of racial prejudice: 'If the figure of the Wandering Jew represents the stranger in our midst, it also represents an essential part of ourselves.'

After the lecture I was approached by a distinguished looking gentleman with a grey beard, who reminded me of the Jewish prophets portrayed by Rembrandt. 'My name is Emanuel,' he said. 'Do you know what that means?' There was a pause. I *should* have known – had we not sung during my schooldays 'O come, O come Emanuel / and ransom captive Israel'? It means 'God with us' he explained. Were we about to receive blessings from above? As our conversation continued, Ralph Emanuel explained that he and his wife Muriel lived in London, but he felt an affinity with Brighton, where he had spent his childhood. Both his parents had been immigrants from Germany – hence his fascination with our project.

Our next public event took place on 5 December 1995, when a packed Meeting House heard Rabbi Julia Neuberger speak about her new book, *On Being Jewish*. Her account of the diverse strands of Judaism high-lighted the liberal tradition that encourages women to play an active role, but students were even more intrigued by the contrasts with Christian asceticism. 'Within Judaism, married women have a right to sexual pleasure, and there are recommendations for the frequency of the sexual act,' she explained. 'For scholars it should be weekly!' Her talk provoked a voluble debate, chaired by Gordon Conway, the new Vice-Chancellor. Rabbi Neuberger spoke with pride about her German heritage and the campaign to assist refugees. For Professor Conway this was a moment of truth. He suddenly realized that Hans Woyda, the maths teacher at Kingston Grammar School who had kindled his interest in science, must have been a refugee.

'What an inspiration to launch a German-Jewish studies programme when you arrived at Sussex,' Julia said that evening over supper at Swanborough Manor, the Vice-Chancellor's residence.

It wasn't as simple as that. Soon after his arrival, Gordon Conway had made a point of meeting small groups of academics and listening to their ideas. At his suggestion, we applied to the Research Development Fund for a grant to organize an international conference. Moreover, Conway continued the Sussex tradition of encouraging innovation.

'Why only a single conference?' he asked, after our grant was approved. 'Why not a series, indeed a research centre?'

The Centre came into existence through a process described by Robin Street, the genial Development Officer, as osmosis. Writing to Gordon Conway, I asked for permission to print publicity materials and headed paper with the postal address of the Centre and an eye-catching logo derived from what had once been the Great Synagogue in Dresden. In lieu of a formal appointment, my position was confirmed by the arrival of a ream of headed paper with my name as Director. We were already filling in the blanks. Our research colloquium had mutated into a weekly seminar that explored German-Jewish culture and politics from multiple angles. Sussex colleagues led the way with papers on the novelist Anna Seghers (by Barbara Einhorn), Kaiser Wilhelm II and Antisemitism (John Röhl), Women in the Resistance (Sybil Oldfield), the BBC German Service during World War II (Christina Brink), and the German Occupation of Greece (Mark Mazower). Doctoral researchers added to the multicultural mix: Stephen Nicholls speaking on The Forgotten Jews of Pomerania, Andrea Hammel on Jewish Women Authors Exiled in Britain.

A grant from the Dean of European Studies towards travel expenses enabled us to host talks by visiting speakers, including Peter Pulzer (from All Souls Oxford) on Jewish Life in Germany during World War I, and Arnold Paucker (Leo Baeck Institute, London) on Jewish Resistance in Nazi Germany. In some cases we saved on hotel bills by welcoming visitors to 4 The Cliff, the spacious house overlooking Brighton Marina to which Saime and I had moved in May 1993. Ritchie Robertson (St John's Oxford) spoke on the Concept of Jewish Self-hatred, Jeremy Adler (King's College, London) on the Archive of H. G. Adler, Rabbi Rodney Mariner (Belsize Square Synagogue) on Judaism and Homosexuality, Tony Kushner (from the Parkes Institute at Southampton) on the Post-war Image of Anne Frank, and Louise London (Royal Holloway) on Refugees from National Socialism. We also invited some of the refugees themselves give an account of their experiences. They included Lord Weidenfeld on Growing up in Vienna before the Anschluss, Richard and Liesl Grünberger, who spoke about Gallows Humour as a Response to National Socialism, and Judith Kerr on Writing about Being a Refugee.

These seminars coincided with a surge of interest in the Holocaust. The opening of the United States Holocaust Memorial Museum in Washington in April 1993 was followed by the release of Stephen Spielberg's film *Schindler's List*. It was astonishing to see a work of such historical substance created by a director famous for entertainments like the dinosaur fantasy *Jurassic Park*. But Spielberg had been profoundly impressed by Thomas Keneally's prize-winning novel *Schindler's Ark*, based on events that took place after the German invasion of Poland. To avoid sensationalism, he filmed in black-and-white, echoing the documentaries of the period. And where earlier treatments of the Holocaust had contrasted jackbooted Germans with pathetically helpless Jews,

Spielberg's approach was more subtle. The film has two heroes: a Nazi businessman on the make named Oskar Schindler (played by Liam Neeson) and the Jewish accountant on whom he comes to depend, Itzhak Stern (played by Ben Kingsley). From the beleaguered Jewish community in Krakow, Schindler obtains funds to set up an enamel goods factory, hiring Jews to work for him because their labour is cheap and obtaining lucrative contracts from the German army. He succeeds in protecting his Jewish workers from deportation by ingratiating himself with Nazi officials, especially the sadistic commandant of the Plaszow Forced Labour Camp, Amon Goeth (played by Ralph Fiennes).

Spielberg's film set a new agenda for German-Jewish studies, for it dramatized to the cooperation between Germans and Jews within an overwhelmingly antisemitic environment. The thrusting businessman could never have prospered without his skilful accountant, and the plucky Jewish workers would have perished without their resourceful German boss. Such synergies, so exceptional in the age of the Holocaust, could be traced back to earlier periods, as I suggested in a further article in the *Jewish Quarterly*. During the 150 years preceding Hitler's seizure of power, the Jews of Germany had become so integrated that some historians spoke of a 'symbiosis', notably Ruth Gay in *The Jews of Germany*. In adopting this approach, she did not ignore the barriers to emancipation, but showed how obstacles acted as a spur. I contrasted this positive picture with other publications depicting a nation so riddled with prejudice that it seemed incredible that Jewish communities should have survived in Germany for over a thousand years. For those authors, antisemitism led with deadly logic to Auschwitz. The dilemma for historians was how to reconcile the two competing paradigms, which I defined as Holocaustism and Symbiotics. While a focus on symbiosis highlights the values of the diaspora, Holocaustism plays into the hands of militant Zionists by mobilizing support for Israel.

Our Centre caught a rising tide of interest in refugees. During the 1980s Dr Julius Carlebach, the son of a celebrated Hamburg rabbi, had been Reader in Sociology at Sussex. Now he was Director of the High School for Jewish Studies in Heidelberg, but he and his wife Myrna had a home in Brighton. Myrna ushered me into a room lined from floor to ceiling with books in Hebrew and other Judaica. A dozen years earlier, Julius recalled, he had attempted to establish a programme of Jewish studies at Sussex, but his efforts had been frustrated. Even now he was dubious about our prospects, although he promised his support.

'How many battalions do you have?' he asked, giving me a piercing look. It was several moments before it dawned on me that he was referring to funding.

'Only a Research Development grant,' I said, 'but there is an enormous fund of goodwill and I'm working with wonderful people.'

By this date both Arthur Oppenheimer and Diana Franklin were contributing hours of unpaid effort, while Ralph and Muriel Emanuel had arranged for me to address a group of sympathizers at their home in Hampstead. This led to the creation of our London Support Group, chaired by Max Kochmann, who coordinated efforts to raise funds on our behalf, while Peter Pulzer agreed to chair our Academic Advisory Board. The next milestone was the conference on The German-Jewish Dilemma, staged at Sussex in March 1995. The aim was to challenge the lachrymose model of Christian–Jewish relations and refute monocausal explanations of the Holocaust. In a keynote lecture entitled Emancipation and its Discontents, Pulzer analysed the constraints that had confined Jews to the status of second-class citizens. The failure of the Enlightenment project, he concluded, was not inevitable, but in Germany it was more vulnerable than in other advanced countries.

The sources of this vulnerability were analysed by further contributors, including the historians Robert Wistrich and Arnold Paucker, Julius Schoeps and David Bankier. The interdisciplinary conference also drew literary scholars like Gabriel Josipovici into its ambit, enhancing political analysis by a focus on texts. Josipovici's paper emphasized the fundamental value of the Hebrew injunction to remember – 'zakhor', given that the Nazis had attempted to eradicate all memory of their crimes. But a balance should be struck between too little memory and too much. Communal memory, he insisted, is a dialogue involving complex adjustments to protect us from the kind of myth-making that allows the past to poison the present. Further papers traced the tensions between German policies and Jewish responses, elucidating the testimony of Theodor Herzl and Arthur Schnitzler, Victor Klemperer and H. G. Adler. For my colleague Margarete Kohlenbach, it was Kafka who came closest to defining the inescapable German-Jewish double-bind: 'whatever he does or does not do, he seems to be in the wrong.'

My own paper, on Antisemitism in the Universities and Student Fraternities, attempted to explain how educated Germans and Austrians came to believe that *they* – not the Jews – were the victims. This reversal of roles, which sanctioned aggressive conduct as legitimate self-defence, was facilitated by the 'numerus clausus' debate:

The 'numerus clausus' argument provided an algebra for antisemitism. If 'x' is the number of Jews in Vienna and 'y' is the total Viennese population, then 'x-over-y' provides a formula for calculating how many should be admitted to any university faculty or liberal profession. If the proportion is one-in-ten, as indeed it approximately was, then the admission of Jews to study Medicine or Law should be limited to 10% of the total intake.

Antisemites became amateur statisticians, compiling figures to demonstrate an alleged Jewish take-over. According to a survey from the early 1930s, 85% of the lawyers in Vienna were Jewish, 70% of the dentists and 52% of the doctors.

These figures were exaggerated, but the over-representation of Jews in law and medicine has been confirmed by recent research. According to Steven Beller, Jews constituted 40% of those enrolling in the Vienna Medical Faculty in 1914. Such figures reflect the rapid assimilation of young Jews into the professional middle class. The majority wanted nothing more than to become good Germans or Austrians, or rather, better Germans and Austrians – better educated, better qualified, better attuned to the professional requirements of an increasingly sophisticated society. This (I argued) formed the crux of the German-Jewish dilemma: 'The dynamics of contemporary life required a rapid adjustment to the demands of modernity; but successful adaptation exposed the Jews to the envy of their more conservative and less adaptable fellow citizens.' What made the 'numerus clausus' argument so insidious was that it claimed to be egalitarian. Christians concerned about their job security and educational opportunities for their children felt that Jews should not be allowed to become unduly dominant.

The approach challenged the generalizations about antisemitism by Daniel Jonah Goldhagen in his controversial bestseller, *Hitler's Willing Executioners: Ordinary Germans and the Holocaust*. Written with intellectual passion, the book cited chilling evidence to demonstrate the brutality of the police battalions and the gratuitous cruelty of the death marches. But Goldhagen overstated his case when he spoke of a 'genocidal community in which the killing of Jews was normative' and attempted to trace 'eliminationist antisemitism' back through previous generations. Drawing on an analysis of anti-Jewish publications of the years 1861 to 1895, he insisted that leading authors were already calling for the extermination of the Jews.

This type of monocausal argument was challenged by the Sussex programme. At a public discussion in the Meeting House, Goldhagen's account of genocide was criticized as a form of Holocaustism that implied that the German racism was unique. Why then was a 'numerus clausus' quota also applied to Jews by American universities, including Yale and Harvard? There was widespread anxiety about Jewish influence in the English-speaking world, encapsulated by T. S. Eliot's assertion in *After Strange Gods* (1934) that 'reasons of race and religion make any large number of free-thinking Jews undesirable'.

To define what was exceptional about Germany required a more differentiated approach, exemplified by the conference on Two Nations: British and German Jews in Comparative Perspective, organized at Cambridge in autumn 1997 by the Leo Baeck Institute. It was salutary to be reminded how oppressive British attitudes towards Jews have been. Recalling the anti-Jewish stereotypes of popular culture and anti-Jewish feeling in English society, David Cesarani suggested that the fact that these attitudes did not lead to violence may have been an 'accident of history'. And a paper by Ritchie Robertson reviewed negative Jewish stereotypes in English literature, from Shylock and Fagin through the ambiguous Melmotte and the sadistic Svengali to the programmatic antisemitism of Eliot, Pound and Wyndham Lewis. The infiltration of the ruling class by 'Jewish plutocrats', he noted, was a favourite theme for popular novelists like Hilaire Belloc and H. G. Wells.

This questioning of the myth of English liberalism created a further conundrum. If anti-Jewish *attitudes* were as pronounced in Britain as they were in the German Reich, why did they not lead to anti-Jewish *actions*? Challenging the notion that this was a historical accident, my own contribution drew attention to the divergent effects of German antisemitism and British xenophobia. The culture of the Empire was shaped by a pronounced hostility to foreigners, but British attitudes were xenophobic in a pluralistic way. In the adventure stories of my childhood virtually all foreigners were despicable: 'Frogs' and 'Huns', 'Wogs' and 'Chinks', 'Kaffirs' and 'Dagoes'. This problematic ideology had one merit: it made it difficult to demonize any single group as *the* enemy. This contrast was echoed in the writings of national leaders. Churchill's *My Early Life* portrays a global drama in which it is hard to guess who will be next to challenge the overstretched resources of the Raj: intrepid Pathan tribesmen or fanatical Dervishes; but in *Mein Kampf* the Jews become the only enemy.

By this date I had become acutely aware of the dangers of dualistic thinking when it lacks dialectical flexibility. German social theory in the early twentieth century was dominated by crude oppositions like 'Kultur' versus 'Zivilisation', 'Gemeinschaft' versus 'Gesellschaft'. In was on such antitheses that Hitler's mentor Houston Stewart Chamberlain drew when he pictured politics as a life-and-death struggle between Germans and Jews. At Sussex these issues came into focus during three-cornered interdisciplinary discussions with the sociologist William Outhwaite and our doctoral student, Franz Solms-Laubach, later a leading German journalist. Franz's dissertation was published as *Nietzsche and Early German and Austrian Sociology*.

When the Cambridge conference papers were published under the title *Two Nations*, I was particularly impressed by Reinhard Rürup's analysis of Jewish Emancipation. In the German states of early modern period there were laws restricting the rights of the Jews. By contrast, there was no specifically anti-Jewish legislation in England, although the privileges reserved for the Anglican Church placed all others at a disadvantage: Catholics and Non-Conformists, as well as Jews. It was only after the barriers against Catholics and Non-Conformists had been removed that a campaign to confer legal equality on Jews began, strongly supported by the House of Commons – but delayed by the Lords. Jewish emancipation was merely a side issue in the British power struggles between Church and State, the Commons and the Lords. But in Germany, Rürup concluded, there was a tendency to regard Jewish achievements 'less as contributions than as threats to German society as a whole'.

It was not the Jewish Question that bedevilled British politics but the Irish Question, which came close to causing what George Dangerfield, in an influential book, called *The Strange Death of Liberal England*. Things looked very different when you tried to enter what Hans Kohn, in another book that impressed me, defined as *The Mind of Germany*. Why were anti-Jewish feelings allowed to fester for so long in a nation led by such enlightened spirits as Lessing, Kant and Moses Mendelssohn, Goethe, Schiller and Heine? In 1809 Wilhelm von Humboldt had called for action to counteract the mentality that 'judges a human being not by his specific qualities but by his descent and religion'. The state could do this, he continued, 'by saying loud and clear that it no longer recognizes any difference between Jews and Christians'. This is precisely what did *not* happen in Germany – but why?

This question sent me back to the debate about Jewish emancipation at the Congress of Vienna. In April 1999 we hosted a conference on Progress and Emancipation in the Age of Metternich, organized with the support of the Austrian Cultural Institute under its new director, the historian Dr Emil Brix. The title was a provocation, designed to challenge the standard view of Clemens Metternich as the prince of darkness. At the Congress of Vienna proposals to grant full civil rights to German Jews had been supported not only by the Prussian reformers Karl von Hardenberg and Wilhelm von Humboldt, but by Metternich himself. My paper on the debate about Jewish Emancipation showed how these reforms were frustrated by the representatives of the north German city-states Hamburg, Bremen and Lübeck, who resented the rights granted to Jews under the Napoleonic occupation. That debate was approaching its climax in March 1815 when the delegates heard that Napoleon had escaped from Elba. In the ensuing panic, proposals for Jewish emancipation were overtaken by the need for military action. Hatred of France became transferred to those who were perceived as France's protégés, and German nationalism became suffused with anti-Jewish sentiments.

It has been estimated that between 1815 and 1850 some 2,500 books, pamphlets and articles were published in Germany on the Jewish question. But that flood of publications, I argued, was not the cause but the consequence of the stalemate over Jewish emancipation. One good law is worth a thousand pamphlets, and the Congress of Vienna had provided an unprecedented opportunity for changing the direction of modern politics. This was my answer to the 'Sonderweg' question – the point where German society took its fateful wrong turning. In 1814, and again after the revolution of 1848, reforms were proposed that might well have carried the day. The failure to amend discriminatory legislation reinforced what might be called state-sanctioned antisemitism. An educated German or Austrian Christian could despise the Jews with a good conscience, knowing that he had the law on his side, quite apart from the blessing of the churches.

Even after Jews were granted full citizenship the resentments persisted. By the 1890s they had become so virulent in Vienna that some Jews were promoting emigration. Hence the theme of further conference on Theodor Herzl and the Origins of Zionism, which we organized in London in April 1996 to mark the centenary of Herzl's pamphlet *Der Judenstaat*. Once again our aim was to avoid the black-and-white picture painted by partisans. From John Röhl we learnt that Herzl's supporters included Wilhelm II, who was planning a visit to the Ottoman Empire. Although the Kaiser shared the anti-Jewish prejudices of the day, an interest in Zionism prompted him to declare that he would be willing to establish a German protectorate over the proposed Jewish state, which would lead to an economic revival in Asia Minor. At first everything went according to plan. Herzl had an audience in Istanbul with the Kaiser, who promised to use his influence with Sultan Abdulhamid in favour of the plan. But during the ensuing conversations between Wilhelm and Abdulhamid, the Sultan brusquely rejected the plan for a Jewish state under German protection.

The German-Jewish dynamic, we concluded, was far too complex for any schematic explanation, let alone the claim that it led inexorably to the Holocaust. It was only after the trauma of the First World War that antisemitism entered the mainstream of German politics. It was the catastrophe of 1918 that led to the concentration on a single scapegoat, as the Manichean fantasies of the antisemitic sub-culture came into their own. This sense of the pivotal significance of the Great War gave an additional impetus to my research on Karl Kraus, for my second volume would highlight his satire on the rise of the swastika. The problem was how to combine archival research with my duties as Head of Department and Director of the Centre. Further resources were needed to expand the staff and place our work on firmer foundations. Fortunately, we succeeded in attracting funding not only from statutory bodies like the British Academy and the Arts and Humanities Research Council, but also from the British retailers Marks & Spencer, the Swiss-based ANNE FRANK-Fonds, and even the international film industry.

The Attenborough Connection

During the early days of the University of Sussex, the director Richard Attenborough was on location in Brighton filming the musical *Oh What a Lovely War!* Needing extras for key scenes, some of which were filmed on the West Pier, he applied to the Vice-Chancellor, Asa Briggs, for permission to use Sussex students. Thus began a connection that was to last for forty years, as Attenborough became one of the Pro-Chancellors. In the mid-1980s he helped to endow the Nelson Mandela Scholarship scheme to provide a university education for black South Africans. This reflected the commitment to decolonization that inspired his award-winning films *Cry Freedom* and *Gandhi*. As an admirer of both the Mahatma and Mandela, he shaped these films to celebrate friendship across the racial divide.

When Gordon Conway became Vice-Chancellor in 1993, he asked Attenborough whether there was any other programme at Sussex that he would like to support. The consequences were unexpected. In January 1995 the *Times Higher Education Supplement* announced that Steven Spielberg had pledged $100,000 of the profits from *Schindler's List* to the Centre for German-Jewish Studies. At Attenborough's suggestion, Spielberg was making the donation through his Righteous Persons Foundation, set up to support Holocaust research. Interviewed in the *Higher Education Supplement*, I explained that grant would help us research the experiences of refugees. Their testimony would complement the Sussex-based Mass Observation Archive, a unique collection documenting British attitudes during the Second World War. 'Even those refugees who came to the UK as children are reaching retirement', I explained. 'It is time to put their memories on record.'

Why had Richard Attenborough become so interested in the Holocaust? When we met, Richard recalled that in September 1939, at the age of sixteen, he was called into his father's study with his brothers. Their mother Mary, working on the refugee committee, had arranged for two girls, Irene and Helga Bejach, to join their uncle in New York. But the declaration of war meant that these two young Jews would have to remain with the Attenborough family, providing the boys agreed. So Inge and Helga became their sisters. 'They brought into our ordered household an awareness of a wider and more dangerous world,' Richard explained. 'When the war was over, we learnt that both their parents had perished.'

The more closely we worked with Attenborough, the stronger the synergies. My parents, too, had welcomed a Jewish refugee girl into their home, leaving memory traces that deeply affected me. And now, co-inciding with the launch of the German-Jewish Centre, he accepted the position of Chancellor of the University of Sussex. Thinking more carefully about his films, I realized that they chronicled my generational experience from the traumas of the Second World War through the defeat of xenophobic nationalism to the emergence of multicultural societies. Moreover, he was a lifelong socialist with a hatred of racism. Above all, his films chronicled changing attitudes towards military conflict. It was an extraordinary achievement to reshape the anti-war musical *Oh What a Lovely War!* for the cinema. The parallels with Kraus's *Last Days of Mankind* made this one of my favourite films. But while criticizing the First World War for its futility, Attenborough took a different line towards the struggle against fascism. As a young man he had served as an airgunner cameraman on missions over Nazi Germany, so he knew this was a war we had to fight. Hence his treatment of fortitude in adversity in war films like *A Bridge Too Far*. And in *Shadowlands* he depicted the poignant relationship between the Christian author C. S. Lewis and Joy Gresham, a Jewish divorcee, capturing the creative turmoil of an Oxbridge college in exemplary terms.

Such resilience also struck a personal chord. In April 1997 the Timms family gathered to celebrate my mother's ninetieth birthday. She was in great spirits, especially when we presented her with a fine portrait created by our friend John Chaltas from a photograph. That summer I gave a lecture entitled A Gemini in German Studies to mark my sixtieth, gently suggesting that being born in June encouraged dialectical thinking. Breaking free from mainstream German studies had enabled me to explore Jewish experience, but given the Centre's ambitious aims, there was so much to do – and not enough time to do it! For me this had become more personal, for my neurologist had diagnosed a progressive form of Multiple Sclerosis which was affecting my mobility. 'Don't forget,' I concluded, 'even a Gemini cannot do it all on his own.' Fortunately, the Centre was expanding its network on campus and beyond. During my absence on a visiting fellowship in Vienna, Laci Löb acted as Director and edited the Newsletter which we were publishing twice a year.

Through the Newsletter we reached five thousand readers, bringing word of our activities to both Friends of the Centre and subscribers to the journal of the Association of Jewish Refugees. An enterprising fund-raising campaign enabled us to make fixed-term appointments that extended our research in three fields, starting with pioneering projects on Jewish religious thought: the work of Franz Rosenzweig and Martin Buber, studied by David Groiser (supported by the Righteous Persons Foundation); and the Wissenschaft des Judentums Movement, by Henri Soussan (Lucas Research Studentship). Refugee studies formed a second cluster: the Testimonies of Women Refugees, by Christina Brink (Hulse Trust); the Educational Experiences of Refugees, by Monica Lowenberg (Schild Scholarship); Contributions to British Public Life, by Ulrike Walton-Jordan (Manja Leigh Fellowship); the History of the Belsize Square Synagogue, by Bea Lewkowicz (Belsize Square); and the Transfer of Technological Expertise to Britain, by Gerhard Wolf (Goldsmith Scholarship). This research complemented the course on the Jewish Holocaust introduced by John Jacobs, a colleague who wrote for the *Jewish Chronicle*. The format was flexible enough to include comparisons with other genocides like the Armenian massacres in Ottoman Turkey and the recent atrocities in Rwanda. The student response was so strong that John enlisted several of us as course tutors, led by Chana Moshenska, our Director of Educational Programmes, whose work was supported by the ANNE-FRANK-Fonds.

We welcomed the government announcement that 27 January – the anniversary of the liberation of Auschwitz – would be nationally commemorated as Holocaust Memorial Day. Given my double commitment as Professor of German and Director of the Centre, there was little time for conventional political activities, although Saime was an active member of the Labour Party. During the General Election of 1997 she was out canvassing, just as she had in her student days. Then the first ever Labour victory in Kemptown had brought Harold Wilson to power with a wafer-thin majority. This time the celebrations were ecstatic as Tony Blair led New Labour to a landslide victory. The hospitality suite at the Racecourse was heaving as we joined out friend Joe Townsend, formerly mayor of Brighton, in congratulating our new Member of Parliament, Des Turner. There was a sense of reconciliation after the divisive politics of the Thatcher years – the confrontations with the industrial working class and the hand-bagging of fellow Europeans. 'There is no such thing as society' had been her mantra, but Labour was committed to more inclusive forms of identity politics. Tony Blair's focus on educational reform, which gave priority to primary schools, was particularly welcome, for we now had a grandson named Jamie, born in April 1995 to our daughter Daphne and her husband Nigel Leff.

The political changes were echoed in academia. Shortly after Richard Attenborough became University Chancellor (after a contested election), Alasdair Smith, another supporter of our Centre, took over from Gordon Conway as Vice-Chancellor. When the new Labour government, sensitive to racial tensions within an increasingly multicultural society, announced that there was to be a Holocaust Memorial Day, we rose to the challenge. After a meeting with Diana Franklin and Chana Moshenska to plan the first such event on campus in January 2001, we booked the largest lecture theatre in the Arts Building. Supported by the Association of Jewish Refugees, the Centre screened films not only about the sufferings of Jews, but also those of homosexuals, Jehovah's Witnesses and gipsies. Our speaker, Janina Fischler-Martinho, impressed the packed auditorium with her first-hand narrative of survival in the Krakow Ghetto. Linking the programme with the persistence of prejudice in British society, the broadcaster Simon Fanshawe pinpointed the action-reaction problem: the more liberal social practices become, the more violent the potential reaction, as in the Weimar Republic.

This marked the point where national policy and academic endeavour coincided. 'What splendid synergies!' said Margaret McGowan, Pro-Vice-Chancellor for the Humanities. But it was quite a challenge to coordinate the research of such a diverse team, and problems arose when donors became impatient with delays (not all our projects went according to plan). Academics are not appointed for their managerial ability, so I welcomed the chance to improve my interpersonal skills under the guidance of David Cornthwaite, a consultant who had worked with Arthur Oppenheimer at American Express. David focused on the need to improve the organizational structure of the Centre and the handling of colleagues identified as underperforming. Questionnaires were completed by the ten people closely associated with the Centre, asking them to rate my skills in areas like Strategic Thinking and Managing Change. The principal finding was a reluctance to delegate (I certainly failed in my attempts to groom younger colleagues for the role of Deputy Director).

The crucial factor was a commitment to collaborative research – there was no place for self-absorbed individualists. While working on her doctorate, Andrea Hammel proved a reliable Research Assistant, helping to edit the German-Jewish Dilemma proceedings as well as completing her thesis on Women Refugee Writers. We could also count on the increasingly experienced Diana Franklin, now appointed Administrative Liaison Officer, to coordinate events at Sussex and in London. These included a public discussion at the Spiro Institute in September 1997 between two eminent refugees: the publisher Lord Weidenfeld and Sir Claus Moser, director of the British Museum development campaign. More provocatively, we also staged the Trial of Richard Wagner, debating in courtroom style the consequences of the composer's antisemitism. Another musical evening, featuring German Lieder, was hosted by Ralph and Muriel Emanuel, and we continued to enjoy Richard Attenborough's support. He hosted fund-raising events at the House of Lords, and when his new film *Grey Owl* was completed, we arranged a preview on campus.

By the turn of the century, despite occasional glitches, the work of the Centre had gathered such momentum that Sussex awarded an honorary doctorate to Max Kochmann, chairman of our London Support Group, which regularly met in the library of Belsize Square Synagogue. Photographs taken during a meeting attended by our research team illustrate the synergies between senior members of the Association of Jewish Refugees, such as Theo Marx, and youthful researchers like Lori Gemeiner from the United States. We all enjoyed the traditional home-baked pastries provided by Hilde Kochmann, which Arthur Oppenheimer claimed was his main reason for coming (actually, both he and Hilde made invaluable contributions to project planning). Although travelling to

London was becoming more arduous for me, there was a further reason why I felt at home at Belsize Square. The synagogue library was located in what had once been an Anglican vicarage.

At the degree ceremony, where we were honoured by Richard Attenborough's presence, I was called on to deliver the eulogy to Max Kochmann. As Chancellor, Attenborough was an inspiration for the innumerable graduates on whom he conferred degrees, stressing in his heart-warming speeches the transformational power of education. On that same day, 27 January 2000, he inaugurated the Centre's Archive in the University Library. After movingly recalling his family's involvement with the Jewish refugee girls, he unveiled a plaque with the Centre's logo, designed by Christopher Calderhead. This featured the Star of David encircled by a rose, symbolizing the ideal of cooperation between Jewish and Christian communities. It was essential, the Chancellor said, to teach the younger generation how the murder of Jews and other people deemed 'unworthy of life' could have occurred. The Sussex Archive would help to ensure that those events were never forgotten. These ideas were echoed in the vote of thanks by Henri Soussan, who cited that exalted concept from Jewish liturgy: 'shamor ve-zakhor'. Remembrance combined with remedial action was needed to reshape the future.

Adventures in the Archives

In addition to family papers my father bequeathed to me a reluctance to throw anything away, but fortunately the house at The Cliff overlooking Brighton Marina, where we settled in May 1993, had a basement with ample storage. Within a couple of years one of the bedrooms was converted into a study for ease of access when inspiration came during the night, but it was difficult to stem the tide of books lapping against the walls, reminding me of the Vicarage. In some cases they were the same books, hoarded in the hope of grandchildren. Our taste for communal living meant that we welcomed congenial housemates, including a teacher of West Indian parentage named Antony Edkins, hired by the Local Authority to rescue a failing school. When he began researching for a Doctorate in Education at Sussex, we had lively debates about the governance of schools and colleges, balancing the claims of interventionist leadership against more traditional models of consensual teamwork.

Saime presided over a household where visitors were always welcome. New friends included a therapist named Joy Ramsay, married to the artist John Chaltas. While John painted subtle portraits and flowing landscapes, Joy's bioenergetics class was more challenging. 'Why do we have to sprawl on the floor like kids having a tantrum?' I wondered after one strenuous session. 'Vibrant health,' she replied, 'involves an opening of the heart and an integration of history with the present through attention to the body and its holding patterns of trauma.' Some people found our life-style disturbing. 'People like you shouldn't live here,' said a straitlaced neighbour after one of our parties. But Brighton was changing and we were part of the transformation.

Saime had her own personal space – a counselling room in the basement for individual clients and ample scope for group work with fellow Co-Counsellors. In her study a growing collection of Turkish books and papers jostled for space with the overflow from my library. We were poised for adventures in the archives that were to lead to substantial publications, following the paper trails left by half-forgotten figures like Hikmet, Wittels and Daghani. This enabled us to reassess, from the margins of history, the most potent ideologies of the twentieth century: Communism, Psychoanalysis and National Socialism.

ROMANTIC COMMUNISM

The sources for our biography of Nazım Hikmet, mainly in Turkish, were scattered across several countries, so Saime set out on her travels, supported by a grant from the British Academy. During visits to Moscow she worked on the Hikmet papers at the Central Archives for Literature and Art as well as the Soviet Peace Archives. She was able to access documentation in Russian with the help of Rady Fish, author of an earlier biography. In the Budapest Theatre Archives she discovered a list of Nazım's plays staged in the eastern bloc, while the Radio Archives contained recordings of his broadcasts. Further radio transcripts were came to light at the International Institute for Social History in Amsterdam, while the Comintern archives helped us piece together Nazım's distinctive position during the Stalinist period. It was Stalin's daughter Svetlana Alliluyeva who provided us with the title for our book. Her memoirs identified Hikmet as the exponent of a form of 'romantic communism' that challenged the party apparatus.

Visits to Turkish archives yielded further insights. The frenzied anti-communism of the post-war period was reflected in the Ankara parliamentary records, which she accessed with the aid of her friend Ülkü Özen. In 1938 Nazım had been sentenced to twenty-eight years imprisonment for allegedly inciting a revolt in the Turkish armed forces. During the discussions about an amnesty that finally led to his release in 1950, one Deputy argued that murderers should be amnestied because they had only killed one person, but not communists – for they threatened the life of the nation! Further collections, especially the Aziz Nesin Archive at Çatalca, illuminated the poet's private life.

Among the most revealing items were three letters written by Münevver Andaç, the woman with whom Nazım lived before fleeing to the Soviet Union in 1951. During our Cambridge days we had already been introduced to another romantic communist, the artist Abidin Dino, who was sharing French exile with his wife Güzin. From them we learnt that Münevver was living in seclusion in Paris. In the thirty years since Nazım's death, she had refused to give any interviews about the relationship that had led to the birth of their son Mehmet in 1951. But we had drafted a chapter about those days entitled A Sad State of Freedom, and we asked

Güzin to show the print-out to Münevver. The outcome was that the poet's lover, now a gracious silver-haired lady, agreed to meet us in Paris to set the record straight.

We were taken further back in time by Nazım's stepson Memet Fuat, the son of Piraye, the married woman with whom the poet had fallen in love in 1934. In our original draft we had tried to define Piraye's ambivalent attitude towards communism. Memet Fuat elucidated this question, describing how Piraye supported her husband through thick and thin, inspiring him to write his poems from prison. He also helped us to understand her feelings when Nazım fell for other women. In principle Memet Fuat avoided commenting on mistakes made in the popular accounts of the poet's life that were circulating in Turkey. But he generously answered all our questions, annotating the margins of draft chapters sent to him before publication. In all, we interviewed thirty-five people who had known the poet personally from the painter Ibrahim Balaban, who had taken lessons from him in Bursa Prison, to the singer Semiha Berksoy, who had starred in his version of *Tosca*, and the architect Nail Çakırhan, co-author with Nazım of a volume of poems entitled *1 + 1 = 1*. In such distinguished company we felt like time-travellers, reliving the golden age of the Turkish avant-garde.

Unsupported oral testimony is a questionable source, but our approach was pluralistic. While Saime's listening skills elicited a wealth of reminiscences, we would always check the interviews against archival sources. My main responsibility was to edit – indeed rewrite – the rough drafts which she entered on computer after her research trips, including her translations of photocopied documents – poems, speeches, letters, memoirs, newspaper articles, radio transcripts and court proceedings. It was not easy to transform this medley into a coherent narrative. 'No, that's not what I meant at all!' Saime might say in response to a passage which struck her as too polished, and there were days when we argued over every word. Having taken a creative writing course in Cambridge, she was keen to make events more tactile. 'Let the reader hear the snow crunching under their feet,' she said, recalling how the young Nazım and his closest friend kept up their spirits by reciting poetry as they trekked across Anatolia. But my academic approach required a source for circumstantial details, for the aim was to achieve scholarly authority by through a rigorous documentation of the factors that shaped his poetry. The disruptions of lyrical mood could be extremely daring, for example in the poem 'After Getting out of Prison', where Nazım broaches the great taboo of Turkish politics, the Armenian deportations and massacres.

By the spring of 1997 we had covered the poet's whole career. Just as we were finishing the book, we learnt that another of his friends, Yevgeny Yevtushenko, was due to give a reading at the Brighton Festival. Thrilled to hear about our project, the Russian author agreed to contribute a

Preface describing the contrast between the Leninist Moscow of Nazım's youth and the Stalinist world to which he returned. Within a few months we had this manuscript in our hands, arranging for it to be translated by Milner-Gulland. The quality highlighted in this Preface was Hikmet's internationalism, which entitled him in Yevtushenko's eyes to a 'universal passport'. We later heard that Hikmet's poetry had been an inspiration for Che Guevara.

It was a challenge to find a publisher for a book about a Turkish communist poet. Initially we were encouraged by Nicholas Jacobs, who had worked for Lawrence & Wishart before setting up Libris, his own imprint. But at Libris he promoted an interest in German authors, whereas we needed a publisher committed to the developing world. During a visit to New York, I called on Michael Braziller of Persea Press, publisher of fine translations from the Turkish by Randy Blasing and Mutlu Konuk. But it was in London, in a tiny office overlooking Covent Garden, that we found the ally we needed: Christopher Hurst, an independent publisher with an interest in Mediterranean cultures. He took our manuscript in hand, producing a beautifully illustrated book running to almost four hundred pages. When *Romantic Communist* came out in summer 1999, it coincided with the publication of *The German–Jewish Dilemma* (Edwin Mellen, another academic publisher). The double book launch brought together historians, translators and communists, Turks, Germans and Jews, with Julius Carlebach there to bless the multicultural gathering.

To Turkologists I was an amateur while Saime's background was in theoretical physics, but the synergies produced the first comprehensive biography of a fine poet. A groundbreaking chapter reconstructed the genesis of Hikmet's epic political poem, *Human Landscapes*. Although his main focus is on the Turkish War of Liberation and the defeat of Nazi Germany, we also identified a significant shift in Hikmet's attitude towards Britain, expressed by a soldier named Harry Thompson. This passage anticipates that the military struggle will lead to a programme of social reform: 'We won't go hungry and jobless after the war. / One of our Lords has devised a solution: / justice without revolution' – an unexpected tribute to the Beveridge reform proposals which the Labour government implemented after 1945.

Soon after *Romantic Communist* appeared we received invitations to speak in London and Oxford, Paris and The Hague, and our review of archival sources was assigned pride of place in the French collection *Nazım Hikmet: Héritage et modernité*, edited by Michel Bozdemir and Timour Muhidine. The English edition of our biography went into paperback, and we were delighted by the success of the Turkish edition, translated by Barış Gümüşbaş, the son of our Ankara friends. Within weeks it was on the bestseller list, next to the latest Harry Potter story by

J. K. Rowling. Our Turkish edition had a laudatory preface by Memet Fuat, sealing the success of a venture that had involved many hands.

ANALYSIS DECENTRED

It was not the dogmas of psychoanalysis that fascinated me, but creative spin-offs associated with the erotic domain. Since adolescence the seminal force of wish-fulfilment had haunted my dreams, a kaleidoscope of images which often resolved some question that had troubled my daylight hours. Academically, this approach was reflected in the title chosen with Ritchie Robertson for an early volume Austrian Studies: *Psychoanalysis in its Cultural Context*. And when the journal *Psychoanalysis and History* was launched, my Sussex colleague Laura Marcus joined me in editing a special number to mark the centenary of *The Interpretation of Dreams*. The journal's aim was to give the subject a firmer historical grounding. A further objective was to counter the campaign to discredit Freud's professional integrity. Thus our conference on Dreaming, Therapy and Creativity, staged in London in May 2000, included a paper by the neurosurgeon Mark Solms. His colour scans of the dreaming brain correlated Freudian theory with the findings of Magnetic Resonance Imaging.

Within this framework we welcomed to Sussex a series of gifted speakers, including Malcolm Pines of the Group Psychoanalytic Practice in London, who reconstructed the Jewish Context of Psychoanalysis; Martin Stanton, Director of the Centre for Psychoanalytic Studies at the University of Kent, who spoke about Family Secrets in Post-War Germany; John Gatt-Rutter from La Trobe University Melbourne, who spoke on Freud and History in the Work of Italo Svevo; and my doctoral student Francis Clark-Lowes, who reassessed the career of Freud's great rival, Wilhelm Stekel. Far more fanciful were the speculations of the maverick Peter Swales about Freud's alleged affair with his sister-in-law, Minna Bernays. Although Swales's racy topic attracted a large audience, the reaction was sceptical: 'If so, so what?'

The two most eminent speakers, Paul Roazen and Jacques Derrida, represented the polarities of empiricism and deconstruction. Roazen's meticulously documented study *Freud and his Followers* had fuelled my interest in minor figures, so it was fascinating to hear his talk about James and Alix Strachey. The seminar by Derrida, invited to Sussex by our colleague Geoffrey Bennington, was more speculative, for his playful approach relied on fortuitous French homophones. But meeting Derrida sent me back to his published writings including his paper on Freud and the Scene of Writing, a meditation on the Mystic Writing-Pad ('Wunderblock'). Freud uses a motif from childhood, the plastic pad that enables you to scribble and erase, to exemplify the persistence of memory traces. In elucidating this text, Derrida gave the concept of 'erasure' an existential weight, foreshadowing the fear of death.

The tension between empiricism and deconstruction shaped my own research about networks of creativity, extending from Vienna to New York. Psychoanalysis was the catalyst that shaped the career of Fritz Wittels, a member of Freud's circle whose stormy relationship with Karl Kraus featured in the first volume of *Apocalyptic Satirist*. After a quarrel, he had taken his revenge by publishing a scurrilous novel about Kraus and his circle, traducing his character in a paper presented to the Psycho-analytic Society on 'The Fackel-Neurosis'. However, I began to take Wittels more seriously after studying the book that paved the way for his emigration to the United States, *Sigmund Freud: His Personality, his Teaching and his School* (1924). Seated at my desk in college (we had not yet moved to Sussex), I found myself identifying with this versatile author. What would I have done, as a successful analyst in New York, looking back on my friendship with both Kraus and Freud? – I would have written my memoirs!

During a visit to the Museum in Hampstead I mentioned this possibility to the historian Peter Gay, author of a highly regarded Freud biography. 'Why not check out the Abraham Brill Library at the New York Psychoanalytic Institute?' he said. A few weeks later I was attending a conference in the States, so I made a point of visiting the Brill Library. They did indeed hold unpublished Wittels papers, deposited after his death in 1950. To my delight I discovered that the memoirs conjured up in my imagination actually existed – amid a copious collection of other unpublished typescripts.

Thus began the adventures that inspired my most controversial book, *Freud and the Child Woman*. The first task was to discover who had inherited the copyright after the death of the author's widow, Poldi Goetz Wittels. Inquiries at the New York Public Library led me to the County Surrogate's Court in Chambers Street near Brooklyn Bridge, where copies of wills were filed. This enabled me to identify the author's son by an earlier marriage, John Ralph (originally Hans Rudolf) Wittels, born in Vienna in 1922, who was working as an engineer in California. John Wittels was delighted to learn that his father's work was being re-discovered, sharing further details about his family heritage. After putting him in touch with Robert Baldock of Yale University Press, I was able to arrange for the memoirs to be published under my editorship.

Why had those memoirs been allowed to gather dust for forty years? An answer was provided by a handwritten note discovered in the Brill Library, probably by Poldi Goetz Wittels. After her husband's death she had tried to find a publisher for the memoirs, only to be warned that they would be unacceptable to 'Jehovah's children'. Since Wittels had criticized Freud's 'Jehovah complex', this alludes to loyal disciples who wished the great man's authority to remain unchallenged. They would be shocked by the frankness with which Wittels wrote about early controversies. Composed in English during the 1940s, those intimate memoirs revealed how the investigations of the Psychoanalytic Society were entwined with the cult of the 'child woman', the actress Irma Karczewska.

My preliminary findings were published in Austrian Studies under the title 'The "Child Woman": Kraus, Freud, Wittels, and Irma Karczewska'. Here we seemed to have the makings of a 'classic erotic triangle', I wrote, 'with Wittels as the ardent young lover competing for Irma's favours against Kraus, his friend and mentor'. But Wittels's memoirs revealed that, tiring of his relationship with Irma, Kraus actually wanted to pass her on to him – and even to induce him to marry her. The resulting tension was a form of jealousy *in reverse* – an inverted erotic triangle that was not without its humorous side. When Wittels portrayed these relationships, thinly disguised, in his satirical novel *Ezechiel or the Visitor from Abroad*, he alienated both his mentors.

Freud expelled him from the Psychoanalytic Society (he was readmitted a dozen years later), while Kraus banished him from his coffeehouse circle. Wittels's emotional ambivalence prompted him, even as he was composing his novel, to send Kraus two handwritten notes so affectionate in tone that they amounted to 'love letters'. However, Kraus (as the memoirs confirm) remained implacable. Towards Irma on the other hand his attitude was more generous. The memoirs reveal that their relationship was by no means as short-lived as I had supposed. In the words of Wittels, Kraus 'remained her protector – often against his will – for over twenty-five years until she died and I think he will be forgiven all his sins for that'.

During those controversies, which culminated in a sensational court case, Freud became closely involved. On 29 May 1907 Fritz Wittels – with Freud's encouragement – presented his paper about the 'child woman' at one of the meetings of the Psychoanalytic Society under the title 'Die grosse Hetäre' ('The Great Courtesan'). When I studied the *Minutes of the Vienna Psychoanalytical Society*, it became clear that details of the discussion had been erased, after Freud expressed his disapproval. 'The ideal of the courtesan has no place in our culture,' he declared. 'A woman who, like the courtesan, is not trustworthy in sexuality is altogether worthless. She is simply a *Haderlump* [a ragamuffin].' Wittels's celebration of female sexuality was too scandalous to be included in the record, though later in the *Minutes* there are cryptic references to the 'Kraus affair'.

Basic questions still needed to be resolved. It proved difficult to establish Irma's date of birth, for her name kept changing – first through adopted stage names and later through marriage. Was she a real woman or some kind of collective fantasy – a figment of male desire? Records discovered at Vienna City Hall finally yielded a reliable date of birth, 30

January 1890. So Irma was just fourteen-and-a-half when she joined Kraus's circle and became his mistress (in Austria the age of consent was fourteen). This correlated with Wittels's celebration of polymorphous infantile eroticism, while raising questions about what would now be regarded as sexual abuse.

Correspondence unearthed at the Library of Congress in Washington showed that the protagonists were haunted by those controversies until the end of their days. Writing to Freud in December 1923, shortly after publication of his book about the psychoanalytic movement, Wittels enclosed a chapter he had drafted about the Kraus affair – and then decided to omit. After reading the suppressed chapter, Freud composed a reply dated Vienna, 24 December 1923, which begins: 'You were very right not to insert in your book the chapter which you sent me. It belongs to a different continuity.' Unfortunately, it has not been possible to trace a copy of the missing chapter, but Freud's response shows that it stirred potent memories, not least about an essential detail that was omitted. He explains that it was the affectionate letters Wittels had written to Kraus that caused his expulsion from the Society: 'You yourself did not deny these letters and claimed the right of acting that inconsistently because your feelings were ambivalent.' After receiving this letter, Wittels realized that he had repressed the memory of those notorious 'love letters'.

Wittels's memoirs also record the sequel in the 1930s. After settling in New York, he became a respected member of the American psychoanalytic community, but the Kraus affair was still not closed, as became evident when he visited Freud for the last time in 1933. They started talking once again about the passages in Wittels's biography which Freud had found objectionable. Suddenly Freud changed the subject and, growing angry, said: 'It wasn't the biography alone; there are those letters that you wrote to Kraus – regular "love letters", while you were occupied in attacking him.' Wittels was stunned. 'Professor', he said, 'do you realize that this was twenty-five years ago?' Freud made a soothing gesture. 'I know,' he said, 'but you were close to me.'

This final conversation, at a time when Freud was approaching his eightieth birthday, shows that the affair left indelible traces. Freud had attempted to draw a line between the scientific and sexual spheres, consigning the latter to a different 'continuity'. But my research suggests that the circles of creativity in Vienna form a three-dimensional jigsaw puzzle. Intellectual and artistic life is nourished by an erotic subculture, as well as by financial resources to be mapped by a cash-flow diagram. The most powerful inspirations involve complex synergies with an underlying homoerotic charge.

Further research in Vienna was required to complete the picture. Once again, my path was smoothed by personal contacts. During our coffeehouse conversations, my mentor Sophie Schick drew my attention to intimate letters from Fritz Wittels to Irma Karczewska in the City Library. 'Beloved Irmerl,' he had written on 21 July 1907, 'I am already deep in memories – how I dragged you out of Kraus's bed and you said: "You can love me your whole life long".' The Library gave permission to reproduce these letters in facsimile, but Frau Schick was still unwilling to let me read Irma's handwritten diary, hidden in her private collection. Fortunately, an Austrian friend named Gerald Krieghofer had discovered a typewritten transcript of the diary, made after Irma's death (fearing that she had a terminal cancer, she committed suicide in January 1933). So now it was possible to hear Irma speaking in her own voice, recalling her passionate feelings as a teenage member of Kraus's circle, as well as her grief after losing his favour later in life.

By this date I had assembled dozens of illustrations to enhance the memoirs without locating the image that really mattered – a photo of Irma herself. However, a chance encounter in London during a conference at the Austrian Cultural Forum in February 1994 set me on a new tack. Hanging above the fireplace in the first-floor auditorium was a portrait of the poet Erich Fried, a refugee from National Socialism who had lived in London for decades – but had recently died. 'Typical,' I remarked to the grey-haired man with a magnificent moustache who happened to be standing next to me. 'They ignored him while he was alive because he was far too radical for their taste, but now that he is safely dead they are proud of him.' The man seemed to agree with me, so I added: 'By the way, what is your name?'

'Jakov Lind,' he answered, 'and this is Silke Hassler, a student from Vienna who is helping me sort my papers.'

Jakov Lind? The name rang a bell. History was repeating itself, for here was another refugee writer living in London who was in danger of being ignored – by researchers like myself! Within minutes we had exchanged addresses and I was inviting them both to Sussex. By the time of their visit to Brighton that autumn the three of us had become good friends, and Silke Hassler and I started planning a symposium to mark Lind's seventieth birthday.

During my next visit to Vienna in January 1995 Silke and I met again, for she wanted advice about her dissertation. By this date Sophie Schick had revealed that she actually had a photograph of Irma Karczewska in her private collection. When Frau Schick finally consented to show me the photo, Silke came along for company, braving the heavy snow. As we sat drinking tea at her flat in the Johannisgasse, Frau Schick produced the long-sought photograph. To my astonishment, the features in the photo seemed identical with those of Silke, the young woman seated beside me – the same dark eyes, high forehead, full lips and lustrous hair! Frau Schick replaced the photo, and we took our leave. Sanding outside in the snow we hugged each other in delight, for Silke too was struck by the coincidence. To me it felt as if the 'child woman' had stepped out of a photo album to share my life.

This encounter solved my editorial task, for Silke was due to visit England a few weeks later. So we transformed our sitting-room into an artist's studio and John Chaltas made a line drawing of her head and shoulders in that provocative 'child woman' pose. This drawing was duly included in the book with the caption: 'Irma Karczewska: artist's impression'. In autumn 1995 *Freud and the Child Woman: The Memoirs of Fritz Wittels* was launched at the Freud Museum in Hampstead. Translations followed into French, German, Spanish and Portuguese, earning the book an international readership. By the time the German edition appeared, Sophie Schick had passed away, bequeathing her collection to the Vienna City Library. So the publisher was able to substitute the original photo for our artist's impression.

Some readers were disconcerted by the title *Freud and the Child Woman*. Wittels's typescript, originally entitled 'Wrestling with the Man: The Story of a Freudian', was at certain points incomplete, and he had left behind three chapters for a second volume to be entitled 'When Vienna was Vienna: Reminiscences of a Former Resident'. After consulting the author's son, we decided to conflate the two sources, reshaping Wittels's memoirs in order to produce a coherent narrative. Details of the changes were given in the Notes at the end of the book, but this did not prevent a German reviewer from accusing us of marketing the memoirs under a misleading label. This was to misconstrue the essential aim – the decentring of standard accounts of psychoanalysis by foregrounding what would normally be regarded as marginal phenomena. The focus was not on high-minded intellectuals, but on the nether world of coffeehouses and nightclubs, theatres and cabarets, sensational novels, court cases and journalistic rivalries. The key to this counter-narrative was Wittels dragging Irma out of Kraus's bed – and then presenting his findings to Freud's learned society.

Did Freud really exclude from his theorizing the ragamuffin type that he saw in Irma? An answer is provided by the paper he wrote at the height of the imbroglio, 'A Special Type of Choice of Object Made by Men'. This paper, presented to the Psychoanalytic Society in May 1909, deals with 'the openly promiscuous way of life of a *cocotte*' and with men of outstanding qualities who become obsessed with 'love for a prostitute'. It is the knowledge that the polygamous type is unfaithful which makes her attractive to men: 'It is only when they are jealous that their passion reaches its height,' he argues. 'In glaring instances the lover seems perfectly comfortable in the triangular situation'. It is not hard to guess which glaring instance he had in mind. Freud attempts to transpose the Kraus–Irma–Wittels affair into psychoanalytical terms by tracing it back to the Oedipus complex. The man who attempts to rescue the prostitute, he concludes, is fixated on a mother-surrogate, while the rival is a displacement of the father.

It was the discovery of such linkages that made archival research so rewarding. There were further traces to be found – literally on the margins, when I examined books in Freud's library. His habit of annotating publications that impressed him was familiar from earlier visits to the Museum in Hampstead. Taking a closer look at the original German edition of *Sigmund Freud*, presented to him by Wittels, I found the book peppered with marginal comments. 'Too much Stekel!' was a repeated phrase, showing that he was far more annoyed by the book than he had admitted in his letters. Since their dispute in 1912 about the control of a journal, Freud had regarded Wilhelm Stekel as a renegade, and it was galling to discover that Wittels admired him. Wittels also recalls that it was not Freud but Stekel who enabled him to free himself from his fixation on Kraus and Irma. His summing-up of that triangular relationship can be found in the book on Freud: 'The immense success of women who are ardently desired and greatly loved depends upon homosexual impulses in men. What a man loves in the hetaera is the other men who have lain and will lie in her arms.'

In December 1995 *Freud and the Child Woman* was greeted by Colin Wilson in the *Literary Review* as one of the major literary discoveries of the year. The following month is was the subject of an extended article by Adam Phillips in the *London Review of Books*. Linking Wittels's memoirs with the proceedings of the Vienna Psychoanalytic Society, he argued that they illuminated two of the most contentious issues in psychoanalysis: the concept of 'sexual liberation' and the 'problem of women'. For all their faults, he concluded, the Wittels memoirs encapsulated the most disturbing of Freud's discoveries: that infantile sexuality is the paradigm of erotic life. This was by far the most thought-provoking response to a book that was widely reviewed. In the *German Quarterly* the American scholar Leo Lensing questioned the strategy of conflating two different sources. However, the French edition was welcomed in *Le Monde des Livres* under the headline 'Lolita à Vienne'.

The feminist decentring of psychoanalysis had to be based on other sources. Interviews with Ilse Hellman, who had fled to England after the annexation of Austria, had put me on the track of another tradition – developmental child psychology. In 1935 Hellman's teacher Charlotte Bühler had published a pioneering study entitled *Testing Children's Development from Birth to School Age*. Hellman's work at the Hampstead Nursery marked a convergence between Bühler's empiricism, Anna Freud's pedagogical approach, and the speculative psychology of Melanie Klein. Those ideas transformed attitudes to child development, as argued in my paper on Approaches to Child Psychology: From Red Vienna to the Hampstead Nursery, first presented at a Sussex conference organized (with my colleague Jon Hughes) on Intellectual Migration and Cultural Transformation. Soon I was invited by Friedrich Stadler of the Vienna Circle Institute to present my findings in Vienna. The theme of that conference, held in June 2003 in honour of the biochemist Ernst Kandel, was the consequences for science and the humanities of the Nazi seizure of power.

NARRATIVES OF SURVIVAL

The third strand of our investigations was National Socialism, using the methods of Life History to record the voices of the victims. In the first volume of *Nazi Germany and the Jews* (1997) Saul Friedländer systematically cites their testimony in order to put Nazi policies into perspective. This book was an appropriate birthday gift from my colleagues Andrea Hammel, Diana Franklin and David Groiser, for we too were committed to recording the voices of survivors – not merely as a methodological imperative, but as an act of moral solidarity. Survivors invited to Sussex to speak about their ordeals included Jack Kagan, who gave an eyewitness account of the German Occupation of Novogrudek; and Holocaust Testimonies from Lithuania and Auschwitz by Ibolya and Waldemar Ginsberg.

We were fulfilling the mission defined by Richard Attenborough when he inaugurated the German-Jewish archive – to collect and evaluate the testimony of those regarded as unworthy of life. Documenting the experiences of survivors required systematic collaboration. To balance my focus on culture and politics, the Centre recruited researchers with complementary skills. Our study of Racist Materials on the Internet was undertaken by Information Technology experts led by Stella Rock. A further project, funded by the British Academy, related to those who fled from Nazism as children on the Kindertransport. Andrea Hammel took the lead in compiling interviews with refugees from that generation, exploring the international context in collaboration with Wolfgang Benz, Director of the Centre for Antisemitism Research at the Technical University in Berlin. An archive-based study of Refugee Experiences in London and New York was completed by a young American, Lori Gemeiner, while Iris Guske from Bavaria undertook oral history interviews for her project on the Kindertransport Experience: A Socio-Psychological Study.

Further educational projects were developed by Cathy Gelbin and Chana Moshenska with the support of the ANNE FRANK-Fonds. As Director of Educational Programmes, Chana arranged a remarkable series of speakers to mark Holocaust Memorial Day. In January 2002 we heard the testimony of two Auschwitz survivors, Trude Levi and Fred Knoller.

Sensitive to the atmosphere of xenophobia resulting from the destruction of the World Trade Building in New York, we began the day with an inter-faith service on the theme of Remembrance and Hope. Our theme the following year, Survivors and Refugees 1933–2003, connected the experiences during the Nazi period of Janina Fischler-Martinho with the more recent ordeal of a refugee from Afghanistan, Abdul Lazlad, whose escape from the clutches of the Taliban gave a personal edge to his analysis of British Asylum Policy. During the following years we explored further topical themes, especially relating to genocide. In January 2008, after Rabbi Jonathan Wittenberg had analysed the obstacles to inter-faith dialogue, we were warned by Mark Levene (of Southampton Parkes Institute) that the competition for scarce resources caused by climate change could have apocalyptic consequences.

In creating an archive we gave priority to family papers of refugees from Nazism that trace the fortunes of German-Jewish families through several generations. The quest took me, on a single day in February 1997, to Kilburn to interview Elli Kamm, a teacher originally from Aachen; to Hendon to collect archival papers from a lawyer from Düsseldorf named Fritz Hellendall; and to Hampstead to meet a textile manufacturer named Clemens Nathan, originally from Hamburg. On the train back to Brighton I read the draft memoirs of another lawyer named Gary Leon, who had asked me to assess them for publication. We also received typescripts of unpublished novels by Selma Kahn about Jewish life in southern Germany (from her son Michael Kean) and illustrated albums of poems by a school-teacher named Ludwig Marx (from his son Robert Miller). These personal contacts with donors enhanced the value of their gifts. The Ehrenberg papers, presented by Lewis Elton, illuminated intellectual developments from the Enlightenment through to the scholarly legacy of refugees. This was soon joined by the Mac Goldsmith archive documenting the career of an innovative engineer, presented by his widow Ruth Goldsmith.

Sussex appealed to donors who wished their papers to become a focus for research. Hellendall's collection included correspondence about his – ultimately successful – campaign to persuade his native city of Düsseldorf to name its university in honour of another of its sons, Heinrich Heine. This formed the basis for a thesis by Stella Joory within the framework of our Masters course in German-Jewish Studies. The Ehrenberg collection was catalogued by our archivist Samira Teuteberg, noted for her skill in palaeography, while Professor Elton collaborated on a research paper on the intellectual legacy of his mother Eva Ehrenberg, entitled A Dialogue about Languages, Multiculturalism and Exile. The Selma Kahn papers were researched by Andrea Hammel, who edited one of the novels for publication, *Der Weg ins Dritte Reich*. And the career of Mac Goldsmith was chronicled by Gerhard Wolf, a postgraduate from Berlin, leading to the publication of an illustrated biography entitled *The Life and Work of*

a Refugee Engineer. We also welcomed to Sussex a Visiting Fellow from
Tel Aviv named Ernest Stock, helping him prepare personal diaries from
the Nazi period for publication under the title *Jugend auf der Flucht.*

Our three most ambitious projects related to refugees born in Austria.
Not long after the founding of the Centre the phone rang in my office.
'What has happened to the Daghani collection?' asked an anxious voice.
The Sussex archives, the Librarian had assured me, held no Jewish collections (the emphasis was on Mass Observation Archive, the Kipling papers
and the Bloomsbury Group). But on the line was a journalist from Hove,
Mollie Brandl Bowen, insisting that only a few years earlier the university
had acquired the work of a Holocaust survivor. Asked where this mysterious collection was located, the chair of the archives committee, Margaret
McGowan, took several weeks to find the answer. Locked away in a storeroom in the Education Building we then discovered a treasure trove – the
artistic and literary estate of Arnold Daghani.

This strengthened our sense of mission, for the artist was born in 1909
in an eastern frontier town of the Austro-Hungarian Empire as a member
of a German-speaking Jewish family. After enduring persecution, deportation and exile, Daghani had died in 1985 in Hove, where he and his wife
Nanino had finally found sanctuary. The Trustees, his sister-in-law Carola
and her husband Miron Grindea, had the task of finding a home for the
works that had been displayed at the artist's apartment. When the collection was offered to the Israel Museum in February 1987, the offer was
politely refused by the Mayor of Jerusalem, Teddy Kollek. But Miron and
Carola found an ally closer to home: Norbert Lynton, Professor of the
History of Art at Sussex. 'As a refugee who has lost many relatives and
some childhood friends in the Holocaust,' Lynton explained to me, 'I
could not but be sympathetic.' He was supported by Sir Hugh Casson,
past president of the Royal Academy of Arts, who confirmed that the
complete collection would be of more interest to scholars and students
than a few isolated pictures. When the Trustees offered Daghani's estate
to the university, Lynton ensured that the collection found a haven on the
campus.

'MAJOR ART COLLECTION COMES TO SUSSEX' proclaimed the
University Bulletin on 12 May 1987. But at Sussex, despite its interdisciplinary ethos, the collection fell between two schools. Professor Lynton
took early retirement, and his colleagues in History of Art had other priorities. The gift, which was to form part of the University Art Collection,
was not their departmental responsibility. For political historians, on the
other hand, it was too subjective to be regarded as a reliable source, while
it was too pictorial to be acceptable as part of the Manuscript Collection
in the Library. Moreover, there was no funding to catalogue the collection, so for ten years it languished in storage, virtually forgotten.

With colleagues at the Centre I rescued key works from the dismal storeroom and raised funding to have them catalogued. A grant from the Ian Karten Trust enabled us to employ a young art historian, Deborah Schultz, to compile an inventory and develop a strategy for conservation and analysis. Daghani's estate included approximately 6000 artistic and commemorative works – the most significant collection of work by a Holocaust survivor at any British institution. Further items were added after Deborah and I visited Carola Grindea at her West London home.

Calligraphic Portrait of a Woman Prisoner (by Arnold Daghani)

The wall of her music room was covered with paintings, while half the floor space was taken up by a grand piano. 'Have a look under the piano,' Carola said, and several hours later we were still marvelling at the treasures that lay there. Archival research became a blessing as I drove home with Daghani's monumental album *1942-1943* in the back of the car, a unique compilation of commemorative paintings and writings.

To draw attention to the achievements of this idiosyncratic artist, the Centre published our initial findings in a research paper entitled Memories of Mikhailowka: Labour Camp Testimonies in the Arnold Daghani Archive. One of his albums concludes with an account of how more than a hundred and fifty Jews from the camp were executed by the Germans in December 1943, followed by a calligraphic portrait of a woman prisoner incorporating their names (FIGURE: Calligraphic Portrait of a Woman Prisoner). Daghani's aim was to rescue the victims from oblivion and remind us that each of them had a human face.

The interest in text and image, which Deborah and I shared, enabled us to obtain a grant from the Leverhulme Trust that supported further archival research, assisted by Petru Weber, a Romanian postgraduate.

The resulting publications included *Pictorial Narrative in the Nazi Period: Felix Nussbaum, Charlotte Salomon and Arnold Daghani*, which appeared in a special number of the journal *Word & Image* before being published by Routledge as a book. Pictorial narrative, we argued, should be seen not as a pre-modern resource for the simple-minded, but as an art of crisis. This creative engagement with fascism could already be discerned in the exile paintings of Felix Nussbaum, which we analysed as a narrative sequence. The interactions between word and image became even more compelling in Salomon's evocation of German-Jewish family life under the shadow of the swastika, *Life? or Theatre?* Visits to archives, particularly the Jewish Historical Museum in Amsterdam and the Felix Nussbaum Museum in Osnabrück, gave our aesthetic analysis a firm historical foundation.

Text and image combinations were also at the heart of a further project about David Josef Bach, who was born into a Jewish family in Lemberg in 1874 and died in London in 1947. As director of the Social Democratic Arts Centre in Vienna, his organizational flair had won him the admiration of a whole generation of writers, artists and musicians, including Hofmannsthal, Kokoschka and Schoenberg. When he fled to England after the annexation of Austria, he brought with him the casket containing original tributes from ninety of his admirers. This collection, now owned by Bach's great nephew by adoption, Dr Philip Marriott, had formed the focus for an Austrian Study Group meeting in Cambridge.

Since the collection was actually located in Sussex, where Dr Marriott was a general practitioner, I now began to study it more systematically, assisted by the musicologist Jared Armstrong and the Centre's archivist

Samira Teuteberg. In the spring of 2003 the Centre arranged an exhibition of works from the Bach collection at the Austrian Cultural Forum in London, accompanied by a workshop on Austrian Culture between the Wars. Papers from this workshop then formed the core of *Culture and Politics in Red Vienna*, the title of special number of Austrian Studies masterminded by the yearbook's new editors, Judith Beniston and Robert Vilain. In this illustrated volume we were able to identify all but one of the contributors to the casket on the basis of collaborative archival research.

To deal with the multifaceted work of a living author, Jakov Lind, we coordinated research from Germany and Austria, Israel and the Netherlands. This resulted in *Writing After Hitler: The Work of Jakov Lind*, co-edited with Silke Hassler and Andrea Hammel. After the success of his early writings, notably the satirical stories in *Seele aus Holz* (Soul of Wood) and his narrative of survival in Nazi Germany, *Counting My Steps*, Jakov's reputation had gone into eclipse, so he was gratified by this comprehensive reassessment. Our personal contacts continued inter-mittently until his death in 2007 at the age of eighty. The interactions with Silke Hassler proved rewarding in other ways, enabling me to keep my finger on the pulse of life in Austria.

In April 2002 Saime and I had been invited to Vienna for the award of the State Prize for History of the Social Sciences, with a laudation deliv-ered by the historian Moritz Csáky. The Centre's work received further recognition when the Arts and Humanities Research Council awarded us a grant to compile a database of British Archival Materials Relating to German-Speaking Refugees, 1933-1950 – the BARGE project. The field-work was undertaken by Andrea Hammel and Samira Teuteberg, assisted by Sharon Krummel. Their archival adventures took them to all corners of the British Isles, from London to the Isle of Man, from Norwich to Aberdeen. My own role, given the constraints on my mobility, was to coor-dinate their work and welcome participants to a conference at Sussex in April 2007 on Refugee Archives – Theory and Practice. When the papers were published in the *Yearbook of German and Austrian Exile Studies*, the dynamics of archival research were pinpointed in my introduction:

> According to Derrida's *Archive Fever*, a book inspired by the Freud Museum in London, archives form a defence against the death drive, which threatens to reduce everything to nothingness. With the National Socialist regime intent on annihilating the Jews of Europe and erasing their heritage, the preservation of personal papers and historical records [becomes] a political imperative.

The projects outlined above were well on the way to completion by the time I handed over the leadership of the German-Jewish Centre to my successor, Dr Raphael Gross.

The Centre's work was complemented by other Sussex colleagues. Childhood memories of hiding from the Nazis in Vichy France form a focal point in *A Life*, Gabriel Josipovici's tribute to his mother Sacha Rabinovitch. A grimmer story is told by Ladislaus Löb in *Dealing with Satan: Retzo Kasztner's Daring Rescue Mission – A Survivor's Tale*, which reconstructs the circumstances under which 1,670 persecuted Hungarian Jews were enabled to escape to Switzerland. On a lighter note, John Röhl took time off from his monumental study of Wilhelm II to publish an article entitled 'The Kaiser's Germany as Seen from Beachy Head', incorporating memories of his early life in Nazi-occupied Europe.

Archival excursions delayed the completion of my own major project, the second volume of *Apocalyptic Satirist*, but they gave the book a sharper focus. Politically the impact was enhanced by drawing out the links between Kraus's satire of the First World War period and the dramatic developments of the early twenty-first century. For years I had been puzzling over the predictions made in *Die letzten Tage der Menschheit* that China was destined to become a dominant power, using its economic potential to bring peace to a troubled world. Now, with Chinese industry booming, the prophetic implications of Kraus's analysis had become unmistakably clear.

Kraus's image of China, I suggested, was shaped by his reading of Ku Hung-Ming's *Letters from a Viceroy's Yamen*, a forceful critique of western imperialism. If there is a conflict of civilizations, the Chinese author argues, it is not between races. It is the struggle of western people to free themselves from the fatal combination of modern gunboat policy and medieval religious prejudice. That was written almost exactly a hundred years before George W. Bush and Tony Blair joined hands in prayer before launching their crusade against Iraq.

A mystery of a more personal kind was resolved through my scrutiny of the diaries of Sidonie Nadherny, the Bohemian aristocrat with whom Kraus enjoyed a tangled relationship extending over twenty years. Through my Canadian colleague Murray Hall, who had compiled a checklist of literary estates, I learnt that Sidonie's papers could be consulted at the Statni Oblastni Archive at Horská 8, an address in an eastern suburb of Prague. The invitation to attend a conference about Kraus's links with the Czech Republic provided the opportunity to visit the archive, but locating it was a challenge. Horská proved to be a road winding up a hillside which suddenly petered out into a footpath, and my taxi driver dropped me at the wrong end. For twenty minutes I toiled up the hill with a Kafkaesque sensation that my goal was continuously receding. When the Horská footpath at last became a road, I discovered the archive in the attic of a disused convent.

The precious diaries enabled me to reconstruct the personality of a woman whom earlier researchers had seen as something of a cipher. They chart the journey towards self-discovery of an emancipated woman who enjoyed foreign travel, skiing, cycling and other outdoor pursuits, but was also independent-minded and widely read. Where others had suggested that there was no meeting of minds between Karl and Sidonie, the diaries tell a different story, showing that there were deep affinities, quite apart from the sexual chemistry. Just as she conformed to his ideal of the polygamous woman, so her cosmopolitan outlook appealed to a writer opposed to nationalism in all its forms. She shared Kraus's hostility to what she calls 'the German spirit of destroyance', and her comments in November 1916 on the death of Emperor Franz Joseph are equally radical: 'He ended his reign as he began it: with a bloody war.'

Above all, the diaries reflect her efforts to maintain emotional equilibrium amid the turmoil of competing relationships. Sidonie's attachment to Kraus continued – with intermissions – until her dying day. She too was a lifelong letter-writer who could stay up scribbling all night. Her correspondence with a Czech friend during the early 1940s, when the Germans transformed the park at Janowitz into a military training area, makes her hatred of war even more explicit. And she showed great fortitude, after the estate was confiscated by the communists in 1948, when she fled on foot across the border to spend her final years in exile in Britain. Sidonie emerges from the letters and diaries as a courageous woman who shared with Kraus a relationship of exceptional amplitude, shaping Janowitz into a touchstone for civilized existence. Now at last I had the missing pieces in my hands that would enable me to complete my study of the apocalyptic satirist.

Connecting the Past with the Future

During a multicultural party to welcome the new millennium, our guests recorded the date according to their calendar. For Chinese or Hindus, Muslims or Jews the year 2000 was an arbitrary construct, and we certainly did not imagine we were entering a golden age of democracy and peace. But as we joined hands to sing Auld Lang Syne, there were grounds for guarded optimism. With the ending of the Cold War there had been significant moves towards détente, while internet and email were extending the frontiers of communication. Bitter conflicts in the Balkans had been resolved by peace-keeping forces, while plans for an International Criminal Court promised to bring warlords to justice. Even misfortunes like the Turkish earthquake earlier that year had created a sense of solidarity. Greece was among the countries to send rescue teams, while friends in Brighton responded generously to the appeal for funds and clothing. Even in the Middle East hopes were raised by President Clinton's proposals for a two-state solution to the dispute between Israel and the Palestinians.

At the university the German-Jewish Centre was relaunched with an updated mission statement, Connecting the Past with the Future.

The cover design (FIGURE: Connecting the Past with the Future), featuring young people watching apprehensively as armed men emerge from their computer screen, served as a reminder that new media could be misused. Monitoring racism on the internet had revealed that antisemitic forgeries like the Protocols of the Elders of Zion were being disseminated in dozens of languages, but this strengthened our sense of purpose. 'The Centre owes its existence to a partnership between researchers at a leading British university, educational foundations and individual supporters who value their Jewish heritage,' the leaflet

Connecting the
Past with the
Future (Centre
for German-
Jewish Studies
leaflet, 2002)

*Connecting the Past
with the Future*

explained. 'We are fighting to preserve the history and culture of German-
Jewish life for generations to come.'

Our work was showcased at a series of international events.
Remembering for the Future: The Holocaust in an Age of Genocides was
the theme of the conference organized by Dr Elizabeth Maxwell at Keble
College Oxford in July 2000, attended by over five hundred historians and
survivors. My paper dealt with Labour Camp Testimonies in the Arnold
Daghani Archive, while Deborah Schultz staged an exhibition of the
artist's watercolours from the years 1942–43. This was followed by work-
shops at Sussex on Racism on the Internet, attended by Lord Bassam,
Minister of State for the Home Office, Neil Stevenson of the Race Equality
Unit, and Barry Kosmin, Director of the Institute for Jewish Policy
Research. A presentation by Stella Rock analysed the revival of anti-
Judaism in Russia, while Rebekah Webb showed how German legislation
against Holocaust denial was being circumvented. Rebekah went on to
present these findings at the United Nations World Conference against
Racism in Durban in August 2001.

The next major conference, organized the following month in
Cambridge by the Leo Baeck Institute, dealt with German-Jewish relations
under the title Towards Normality. This proved ironic: midway through

the proceedings came the news of the destruction of the World Trade Centre. In the television room of Clare College we watched in disbelief as the Twin Towers crumbled under the impact of planes hijacked by terrorists from Saudi Arabia. By this date the Republicans had regained control of the White House under George W. Bush, and US foreign policy reflected the hawkish views of Donald Rumsfeld, Secretary for Defence. So in some quarters there was an astonishing outbreak of schadenfreude. An article in the *London Review of Books* asserted that the United States 'had it coming'. But at Sussex we were mourning the death of Karlie Rogers, one of our German majors, who had perished during the attack.

We redoubled our efforts by extending the range of Holocaust Memorial Day and launching a new project on Nationalist Myths and Modern Media. Moreover, the impending conflict made it all the more urgent to complete my study of Karl Kraus, connecting his satire on militarism with more recent critiques, like that of Robert Fisk. For Fisk, the western powers believed they were fighting a Great War for Civilization – the title of his best-known book. Although the main focus of his reports was on the Middle East, Fisk too sees the First World War, in which his father had served, as the source of unmitigated disasters.

MILITARISM AND THE MEDIA

'How is the world governed and made to fight wars?' Kraus had asked in autumn 1915 and provided an answer: 'Diplomats tell lies to journalists and believe them when they see them in print.' His critique of propaganda during the Great War was analysed in the first part of *Karl Kraus - Apocalyptic Satirist*. My second volume, approaching completion at the time of the Twin Towers disaster, focused on the inter-war period, stressing his critique of militarism and the media. An opportunity to test out these ideas was provided by an Anglo-American conference on Changing Perceptions of the Public Sphere, organized at Trinity College Cambridge in July 2006 by my former colleague David Midgley. For Kraus (I explained) the media had become 'the lethal organization of moral and intellectual irresponsibility, itself creating events'. Wars occurred because irresponsible politicians could claim 'to represent the will of a nation which they have first intoxicated with clichés'. His most compelling example was the phrase 'standing shoulder to shoulder', cited in *Die Fackel* a hundred times. The politician who proclaimed that Austria and Germany – or indeed Britain and the United States – should stand shoulder to shoulder, was mystifying the realities of war.

The effect of such mind-numbing slogans was illustrated by Kraus's critique of the inter-war campaign for Anschluss – the unification of Austria and Germany. The key concept was 'das deutsche Volk', a slogan with populist and racist implications that helped to bring the Nazis to power. In an article of May 1926 he demonstrated how such images created a world of plausible delusion. Responding to the nationalistic agitation, Kraus denounced the press for disseminating a 'counterfeit reality'. Newspapers in Berlin and Vienna were generating a circular discourse that had no basis in any actual political or diplomatic event: 'A world is created out of headlines and soundbites where nothing is real except lies'. But this gigantic apparatus had the capacity to turn non-events into 'action and death'.

An earlier instance had been provided by the Friedjung Affair. In 1908 the neo-conservative historian Heinrich Friedjung had published an article in the leading daily newspaper, the *Neue Freie Press*, citing documents which supposedly proved that Austria was threatened by a conspiracy in the Balkans. The aim was to justify a pre-emptive attack on Serbia, but the war scare passed as Austria annexed Bosnia-Herzegovina without the expected military conflict. A year later Friedjung was sued for libel by Croatian politicians, whom he had accused of treason. His documents were exposed as forgeries fabricated by the Austrian Foreign Office, and he was publicly humiliated. Challenging the notion that the country was 'in danger', Kraus concluded: 'Austria is the most willing victim of the media; it not only believes what it sees in print, but also believes the opposite, when it sees that in print, too.' Sadly, the political lessons of the Friedjung affair were ignored, and in 1914 the militarists had their way.

My lecture suggested that Kraus's diagnosis was confirmed by the fabrications of the British and American governments in the run-up to the Second Gulf War. The evidence used to justify the invasion of Iraq in March 2003 was just as suspect as that cited by Friedjung. On 3 February 2003 journalists in London were issued with a briefing document entitled *Iraq's Weapons of Mass Destruction*, with a Foreword by Prime Minister Tony Blair. This purported to be a well-researched account of Iraq's Chemical, Biological, Nuclear and Ballistic Missile Programmes. Compiled by Blair's Director of Communications, Alastair Campbell, this document became known as the 'dodgy dossier', since its evidence was cobbled together from dubious sources. Worse was to follow three days later when the US Secretary of State, Colin Powell, presented the United Nations with an elaborately illustrated – but equally fallacious – account of Iraq's Biological Weapons, Chemical Weapons and Ties to Al Qaeda.

We now know that there were no weapons of mass destruction in Iraq and that Saddam Hussein had no connection with Al Qaeda, let alone with the attack on the Twin Towers. But these myths were so insistently repeated by the patriotic media that a majority of the British Parliament and the American Congress came to believe them. The Friedjung fiasco was being repeated, but it was now America that was allegedly 'in danger' and Britain that was standing 'shoulder to shoulder' (Blair's phrase) with the dominant power. At least there was a modicum of logic in the Austro-Hungarian invasion of Serbia in August 1914, since the plot to assassinate Archduke Franz Ferdinand really was hatched in Belgrade. But how could an act of terrorism committed by Saudis trained in Afghanistan justify the invasion of Iraq? This was counterfeit reality on a global scale.

The most senior figure present at the Public Sphere conference, Lord Wilson of Dinton, ruefully acknowledged the justice of this critique. As a recent Secretary of the British Cabinet, he was intrigued by my suggestion that Bush and Powell, Blair and Campbell actually came to believe the myths they were disseminating. This was the paradox of sincere deceit pinpointed by Kraus's aphorism: 'Diplomats tell lies to journalists and believe them when they see them in print.' However, conference participants from the United States were disconcerted to find national policy subjected to such radical scrutiny. There were similar reactions from American reviewers after the second volume of *Apocalyptic Satirist* was published in 2005. They found it hard to accept that lessons for the future could be drawn from historical scholarship. My insistence on the topicality of Kraus's writings struck a stronger chord in Vienna, where I was invited by Werner Welzig to lecture at the Austrian Academy of Sciences; and in Paris, where I contributed to a conference organized by Jacques Bouveresse at the Collège de France.

May 2005 was the date of the British General Election that might have removed the Labour government from office. Their one hope was that prosperity at home, fuelled by low inflation and easy credit, would compensate for mistakes abroad. Saime and I had left the Labour Party in protest against the invasion of Iraq, but the post brought almost daily appeals to rejoin the party and contribute to funds. The envelope that arrived just twenty-four hours before the vote was from the Office of the Prime Minister. 'They must be desperate!' I remarked, and was about to bin it with other junk mail when Saime said: 'Open it and see'. It was a letter from 10 Downing Street, explaining that the Prime Minister was minded to make me an officer of the Order of the British Empire for services to scholarship. The following day the Labour government won a comfortable majority, so they too were pleasantly surprised. Saime was too much of a republican to attend the ceremony at Buckingham Palace, but our daughter Daphne and grandson Jamie accompanied me. We were escorted to the ceremony by Diana Franklin, whose service to the Centre deserved just as much recognition as mine.

The politics of the period were explored on a broader front during our conference on Nationalist Myths and Modern Media, staged at Chatham House in London. The programme, funded by the Arts and Humanities Research Council, was organized Stella Rock and Jan Herman Brinks, a researcher from the Netherlands. Academics, journalists and policy makers from a score of countries explored the recycling of racial and religious prejudices through newsprint, film, television, radio and the internet. David Binder of the *New York Times* gave a riveting lecture on Reporting Civil Wars, showing how partisanship distorted coverage of the conflicts between Serbia, Croatia and Bosnia. Other politically experienced speakers included our Sussex colleague Stephen Burman, an expert on American foreign policy; Gerry Gable, founder of the anti-fascist journal *Searchlight*; Franziska Augstein of the *Süddeutsche Zeitung*; and Tanya Lokshina, director of the Moscow Helsinki Group.

A total of sixty papers explored questions like: Has the United States become the ultimate imperial nation? How does the gender of Palestinian suicide bombers influence the press coverage? Why has Hitler's deputy Rudolf Hess become a cult figure among the Far Right in Germany? The role of religion in the formation of national identity formed a further leitmotif. There were also papers on the constructive function of the media in democratic societies. James Miller, Professor of Communications from Amherst Massachusetts, described the UNESCO-backed effort to establish western models of journalism in formerly communist countries. But the most surprising finding, summarized in my introduction, was the enduring power of political myths in an age of educational advance. When selected papers appeared in book form in 2006, the picture had darkened. The hopes with which we had greeted the millennium were evaporating in the aftermath of the wars in Afghanistan and Iraq.

LANDSCAPES AND MEMORIES

Cultural historians have become increasingly preoccupied with the politics of memory. At Cambridge my outlook was influenced by the sociologist Paul Connerton, a witty raconteur who would test out his ideas over a convivial drink. In his pioneering study *How Societies Remember* (1989) he redefined collective memory by emphasizing the function of rituals and performances, especially in Nazi Germany. During the following years the literature expanded, with Simon Schama's magisterial *Landscape and Memory* (1995) exploring the national myths inscribed in mountains, forests and rivers. More recently the television series *Coast*, produced by the BBC and the Open University, has mapped the British Isles through explorations of a littoral scoured by the tides of history.

These developments coincided with a vogue for Life History that encourages ordinary people to record their experiences. Sussex led the way with publications like *Wartime Women: A Mass Observation Anthology* edited by Dorothy Sheridan. My own contributions include recordings made with my mother, which highlight the continuities of rural life. Even in her eighties her memory was unclouded as she recalled the West Country farming communities of her childhood: her parents setting up their stall in Barnstable market, the lamp-lit farm kitchen at Collery, the pony and jingle that carried the family to Sandymouth for picnics, a postman announcing the outbreak of the First World War, the village school where she first set eyes on her future husband. In a panoramic narrative lasting several hours she evoked a landscape to which they 'belonged' – and to which they returned at the outbreak of the Second World War.

After Mother's death at the age of ninety-seven the family gathered for the funeral at St Luke's Church Buckfastleigh, no longer the dingy edifice of earlier days. After the burning-down of Holy Trinity, the insurance payments had funded the construction of a fine new building in the heart of town, designed by one of Father's protégés, the architect Ronald Weeks. My elder brother David delivered the eulogy with an apple in his hand, an emblem of our parents' lives. Echoes of the Garden of Eden became fused with anecdotes about Father's apple-picking exploits in the Vicarage orchard and the succulent fruit pies baked by Mother in the breakfast room. The epitaph was from a poem by Robert Frost: 'But I am done with apple-picking now, / Essence of winter sleep is on the night.' Tides of memory carried the cortège up the hill to the ruins of Holy Trinity, where Mother was laid to rest beside her husband. From the churchyard there were glorious views of the moors as four of the grandchildren performed 'The day Thou gavest Lord is over'.

To complement Mother's account of Collery, my uncle George Timms has produced a personal memoir of Rowden, the farm where Father spent his boyhood and where George and his wife Peggy raised their four children. This meticulously reconstructed narrative takes us back to the 1920s, when Granfer Bill Timms was running the farm and threshing machines were first introduced. As an enduring contribution to local history, it maps the rhythms of rural life within the ten square miles of borderland between North Devon and North Cornwall where George has spent almost his whole life. He insists that he never intended to be a farmer. But after interludes at college and in the army, serving as a Platoon Commander after the Normandy landings, he took over the farm after Granfer had suffered a stroke.

An evocative section of George's memoir is devoted to Cranham Mill near Welcombe, the watermill where Grandma Rhoda Timms (née Knight) was born. As a girl it was her job to guide the donkey laden with sacks of freshly-ground flour back to the farms. A further serendipitous chapter has been added to this story by the poet John Moat, the boy who shared his governess with me sixty-five years ago in that cottage on the edge of Dartmoor. For John has made his home in the disused mill where Grandma was born, celebrating the life of the region in a collection entitled *Welcombe Overtures*, while his *Ballad of the Leat* describes the restoration of the waterwheel.

Such continuities are hard to match from my reading of German authors. The concept of 'Heimat', a life embedded in rural rhythms, was devalued by the Nazi cult of 'Blut und Boden', while the defeat of 1945 forced millions of Germans to flee from their ancestral homes. Attempts at 'Vergangenheitsbewältigung', the mastering of a troubled past, tend to be shaped by fractured narratives and occluded memories. A notable example is the novella by Günter Grass, *Im Krebsgang* (Crabwalk), published in 2002. This fictionalized historical inquiry recalls an episode from January 1945 that had been erased from public memory: the sinking by a Soviet submarine of the *Wilhelm Gustlow*, a cruise ship carrying over nine thousand German refugees from East Prussia. Numerically, this may have been the greatest naval disaster of all time, for very few survived the icy waters of the Baltic. How could this have been forgotten? The question became connected in my mind with the loss of the *Struma*, a ship carrying hundreds Jewish refugees from Romania, which sank in the Black Sea in February 1942 after a mysterious explosion. Rumours about the *Struma* had reached us from relatives in Istanbul, but that disaster, too, seemed to have been expunged from the record. Could there be a link between these parallel universes?

My approach to this conundrum was through passages from the Old Testament about the defeat of Amalek, a paradigm showing that events associated with a specific place and perpetrator are easily remembered. By contrast, losses at sea tend to sink into oblivion. Countries with maritime traditions, like Britain and the United States, may incorporate such disasters into their narrative, but for both Germans and Jews national memory seemed curiously landlocked: hence the forgetting of the *Gustlow* and the *Struma*. Incidents at sea are of marginal significance for cultures that conceptualize their heritage in territorial terms – the longing for 'Lebensraum'. There seems to be a parallel with the State of Israel. My argument ended by contrasting the Zionist dream of a 'promised land' with the more open attitude of post-Zionist thinkers towards the Palestinians. Jewish and Islamic fundamentalists may base their claims to holy lands on scriptural authority, but the focus should surely be on the practical politics of dividing the land. The final linkage made in this article was with another contemporary problem – the plight of African refugees fleeing across the Mediterranean in flimsy boats.

These challenging questions, first canvassed in July 2002 at a conference in London, were fine-tuned for publication, taking account of the responses of Jewish audiences in Hampstead and Hove. One irate rabbi, distressed by the parallel between German and Jewish territorial claims, protested to the Vice-Chancellor, Alasdair Smith. Perhaps I should have been forewarned by the tumult caused by an earlier seminar at Sussex, when an elderly German-Jewish refugee, formerly a Zionist, was billed to speak about her experiences in Palestine. The packed auditorium erupted as members of Palestine Solidarity passed around maps showing illegal Jewish settlements – only to see them torn up by Zionist sympathizers. The furore was impossible to moderate, since neither side wanted to hear what the other had to say.

The debate about national memory received a further impetus from W. G. Sebald, the melancholy laureate of the declining century. Meeting Max, as he was known to his friends, was a defining experience for British Germanists. Born in 1944 in a small town near the Bavarian Alps, he had come to Manchester in his early twenties as a Lector. By the time we became acquainted he was teaching at the University of East Anglia and living in the Old Rectory at Poringland near Norwich. He was among the audience for my first lecture on the Vienna Circles, and we had shared interests. Max, too, was inspired by the Frankfurt School, balanced by an interest in Austrian literature that brought us together at conferences. There was something uncanny about his double identity: Max the witty raconteur, full of quirky anecdotes, seemed at odds with Sebald the archival researcher, author of academic articles. These gifts had yet to merge into the creative synthesis that produced *Die Ausgewanderten* (*The Emigrants*), his first work of documentary fiction. When the German paperback appeared in November 1994, a copy was presented to me by our new Sussex lector, Caroline Welsh. She too was impressed by these narratives of exile with their haunting visual images.

Sebald had served on the Editorial Board of Austrian Studies, and the affinities were strengthened as he engaged with the trauma of the Second World War and the ordeals of Jewish refugees. Given this convergence we invited him to speak at Sussex, but in an era of instant emails he was living at a more measured pace, reflected in the elegant longhand of letters from the Rectory. 'The last lap in the old millennium,' he wrote on 6 January 1999, 'promises to be difficult on several fronts, not least here at East Anglia, where we are in the process of dismantling the remainders of our modern languages sectors. But perhaps we can talk about my coming down to Sussex once things are more settled.' With reference to Austrian Studies he wrote: 'I had always meant to write to express my sense of guilt about not having helped more with the Austrian Yearbook which has become such an admirable collection. It is not that my interest in AUSTRIACA has waned; rather my various other preoccupations getting the better of me. [. . .] I greatly admire the work you are doing at the Centre,' he concluded, 'and would like to do something at Sussex.' After the publication of *Austerlitz*, his most ambitious German-Jewish narrative, we renewed our invitation, but sadly it was not to be. In December 2001 we were shocked to hear that Max had been killed in a traffic accident.

While untimely death set the seal on Sebald's melancholy vision, books like *Die Ausgewanderten* and *Die Ringe des Saturn*, fluently translated into English, were winning him a cult following. By highlighting British tolerance towards refugees, while writing more critically about Germany, he was being generous towards his adoptive country. On closer reading, however, even narratives like *The Rings of Saturn* prove extremely probing. Sebald's account of his wanderings through the East Anglian countryside contains reminders that British history, too, consists of atrocities and disasters. Chance encounters recall not only the bombing raids on German cities launched from East Anglian airfields, but also the slave-labour on sugar plantations that became the source of British prosperity.

Near the Suffolk coast the solitary wanderer comes across a narrow-gauge railway bridge over the River Blyth, featured in one of the photographs that punctuate his narrative. Recalling that the railway was originally designed for the Emperor of China, he takes us back to the military adventurism and commercial greed of the Opium Wars, with telling asides on of the imperialist mentality of warmongers in Westminster. Within a couple of pages we are witnessing the mass suicides that followed the siege of Nanking – and reminded that such horrors occurred with the complicity of the British army. This technique connects the affluence of imperial London or Brussels with the sufferings of impoverished labourers in China or the Congo.

History, as defined in *The Rings of Saturn*, consists almost entirely of calamities, and Sebald's readers look in vain for an affirmation of social institutions. An eloquent passage describes how relentless coastal erosion caused the thriving medieval port of Dunwich to sink into the sea. But measured against my own experience, this seems undialectical. Over the centuries, while the coast of Suffolk was eroding, the north-facing shoreline of Norfolk was silting up, creating those magnificent beaches which our family had explored in Snettisham days. Moreover, without millennia of coastal erosion Britain would never have become an island, exposed to the sea but protected against land-borne invasion.

Sebald's pessimism can be traced to the fracturing of historical continuity in the Germany of his youth – cities in ruins, discredited father figures, crimes furtively concealed. 'Such are the unplumbed depths of history,' he said, looking back on his childhood. 'When you look down you feel dizzy and terrified.' This passage occurs in lectures he delivered in Zurich, published in 1999 under the title *Luftkrieg und Literatur*. In English this book appeared as *The Natural History of Destruction*, though a less misleading title would have been Literary Responses to the Bombing of German Cities. The question for Sebald was not whether the bombing of civilian targets was justified, but why the cataclysmic consequences had been virtually erased from the record after 1945, as the survivors got on with the task of reconstruction. The Germans, he claimed, lacked the passionate interest in the past so perceptible in the British Isles. Germany had become a nation blind to history.

These claims provoked a controversy with political consequences. The debates about aerial warfare intensified after the publication of a more exhaustive account by the historian Jörg Friedrich, *Der Brand: Deutschland im Bombenkrieg, 1940–1945*. Serialized in *Bild*, the mass-circulation daily, this book left readers in no doubt about the magnitude of the crimes committed by British and American air power (the subtitle of the English edition, *The Bombing of Germany*, makes the intention even clearer). This radical rethinking about the Second World War coincided with growing apprehensions about US foreign policy in the run-up to the German general election of autumn 2002.

Discussions with German friends during our visit to the Felix Nussbaum Museum in Osnabrück that summer had indicated that the Social Democratic/Green Party coalition, led by Chancellor Gerhard Schröder, was so unpopular that he was certain to lose. But the campaign coincided with American efforts to mobilize support at the United Nations for the planned invasion of Iraq. Fearing that a Christian Democratic/Christian Social government would support the war, the electorate swung behind Schröder and his Foreign Minister, Joschka Fischer. Their promise that no German troops would be sent to Iraq helped the Social Democratic/Green Party coalition to a historic victory.

A highlight of the Iraq debate was the confrontation between Joshka Fischer and Donald Rumsfeld at a Munich conference in February 2003. Fischer represented the success of that long march through the institutions advocated by Rudi Dutschke. After making his name as a left-wing activist during the 1970s, Fischer had risen through the ranks of the Green Party to hold high office. In 1999 he authorized the deployment of German troops in the Balkans as part of a European peace-keeping force. As a veteran anti-war campaigner, he justified the decision by the need to protect Kosovo Albanians against the threat from Serbia. This showed that Germany had acquired an independent geo-political voice, as Franziska Augstein noted at our conference on Nationalist Myths. Fischer's response in Munich to Rumsfeld's call for action against Saddam Hussein was even more decisive. Discarding his prepared text, he switched to English as he turned to face the Secretary for Defence. 'My generation has learnt you must make a case,' he said, 'and I am not convinced!'

For students of German affairs, there was a link between the refusal to support the invasion and the controversy about bombing civilians. In the *Times Literary Supplement* Daniel Johnson accused Schröder and Fischer of a 'cynical exploitation of anti-Americanism'. But for me this was an attempt to save the Americans from themselves, or rather from the military adventurism of Bush and Rumsfeld. Germans of Fischer's generation had learnt the lessons of the past – if only British parliamentarians had done the same!

When Tony Blair called on Members of Parliament to vote for war, a large majority supported him, defying anti-war demonstrations by millions of citizens (Saime joined the march in London). The mystery was why British politicians were so easily deceived by the dodgy dossier concocted in Downing Street. One answer lay in the belief, endlessly repeated by Blair, that it was morally 'right' to overthrow Saddam and his 'evil empire', even if there was no immediate threat from weapons of mass destruction. Saddam was indeed caught, tried and hanged. As a result of the invasion and its uncontrollable aftermath, an estimated one hundred thousand other Iraqis also suffered violent premature deaths.

My disability prevented me from attending the anti-war demonstration. However, shocked by the bombing of Baghdad, I had a series of conversations about Allied strategy with our neighbour John Beck, an RAF veteran. Although now in his mid-eighties, John's memories of missions carried out in the summer of 1944 were undimmed. Then there had already been debates about the bombing of densely populated areas, but at least it was an equal contest. John showed me the Operational Diary of the Bomber Command squadron with which he had served as Flight Engineer after the D-Day landings. Of sixteen aircraft that set out on the night of 7 July 1944 to attack German positions near Criel (St Leu), two went missing without trace. John recalled poignant details about comrades who failed to return from those missions. While they perished in a life-and-death struggle for democracy, there are few risks for the protagonists of today's asymmetrical warfare.

MULTICULTURAL MOSAICS

Despite these controversies, making sense of history is easier in England. 'I can't bear to watch the BBC,' a German friend remarked. 'Every night another programme about the British Empire!' This undervalues the collaboration between broadcasters and academics. Avoiding a simplistic Whig view of history, the BBC programmes have created narratives that reach back beyond imperial days to the Vikings and Anglo-Saxons. For makers of German television series such as Guido Knopp the task of establishing a coherent national narrative has proved a challenge. But Britain is fortunate in having historians like Simon Schama and David Starkey, committed to dramatizing the links with the past. The 'continuity of institutions' was one of the values affirmed by Churchill in his broadcasts of June 1940. As his cherished Empire mutated into a looser Commonwealth, new patterns emerged through the migrations of the post-colonial period.

The transformation of Britain into a multicultural society now heads the agenda both for both policy makers and educationalists. At Sussex the achievements of immigrants form a focal point for research, not only at the German-Jewish Centre. It is not only historical curiosity that makes immigration a compelling theme, for the Britain of my childhood has been transformed from a monolithic white community into the colourful post-imperial diaspora of today. Successive waves have brought new communities to our shores: the *Windrush* generation from the West Indies during the late 1940s, followed by groups displaced by the break-up of Empire: Greeks and Turks from Cyprus, Chinese from Hong Kong, Muslims from Pakistan, and East African Asians. Political refugees from as far away as Chile form further sub-groups, but it is the European treaties promoting social mobility that have completed the transformation.

At Cambridge in the 1970s we needed to make the case for a work permit before the Ministry of Labour would allow the college to employ a single French or German lector. Thirty years later, Britain has opened its doors to European workers from as far afield as Poland and Romania, while refugees from Afghanistan and Iraq increase the numbers. Multiculturalism is an audacious experiment for a small island. Can rival ethnic groups live in relative harmony, forming stable communities within their regions of resettlement? Britain may have neither the time nor the space to become a melting-pot on the American model, but the migrations have created a colourful ethnic mosaic.

During the general election of May 2010 the effects of unregulated immigration damaged the authority of Gordon Brown after he succeeded Tony Blair as Prime Minister. Although Brown won plaudits for his handling of the banking crisis, the Labour government lost touch with working-class voters, after failing to opt for phased immigration when Poland joined the European Union. The campaign was dominated by competing plans for reducing public expenditure, but ethnic tensions lurked in the background, with David Cameron's Conservatives claiming that Britain had become a 'broken society'. Even the *Guardian* described the UK as 'politically fragmented and chaotic', after the result proved inconclusive. The outcome pivoted on Nick Clegg, leader of the Liberal Democrat minority, who insisted on electoral reform as a precondition for joining Cameron's coalition government. Clegg's cosmopolitan background may prove an asset, given that his grandfather came from imperial Russia, his mother is Dutch and his wife Spanish.

Universities are in the forefront of the move towards multiculturalism, countering hostility towards immigrants by encouraging diversity. At the Sussex degree ceremony in January 2010 we watched graduands from over a hundred different countries receive their awards from our new Chancellor, an actor of Indian heritage named Sanjeev Bhaskar. Years of research have revealed the consequences of racial prejudice, for in Britain, too, there have been waves of xenophobia, epitomized by the inter-war campaign led by Colonel A. H. Lane, author of *The Alien Menace*. Our strategy is to show how much Britain has benefitted immigration, from the Huguenots through to the economic migrants of today.

Contested Identities in the Age of Globalization is the subtitle of our book *Nationalist Myths and Modern Media* (2006), a volume of conference papers that includes a critique of The British Media and the Far Right, written by Chana Moshenska together with Gerry Gable, editor of the anti-fascist journal *Searchlight*. This was followed by public events at the British Academy, which has provided me – as a newly elected Fellow – with a forum in central London. There was a full house in June 2008 for a workshop on German-Speaking Refugees of the 1930s and their Legacy to Britain, followed later that year by Kristallnacht and its International Aftermath. Lessons for the future were drawn in a concluding public discussion on Immigration, Diversity and Integration: Past Experiences and Present Trends.

Multiculturalism is a cause close to my heart. Forty years of family life shared with a woman from Ankara has accustomed me to living transnationally, absorbing Turkish culture with its mix of religious traditions and secular institutions. Republican Turkey, encouraged by the European Union, is experimenting with new forms of Islamic democracy. Here in Britain our friends include Turkish immigrants who are contributing to innovative sectors of the economy. The Mobile Government Consortium founded by Ibrahim Kushchu, after gaining a doctorate in Artificial Intelligence at Sussex, promotes the use of sophisticated cell-phone systems for both business and the public services. His international projects include a scheme funded by the Bill Gates Foundation to extend computer access in Turkish public libraries. And when a Turkish jurist named Seyran Uz rented our basement room, our breakfast table was transformed into a forum for discussing the political and environmental issues raised by oil extraction around the Caspian Sea. Lawyers may never have discovered a single drop of oil, we concluded, but they deserve credit for safeguarding energy supplies through international arbitration.

In other parts of Europe attitudes towards immigrants may be hardening. Parties using anti-Islamic slogans have achieved electoral success in the Netherlands and Scandinavia. Even in Germany, with its stable democracy and thriving economy, foreign workers are seen as outsiders, and 'Multikulti' is used as a term of abuse. Under the provocative title *Deutschland schafft sich ab* (Germany Does Away With Itself), a banker named Thilo Sarrazin has argued that Turkish and Arabic immigrants are taking over the country. And alarm bells began to ring all over Europe when this rhetoric was taken up by Chancellor Angela Merkel, who declared that in Germany multiculturalism had 'utterly failed'.

The multicultural project certainly entered a testing phase after the September 2001 attacks in New York and Washington and the London bombings of July 2005. There has been a spate of publications warning that western civilization is under threat from Islamic jihad. The British government introduced legislation making it possible to detain terrorist suspects without trial for twenty-eight days, and the security forces remain on high alert. But terrorist atrocities have actually diminished as a result of the settlement in Northern Ireland, and historical reflection yields further lessons. Around the year 1900 there was panic about Jewish anarchists arriving from Eastern Europe, allegedly intent on destroying British institutions. But their descendants have prospered and become solid citizens. Now it is Islamic terrorists that are regarded as a threat. But the majority of British Muslims are law-abiding and industrious, so with the passage of time this latest panic may proved misconceived.

These issues are judiciously reviewed in *The Changing Face of Religion and Human Rights* by Clemens N. Nathan, one of the German-Jewish Centre's most dedicated supporters. Here, religion and human rights are seen as complementary forces in the evolution of civilized societies, providing they are capable of dialectical adjustments. In an exemplary chapter on the Impact of Religious Symbolism in Europe: Wearing the Hijab and Burqha, Nathan illustrates what he sees as Best Practice Policies for the running of a 'multi-cultural, multi-faith secular school'. The Case of Shabina Begum against Denby High School illustrates the judiciously balanced policy adopted towards Islamic pupils with respect to school uniforms. Nathan's review of diverse approaches in other European countries does not minimize the difficulties. But a short section on Turkey suggests that there, too, compromises may be possible between religious and secular principles.

Our research has highlighted the role of institutions in facilitating integration while sustaining a distinctive identity. The most significant bodies established by the refugees of the 1930s are still thriving: the Warburg Institute, the Wiener Library, the Freud Museum, the Leo Baeck Institute, the Belsize Square Synagogue, the Association of Jewish Refugees and its monthly magazine, the *AJR Journal*. In certain fields of innovation, including photo journalism, child psychology and art history, Britain has adopted the ideas of the immigrants – acculturation in reverse. A systematic study by one of our doctoral students, Lori Gemeiner, focused on the grass-roots organizations that eased the process of resettlement in both London and New York. And my own research has highlighted the function of groups like the Quakers, the German-Jewish Aid Committee and the Academic Assistance Council.

This research prompted me to reassess the account of refugee experiences in Sebald's *Die Ausgewanderten*, which portrays emigrants as loners and eccentrics. The most compelling of the four stories deals with the artist Max Aurach, a composite figure based on real-life models. Re-reading the opening pages, which describe the artist's technique of continuously applying layers of paint, scraping it off, and then adding new layers, my

Catherine
Lampert
(drawing by
Frank Auerbach)

eye was caught by a striking chalk drawing (FIGURE: Catherine Lampert). There was no caption, but a clue was provided by the jacket design of the German paperback, incorporating a street scene identified as 'Strasse mit Laufenden' (Street with Running Figures) by Georg Eisler. As a refugee from National Socialism, Eisler did indeed spend several years in Manchester, but his cityscapes are in a different idiom from the chalk drawing reproduced in Sebald's text. The mystery was resolved when Richard Murphy, my successor as Professor of German at Sussex, explained that the drawing was by Frank Auerbach, another well-known refugee artist. This made the matter more intriguing, for Auerbach worked at a studio in Camden Town, purchased from our friends Trevor Tennant and Dorothy Annan.

Murphy explained that the blurring of boundaries between fictional characters and living persons defined Sebald's aesthetic strategy. But I wondered whether he had obtained Auerbach's permission to attribute one of his works to Aurach. In response to my inquiries, the seventy-five-year-old artist agreed to meet me in Camden Town, accompanied by our son Yusuf, who lived nearby. Auerbach had come to Britain in 1939 at the age of eight, leaving his parents in Germany, and for sixty years he has been living in London. In answer to our questions he recalled his schooldays at Bunce Court, the co-educational boarding school in Kent. The progressive curriculum stimulated his interest in the arts, and those formative experiences proved so liberating that memories of his parents rapidly faded. Six years were spent at art school, where his teachers included David Bromberg, and he was further inspired by the friendship of Leon Kossoff.

Auerbach welcomed questions about his work, including the parallels with the émigré artist in *Die Ausgewanderten*. It turned out that he had never met Sebald, nor had the author asked for permission to reproduce his drawing, a study of Catherine Lampert, one of his favourite models. The artistic technique described in *Die Ausgewanderten* certainly matches the style for which Auerbach is famous, and yet the details don't fit. Aurach comes from Bavaria and lives in Manchester, whereas Auerbach comes from Berlin and lives in London. Moreover Sebald's hero is depicted in almost complete isolation, whereas Auerbach acknowledges a range of formative influences, including college tutors, fellow artists and of course his models, some of whom have patiently sat for decades. By contrast Sebald's description of an outsider working in a derelict warehouse implies that self-denying solitude is the basis of artistic integrity.

It is not simply the life of a refugee that is decontextualized but the whole process of becoming an artist. To insist on this point would be pedantic, were it not part of a wider pattern, for Sebald's work plays down the value of institutions. His figures are seized by a melancholy solitude, existentially vulnerable and ontologically insecure, while the narrator makes a virtue of isolation. There may be moving pen portraits of individual authors, friends and colleagues, but Sebald scarcely ever speaks for a community. He must later have realized that his portrait of Aurach/Auerbach was misleading, for when *The Emigrants* appeared in English translation, the name of the artist was changed to Max Ferber – and the Auerbach drawing omitted.

Sebald appeals to me because, like Karl Kraus, he sustains an apocalyptic vision by means of a narrative persona imbued with complex cultural memories. However, the misfortunes described by Sebald appear inescapable. This fatalism distances his writings from those of Kraus, for the satirist suggests remedies where the novelist chronicles calamities. While Sebald ultimately envisages a world in flames, Kraus's Torch (as continuing research reveals) carries a message of hope.

Tending the Flame

My sense of an ending has several strands, interweaving Greek mythology and Judeo-Christian prophecy with the philosophy of the Enlightenment and the dialectics of history. In different registers they convey a message of defiant hope, checked by the awareness of conflict and suffering. The faith in evolutionary advance, classically defined by Lessing's essay *On the Education of the Human Race*, is shadowed by fears of backsliding and intuitions of disaster. This was the dilemma explored by my lectures on German Philosophy of History during the early 1970s, a period haunted by the nuclear threat. Forty years on, in a war-torn and environmentally ravaged world, the question remains: How can hope survive in a civilization capable of self-destruction? If after all these years Karl Kraus remains a defining presence, it is because these dilemmas are so forcefully expressed in *Die Fackel*; but the Torch casts disparate shadows, making it hard to reach an unambiguous conclusion.

RECONFIGURING THE TORCH

The first volume of *Apocalyptic Satirist* opened under the heading City, Masks and Torch. After noting that the mask was a characteristic symbol of fin-de-siècle Vienna, I argued that the grinning mask of comedy and the goatish face of the satyr in Kraus's cover design announced the intention of comic and satirical stylization. The aim was to break through the clouds of mystification and shed light behind the scenes. In those early days I was only marginally interested in Torch symbolism. After all, Kraus had discarded the original cover of *Die Fackel* in October 1901 after courtroom battles with his printer, and the artist was unknown. However, research by Werner Kraft suggested that one of Kraus's models might have been *La Lanterne*, the polemical magazine edited by Henri Rochefort in

Paris during the late 1860s. Perhaps Rochefort's cover might provide a clue?

Sitting in the domed Reading Room of the British Museum awaiting the Rochefort file, I fantasized about decadent aristos being strung up by the Paris mob. But *La Lanterne* proved uninspiring, for the pallid cover featured an antiquated lantern such as a weary night-watchman might have carried (FIGURE: Vignette from *La Lanterne*). There was nothing that could have caught the imagination of an Austrian author or illustrator – no wonder they preferred the flaming torch. Kraus remained attached to this emblem even after the court compelled him to abandon the original cover. For a dozen years the familiar vignette of the Torch (FIGURE: Vignette from *Die Fackel*) punctuated the pages of *Die Fackel*, marking breaks between sections.

By contrast with Rochefort's antiquated contraption, Kraus's emblem dramatizes an archetypal quest. However, my original idea that his aim was to shed light behind the scenes seemed too simplistic, as the satirical masquerade became increasingly apocalyptic. 'Is this the promised end?' he asked, echoing the climax of *King Lear*, after an earth tremor had exposed the complacency of his contemporaries. And in November 1914 the horrors of the battlefield prompted him to quote verses from chapter 8 of the Revelation of St John (in Luther's translation), describing how – after the breaking of the Seventh Seal – a star fell from heaven which 'burnt like a torch' ('brannte wie eine Fackel').

Kraus was associating his journal with the flames of divine retribution. Although by no means the only writer of his generation to be inspired by a sense of doom, he was by far the most articulate prophet of the impending Apocalypse, sustaining the idea through to the visionary climax of *The Last Days of Mankind*. In the final scene we are confronted by a wall of flames, and a Voice from Above proclaims: 'This was not what I wished'.

Vignette from *La Lanterne* (1868)   **Vignette from *Die Fackel* (1910)**

Apocalypse Postponed, the heading that introduced my second volume, marked a turning point, as Kraus committed himself to post-war reconstruction. During the 1920s he defended the polis against recalcitrant citizens and the republic against implacable adversaries. This prompted me to reflect on the more positive associations of the Torch within the framework of comparative iconography. For further guidance I approached the staff of the Warburg Institute, which had migrated from Hamburg to London after the Nazi seizure of power. We admired Ernst Gombrich as the most influential of the art historians who came to England at that time. But the founder of the Institute was the late Aby Warburg, whose conception of 'trade routes of the mind' had been elucidated by Dorothea McEwan during our conference on Intellectual Migration and Cultural Transformation. Warburg had studied the multifarious ways in which symbols from classical antiquity had been adapted by other cultures. Surely this approach would assist my inquiry. Taking up the Torch could be retraced to its origins.

By this date my disability was making visits to libraries and archives more difficult. Fortunately, the trade routes of the mind could be explored electronically – through the worldwide web. At Cambridge fifteen years earlier the discovery that it was possible to consult the University Library catalogue online from my desk in Caius had come as a revelation. Now the touch of a keyboard gave effortless access to Google or Wikipedia, not to mention more specialized scholarly resources. The seduction of web research lies in its unbounded frontiers; but the argument becomes more speculative when a person good at jigsaw puzzles begins playing with this electronic kaleidoscope.

Googling 'Symbolism of the Torch' produced 23,000 results, many relating to sporting activities; and there were almost as many for 'Symbolik der Fackel', with a more scholarly focus (for example on numismatics) and a photo of the young Karl Kraus on the second page. Within this cornucopia of unsorted images I detected a basic polarity between the ideas of dynamic activity and bold illumination. Searching for the motif of light breaking through the clouds, I discovered it in the iconography of the Enlightenment, notably on the cover of Diderot's *Encyclopédie*. But an unresolved tension emerged between the idea of fire as a source of knowledge, deriving from Classical Antiquity, and the eschatological imagery of Judeo-Christian prophecy. In Dürer's woodcuts for the *Apocalypse*, published in 1498, fire and brimstone rain down from heaven at the Day of Judgment. At the other extreme, the frontispiece of Rousseau's *Discours sur les sciences et les arts* (1750) shows Prometheus breaking through the clouds with a flaming torch in his hand (FIGURE: Frontispiece of Rousseau's *Discours sur les sciences et les arts*).

The Rousseau frontispiece proved particularly intriguing. 'Could this have been one of the inspirations for Kraus's cover design?' I wondered.

Frontispiece of
Rousseau's *Discours
sur les sciences et les
arts* (1750)

There are relatively few references to Rousseau in *Die Fackel*, but Kraus
was familiar with his seminal ideas. In the number published at the end of
January 1901 he quoted (in French) Rousseau's fundamental claim: 'Les
hommes sont méchants, cependant l'homme est naturellement bon'.
Kraus's view of how human instincts become perverted was more complex
than Rousseau's, but I sensed a parallel between the two iconographies.

In both cases the design is centred on a flaming torch breaking through
the clouds. The French engraving, by Jean-Baptiste Pierre, places it in the
hand of Prometheus. Fire stolen from the gods, the source of scientific
knowledge, is bestowed upon an idealistic youth, who represents the
natural goodness of mankind. But the value of this gift is threatened by
the goatish figure of the satyr, lunging forward to grab the torch and abuse
its power. This scene, based on one of Plutarch's fables, enacts Rousseau's
essential theme: that knowledge is easily perverted.

The features of the satyr provide a further link between the two designs.
For Rousseau, as his text explains, flaming torch and bearded satyr repre-

sent antagonistic forces. The creative potential of science is contrasted with the bestially destructive purposes to which it will be put when it falls into the wrong hands. What follows is his celebrated attack on the arts and sciences for corrupting the morals of mankind. However, Kraus's design reverses the dualism of torch and satyr, challenging the fable featured by Rousseau. The grinning masks on his cover affirm the creative potential of comic and satirical stylization. By transforming the satyr into one of the torchbearers of enlightenment, *Die Fackel* reconfigures Promethean myth as the inspiration for a modern critical crusade.

HERMETIC SOURCE AND PROMETHEAN FIRE

The symbol of the Torch is complemented in Kraus's writings by a second leitmotif, the Source ('Ursprung'). It has proved difficult to interpret this motif, which features in the eight-line poem 'Two Runners' ('Zwei Läufer'), published in April 1910 on the final page of the celebratory 300th number. The placing of the poem just above a boldly printed Torch vignette suggests that Kraus sensed the archetypal interplay between 'Fackel' and 'Ursprung'. Further study has revealed that this marked the moment when Kraus decided to remove the Torch vignette from the pages of *Die Fackel*. There may have been some practical reason of this change, but to me it seems symbolic. After a decade of crusading for enlighten- ment, the torchbearer is making way for the runner who returns to the source. Kraus's work was entering a religious phase (in 1911 he was received into the Catholic Church). However, this did not reduce the fervour of his writings, for the dialectic between Source and Torch increased the force of his satire.

Although these motifs remain hermetic, I sense an underlying parallel with the polarity of Oceanic flow and Promethean fire in Greek legend. Digging a little deeper, I discover that Oceanus is named in Homer's *Illiad* as the source from which the gods are sprung. Moreover, Aeschylus stages a memorable dialogue between Oceanus and Prometheus at the heart of *Prometheus Bound*, in which Oceanus urges the chained Titan to make his peace with Zeus. In Kraus there are only distant echoes of this formal mythology, but the tension between fire and water forms a recurrent motif in his poetry. Inspired by Goethe's dramatic fragment *Pandora* he composed 'Die Flamme der Epimeleia', a poem which reconfigures the motifs of flame and source as a tribute to creativity. The visionary fire that draws Goethe's heroine heavenwards 'redeems the source / of all woman- power' ('Rettet Ursprung / Aller Weibmacht'). This cryptic verse first appeared in *Die Fackel* in May 1918, contrasting the inspirational flame of poetry with the cataclysmic violence of war.

My web search also led me to more modern images of fire and water.

A leap of the imagination takes us to the Prometheus fountain at the Rockefeller Plaza in New York. During my early research trips to the States, the art deco ensemble of the Plaza had made an overwhelming impression; but it is only recently that I have grasped the full significance of the sculpted fountain. The gilded figure of Prometheus, designed in 1934 by Paul Manship, rises above the waters holding the flaming torch in his hand (FIGURE: *Prometheus Fountain*).

The figure is encircled by a decorative ring of gold, symbolizing the applications of the gift of fire. Powerful jets of water form a mobile curtain, above which the words of Aeschylus are inscribed: PROMETHEUS TEACHER IN EVERY ART BROUGHT THE FIRE THAT HATH PROVED TO MORTALS A MEANS TO MIGHTY ENDS. As Oceanic flow balances Promethean flame, a display of flags in the background suggests international harmony.

The Torch is especially prominent in American iconography, representing Freedom on the Statue of Liberty, Learning on the Dome of the Library of Congress. The symbolic resonance is enhanced by linguistic usage. In the States 'torch' implies a living flame, while the battery-powered device you slip into your pocket is a 'flashlight'. You even find a burning torch on that most common of coins, the dime. In Britain the symbolism is less pervasive, but for years the flaming torch was depicted on traffic signs marking the approach to a school (FIGURE: The Torch of

Prometheus Fountain (by Paul Manship, 1934)

The Torch of Learning

From the British Highway Code   On an American postage stamp

The Torch of Learning: British traffic sign and American postage stamp

Learning). For a time the Conservative Party used it as their emblem, and as London prepares to host the 2012 Games, the Olympic Torch again recalls the rituals of archaic Greece. But for me it is above all the Torch of Knowledge, transposed more modestly into the oil lamp featured on an American postage stamp celebrating higher education (FIGURE: American postage stamp).

That lamp needs to be tended if our work is to endure, for these are challenging times for universities. Several times, since the foundation of the University of Sussex fifty years ago, the state-funded higher education sector has been crippled by economic crises. In July 1981 the government of Margaret Thatcher announced that funding would be reduced by 20 percent. She also deprived academics of security of tenure and abolished the University Grants Committee, which had sheltered them from direct state interference. Currently, universities face even more severe pressures introduced by Gordon Brown's Labour government. It was scant consolation that Labour were voted out of office in May 2010, for the public-spending cuts announced by the incoming Conservative–Liberal Democratic coalition were even more draconian.

It was hardly the fault of the universities that the international banking system collapsed, requiring government bail-outs that reduce funding for public services. 'Cuts will bring us to our knees,' the *Guardian* reported on 12 January 2010, quoting the claim that one of the world's greatest educational systems, which had 'taken 800 years to create', was now under threat. The allusion to the eight-hundredth anniversary of Cambridge University was misleading, for the state-funded system is a recent creation. By contrast, Cambridge with its well-endowed colleges is financially secure.

Keeping in touch as a Life Fellow of Caius, I could not fail to be impressed by developments. In the perennial debate between pure and applied research, the balance at Cambridge has shifted towards techno-logical innovation and enterprise culture. The pace accelerated under the leadership of Sir Alec Broers, Vice-Chancellor from 1996 to 2003, who had worked in the US with IBM before returning as Professor of Electrical Engineering. Moreover his successor, the anthropologist Professor Alison Richard, led a campaign to mark the eight-hundredth anniversary that strengthened the university's financial base and enhanced its global repu-tation. All this was achieved through a democratic system of governance that provides protection from the autocratic decision-making that is the bane of other universities.

It is the centralized universities of more recent date that are most vulnerable in the aftermath of the banking crisis. Events at King's College London, as analysed by the novelist and historian Iain Pears, show what can happen if academic planning passes into the hands of professional managers. In a widely circulated memorandum, Pears argued that the proposals for staff reductions at King's were notable not only for their severity, but for the way they were being implemented. He feared that a managerial elite was reorganizing British universities on the model of busi-ness enterprises. The concept of the university as a place where disciplines combine to stimulate fruitful ideas had been replaced (he concluded) by a situation where any subject lacking a measurable pay-off was under threat.

At Sussex there have been comparable changes, for new pressures are eroding the interdisciplinarity that has been one of our hallmarks. This commitment still inspires the dining club hosted by Margaret Boden, author of *The Creative Mind*, which explores the affinities between arti-ficial intelligence and imaginative creativity. But while such subjects flourish during the discussions over which she presides at the Hungry Monk or English's Oyster Bar, the departmental structures on campus make the linkages harder to sustain.

Sussex has undergone two waves of structural reform imposed by Senior Managers, partly in response to signals from central government. The first reforms were implemented by Alasdair Smith after he succeeded Gordon Conway as Vice-Chancellor. His enduring achievement was the founding of a Medical School (jointly with the University of Brighton). This strengthened the position of the sciences, which were experiencing difficulties in recruiting students and retaining staff, despite outstanding research. 'There was a standing joke in Chemistry,' Alasdair explained, 'about a football match between the five full-time students and the five Fellows of the Royal Society.' These included the winner of the 1996 Nobel Prize, Sir Harry Kroto.

A further far-reaching decision swept away the Schools of European

Studies, English & American Studies, and Afro-Asian Studies, to be replaced by a more inclusive School of Humanities, with Stephen Burman as Dean. The rationale behind this reform was that existing structures were so complex that student recruitment in the humanities was affected. The interdisciplinary structure also made it difficult to meet the demands of the Research Assessment Exercise and the Quality Assurance Agency, on which substantial government funding depended. Longstanding colleagues shared my grief over the loss of European Studies, but a decline in the numbers studying languages made that original model difficult to sustain. There was no longer a Modern Languages group, and my successor as Professor of German, Richard Murphy, was transferred to the newly created Department of English.

When Alasdair was succeeded in autumn 2007 by Professor Michael Farthing, formerly Principal of St George's, University of London, the modernization of the Sussex campus continued. The Schools of Humanities, Social Sciences and Cultural Studies were abolished, and we now have Schools of Business, Management & Economics, Education & Social Work, Global Studies, and Informatics, while the German-Jewish Centre forms part of the History Department within the School of History, Art History & Philosophy. These changes coincided with economies imposed as a result of the financial meltdown. In December 2009, after a systematic financial review, more than a hundred Sussex staff found themselves facing redundancy. The individual hardship was all the more resented because it was imposed by a Management that seemed out of touch with the ideals that had inspired the founding of the university. There was a loss not only of valued colleagues but of something less tangible – institutional memory.

For six months the campus was intermittently in turmoil as the Universities and Colleges Union consulted with Management in an effort to mitigate the damage. Students were so alarmed to see dedicated teachers being dismissed that in March they occupied the university administration, Sussex House, causing significant damage. Where in the past such incidents would have been resolved by negotiation, the new regime summoned the police and several students were arrested. The suspension of six of the demonstrators provoked a student occupation of the main Arts lecture theatre, and the protestors refused to leave until the suspensions were lifted. Meanwhile, the Union was organizing a series of one-day strikes, while nationally there was a proposal to blacklist Sussex for its heavy-handed treatment of its staff. After protracted negotiations, those threatened with redundancy were offered a financial sweetener known as Early Retirement Voluntary Severance. The word voluntary had a hollow ring. On the credit side, the university succeeded in strengthening its financial position so that it was able to complete new buildings and support further innovative developments.

A wide-ranging debate about the future of the humanities began in the *Times Literary Supplement* after our Sussex colleague Gabriel Josipovici had castigated the new approach. The crisis had the merit of encouraging a return to first principles. 'What are universities for?' asked the historian Keith Thomas in a magisterial article, published on 7 May 2010. While stressing that they have always served the needs of society, he argued that those needs go beyond economic success and technological advance. A further role is to carry 'the torch of literary culture'. The primary aim should be to develop the intellectual skills, independence of judgment and mental flexibility required by a rapidly changing society. 'In multi-ethnic Britain and a troubled world,' Thomas concluded, 'a liberal education is a precondition for intelligent citizenship.'

At Sussex I particularly regretted the decision that there would no longer be research-led teaching of European History before 1900. But these changes coincided with a Strategic Plan for the period 2009–15 that has genuine merits. New buildings are being constructed to enhance facilities on campus, while measures to attract more international students are generating additional income. The choice of a second-genearation British Asian, the actor Sanjeev Bhaskar, to succeed Richard Attenborough as Chancellor, strengthens our commitment to multiculturalism. A further hopeful sign is that Sussex continues to earn accolades both as a learning environment and for outstanding research. The university has been placed in the top ten by national student satisfaction surveys and in the World University Rankings, published in September 2010 by *Times Higher Education*, Sussex was placed eighth among British Universities, scoring especially well for research.

The Centre for German-Jewish Studies continues to make a distinctive contribution. The current Director, Christian Wiese, has transformed it into a hub of international cooperation that impresses even the skeptics. Now that Wiese's outstanding achievements have earned him the Martin Buber Chair of Jewish Philosophy at Frankfurt, a Readership in Jewish Studies has been advertised at Sussex, to be held jointly with the Directorship of the Centre. Our latest Newsletter, number 31 in a series that has been running for fifteen years, reviews activities ranging from a symposium on the Reform Philosophy of Rabbi Samuel Hirsch to a multimedia exhibition entitled Surviving History: Sites of Memory. My own contribution has been to attract funding for a three-year project on the Quakers as Rescuers during the Nazi Period. This will be supported by a generous gift from Dr Alfred Bader, channeled through the American Friends of the University of Sussex.

While British academics feel under pressure, developments in the United States are more encouraging. From visits to the State University of New York at Albany, where the Austrianist Joseph Peter Strelka hosted several rewarding conferences, I know that Minerva, goddess of wisdom, features in their college song: 'Ever in Minerva's thrall, / Pass the torch from one to all'. Martha Nussbaum, Professor of Law and Ethics at the University of Chicago, makes the case more systematically in her book *Not for Profit: Why Democracy Needs the Humanities*. 'Responsible citizenship,' she writes, 'requires the ability to assess historical evidence, to think critically about economic principles, to compare differing views of social justice, to speak a foreign language, and to appreciate the complexities of major world religions.' More recently I heard welcome news from further south. Seeing no future at Sussex, Richard Murphy has accepted the Chair of German at the University of South Carolina. There he heads a large and thriving department that provides scope for innovative teaching and research.

Politically, too, America's democratic traditions have proved resilient, even though the presidency of George W. Bush was scarred by setbacks and disasters: the destruction of the World Trade Centre, the invasion of Afghanistan followed by stalemate in the campaign against the Taliban, the even more controversial military occupation of Iraq, the environmental disaster of Hurricane Katrina, and finally the global financial crisis. The failures of American intelligence became so notorious that Donald Rumsfeld glossed them as a virtue. Reviewing the unstable situation in post-invasion Afghanistan, he declared: 'There are known unknowns. That is to say, there are things we know we don't know. But there are also unknown unknowns. These are things we don't know we don't know.'

The Republicans were forced on the defensive by the financial meltdown, as Barack Obama became the first African-American to win the Democratic Party nomination. Having voted in the Senate against the invasion of Iraq, he had impressive foreign policy credentials, in addition to his record as a social reformer. His campaign for change, which mobilized thousands of youthful activists, proved a spectacular success. No one should underestimate the difficulty of healing the wounds of a financially crippled and ideologically divided society, but after the multiple failures of the Bush administration it was time for new leadership. For right-wing ideologists Obama's victory was further proof that the US was succumbing to socialism, but there could hardly have been better news for multiculturalists. 'What a relief to have an American President who thinks clearly and writes well!' I noted in my end-of-year circular to family and friends.

I had been reading *Dreams from my Father*, a personal memoir in which Obama links racial toleration with progressive politics. His parents would never have met had there not been a scholarship scheme to enable gifted young Africans to study in the States. After Barack Obama Senior met Ann Dunham during a Russian language class at the University of Hawaii, they decided to get married. In many states, marriage between a white woman from Kansas and a black man from Kenya would have been banned as 'miscegenation'; but in April 1961 multi-ethnic Hawaii became the birthplace of the future President.

Educational attainments provide the key to Obama's career. When his parents divorced, his father returned to Kenya and his mother remarried. Her second husband was from Indonesia, and it was in Jakarta that Barack started school, attending first a Muslim and then a Catholic institution. During the following years, back in Honolulu under the care of his grandparents, he proved an outstanding student, gaining admission to Columbia University in New York in 1981 to major in Political Science. The central section of his memoir chronicles his campaign on behalf of impoverished blacks in Chicago as organizer of the Development Communities Project. The unsparing narrative conveys the rawness of racial antagonism and the desperate struggle to overcome it. The turning point came in 1988 when he was offered a place at Harvard Law School. Would this mean abandoning the social projects which he and his supporters had so painstakingly built up in Altgeld and Roseland, two of Chicago's most impoverished suburbs? A key paragraph recalls how he reached his decision. At Harvard he would be able to learn things that would have compromised him if he had gone to law school before coming to Chicago. Now he would be able to return to Roseland and Altgeld bearing what he describes – with a characteristic flourish – as Promethean fire. After being elected as the first black president of the *Harvard Law Review*, Obama returned to Chicago to work as a civil rights lawyer and serve on the Illinois Senate. The rest is a tumultuous history in the making.

THE FLAME OF HOPE

If Rousseau provided one of the sparks that ignited *Die Fackel*, it was the philosophy of Kant that underpinned Kraus's campaign for a better world. The most significant paradigm carried over from his apocalyptic writings into the more sober polemics of the 1920s was the concept of a Day of Judgment. This was partly inspired by Kant's essay on Perpetual Peace, 'Zum ewigen Frieden'. Writing amid the conflicts of the 1790s, Kant knew that the goal of a peaceful federation was a distant dream. But he insisted that although the progress of the human race may at times be interrupted, it is never broken off. Kraus was particularly inspired by a passage in which Kant affirms his faith in the future:

> Confronted by the sorry spectacle not only of those evils which oppress the human race from natural causes, but also of those which men inflict upon one another, our spirits are still raised by the prospect that things might get better in the future: moreover with a sense of unselfish good-

will, since we shall be long in the grave and unable to harvest the fruits we helped to sow.

For Kraus, this altruism offered an antidote to the madness engulfing Germany, and he followed Kant in stressing the need to create new international institutions. Implicit in these arguments are the concepts of a League of Nations (with the power to settle disputes) and an International Court of Justice (to punish breaches of the peace). For over a century after Kant's death these proposals remained utopian, but in 1918, in the climate created by President Wilson's Fourteen Points, a first attempt was made to put them into practice. Kraus greeted Wilson's 'immortal deed', the liberation of Europe from military tyranny, as the fulfilment of Kant's 'immortal idea'.

Kant's words express the impulse that has shaped my teaching – the spirit of hope. If hope is steadfastness in adversity, the most compelling examples are provided by those imprisoned for their ethnicity or their beliefs, whether as communists or democrats, Jews or blacks. For me, the testimony of Nelson Mandela, Nazım Hikmet, Anne Frank, Charlotte Salomon and Vaclav Havel has proved exceptionally inspiring. When Saime first introduced me to Hikmet's poetry, I marvelled at the courage with which he upheld the flame of hope: 'If we don't burn, / How will the darkness turn into light?' Researching for *Romantic Communist*, we worked together through the letters and poems he sent from Bursa prison to his wife Piraye. 'You can't live without hope' is the title of a characteristic poem.

A similar vision of hope can be found in the *Diary of Anne Frank*. A highlight of my years as Director of the German-Jewish Centre was the visit to Basel to meet Buddy Elias, cousin of Anne Frank and chair of the ANNE FRANK-Fonds. It was inspiring to hear at first hand about their days together before the Second World War and to see the treasured original photographs of the Frank family's life before they were forced into hiding in Amsterdam. In a lecture delivered at the Dear Diary conference, organized at Sussex by Chana Moshenska, I tried to recapture the spirit that sustained Anne Frank during those terrifying years in the secret annex. Her greatest wish – beyond personal survival – was to express her faith in a better world. Something similar was achieved in painterly terms by Charlotte Salomon before she too was deported to Auschwitz. Hence the tribute paid to her achievements in *Pictorial Narrative in the Nazi Period*, co-authored with Deborah Schultz. Responding to those courageously creative figures, we concluded that hope is not a philosophical principle but an existential commitment, transmitted through luminous words and images.

Studying the career of Vaclav Havel was also a shared experience, for he was a favourite of my mentor Peter Stern, an exile from Czechoslovakia. When Ritchie Robertson and I were editing the Austrian Studies volume on *Theatre and Performance*, we invited Peter to contribute an article on Havel's satirical dramas of the 1960s, *The Garden Party* and *The Memorandum*. After subverting the language of Stalinist oppression, Havel became a leading human rights campaigner, imprisoned by the regime as one of the signatories of Charter 77. The letters to his wife Olga, written from prison between 1979 and 1982, testify to human solidarity. And in a series of clandestine interviews, published under a samizdat imprint in Prague in 1986, he defined the Politics of Hope: 'Hope is definitely not the same thing as optimism,' he maintained. 'It transcends the world that is immediately experienced and is anchored somewhere beyond its horizons.' Havel's faith was rewarded during the Velvet Revolution of 1989, when he emerged as leader of Civic Forum, and – within a dazzlingly short span – had become President of the Republic.

Disaster may confront us daily in reports of economic and environmental crises, armed conflict and enforced migration, but hope clings to the wreckage. My mind is carried back to *The Wreck of the Deutschland*, the poetic tribute by Gerard Manley Hopkins to the Franciscan nuns drowned off the Kent coast after being forced to leave Germany by the Falck Laws. 'Is the shipwrack then a harvest, does tempest carry the grain?' Hopkins asks towards the end of the poem, transcending those mournful lines about 'hope twelve hours gone'. From the testimony of more recent refugees I know that poetry can literally help people survive. In July 1940 the *Arandora Star*, carrying over a thousand people interned by the British government as enemy aliens, was sunk by a U-boat off the northwest coast of Ireland. Among those who survived was the Italian-Jewish refugee Umberto Limentani, a Dante scholar who was later to become a colleague at Cambridge. During those hours in the water, as he recalled, he kept up his courage by reciting verses from the *Inferno*.

Interviewing refugees from Nazism has increased my faith in the flame of hope. Their dream of a German-Jewish symbiosis was in ruins and behind them lurked the horror of the Holocaust, but they embarked on new lives with extraordinary resilience. The creation of the Centre for German-Jewish Studies paid tribute to that spirit of endurance. Working with refugees, their children and grandchildren, confirms the value of connecting the past with the future.

Moments of hope run through my personal life like leitmotifs in a composition: Father explaining why Christians have the right to resist aggression; Hilda singing of the home to which she longed to return; St Paul (in Brangwyn's mural) surviving shipwreck to proclaim the gospel. It was hope that sustained us through the darkest days of the war as a disembodied voice spoke of sunlit uplands and a military cavalcade thundered through country lanes. Books and teachers opened my eyes to a wider world: the generous vision of the *Children's Encyclopedia*; the language teacher who praised me for reciting a tricky passage of German; the poetry of Goethe and Heine. At Cambridge a gentle teacher shared his faith in love, and a classmate insisted on the power of positive thinking. Liberation then came from abroad: from a German girlfriend with artistic gifts; a Jewish Monsignor who revered Karl Kraus; a Turkish woman who took the train to Munich for a life-saving operation; and the smile on an infant's face in an Ankara orphanage.

Universities, writers and intellectuals created a further surge: Bertrand Russell's hopes for a changing world; Sussex with its innovative map of learning; Kemalist Turkey attempting a marriage between divergent traditions; Hegel and Marx on dialectical contradictions; the legacy of Austria-Hungary as a multinational empire; and Karl Kraus in affirmative mode, celebrating the legend of Pandora – embodiment of Hope amid the evils besetting mankind. A further stimulus comes from studying the artists and writers of the Avant-garde, especially their visions and blueprints for the future. Like Hikmet, they dreamed of a better world to be salvaged from the ruins of history. 'That's how it is, my friend,' he wrote in a late poem. 'Being taken prisoner is not the problem, / The problem is how to avoid surrender'.

It may appear perverse to hold on to hope amid the catastrophes of the twenty-first century, but for those living in pluralistic societies like the British Isles there are grounds for optimism. Life in Britain, home to a mere one percent of the world population, is far from typical of the human condition, but its cultural history, educational institutions and tolerant democracy have proved paradigmatic. The Welfare State created by the socialist government of my childhood may be under pressure, but the National Health Service forms the cornerstone in an edifice of mutual aid. I grew up under the sign of the Cooperative Society, and the commitment to collaborative endeavour has lasted a lifetime.

Our watchword is not the 'me-first' individualism of the Thatcherite era, but Barack Obama's 'yes-we-can'. The emphasis (as so often in these memoirs) is on the word 'we'. While Britain is becoming a more plural society, a dramatic leap towards inclusiveness took place in the United States with the election of the forty-fourth President. Obama's campaign for practical reforms is rooted communal traditions. Re-reading *Dreams from my Father*, my eye was caught by his description of a church service in Chicago, celebrating the biblical message of hope. He imagined the stories of ordinary black people merging with the stories of David and Goliath, Moses and Pharaoh, and the Christians in the lion's den. Then a phrase leaped at me from the foot of the page, condensing these ideas into the image that was to form the title of his second book of memoirs, *The Audacity of Hope*. These books make inspiring reading even for those not involved in political struggles. As teachers we may not march victoriously with the modern world, but we keep open our communications with the future.

CHAPTER EIGHTEEN

The Autobiographical Pact

On the point of completing these memoirs I attended the biennial conference of the International Auto/Biography Association at Sussex in July
2010. There were almost a hundred presentations covering an astonishing
range of topics from Animal Lives through the Drama of Ageing to
Researching beyond Death. They included a panel on Life Writing and the
Photographic Image, shared with my colleague Deborah Schultz, co-
author of *Pictorial Narrative in the Nazi Period*, and Julia Winckler,
Lecturer in Photography at the University of Brighton. 'Photographic
traces,' Julia explained, 'can evoke powerful emotions and become sites
of remembrance.' For me, too, visual images act as memory triggers,
releasing additional skeins of narrative – hence the positioning of figures
within the text of this book.

At such a large international gathering there could be no consensus
about the aims of autobiography, but three basic definitions came into
focus, framing my own approach. In *Le pacte autobiographique* Philippe
Lejeune defines the relationship with the reader as a *pact* which commits
the author to a faithful narrative of personal experience. But in *Design
and Truth in Autobiography* Roy Pascal distinguishes autobiography,
which focuses on the development of the *self*, from memoirs, which
describe encounters with *others*. Equally significant is Northrop Frye's
emphasis in the *Anatomy of Criticism* on the *patterning* of experience.
Most autobiographies, Frye observes, 'are inspired by a creative, and
therefore fictional, impulse to select only those events and experiences in
the writer's life that go to build up an integrated pattern'. Can autobiography really be faithful and fictional at the same time? My response to this
conundrum is to recall how personal experience is refracted through
superimposed patterns and enriched by interactions with others.

Dialectical Patterns

Sharing memories with Saime, I am aware that it is not only the attraction of opposites that drives our personal dialectic, for we are both attached to triadic patterns. Her method, when approaching some challenging task, is to divide a sheet of paper vertically into three columns. On the left she formulates her aims and objectives while the central column lists the drawbacks and obstacles. After balancing the pros and cons, she is usually able to enter some ingenious solution in the right-hand column. Many years after our marriage she recalled how this had helped her in April 1966 accept my proposal. Yes, she wanted to share her life with me, but against this (middle column) she would have to resign her lectureship in Ankara and leave her parents behind. The solution (right-hand column) was to sell her car so that her parents had the funds to move into a new apartment, and obtain leave of absence from her university so as to undertake research in Cambridge. Retaining her lectureship meant she could always return to Ankara, if the marriage did not work out.

For me the dialectic has a different axis. It may be pictured as a triangular movement ascending towards an apex, echoing the Hegelian idea of thesis, antithesis and synthesis. If some purposive activity encounters a constraint, the contradiction itself generates energies that make it possible to build towards a positive outcome. Hence the triadic patterning in each chapter of these memoirs: from Religion through Discipline to a sense of Vocation (in Lessons of Boarding School); from Unanswered Questions through Probing the Past to the discovery of a Critical Heritage (in Exploring the New Germany). For some readers this will seem overly schematic, but for me it reflects the rhythms of a lifetime. I was a closet Hegelian long before reading the *Phenomenology*. The rhythm arose from stories heard at Mother's knee – from the folktale of the Three Billy Goats Gruff through the parable of the Good Samaritan to the carol about Three Kings bringing gold, frankincense and myrrh.

There is no denying that patterns prettify experience. The memoirs of the poet Francis Warner, my contemporary at Christ's Hospital and Cambridge, have appeared as an elegantly versified autobiography, *By the Cam and the Isis, 1954–2000*. Here the reminiscences of an Oxbridge don flow serenely through rhyming quatrains, celebrating inspirational encounters with colleagues and mentors. At the other extreme *The Shaping Season* by the historian Norman Longmate gives a grim account of experiences at Christ's Hospital that fills six hundred pages. My aim, avoiding an overcrowded canvas, has been to steer a middle course, selecting and simplifying without glamorizing or distorting. Twenty pages suffice to convey the enduring lesson of my schooldays: that nothing worthwhile is achieved without a struggle.

That struggle does not diminish with advancing years, least of all for someone with a progressive illness. For people with multiple sclerosis the word 'progressive' does not mean that things are getting better, for gifted clinicians have yet to find a cure. My neurologist George Ebers of the Radcliffe Infirmary is sceptical about the costly 'miracle cures' promoted by alternative therapies. 'Don't waste your money on unproven treatments with unpredictable side effects,' he said. 'Take a good holiday instead!' Following this advice, Saime and I spend two months each year in Marmaris on the southwest coast of Turkey, where the weather is fine and the swimming easy. Onlookers sometimes become concerned about my safety as I strike out towards the horizon, enjoying invigorating exercise combined with a blissful sensation of weightlessness (I can swim further than can walk). Although we are both in our seventies, the sea is so warm that Saime and I even swim together by moonlight. Moreover at Marmaris a rehabilitation therapist from Uzbekistan named Elena Nerova keeps me on my feet by means of physiotherapy and massage.

Back home in Brighton we have caring friends and housemates who add energy and colour to our lives. After one of our trips to Marmaris we returned to find a scruffy upstairs room transformed into a paradigm of modern living by our Turkish friends Hale and Tekin Uçar. More recently an artistically gifted potter named Fay George has redecorated the whole interior in a harmonious blend of blues, greens and terracottas. The garden, too, has been transformed, with a Greek olive tree planted on the lawn to complement the Turkish fig trained along a sheltered wall. This is surely the most important dialectic of all – the interaction with others.

The Self and Others

In *The Self and Others*, one of the cult books of the 1960s, R. D. Laing has a chapter on Complementarity – 'that function of personal relations whereby the other fulfils or completes the self'. It has been my good fortune to live among people who have completed me in this way. Cultural history reconstructs the experiences of a community, and these memoirs could never have been written without the help of valued individuals and institutions, from parents and families to universities and colleagues. My debt should be clear from numerous passages, but I would like to express my thanks more explicitly. First to Saime, who has shaped my life in innumerable ways; then to my siblings for shared memories and helpful comments on draft chapters: Owen, Helen, David, Robert, Christopher, Jonathan, Margaret and Simon. Then to friends from school and college days, especially John Moat, John Woods, John Rice and David Wells.

Two Oxbridge colleagues, Christopher Brooke and Ritchie Robertson, have been particularly generous with their time, reading and helping me improve whole sequences of chapters. And I am grateful to Sussex colleagues who have commented on substantial excerpts: Stephen Burman, Brian Easlea, Diana Franklin, Andrea Hammel, Gabriel Josipovici, Sybil Oldfield, John Röhl and Alasdair Smith. The input of others has also proved invaluable: Mick Brown, John Chaltas, Christine Crow, Susan Drucker-Brown, Ralph Emanuel, Yeter Göksu, Irmak Gümüşbaş, Nicholas Jacobs, Partha and Swasti Mitter, Gila Pollich, Joy Ramsay, Naomi Segal, Gavin Wraith, and W. E. Yates. And special thanks are due to Julia Winckler for her professional skill and personal kindness in helping me prepare images for publication.

Life writing is a two-way traffic, and passages referring to living persons have been checked with those concerned, eliciting helpful responses. The method, trialled while writing the biography of Nazım Hikmet, has been to send them a draft of my proposed wording, asking for corrections to be written in the margins. While generating a further archive of annotated typescripts, this has sometimes provoked dissent. 'You must be dreaming, Ted!' wrote one of our friends from the 1960s. 'It wasn't like that at all.' He had difficulty in recognizing his younger self in my perspective and insisted on modifications. But if these memoirs are inescapably subjective, they are not fabrications. The events and encounters reconstructed in this book actually occurred, at specific times and places, involving people of flesh and blood with distinctive quirks and qualities and minds of their own.

Confirmation in Writing

My memories have been augmented by a multiplicity of written sources – letters and diaries, notebooks and transcripts of conversations, lecture notes and published papers, and innumerable folders and box-files. In addition to dozens of diaries, I have drawn on accumulated correspondence. Father's circulars, together with his diaries and sermons, have proved a primary source. Mother's handwritten letters provide a further reminder of the blessings of parenting, while letters from Aunty Marion (surely not another triad!) add affectionate footnotes to the narrative. Further inspiration has been provided by other collections of letters, especially those exchanged with Amy Colin, Christine Crow, Silke Hassler, Hans Keith, Gila Pollich and Ritchie Robertson – and of course with Saime during periods spent apart. Younger readers will find it hard to imagine the thrill of receiving long-awaited letters in the era before texting and twitter.

Letters have been my life in a further sense – the wording of experience. This is what confirmation in writing really means: using what Kraus called the 'sieve of words' to filter subjective stimuli, mitigate the stresses of separation and bring together hearts and minds. It is no coincidence that almost all my books have been produced in collaboration. In a deeper sense this may even be true of the present volume. Modern theories emphasize the impersonality of authorship, seeing the self as a site of fracture, and there are avant-garde writers who have made their name by composing a whole novel in which the letter 'e' does not occur. For me, it is more tempting to imagine an autobiography from which the pronoun 'I' would gradually vanish, like the smiling face of Carroll's Cheshire Cat. The 'I' can never be a unitary construct, for it too dissolves into a triad – an unstable synthesis of author, narrator and protagonist. The author knows the whole story, the narrator regulates its unfolding rhythm, while the protagonist may still be struggling to find the way.

Happy endings, they say, depend on stopping before the story is finished. The clock is ticking, the crocodile is coming nearer, and sooner or later we have to walk the plank. Perhaps the best way of pushing time away is sharing your later years with the young. My special thanks are due to our children Daphne, Yusuf and Sebastian, whose contributions to my story would have filled many more pages if this had been a family chronicle, rather than a memoir of teaching and learning. The tradition continues with our grandchildren Jamie, Georgia, Joshua and Leon, for story-telling forms a link between self and others. When they crowd around grandfather's chair clamouring to hear about one of their favourite characters, it is likely to be Harry Potter or the Gruffalo rather than Peter Pan or Alice.

'Who Do You Think You Are?' is the title of my favourite television series, screened by the BBC to encourage an interest in genealogical research. Prominent public figures are guided back through archives that may contain startling discoveries. Never trust an autobiography, they say, if it fails to reveal something compromising! I have tried to honour the autobiographical pact by recounting my experiences as faithfully as possible. Postmodern theory may emphasize the Destabilisation of Personal Histories, the title of an article on the autobiographies of German-Jewish survivors by my long-standing colleague Andrea Hammel. The phasing out of European Studies at Sussex means that Andrea will be continuing her career as Lecturer in German at the University of Wales in Aberystwyth. By contrast, when I look back on my experiences, it is the continuities that surprise me.

I still recall the principles of the scholar's oath taken fifty-five years ago at Caius, but deeper soundings surface from dreams. During those nightly visitations I may be struggling to get to a lecture on time – wherever did I put my notes? But there are also flashbacks to the thrills of youth, sliding down the banisters at Buckfastleigh Vicarage or summoned by a joyous peal of bells. The house has long since been sold and the church is in ruins, but the traces remain poignantly imprinted.

Acknowledgements and Picture Credits

'Once the book is finished,' I said to Saime, 'I'll be able to clear my shelves of fifty years of accumulated papers.' She has been patient and supportive, her comments have always been helpful, and the book is dedicated to her. My thanks are also due to other relatives, friends and colleagues, especially those associated with Christ's Hospital, the University of Cambridge, Gonville and Caius College, the University of Sussex, the Centre for German-Jewish Studies, and the Austrian Cultural Forum in London. The physical qualities of the book reflect the professionalism of the publisher, Anthony Grahame, Editorial Director of Sussex Academic Press; and faded photos have regained their lustre thanks to the skills of Julia Winckler, Lecturer in Photography at the University of Brighton. Other debts are acknowledged in chapter 18: The Autobiographical Pact, under the heading 'The self and others'.

Most of the documents and photographs included in this book are from my personal collection. The sources of specific Figures in the Text are listed below, and my thanks are due to the institutions and individuals concerned for allowing them to be reproduced:

Chapter 2, fig. 1: Cooperative Society National Archive, Manchester; chapter 2, fig. 2: based on a design by Phillip Boydell; chapter 3, fig. 1: Christ's Hospital Foundation; chapter 3, fig, 2: the Christ's Hospital Foundation, and Libby Horner, author of *Christ's Hospital Murals*; chapter 5, fig. 2: Verlag Testimon, Nuremberg; chapter 7, fig. 1: Adam Birdsall, Cirencester; chapter 7, fig. 2: Sussex University Special Collections; chapter 8, fig. 1: Hadlow's, Brighton; chapter 8, fig. 3: Pan Books, London; chapter 9, fig. 1: Stina (full name unknown); chapter 10, fig. 1: Telegraph Media Group Ltd; chapter 12, fig. 1: Gila Pollich, Karlsruhe; chapter 12, fig. 2: Jesus R. Delgado, Santillana del Mar; chapter 13, fig. 1: Mitteldeutscher Verlag, Halle; chapter 13, fig. 2: *The Independent*; chapter 14, fig. 1: Barrie Hopson, author (with Katie Ledger) of *And What Do You Do? Ten Steps to Creating a Portfolio*

Career; chapter 14, fig. 2: based on a German print dated 1618; chapter 15, fig. 1: Arnold Daghani Trustees and Sussex University Special Collections; chapter 16, fig. 2: Frank Auerbach, London; chapter 17, fig. 3: staff of the Warburg Institute, London.

The sources of photographs are gratefully acknowledged as follows:

Plate 1: Raphael Tuck & Sons; plates 8 & 9: Nicholas Horne, Totnes; plate 11: Christ's Hospital Foundation; plate 13: Master and Fellows of Gonville and Caius College (photo by Yao Liang); plate 14: Master and Fellows of Gonville and Caius College (photo by Anthony Barrington Brown); plate 15: Gila Pollich, Karlsruhe; plate 19: Verlag PAG, Vienna; plate 24: Avery's, Brighton; plate 26: Central Office of Information, London; plates 28 & 29: Saime Göksu; plate 31: Brian Easlea, Hove; plate 32: Jennifer Drury; plates 36 & 37: Margaret Timms, Buckfastleigh; plates 38 & 39: Master and Fellows of Gonville and Caius College; plate 43: Paul Christie, Histon; plates 48, 49 & 50: underground photographer, Weimar; plate 52: Sussex University Special Collections; plate 67: Yeter Göksu, Ankara; plate 68: Charles Green, Edgware.

Every effort has been made to identify copyright holders, but mysteries remain. I have lost all trace of that East German underground photographer who entrusted me with precious images thirty years ago, which he wished to see published in the West. Then he could not be identified, but now he might be proud to claim his work. And it would be good to know the surname of the gifted artist who signed as 'Stina' on that portrait of Saime as a young woman which stands by my desk. Fortunately, I am still in touch with the writers of treasured letters, who have generously allowed me to quote them. And excerpts from a letter by W. G. Sebald are published by kind permission of Ute Sebald (© 2011, The Estate of W.G. Sebald). But if any copyright has been overlooked, I would like to be informed so that the matter can be rectified on a reprint. Comments can be posted on http://taking-up-the-torch.info

EDWARD TIMMS, January 2011

Index

Index

Index

Index

Index

Index

Index

Index

FINIS